THE STATES SYSTEM OF EUROPE, 1640–1990

The States System of Europe, 1640–1990

Peacemaking and the Conditions of International Stability

ANDREAS OSIANDER

CLARENDON PRESS · OXFORD

Oxford University Press, Walton Street, Oxford OX2 6DP

Oxford New York
Athens Auckland Bangkok Bombay
Calcutta Cape Town Dar es Salaam Delhi
Florence Hong Kong Istanbul Karachi
Kuala Lumpur Madras Madrid Melbourne
Mexico City Nairobi Paris Singapore
Taipei Tokyo Toronto
and associated companies in
Berlin Ibadan

Oxford is a trade mark of Oxford University Press

Published in the United States by
Oxford University Press Inc., New York

First published 1994
Reprinted 1995

British Library Cataloguing in Publication Data
Data available

Library of Congress Cataloging in Publication Data
Osiander, Andreas.
The states system of Europe, 1640-1990 / Andreas Osiander.
Includes bibliographical references.
1. Europe—Politics and government. 2. Peace treaties.
I. Title.
D217.O85   1994   940—dc20   93-47553
ISBN 0-19-827887-X

3 5 7 9 10 8 6 4 2

Printed in Great Britain
on acid-free paper by
Ipswich Book Co. Ltd, Suffolk

ACKNOWLEDGEMENTS

THIS book is the revised version of a thesis submitted for the degree of Doctor of Philosophy in the University of Oxford. My thanks are due to the late Professor John Vincent, of the London School of Economics, who supervised the thesis until it was almost completed, and to Professor Adam Roberts, of Balliol College, Oxford, who took over as supervisor after John Vincent's premature death. Mark Philp, of Oriel College, Oxford, and Robert Evans of Brasenose College, Oxford, provided valuable comments on parts of the manuscript. Needless to say, I am solely responsible for any errors that this book may contain.

This research project would not have been undertaken without the financial and moral support of my parents. I also wish to express my gratitude to the Provost and Fellows of Oriel College, Oxford, and the Master and Fellows of Balliol College, Oxford. By awarding me, respectively, the Rank Xerox Senior Scholarship and the Hedley Bull Junior Research Fellowship, they enabled me to continue my research, not only free from financial worries, but in a highly congenial atmosphere.

Special thanks are also due to my friend Cally Trench for her painstaking perusal of the near-final version of the typescript of this book, and for her profitable efforts to disentangle my thoughts and exorcize some of their stylistic infelicities.

A.O.

Humboldt-Universität zu Berlin
January 1993

CONTENTS

Abbreviations   ix

1. General Remarks   1

2. The Peace of Westphalia   16

3. The Peace of Utrecht   90

4. The Congress of Vienna   166

5. The Peace Conference of Paris, 1919–1920   248

6. Summary and Update   316

Appendix: Kissinger on the Polish–Saxon Question   334

References   337

Index   344

ABBREVIATIONS

APW M. Braubach and K. Repgen (eds.), (1962–), *Acta Pacis Westphalicae* (*c.*60 vols. planned) (Münster). References to this compilation appear in the form APW II C. i. 218, where II C designates the series, i the volume, and 218 the page number.

IPM Instrumentum Pacis Monasteriense.

IPO Instrumentum Pacis Osnabrugense.

Eilt, daß ihr den Verstand zum Nutzen noch gebrauchet,
Eh dann Europa ganz, das goldne Land, verrauchet!
Ach, glaubt mir, einmal sich erretten von den Kriegen,
Ist mehr, als tausendmal unüberwindlich siegen.

[Make haste, use reason to advantage while you may,
Ere all Europe, the golden land, goes up in smoke!
Oh trust me, to be once safe from the scourge of war
Is more, than a thousand times invincibly to conquer.]

ANDREAS SCULTETUS (1622/3?–47)

1

General Remarks

The purpose of this introductory chapter is to point out various aspects of the problem of stability in international politics, and to explain my approach to this problem. I make no claim to sophistication. I will avoid any form of specialist terminology other than the simple terminology that I will explain in this chapter. Much of what I wish to point out, in this chapter as well as in this book as a whole, is really obvious; all of it, I hope, stands to reason.

I must ask the reader to bear with me if the next few pages are a little arid. They will be given over to an exposition of the theoretical approach adopted in this book. The chapters that follow will, I hope, make up for the rather abstract nature of this exposition, by giving concrete illustrations of what I mean.

Politics is determined extensively by the framework of terms of reference used by the decision-makers. Indeed, politics has no reality apart from the way in which it is thought, talked, and written about. I will try to show in this book that international dealings in the states system of Europe during the period covered can be accounted for in a more plausible way than has been done so far if they are explained, not in terms of the (often anachronistic) assumptions made by historians and political analysts, but in terms of the assumptions held by the decision-makers themselves. As far as I am aware, no systematic research has so far been conducted on what these assumptions actually were.

1. THE NATURE OF INTERNATIONAL POLITICS AND THE PROBLEM OF STABILITY

Before we go any further, let me say a word on an expression that will recur frequently in this book. In line with established usage in international relations theory, I will refer to autonomous centres of decision-making in international affairs as 'international actors'.

This may be inelegant, but it has the considerable semantic advantage that it contains no implicit assumptions as to who or what it is that makes decisions and 'acts' in the international arena. It can therefore be applied regardless of the peculiarities that 'actors' may display, either as a result of individual differences between them, or as a result of their belonging to a historical period different from our own. It should also be noted that for simplicity's sake the usage adopted in this book makes no distinction between 'actors' conceived as decision-making centres as such and the territorial and demographic units that these centres represent. (The question then arises of whether decision-making centres that do not have supreme authority over some population and some piece of territory—such as international organizations or multinational corporations—should in certain instances also be called international actors. But, as will be seen, this question is not particularly relevant to the argument of this book and is therefore left open here.)

It is true, of course, that the very expression 'international' contains an assumption about the nature of the decision-making centres in question—suggesting as it does that dealings between these centres will normally be dealings between 'nations'. It is immediately obvious that, while this may be the case with our own historical period, it is not true, for example, of the seventeenth century. Nevertheless, I do use the expression 'international' to describe dealings between decision-making centres of any kind—'nations' or otherwise—that are not subject to some domestic political authority. This, too, is in accordance with established usage even in international(!) relations theory (which one might expect to be more precise). Coined by Jeremy Bentham in the eighteenth century, the expression 'international' has by now become so familiar that we rarely stop to think about its etymology, and it would be too artificial to try to introduce a semantically more correct term. Indeed, the only one that I can think of is 'non-domestic', which is obviously cumbersome.

There is, in international politics, no strong central authority capable of laying down, and enforcing, the rules that international actors will follow. Indeed, this is what defines the international system, as opposed to the sphere of domestic politics. If a system-wide central authority existed, all politics in the system would be domestic; as it is, there is a dichotomy between domestic and international politics. On the domestic level, the highest political authority is centralized, while on the international level it is decentralized and distributed among a multiplicity of self-governing entities.

Although, in the international sphere, there is no supreme political authority overarching the individual actors, the international system is not characterized by disorder—it has a structure, which is normally quite stable. Let me explain immediately what I mean when I speak of the 'structure' of the international system: I am talking about the number and the identity of the international actors, their relative status *vis-à-vis* one another, and the distribution of territories and populations between them. These are the three fundamental aspects of the structure of the international system.

There is another, namely the various kinds of institutions or organizations that actors may share between them. These bodies fall into two different categories. Some are *supra*-'national', which means that the participating actors delegate limited governmental authority to them. Alternatively, and more frequently, these institutions or organizations are *inter*-'national', in which case the decision-making authority of the participating actors is not diminished by their membership. This fourth aspect will occasionally be touched on in this book. But, unlike the other three, its presence presupposes that a reasonable degree of stability of the international system has been *ensured already*, at least as between those actors that support such institutions or organizations and allow them to operate. Since, in this book, we are concerned with the *conditions* of international stability, the main focus will be on the first three aspects.

The sphere of international politics is often perceived to be a conspicuously less stable environment than the average domestic political system. Precisely because they are so conspicuous, manifestations of conflict and disorder in international politics have been studied more extensively than the phenomenon of relative system stability. But even the structure of the international system usually displays considerable overall stability over long stretches of time.

Stability is less eye-catching than conflict. It is of little news value—it cannot be reported the way that conflict is, precisely because it is stability, not conflict, that is the normal condition of the international system, too. There can be no valid theory even of conflict in international relations, let alone of international relations in general, if that theory fails to account for the lack of conflict, or to explain why a certain amount of conflict may be accommodated by the international system without that system losing its overall stability.[1]

2. THE NATURE OF THE INTERNATIONAL SYSTEM: ASSUMPTIONS, PRINCIPLES, RULES

In analysing international politics, one very important thing has to be remembered. This is that the international system has no physical reality. Ultimately, the international system exists exclusively in the mind. It is what people think it is. It is a mental construct, resting entirely on shared assumptions. These assumptions are extremely complex, and, often, they are so deeply ingrained and pervasive that they may seem rock solid. However, unlike a rock, or individuals, or any other object with a physical reality, they can be 'deconstructed'.

Even the most primitive international relations situation is defined by certain assumptions that prevail among the individuals involved. Imagine a clash between two rival Stone Age tribes. This situation is defined by assumptions shared among the members of the two tribes, assumptions to the effect that each tribe is different from the other and that they are rivals. If the individuals concerned did not make such assumptions about themselves and one another, there would be no tribes to begin with. If there were no tribes, they could not be rivals, let alone clash. There may be strong reasons *why* the assumptions involved are made—indeed, assumptions will not prevail in the long run if such reasons are not present. However, such assumptions are never axiomatic. They are always arbitrary to some extent, and capable of modification.

The international system as we know it is the sum of elaborate, widely shared assumptions. What happens in it, whether it is warfare, the absence of warfare, or whatever, is ultimately explained by the manner in which the assumptions that make up the system are interrelated.

---

[1] For an excellent discussion of this point see Blanning (1986: ch. 1).

The problem of stability can be put in the following terms. There will be stability in the international system if the principal assumptions on which the system is founded do not clash. There will be less stability if they do. To put it differently, the degree of stability of the international system will depend on the degree of congruence of the principal assumptions on which the system is founded, or, still more simply, on the degree of consensus present in the system.

In order to illustrate this, let us take the notion of 'frontiers'—something that is obviously of great importance in international relations as we know them. Frontiers have no physical reality, unless they happen to be marked or fortified. But, in the long run, that is neither a necessary, nor indeed a sufficient, condition for having a frontier. A frontier exists by virtue of assumptions, shared by people on either side of it, about where the frontier is located, and, in the long run, about the acceptability of this location. As long as these assumptions concerning the frontier are the same on both sides, the frontier will display a high degree of stability—it will stay where it is. But if on either side the assumptions change, if there is no consensus in this matter any longer, then the frontier will lose its stability. Sooner or later, it will be challenged and, conceivably, redrawn.

It seems promising, then, to look at the international system, not primarily in terms of what the participating actors do, but in terms of certain fundamental assumptions relating to the structure of the system.

This book is concerned primarily with a type of assumptions which I will call *structural principles*. There will be less emphasis on another type of assumptions which I will call *procedural rules*. Structural principles are assumptions that influence the three basic aspects of the structure of the international system: the identity of the international actors, their relative status, and the distribution of territories and populations between them. Procedural rules influence the way that relations between the actors are conducted.

The structural principles are more important to the stability of the international system than the procedural rules. If there is instability in the system, it may be that the structural principles of the system are in some way inadequate. Alternatively, there may be an insufficient consensus on which principles should be respected. A third possibility is that a strong consensus on structural principles exists, but that the international system in its current form does not reflect these principles sufficiently.

3. THE PROBLEM OF CONSENSUS

There is another way of approaching the problem of stability in international relations. This is to posit that stability presupposes reliable expectations. International actors will consider exercising restraint in their mutual dealings only if they can expect such restraint to be universal. There is an inseparable link between stability on the one hand and the predictability of the actors' behaviour on the other. In other words, stability is based on reliable predictions about what the behaviour of other actors will be. Obviously, such predictions can only be reliable if actors are prepared to act in accordance with them themselves. It follows that stability presupposes a code of behaviour.

Strictly speaking, stability is not based on reciprocity, as is sometimes held—although, indeed, the two are concomitant. True, international actors will hardly accept a code of behaviour that is persistently flouted by a majority of the other actors, or even by a significant minority. Nevertheless, stability will not prevail, either, if the actors make their own abstention from disruptive behaviour depend on what other actors *have done* in this respect, rather than on what it is thought that they *will do*. Such a situation would be characterized by distrust and by mutual reluctance to 'take the first step'. It would encourage irrational or pre-emptive aggression, and thereby create a climate of insecurity. Generalized reciprocity (in terms of abstention from disruptive behaviour) is not the precondition, but the result, of the acceptance of a code of behaviour. Failure to reciprocate non-disruptive behaviour indicates that the code of behaviour is not recognized universally.

What provides this code of behaviour? It is nothing other than the sum of the structural principles and of the procedural rules that form the object of a consensus among the international actors. But we are not usually aware of this consensus operating. The reason is because the more important part of this code of behaviour, the structural principles, is not concerned with *promoting* certain types of action, but with *preventing* behaviour that would disrupt the system. In other words, structural principles operate successfully if nothing is seen to happen, nothing, at any rate, that is not routine in character. As a result, the importance of these principles and even their very existence go largely unnoticed.

The international system will be stable, provided that it is in conformity with the structural principles on which there is consensus in the system, and provided, too, that the consensus on these principles is strong enough. If these conditions are not fulfilled, the resulting tension will prompt conflict. This may then lead to a modification either of the system or of the principles that form the object of a system-wide consensus.

4. CONSENSUS AND INTERNATIONAL SOCIETY

If a community is made up of so many individual actors that they cannot constantly coordinate their behaviour individually and on an *ad hoc* basis, there will be stability only if a majority of the actors adhere to a common code of behaviour. Even in domestic society, the presence of a police force capable of enforcing the code would not, in the long run, suffice to prevent disruptive (destabilizing) behaviour. This is only possible if people are, on the whole, predisposed to adhere to this code of behaviour—even when there is no means of compelling them. Adherence to the code must be largely voluntary, although it is potently helped by social conditioning and pressure.

In the international system, voluntary adherence to a common code is even more important, since, at this level, little or no policing is available to enforce the code at all. There is an additional problem in that 'social' pressure within the 'international society' (a notion to which I will return in a moment) will be weaker than it is in domestic society. This is because international actors, largely autonomous by definition, invariably constitute relatively insulated groups of individuals (though the *degree* of insulation from other such groups may vary). In domestic society, it is difficult for individuals or groups to withstand the pressure of society's expectations, because they are fully integrated into domestic society and could not function without it. The sort of pressure found in international society is not so difficult to withstand, because international actors are so much more autonomous.

The answer to this apparent problem is that the code of behaviour of the international society is different from the type of code operating in a domestic society. The code operating in the inter-national society is much simpler, because it has only a single major objective—the preservation of international stability (this has been the situation until the late twentieth century, at any rate). More-over, this objective of preserving international stability can be at-tained simply by mutual restraint. It requires little in the way of active cooperation.

Domestic society is actively engaged in economic and cultural pursuits that are necessary to its continued existence, and also in other pursuits that it considers desirable. As these needs are pro-vided for at the domestic level, international society has tradition-ally had no other goal than to provide the modicum of system-wide stability without which these pursuits could not be engaged in with reasonable success. As pointed out before, the international actors that make up the international society are less dependent on one another than the members of a domestic society, and therefore less vulnerable to 'social' pressure. But they do depend on each other for the stability of the international system (including trans-border economic ties). As a result, they are not, in fact, *immune* to the pressure created by the expectations of international society. And since the goal of that society—international stability—requires less in the way of positive action than the pursuits that have tra-ditionally been the exclusive domain of domestic society, even the relatively less effective social pressure that is found in the inter-national society is usually sufficient to maintain at least a degree of stability. (This, it should be remembered, is not necessarily the same as perpetual peace.)

What I have just said refers to international society as it has functioned, first in Europe and later at a global level, over the last few centuries; and it refers to that society taken as a whole. Each of these two points calls for a qualification. The first qualification is that, in our own time, international society *as a whole* has begun to be faced with tasks that go beyond a shared responsibility for international stability and which cannot be tackled exclusively at the domestic level—for example, global pollution and the possibil-ity of a global climate change. The appearance of such tasks creates increasing pressure on *all* international actors to intensify their cooperation—although it is too early to gauge the extent to which this will transform international society. Shared institutions and organizations that involve (almost) all actors in the global international system exist today as between the members of the United Nations. But these are bodies of the 'inter'-national variety that do not, at present, restrict the autonomy of the participating actors significantly.

The second qualification is that while, traditionally, international society as a whole has only had the simple objective of preserving international stability, this has not prevented *subsets* of actors from accepting a greater degree of mutual integration. They have maintained 'supra'-national bodies invested with some limited governmental authority. The best examples of this phenomenon of 'supra'-national cooperation in Europe are the Holy Roman Empire in the early modern period and the European Community in the second half of the twentieth century. The subsets of actors in question have been characterized by particularly strong mutual bonds resulting from a combination of two factors: first, a relatively developed community feeling as expressed in some form of ideology (German nationalism, the 'European idea'), and secondly, powerful shared interests.

International society can be a reality only to the extent to which the actors that make it up accept voluntarily certain common assumptions, which form what I will call their *consensus agenda*. The consensus agenda is the sum of all the shared assumptions, or *consensus notions*, present among the actors. Most important among these notions are the *consensus principles*, which are concerned with the structure of the international system.

Destabilization will occur if the consensus agenda is violated. However, the degree of destabilization will depend on whether or not the consensus agenda is actually rejected at the same time. For example, in domestic society, a thief or murderer will normally try to evade punishment, but only rarely will he or she reject the consensus notions that give the authorities the right to prosecute deviant (in terms of the consensus notions) behaviour. Even if people get away with deviant behaviour like theft or murder, this is a form of 'cheating' that can only benefit them if a majority of the other actors do not cheat. Cheating must not become too widespread. If it does, the consensus agenda will lapse, and this is likely to leave all the actors worse off in the resulting chaos.

In the international system, actors may disregard the consensus agenda and hope to get away with it. For example, they may run the risk of a limited war, which they may or may not win. As long as such behaviour does not become too serious and widespread, the consensus agenda will remain valid and the overall stability of the international system will be preserved. Actors may, indeed, seek aggrandizement and compete to optimize their relative position in the international system without causing a system breakdown. They will usually seek to avoid such a breakdown, because the likely result, prolonged generalized warfare, involves too many imponderables. Overall system stability is preserved primarily by continued general adherence to a consensus agenda, rather than by any material restraint, such as resource equilibria (a 'balance of power' defined in purely material terms) or deterrence.

A different situation arises if any actors reject the set-up of the system (and with it the structural principles underlying that system) altogether and adopt what Henry Kissinger has called a 'revolutionary' policy.[2] Napoleonic France and Hitler's Germany are classic examples. International society then ceases to exist, at least as between these actors and those willing to uphold the existing consensus notions.

International society may be defined as a situation of general acceptance by the international actors of a consensus agenda. It is characteristic of such a situation that, although the international actors cannot easily be forced to respect the agenda, they will be eager, nevertheless, to justify their actions in terms of the notions that make up the agenda. Typically, a good deal of justificatory discourse, drawing on the consensus agenda and addressed (not necessarily exclusively) to an international audience, will be present in the system.

But it is important to bear in mind that respect for the consensus agenda must be voluntary—certainly in the long run. If the consensus agenda is violated, this is likely to prompt other actors to intervene in order to defend some short-term interest of their own, or the shared long-term interest that they have in upholding the consensus agenda (and thereby the overall stability of the system), or both. But since autonomy is the defining characteristic of international actors, they will inevitably resent being *forced* to respect the consensus agenda, and, unlike individuals in domestic society, they may be in a position to vent this resentment in a way that threatens the stability of the entire system. In particular, the

<hr />

[2] Kissinger (1957: 1).

attempt to promote behaviour that is in accordance with the consensus agenda by *punishing* deviant behaviour (which is different from simply counteracting such behaviour) will almost always be counterproductive. It will leave deep resentment, in other words create antagonism, and this will undermine further the consensus on which the actors' mutual restraint is based.

5. METHOD OF THIS STUDY

The approach to international relations that I have just outlined owes something to the increased interest that international-relations scholars have developed in the past two or three decades in the problem of international 'order', and in exploring the role of norms in international relations. I would like, at this point, to acknowledge the extent to which my own work has been inspired and influenced by the late Hedley Bull's study of the 'anarchical' or rulerless international society.[3] Readers acquainted with Bull's book will easily identify parallels with the present work, though there are important differences as well.

The method and the terminology that I propose in this book are entirely my own—in particular, my definition of the structure of the international system, my concern with international 'stability' (rather than 'order'), and my emphasis on structural principles rather than on procedural rules. Indeed, in my opinion, it is a major shortcoming of the existing literature on international 'order' that it fails to identify the source of this 'order' in a single semantic category—provided in the approach adopted here by the notion of consensus as manifested, most importantly, in the shape of what I call structural principles. So far, authors have limited themselves to reviewing disparate *aspects* of international 'order' (as Hedley Bull has done in his great study), without integrating them into a coherent analytical framework. Most often, the emphasis is more or less exclusively on procedural rules—what Raymond Cohen, to cite a good example, has analysed as 'the rules of the game'.[4] But this emphasis on 'rules of the game' largely ignores fundamental questions like who the players shall be and why, and what the playing board shall look like. Generally speaking,

[3] Bull (1977).   [4] Cohen (1981).

there is an insufficient awareness of the importance of the structure (as defined here) of the international system, and of the importance of the degree of consensus about this structure.

The purpose of this book is to investigate the role of consensus in the international politics of Europe in the last three centuries and a half. Hitherto, research into the international politics of this period has focused largely on conflict. Indeed, conventional accounts of the international politics of Europe in this period usually create the impression that international politics is nothing more than an endless, rather Darwinian, struggle for power. Everything that the authors deem worthy of the reader's attention somehow revolves around warfare. This is true, for example, of the recent volumes by F. R. Bridge and Roger Bullen (1980), Derek McKay and H. M. Scott (1983), and Paul Kennedy (1989). Their approach is, of course, distorting. Kalevi J. Holsti's new theoretical study of the period (published in 1991) shuns the simplistic view that international politics is no more than a power struggle, and features the concept of 'international order' in its title. However, it is essentially concerned with cataloguing causes of wars.

Moreover, the usefulness of these works is also diminished by numerous more or less serious factual errors (Bridge and Bullen being the most reliable among the works mentioned). Unfortunately, this is rather typical of international-relations literature dealing with more remote political events. For example, among other things, McKay and Scott claim that, by the Peace of Westphalia, the German princes were 'allowed to impose their own religion on their subjects'.[5] Holsti also asserts that the peace was based on the concept of *cuius regio eius religio*.[6] In fact, the peace abolished that concept in the Holy Roman Empire and forbade the German princes to impose their religion on their subjects. Holsti, on the very same page on which he makes the statement just referred to, also tells us that the Peace of Westphalia 'established [in Germany] a Lutheran Church with bishops, titles, and honors modeled on the Churches of Sweden and England'— a striking suggestion that bears no obvious resemblance to the facts. McKay and Scott seem to think that the Burgundian Circle was so called because it 'encircled France'[7]—in fact, 'circle' was

---

[5] McKay and Scott (1983: 5).   [6] Holsti (1991: 34).
[7] McKay and Scott (1983: 2).

the name given to the ten administrative provinces into which the various princes and free cities of the Holy Roman Empire were grouped. Kennedy, in a chapter entitled 'The Habsburg Bid for Mastery', wrongly describes the Habsburg dynasty as 'stemming originally from Austria' and then refers repeatedly to one of its scions without recognizing him—he talks about a general in the Thirty Years War whom he calls consistently 'Cardinal-Infante' without the definite article, apparently unaware that he is dealing with a title and not with a proper name. ('Infante' was a title given to Spanish royal princes, and this particular one also happened to be a cardinal.)[8] Moreover, Kennedy is irritatingly fond of sweeping and rather dubious generalizations (such as, to give only a single example, his statement that '[t]he post-1450 waging of war was intimately connected with "the birth of the nation state"'—it would not be difficult to point to quite a lot of post-1450 warfare to which this claim cannot be applied in any meaningful way).[9]

Of course, it is extremely difficult to avoid factual errors when dealing with complicated historical material, and I do not presume to imply that this book is free from such errors. Total veracity is almost impossible to achieve, and I can only refer the reader to Lessing's dictum that historiography must tell the truth, or at least resemble it. However, I have striven to verify the information given in this book carefully, using original sources where this was practical.

It is clear that an exhaustive account of the manifestations of consensus in the international politics of Europe over the last three hundred and fifty years would be beyond the scope of a single book. To make the task manageable, I propose to examine, in the next four chapters, the European international system at four crucial junctures in its development. These are the four major peace conferences that took place during the period under considera-tion: the Congress of Münster and Osnabrück, which convened in 1644 and produced the Peace of Westphalia in 1648; the Congress of Utrecht, which convened in 1712 to terminate the War of the Spanish Succession; the Congress of Vienna of 1814–15, which set up the post-Napoleonic European states system; and the Paris Peace Conference of 1919–20, which followed the First World War. An analysis of these four peace conferences will make up the

---

[8] Kennedy (1989: 40, 56, 61).   [9] Ibid. 89.

main part of the book. A concluding chapter will be devoted to summing up our findings up to that point, and to reviewing the history of the European states system since 1920 in the light of these findings.

The idea is that the best moment to study the assumptions inherent in the international system is that following a general war, a war that posed a severe threat to the system and which, possibly, even involved its partial breakdown. In more tranquil times, the consensus notions prevalent in the international system are largely submerged in the collective subconscious. But they will be invoked and attain a higher degree of visibility when they are challenged in some crisis. The more fundamental the crisis, the more complete the articulation of the consensus agenda is likely to be. A general peace congress, faced with the task of reconstructing (or at least reconsolidating) the international system, is likely to be a particularly rich source of consensus notions, because reconstructing the system must mean first of all reformulating it.

This book therefore relies heavily on original source-material. In all quotations from original material the spelling has been modernized, except in the chapter on the Paris Peace Conference (and except in the titles of publications). Titles of persons or states are capitalized only if they are used as quasi-proper names (e.g. 'the King of Spain', 'the Swiss Confederation'), but not otherwise (e.g. 'the Spanish king'). The titles 'Emperor' (meaning the German emperor before 1806), 'Pope', and 'Sultan' are also treated as proper names, as are expressions designating an office or function used in the original language if that is not English (e.g.: 'the Swedish chancellor', but 'the Rikskansler').

It is perhaps worth pointing out that the frequently used expression 'the Holy Roman Emperor' is peculiar to English-speaking authors, and historically incorrect. At no time in the history of the Holy Roman Empire was the Emperor himself referred to as 'holy'. In the seventeenth and eighteenth centuries he was designated officially as 'Electus Romanus Imperator' or 'Erwählter Römischer Kaiser'. This translates as 'Elected Roman Emperor' or even 'Roman Emperor elect'—because, in contrast to the medieval practice last observed by the Emperor Charles V in the sixteenth century, subsequent incumbents assumed the imperial title immediately on being crowned Kings of Germany. They dispensed with the second coronation by the Pope that had previously been considered necessary to acquire the imperial dignity as such.

Seventeenth- and eighteenth-century Catholic documents used the reformed Gregorian calendar (the New Style), while Protestant documents from that time still clung to the Julian calendar (Old Style). The Julian calendar was ten days behind the Gregorian calendar in the 1640s and eleven days behind in the early eighteenth century. Protestant documents sometimes give the date both in the Old and in the New Styles, but this practice is not consistent. By the early nineteenth century only the Gregorian calendar was used internationally. In this book, dates are normally in the New Style. In some cases (where there is doubt as to which calendar was being used, or where changing the date would not be the normal historiographical practice), I give the dates as they actually appear in the documents, accompanied by the word 'dated'.

In order to keep the material manageable, all extra-European aspects of the peacemaking ventures that we will examine have had to be omitted.

2

The Peace of Westphalia

1. INTRODUCTION

1.1. Historical Background

The history of the Thirty Years War is a complicated one, and cannot be told here in a way that does justice to its complexity. The remarks that follow are only intended as a reminder.

The fragile political consensus of Germany, under increasingly grave strain from religious polarization, only just survived into the seventeenth century. To protect their interests, the Protestant German princes and free cities formed an alliance, called the 'Union', in 1608. The Catholics retorted by setting up a counter-alliance, the 'League', in 1609. Less than ten years later, in 1618, the tension between the two camps erupted into war.

The religious quarrel was compounded by controversy over the respective rights of the Emperor on the one hand and the estates of the Empire (that is, the princes and free cities represented in the Empire's parliament, the Reichstag) on the other hand. Encouraged by the success of his armies, and supported by his Habsburg relative the King of Spain, the Emperor used the opportunity to increase his power. Being Catholic himself, his efforts were mainly directed against the Protestant estates. They culminated in the notorious 1629 Edict of Restitution, which decreed extensive re-Catholicization of Protestant territories.

The threat to Protestantism and to the general political balance in Europe prompted non-German actors to intervene. The first to come to the rescue of the Protestants was the Danish king in 1624. He failed, and withdrew in 1629. The following year King Gustaf Adolf of Sweden landed in Germany. Apart from bringing help to the Protestants, he also sought to consolidate Sweden's position as the dominant power in the Baltic. Even after he was killed in battle in 1632, Swedish troops remained in Germany and continued to play a major role in the war, under the aegis of the Swedish chancellor Axel Oxenstierna. But they failed to defeat the Habsburg party decisively.

This was not even possible when a third power joined the struggle: France. In fact, France had already been largely financing the Swedish efforts, before itself committing troops from 1635 onwards. Despite being a Catholic power, France intervened on behalf of the Protestants. Its aim was to weaken Habsburg—that is, the Emperor and the King of Spain. Their territories largely surrounded France, since, between them, they governed the Spanish mainland to the south, the southern Netherlands to the north, and much of south-west Germany. France perceived this as a territorial stranglehold, which it was keen to break.

At the same time, the Spanish king was fighting the revolt of the northern Netherlands, which had allied itself with France. Later in the war, Catalonia, Portugal, and southern Italy also rose against Spanish rule.

The struggle dragged on for years, with disastrous consequences in Germany in particular, but without giving a permanent advantage to either of the two camps: essentially, the Emperor, Spain, and the majority of the Catholic German estates on the one side; Sweden, France, the Dutch, and most Protestant German estates on the other. The issues being fought over became somewhat obscured as the conflict developed its own dynamic. In the absence of any workable international consensus it fed on itself. To promote such a consensus was the daunting task of the assembly that, after many delays, convened at Münster and Osnabrück in Westphalia in 1644.

1.2. Set-up of the Congress

Münster was assigned to France and Osnabrück to Sweden. The other belligerents divided themselves up between the two cities, depending on which power they were closest to, or, alternatively, which power they wished to negotiate with.

The Emperor had delegations in both cities. As France and Sweden were allies, their delegations each had a permanent resident with the other. The Spaniards were represented at Münster, where they conferred with the French and with the Dutch. (The Dutch were Protestant, but sent their delegation to Münster because they were the allies of the French.) The estates of the Empire also sent representatives. Most of the Catholic estates went to Münster, and most of the Protestant ones to Osnabrück. But there was no strict separation on religious lines.

The presence of the estates meant, in effect, that the international congress also incorporated a meeting of the Reichstag, the Empire's parliament, although the term Reichstag was not itself used. The estates constituted themselves into the three Reichstag councils. The first of these comprised most of the electors—six of the seven princes entitled to elect the Emperor (under the constitution, the seventh, the King of Bohemia, did not participate in the Reichstag deliberations). The second council was made up of the one hundred or so other princes, and the fifty-odd free cities formed the third. In the case of the estates, too, there was close coordination between the two sites of the congress.

Both at Münster and at Osnabrück, it had originally been thought necessary to appoint mediators rather than let the delegations confront one another directly. The Swedes, however, were unhappy about the proposed mediation of the King of Denmark, a rival contender for hegemony in the Baltic and a traditional enemy since Sweden's secession from Denmark in the 1520s. The Swedes rightly suspected that the Danes, who had operated an anti-Swedish *rapprochement* with Vienna, would try to exploit their mediation to weaken them.[1] Sweden declared war on Denmark in 1643, before the congress convened. This effectively ended all talk of mediation at Osnabrück, where negotiations between the Swedish and the Imperial envoys were direct from the start.

In the Catholic camp at Münster, mediation had been entrusted to the Papal and Venetian envoys. But the Papal envoy was too biased against France (allied with Protestants) to be able to assert himself forcefully, and even the gifted Venetian Alvise Contarini found his role diminished as the delegations increasingly resorted to direct contacts at Münster, too.

The negotiations culminated in the signing on 24 October 1648 of the two treaties of peace between the Empire and Sweden (Instrumentum Pacis Osnabrugense or IPO) and between the Empire and France (Instrumentum Pacis Monasteriense or IPM).[2]

---

[1] The Swedish suspicions are borne out by the instruction that the Danish government prepared for its delegates at the congress. Odhner (1877: 84 f.), Lorenz (1969: 38).   [2] Text e.g. in Zeumer (1904: 395 ff.).

The other peace signed at the congress was the Peace of Münster between Spain and the Dutch States General of 30 January 1648. No peace was achieved between Spain and France.

1.3. Key Negotiators

The most important negotiators at the congress were the Swedish, French, and Imperial delegations.

There were three principal members of the Swedish delegation: Johan Oxenstierna and Johan Adler Salvius were the plenipotentiaries at Osnabrück, and Schering Rosenhane liaised with the French at Münster. Oxenstierna was the son of Axel Oxenstierna, the ageing Swedish chancellor (Rikskansler), who had returned to Stockholm to dominate the powerful Council of State (Riksråd). It was Axel Oxenstierna who had kept Sweden in the war, despite the double disaster of King Gustaf Adolf's death in 1632 and the decisive Swedish defeat at Nördlingen two years later.

In doing so, Axel Oxenstierna disregarded pressure from the panicked regency council acting on behalf of the young Queen Kristina. His sang-froid eventually paid off, at the price of fourteen more years of onerous war effort. As a result, the chancellor took on the appearance of a warlord—his personal involvement in the struggle greatly contributed to his power and standing. But he was no Wallenstein. His ultimate commitment was not to himself but to his country (the *fädernesland* or fatherland).

At the congress, Johan Oxenstierna understandably had to defer to his father. This did not facilitate relations with his unusual and brilliant older colleague, Johan Adler Salvius. Although he had previously been a protégé of the chancellor, Salvius increasingly followed a line of his own. This was made possible (though not easy) by the special confidence of the queen. Over her, Salvius enjoyed an influence comparable to that exerted by the Rikskansler on his son.[3] As the negotiations wore on, there was a growing clash between, on the one hand, Salvius and the queen, and, on the other hand, the Oxenstierna party in the Council of State. Salvius strongly favoured a peace based on consensus, even if that meant sacrificing certain Swedish demands. But Axel Oxenstierna

---

[3] Salvius has been described as 'probably the strongest mind she [Queen Kristina] encountered during her time in Sweden, and the man who most influenced her of all Swedes.' Stolpe (1982: 89 f.).

felt that it would be a useless undertaking for Sweden to try to please and reconcile its neighbours. The queen did not oppose the Oxenstierna party while the question of Swedish territorial gains was still unsettled (indeed, she seems to have agreed with them on this point). But as soon as that question was resolved, she turned against them, and in the final phase of the congress leant heavily on Salvius.

As a result, relations between the two Swedish plenipotentiaries tended to be strained. Even stronger animosity existed in the French delegation. This was headed by the Duke of Longueville, a high-ranking nobleman and essentially a figurehead, whose special task was to maintain some outward unity—as the other two pleni-potentiaries, d'Avaux and Servien, were on the worst possible terms. They belonged to different factions at court, and at one stage relations between them were so bad that they refused any contact with each other except in writing.

The Emperor had two plenipotentiaries at each site; in addition, he later dispatched Maximilian von Trauttmansdorff, a gifted dip-lomat and close personal friend, to act as his senior representative. The other remarkable figure in the Imperial camp at the congress was Dr Isaac Volmar, a lawyer and originally second man at Münster. He cooperated closely with Trauttmansdorff and came to play a major role in the congress at large.

2. CONSENSUS: DIFFICULT, DESIRABLE, POSSIBLE

2.1. Difficult

The international system that the congress of Münster and Osnabrück undertook to reorganize was highly complex. More-over, it was in a state of flux and inherently unstable due to a lack of system-wide consensus. During the negotiations, there was no cessation of hostilities—an illustration of the mutual distrust that characterized the international political climate. In a revealing passage, the Riksråd advised the Swedish delegates that, while an armistice might be desirable, they should not lightly take the initiative themselves, considering that 'if we intend by means of an armistice to obtain some breathing space or advantage we would then alienate the few friends that we have and seek to win those as friends of whom we have no friendship to expect.' If someone else were to take the initiative it was not to be rejected out of hand.[4] But if a dominant power like Sweden was not prepared to take the first step, who would?

Salvius, in writing to the French prime minister Mazarin to exhort him to dispatch delegates to the congress, also urged him expressly to intensify the war effort, warning that if the allies laid down their arms then the negotiations would erode the foundations of their common security. He affirmed that 'the shield is what the negotiation must rest on'.[5] These utterances predate the beginning of the congress in 1644, but the attitudes expressed in them prevailed until its conclusion.

In his instruction for Trauttmansdorff of October 1645, the Emperor, too, specified that a general armistice should not be accepted rashly, and that if one were to be concluded it should be only for a brief period.[6] Later, when the fate of Habsburg Alsace was at stake, the Emperor did urgently seek an armistice, but the French saw no reason to grant it. Fighting therefore continued until the treaties were signed or, due to slow communications, even later. (Swedish troops had partially taken Prague when news of the peace reached them—indeed, it appears that the messenger was deliberately held back.[7])

At the congress, there was no shortage of potential consensus notions, but they were vague, confused, largely subconscious, and sometimes contradictory. An adequate consensus agenda was lacking—one did emerge to some extent as a result of the negotiations, but the process was laborious and the result, fragile.

2.2. Desirable

On one point, all the participants in the negotiations were agreed—that peace was to be declared desirable and that no one wanted to be seen to stand in its way. All the interested parties were torn between their aspiration for peace (or, at any rate, their perceived obligation to that goal) and their aspiration to optimize their own position in the international system, if necessary by force. But to take account only of the latter as an input in the decision-making process would be misleading.

---

[4] 26 May 1644, APW II C. i. 218.
[5] 'fulcrum tractatus est clipeus', 10 Sept. 1643, APW II C. i. 25.
[6] APW I. i. 451 f.   [7] Odhner (1877: 288).

Sweden offers a case in point. The Swedish Council of State, in its instruction for the congress, declared Queen Kristina eager 'to remedy the shedding of blood and the devastation of countries, to bring peace to Christendom and help it regain its repose'.[8] On another occasion, it piously reiterated her wish to see the negotiations proceed speedily and successfully, providing for 'the glory of God's name, the repose and comfort of his congregation, and the peace and great benefit of our beloved fatherland'.[9]

If speeches were to be made at the opening of the congress, the delegates were to express 'Her Royal Majesty's grief and compassion on account of this war, the division of Europe and of Christendom, and the desolation of Germany', and the queen's desire to re-establish 'the former good and trusting friendship between the Roman Empire and the Realm of Sweden,' promising 'every cooperation in procuring a secure, honest, general peace'.[10]

Consultations with the French were to be oriented towards 'the general interest of all kings and republics; in the first place should be discussed the situation, welfare, and security of Sweden and France'. The deliberations were then to be extended to the common allies in Germany, and also to others, such as the Dutch States General and the Italian princes:

not so much because we are obliged to act in this fashion or firmly resolved to insist on it, but because we are trying to do what can be done, and in order to show to the world that we are by no means indifferent to what happens in the world; of course this has to be handled carefully and care has to be taken that it is not interpreted as an obligation, but exclusively as courtesy and goodwill.[11]

One is tempted to dismiss this as posturing, and indeed it was in part, but the message it carried was nevertheless genuine. Without being unduly altruistic, the Swedes did wish for peace. Axel Oxenstierna wanted peace for Sweden because the country needed it;[12] but he was not as emphatic about it as was the queen. Queen Kristina wanted peace for Europe. She became increasingly impatient with what she perceived—rightly or not—as the obstructionism of the Oxenstierna party. At one point some three years

---

[8] Swedish main instruction of 15 Oct. 1641, APW I. i. 237.
[9] To J. Oxenstierna and Salvius, 11 July 1643, APW II C. i. 3.
[10] Main instruction, APW I. i. 245.   [11] APW I. i. 242 f.
[12] Lundgren (1945: esp. 295).

into the congress, she added the following revealing missive to the regular office letter for Osnabrück, bypassing the Council of State, which normally supervised the official diplomatic correspondence:

These few words are only added to my public letter so that I might reveal to you with my own hand the fear that I have that this desirable negotiation ... might be upset. In order now to make my will entirely clear to you, I want you to be fully persuaded that above all I long for a secure and honourable peace. ... it is therefore my will that you keep things going in a proper way, ... and assiduously bring the negotiation to a desirable conclusion, making [the terms to be obtained] as good as can be done without breaking the peace, and no longer dawdle with it as hitherto has been done; if it is done differently I leave it to you how you will justify that before God, before the estates of the realm, and myself. Let not the fantasies of ambitious men detract you from this goal, if you are at all keen to avoid my extreme displeasure, and unless you have a mind to answer me for it, going pale and red in turn, in which case you may trust that no authority, nor the protection of powerful families, shall prevent me from showing to the world the disfavour with which I view unreasonable proceedings; for I am sufficiently convinced that, if the negotiation runs into difficulty, I would through your fault be enmeshed in the labyrinth from which neither your lights nor those of them who foment such plans would deliver me, wherefore you need to take great care, which I have no doubt you will do, and I only write this for your information and have every confidence in your cautious conduct, so that with God's help I expect a good outcome in this slow peace.[13]

This letter (which Johan Oxenstierna sent back to Sweden to his father Axel, after Salvius had refused to answer it jointly with him) predictably caused a row between Axel Oxenstierna and the queen; this was patched up but the chancellor temporarily withdrew to a country seat to sulk. In a private letter to Salvius, written on the same day as the above, the queen made it clear that her ire was really directed at Johan Oxenstierna. The allusion to 'powerful families' is, of course, transparent. Salvius, on the other hand, came from a relatively humble social background. Kristina praised Salvius's efforts 'to put an end to this long, perilous, and bloody war, which for such a long time now has burdened nearly all

---

[13] Queen Kristina to J. Oxenstierna and Salvius, 20 Apr. 1647, APW II C. iii. 383 f. On this letter, and more generally on the self-perception of the queen as a bringer of peace to the world, see Stolpe (1982: 150 ff.). See also Odhner (1877: 210 ff., 287 f.), Lundgren (1945: 283 ff., 295).

Europe,' and she again condemned the attempt by some 'at least
to protract the negotiation, if they cannot actually thwart it.' But,
she continued, 'I . . . shall let the world see that not even R. C.
[Rikes Cansler, i.e. A. Oxenstierna] is able on his own to move the
world with one finger; enough said for the wise.'[14]

Kristina may have wished to weaken the ruling élite, traditionally a warrior caste, and whose power competed with that of the
crown. The Oxenstierna party in general, and the person of the
chancellor in particular, epitomized this class. But at the same time,
and probably more importantly, the queen believed with almost
neurotic fervour in her royal calling as a bringer of peace; this was
an essential ingredient in her somewhat unbalanced feeling of self-
worth. Her recurrent use of expressions like 'show to the world',
'let the world see' indicates her defiant resolve to prove herself.
Kristina wanted peace so as to bask in its glory, and if the nobility
stood in the way of this goal, that was reason enough for her to
oppose them. Her father Gustaf Adolf had won fame as a warrior-
king. She intended her own apotheosis to result from the peace.
The chancellor, whom the queen had inherited from Gustaf Adolf
and whose reputation rested on his role in the war, was a substitute
father-figure to rebel against.

Kristina was inundated with poetic outpourings depicting her as
a bringer of peace. In 1649 she commissioned a ballet or masque
entitled *La Naissance de la paix*, with words by Descartes, who
had just arrived in Stockholm and who duly celebrated his new
patron. Kristina seems to have taken all this quite seriously.[15] As
to her clash with Axel Oxenstierna, no sooner was the peace
concluded than a *rapprochement* took place between her and the
chancellor, showing that she did not wish his downfall.

As to Salvius, he had in fact written the Swedish war manifesto
for Gustaf Adolf,[16] but subsequently he campaigned consistently
for peace. He was the moving spirit of the peace party, which
wanted Sweden to pull out of the war, and the only outspoken
opponent of Sweden's involvement after the chancellor had prevailed in this matter. Salvius explicitly stated in 1636, when the

---

[14] 'Jag . . . skall låta världen se att icke heller R. C. förmår allena röra världen
med ett finger, sapienti sat.' Queen Kristina to Salvius, 20 Apr. 1647, APW II C.
iii. 385.   [15] Stolpe (1982: 151 ff., 188).
[16] Lundgren (1945: 26 f.). Text in French: Du Mont (1728: v. 2, 608 ff.); in English: Symcox (1973: 102 ff.).

peace party was at its lowest ebb, that his personal ambition was 'to bring home cherished peace'. His determination to do this was as remarkable as it is difficult to explain, at least in terms of self-interest. It created tensions with the chancellor, on whose good-will Salvius's career depended, and it was a long time before the patronage of the queen, who took power in 1644, compensated for that.[17]

Because of his social origin, Salvius did not share the military ethos of the Swedish nobility, for whom the possibility of more war in the future did not present a problem. War did not endanger the nobility's livelihood, which depended largely on agricultural holdings on the Swedish mainland (itself unlikely to be a theatre of war). Moreover, war opened up the possibility of gaining possessions abroad, as officers were often rewarded with estates in conquered territories. Salvius, on the other hand, was a business-man, whose economic interest was not served by the war. He spent almost twenty years of his life in Hamburg, where he staked considerable sums on commercial ventures. Furthermore, he had long been in charge of the financial side of the Swedish war effort. He therefore understood more clearly than most that, economically speaking, the Swedish colossus had feet of clay. As we will see, he seems to have acted on the premiss that, in the long run, Sweden could not hope to defend its overseas possessions militarily. The only chance of permanently consolidating Sweden's position was to base this position on international consensus and the acceptance of Sweden's neighbours.

The Emperor determinedly pulled out the same rhetorical stops as the Swedes. His main instruction for the Münster delegation stated the congress to have convened in order to restore 'us and the Holy Empire, our beloved fatherland, as well as our laudable house and the electors, princes, and estates who assist us, to the former friendship and neighbourhood, trustfulness, and concord enjoyed with the crown of France and its associates'. It declared this to be a 'highly necessary endeavour in the public interest

---

[17] 'Und muß bekennen', Salvius wrote to Johann Kasimir von Pfalz-Zweibrücken, an uncle of the queen, on 9 May 1636, 'daß ich eine Ambition darin suche, daß ich den werten Frieden nach Hause bringen möge', quoted Lundgren (1945: 148); and again to the same on 31 Oct. 1637 that peace was what he 'von Grund meines Herzens zu Gott wünsche', quoted ibid. 189.

[*dieses hochnotwendige gemeinnützige Werk*]'.[18] The plenipotentiaries were to let it be known that

we had, since commencing our Imperial reign, sought and desired nothing
more eagerly, in order to prevent the shedding of so much innocent blood
and restore the old trust between the Holy Roman Empire and the
neighbouring crowns, than the means to preserve, between, on the one
hand, the Holy Empire and the electors, princes, and estates that faith-
fully serve and belong to it, and on the other, the foreign crowns that,
at present, are found with their troops on the Holy Empire's soil, good
agreeable neighbourhood, to re-establish trade between the subjects on
either side and to restore the old trust to its previous state . . .[19]

Overemphatic and convoluted as this statement may seem, its
message is clear. This message was reiterated on more than one
occasion. In October 1645, in a letter to the Osnabrück delegation, the Emperor spoke of 'our peaceful intention and sincere
desire to re-enter the former trusting relationship with the Queen
and crown of Sweden'. He commanded the delegates to enquire
of the Swedes how they proposed to re-establish 'between us and
the Holy Empire and Her Dilection the Queen and her realm and
lands the former good intelligence and neighbourhood'.[20] The
plenipotentiaries were admonished to contribute everything that
they could to a successful conclusion of the negotiations, if it was
at all compatible with the dignity of the Emperor and the Empire.[21]
They were not to delay dealing with the French and Swedish peace
proposals:

If the crowns should take such delay for an occasion either to break off
the negotiations completely, or with manifold new pretexts—in particular
this one, that they had not received any reply—[to] let the peace-making
come to nothing, then this would, with regard to the beloved fatherland
and the whole of Christendom, be irresponsible to us.[22]

Least vociferous in advertising their desire for peace were the
French. At least part of the explanation lies in the fact that they

---

[18] 15 July 1643, APW I. i. 399.   [19] APW I. i. 401.

[20] APW II A. ii. 513. The Imperial chancery consistently referred to monarchs
other than the Emperor as 'Liebden', 'Dilection' (a traditional medieval form of
address), rather than 'Majesty'. It sought, unsuccessfully, to reserve the title 'Majesty' for the Emperor.   [21] APW I. i. 402 f.

[22] 'so würde alsdann solches uns gegen dem geliebten Vaterland und der ganzen
Christenheit zumalen unverantwortlich sein.' Ferdinand III to the delegates at
Münster and Osnabrück, 15 Sept. 1645, APW II A. ii. 475 f.

were militarily in the ascendant. They had the most reason to believe that they would do well out of continuing the war. Moreover, allowing Habsburg—the Emperor and the King of Spain —time to recover would only encourage them to subvert any settlement in the future. Spain, in particular, could not be trusted in this respect.[23]

Not to join in the call for peace would have been costly in terms of reputation. But if there was to be peace, safeguards against future Habsburg encroachment would be required. For this reason, Richelieu, the author of the main instruction for the French delegates at the congress, envisaged an elaborate collective security system. In the instruction, this is presented as not just a good thing in itself, but as also capable of making a good impression on the rest of the Christian world. This, Richelieu felt, would enhance French credibility.[24] To be seen to be seeking peace was the obligation of any Christian government, and Richelieu in his instruction consequently placed due emphasis on the *repos de la chrétienté*.

2.3. Possible: Based on a Sense of Obligation to the Community

The congress had a double constituency: on the one hand, the European states system at large and, on the other, its central subsystem, known as the Holy Roman Empire. The consensus inherent in these two structures manifested itself as a sense of community which the negotiators could appeal to. It was bound up with the concepts of 'Christendom' and 'Germany' respectively.

2.3.1. Christendom

In the larger European system, a sense of community was expressed in the frequent designation of the congress as *senatus orbis christiani*, or senate of the Christian world. The documents contain references to religious doctrine. The peace proposals emanating from the Imperial, Spanish, and Swedish delegations, as well as the opinions on these proposals voted by the estates of the Empire, were invariably headed by invocations of the Trinity,[25] as,

---

[23] 'l'expérience nous fait connaître que les Espagnols ne gardent leurs traités qu'en tant qu'il leur est utile'. Main instruction for the French delegates, APW I. i. 71.

[24] 'ce sera chose agréable à toute la chrétienté qui donnera d'abord bonne impression du procédé de la France,' APW I. i. 70 f.

[25] These documents will be found in Meiern (1734–6).

eventually, were the treaties themselves ('In nomine sacrosanctae et individuae Trinitatis Amen'). It was clearly seen as politic to insist on one's Christianity, implying acceptance of a common denominator. Indeed, confessional bias was something that the negotiators disapproved of—especially in others. The Frenchman Servien, for example, felt that the Swedish delegates were too little concerned with *raison d'état* and excessively attached to the protestant cause.[26] True enough, the Swedes were instructed to extend their friendship to Protestants and Catholics alike, but primarily to the Protestants.[27] The same somewhat contradictory approach, however, is apparent from a laboured passage from the pen of Brienne, the French secretary of state:

On one point we concur with the Swedes, but not on the means. Weakening the excessive power of the House of Austria, establishing the liberty of the princes of the Empire; that has, indeed, been the aim of our union and of the war. But to reach it by strengthening the Protestants, by weakening the Catholics, that is what we do not concur with and, on the contrary, our goal must be to love [*aimer*] Catholics and Protestants to defend their liberty and to support what is just for each without distinction of religion, but always defending and strengthening our own without allowing ourselves to be induced to weaken it by an ill-founded fear that being Catholic means being dependent on the Spaniards. We have seen that maxim being accepted and defended and it needs to be invalidated and destroyed, making the Catholics understand that when we loved the Protestants, it was not because they were Protestants, but because they were princes who opposed the Emperor . . .[28]

Neither the French prime minister Mazarin nor his protégé at the congress Servien hesitated to sacrifice religion to *raison d'état*. In response to calls by the Imperial delegation for a rapid peace, enabling Christendom to make common cause against the Islamic Ottoman Sultan, Servien warned against 'a misplaced piety, to which our enemies are not susceptible when the fortune in war is favourable to them'. He claimed that '[r]eal charity must begin with the goal of establishing the greatness of the state [*la grandeur*

---

[26] 'Ce qui est un peu fâcheux en traitant avec eux [the Swedes] est qu'il n'est pas malaisé de remarquer dans leur conduite que la faction et l'intérêt de la religion protestante domine beaucoup plus dans leur esprit que la raison d'état.' Servien to Brienne, 31 Dec. 1644, APW II B. i. 824.

[27] The Council of State to the Swedish delegates, 8 Aug. 1643, APW II C. i. 6.

[28] To the French delegates, 18 Mar. 1645, APW II B. ii. 186.

de l'état], and of strengthening it now against the endeavours of its old enemies.'[29] Mazarin, being a cardinal, took the matter more seriously. In his instruction for the French delegates of November 1645, he conceded the need to pacify Christendom in order to put it in a position to combat the Ottoman danger. At the same time, however, Mazarin was unable to resist pointing out that France's willingness for peace was all the more praiseworthy in this respect because it stemmed from pious motives, whereas 'the others [*les autres*]' were acting out of fear for their own territories—situated closer to the Ottoman borders.[30] The Imperial request for aid against the Sultan was answered evasively.[31]

Servien's colleague (and enemy) d'Avaux, an appointee of the pious queen mother, seems to have been the only one of the main delegates to the congress to be both personally devout and prepared to let his religion influence his politics in a systematic way.[32] D'Avaux helped the Catholics where he could, prompting complaints from the Swedish delegates. Servien agreed with the Swedes, but, given the tense relationship between the two French delegates, he was the last person that d'Avaux would have listened to.[33] Longueville, too, aroused Swedish suspicions by stressing France's duty to protect the Catholic religion.[34] But when he was taken to task by the Swedish negotiator Rosenhane, Longueville genially assured him that he would exhort the German Catholics to be pragmatic and to leave the religious quarrel to be decided in the next world.[35] It is also worth noting that the French, with their cross-denominational alliances, uniquely and rather pointedly omitted the customary invocations of the Trinity from the headings of their official proposals, as if to keep theology out of the negotiations altogether.

Of the two main Swedish delegates at Osnabrück, Johan Oxenstierna certainly did not distinguish himself by his religious

---

[29] To Lionne, 11 Nov. 1645, APW II B. ii. 840 f.
[30] APW II B. ii. 888.
[31] See e.g. the French memorandum of 29 May 1646, Meiern (1734–6: iii. 45).
[32] See Dickmann (1985: p. xvii).
[33] J. Oxenstierna to Rosenhane, 15 June 1645, APW II C. i. 636.
[34] APW II C. i, no. 25.
[35] 'så att de måtte låta komma den divisionen, som i religionerna är, att decideras i andra världen ... efter de dock måtte bo uti ett land och under en överhet tillsammans.' Rosenhane to J. Oxenstierna and Salvius, 3 Feb. 1646, APW II C. ii. 107.

zeal, while his colleague Salvius seems to have been completely agnostic. Fascinating evidence provided by Stolpe, the biographer of Queen Kristina, shows Salvius to have been very much interested in the underground 'libertinist', i.e. neo-pagan movement in Italy and France, as, indeed, was Queen Kristina herself.[36] During the congress, Salvius once addressed a remarkable, almost proto-Marxian letter to her, dismissing religious superstructures as a disguise for economic interests.[37] There was no particular reason for him to indulge in such theorizing, except that he clearly saw the queen as a kindred spirit, someone who liked to read that sort of thing.

Even the Imperial court at Vienna thought along relatively secular lines. A group of relatively liberal clerics there combated the extremist Catholic party, headed at the congress by figures such as Bishop Franz Wilhelm von Wartenberg.[38]

The importance of religion in international political processes was clearly on the decline. While religious affiliation retained its significance as a marker of collective identity, the waning of the crusading spirit made a basic consensus possible even between actors of different denominations. All that was required was an agreement that the established religious identity of the actors participating in the system would thenceforth be left undisturbed. This maxim became one of the mainstays of the settlement.

2.3.2. Germany

Declining sectarian zeal, then, diminished the potential for conflict in the international system, and thereby brought consensus within easier reach. But religion itself could not provide the basis for this consensus, nor was there any alternative, stronger ideology available to be held in common by actors in the system at large.

In Germany, on the other hand, a secular ideological bond between the various actors existed. The assembled delegates of the estates of the Empire referred endlessly to what was virtually their shibboleth, the 'beloved fatherland of German nation'. In Germany, the sense of obligation to the community was not based on religion but on a sometimes strident nationalism. There was agreement that the Empire was in danger, both from French and

---

[36] Stolpe (1982: 191 ff.).   [37] 9 July 1646, APW II C. ii. 357 f.
[38] Ruppert (1979: 240 ff.).

Swedish expansionism and from internal dissension. This was accompanied by a general wish, formulated in the following example by the Council of Electors, that

His Majesty the Roman Emperor, the electors, and estates, in their dignity, honour, lands, and population, should as far as possible be kept together and maintained, without any separation or dismemberment, and that, above all, the entire edifice of the Empire be handed down to dear posterity.[39]

It is this pan-German community feeling that explains the existence of a greater potential for stability in the German subsystem than in the European system as a whole. In the Holy Roman Empire, community feeling acted as a bedrock for other consensus notions, as will be seen in more detail later on.

3. TWO BASIC PRINCIPLES: LOYALTY AND STRUCTURAL INVIOLABILITY

It is possible to posit two consensus principles, distinct but interwoven, as being linked to this sense of community. They are, on the one hand, the inviolability of the structures or political framework by which the community was defined, and, on the other hand, loyalty to the community and its members and representatives. The significance of these principles for the Holy Roman Empire is easily established. Why did the Empire not disintegrate, given that the Emperor had essentially become a figurehead with few executive powers? Why did it remain so different from the Italian subsystem, although that, too, had been constituted from the remains of the medieval Empire?

The main difference from Italy was that the German princes and cities retained common institutions and formally acknowledged a common suzerain. This phenomenon did not result from a shared weakness. With about a million inhabitants, the Electorates of Saxony or Bavaria, for example, were as populous as the Kingdom of Sweden,[40] and they were much more developed economically. Through alliances with foreign rulers, the estates of the Empire

---

[39] Resolution of the Council of Electors, presented in the plenary session of the estates at Osnabrück on 16 Apr. 1646, Meiern (1734–6: ii. 921).

[40] According to Dickmann (1985: 47). The new Vasamuseet at Stockholm (1990) puts the population of Sweden under Gustaf Adolf at 1.5 million.

could intervene in the politics of Europe as virtually autonomous actors, and, indeed, they had done so during the war.

The estates could have aimed at complete independence, and the French, as will be seen, fully expected them to do so. But this expectation proved mistaken. The estates operated policies that were not exactly un-self-regarding, but they were careful to respect the limits set by the Empire's constitution. The official aim of the estates was not to weaken the Emperor but to assert ancient and well-established rights. The Emperor, it was argued, had violated these rights during the war, making it necessary to reassert them at the congress. This was the framework for the negotiations, and whatever private ambitions the estates might want to pursue had to be fitted into it.

Nor was this merely a hollow convention. A deeply felt sense of loyalty to the Emperor, and a patriotic pride in the Empire's institutions, were the cement that kept the estates together, despite their jealously guarded autonomy. This attachment to 'Kaiser und Reich' was so strong that actors almost invariably referred to it in justifying their policies.

Here is an example. When, in the final phase of the congress, the negotiations again reached a serious deadlock, the ever-enterprising Elector of Brandenburg, Frederick William, lobbied his fellow Protestant princes with a proposal to revive the Protestant 'Union'. This time, it was to act as an independent third party between the Emperor on the one hand and the two allied crowns France and Sweden on the other. It would use its military weight to support whichever side was more willing to bring about a settlement. In order for this scheme to work, the participation of the other Protestant elector, John George of Saxony, was crucial. The Saxon elector, however, feared that, rather than bring peace, this scheme could only ruin the Empire. In a memorandum to the Brandenburg special envoy, Burgsdorff, he justified his rejection of the Brandenburg proposal by arguing that the scheme would put the 'fatherland' at great risk, a risk that the remaining Protestant demands standing in the way of a settlement did not warrant. The Saxon elector warned that pressing these demands too forcefully would drive the Catholic estates into the arms of the French, rupture the fragile alliance between France and Sweden, and lead to the total breakup of the Empire as a result. This would bring most of it under French influence.

The memorandum culminated in a harangue asking the Brandenburg elector whether he was prepared to admit that

the entire fatherland of German nation should, through alien military power, be altogether ruined; so many prestigious electoral and princely houses brought under foreign sway; the Germans' good name, reputed in all the nations of the world, their dearly bought freedom and much praised constancy and keenness [*Freudigkeit*] trodden under; and finally, through continued warfare, the Germans' memory, like in the old days the Greeks', perish, as must be feared, among their descendants?

He had no doubt, continued the Saxon elector, that the controversial parts of the settlement,

even if they were to remain unaltered throughout (and His Imperial Majesty has, after all, offered to allow for every equitable advice and moderation), are not of such importance that there is reason to have recourse, against His Imperial Majesty, to Swedish or anybody else's troops, because it has to be borne in mind that, otherwise, the estates might be entirely reduced to foreign tutelage and domination, and the constitution of the German Empire, between its head and members, famous among all the other nations, shattered . . .[41]

After Saxony had said no, the scheme collapsed. It is worth noting, by the way, that the Saxon elector followed a completely autonomous policy, for all his emphatic loyalty to the Emperor. At almost exactly the same time as the Burgsdorff mission, the Emperor made soundings to ascertain whether Saxony would give up its armistice with Sweden and adopt a joint policy with Vienna to advance the settlement. Again the response was negative.[42]

A pamphlet that was probably circulated at the congress in June 1648 invokes both the loyalty and the structural inviolability principles in striking fashion. At the same time, it highlights national feeling as a political factor at the congress. The pamphlet sought to rally opinion at the congress against the (allegedly) proposed separation from the Empire of the Burgundian Circle. (Each estate of the Empire belonged to one of ten administrative units known as 'circles' or *Kreise*, each with its own institutions.) The Burgundian Circle had a somewhat special position in that it consisted largely of the Spanish possessions in the Netherlands

[41] Meiern (1734–6: v. 559 ff.). On the Brandenburg proposal, see Odhner (1877: 244 ff.). [42] Dickmann (1985: 451 f.); Ruppert (1979: 322 f.).

and in Burgundy. The King of Spain was an estate of the Empire in his capacity as Duke of Burgundy. As such, he was entitled to assistance by the Emperor and the Empire if he had to defend his possessions. When it became clear that there would be peace between France and the Empire, but not between France and Spain, this created a problem; something had to be done to prevent the Burgundian Circle standing in the way of the Franco-German settlement. In 1548 the Habsburg possessions in the Burgundian Circle had been removed from the jurisdiction of the Empire, but they continued under its protection. Therefore, leaving the Duke of Burgundy (alias the King of Spain) to his own devices could be interpreted as a breach of loyalty. 'What could be more heinous', the pamphlet asked,

what more ignominious, than to allow . . . to be torn from the body of the Empire, not one land, but several, a whole circle, a set of provinces! Let not the Germans' name be soiled by such a crime; let it not be known to posterity that in this turmoil there were Germans—a people once so steadfast in their loyalty—who, at the very moment of peace and to their utter disgrace, would forsake their faithful vassals, old friends, allies, and brothers; forsake their fellow citizens and countrymen; forsake their fellow Germans![43]

In addition to emphasizing the concept of loyalty, the rhetoric of this text is so conceived as to throw the structural inviolability principle into vivid relief, employing the architectural imagery often found where the Empire is discussed.[44] The pamphlet—paradoxically in polished Latin—was anonymous, but it seems likely that it emanated from the Spanish delegation. It did not have the desired effect—not least probably because neither the Spanish Netherlands nor the Spanish possessions in Burgundy were ethnically as German as it implied. The German estates were not willing to put themselves out for the King of Spain—despite his being labelled, in the pamphlet, as 'princeps sanguine Teutonico,

---

[43] Meiern (1734–6: vi. 60).

[44] 'Circulus Burgundicus . . . portionem non minimam sacrosancti huius imperii constituit. . . . Circulum hunc e medio tollere, est aedificii huius pulcherrimi vincula subtrahere; structuram, decem circulis compactam, convellere, corporis molem, quae per tam longam saeculorum seriem stetit illibata, detruncare. Paucis, est Imperii Romano-Germanici statum, heu nimium conturbatum, funditus evertere.' Ibid. 57.

ipsisque Caesaribus ortus' ('a prince of German blood, descended from the Emperors themselves').

Moreover, by this late stage of the congress, the French knew how to handle their German interlocutors. They were careful not to compound the breach of the loyalty principle that they demanded of them *vis-à-vis* Spain (a non-German actor, that is, which made it less bad) with a breach of the structural inviolability principle *vis-à-vis* the Empire itself. Contrary to what the pamphlet alleged, the French steered well clear of even implying that the Burgundian Circle might be detached permanently from the Empire, and they avoided the scare word 'dismemberment'.[45] In the end, it was explicitly confirmed that the Burgundian Circle would remain part of the Empire, although it was laid down that the circle would be excluded from the settlement until the Franco-Spanish war was over, and that the Emperor and the Empire were not to intervene in that war.[46]

The Spaniards pursued a policy of determinedly invoking consensus notions in order to achieve their objectives; we will see how they adopted a similar strategy *vis-à-vis* the Dutch. I would guess that the pamphlet was the work of Dr Antoine Brun, a native of Dôle in the Franche-Comté and the most gifted member of the Spanish delegation. He was famed for his rhetoric; he had already represented Burgundy at the Regensburg Reichstag of 1640–1. (The Franche-Comté or Freigrafschaft Burgund had been part of the Empire for several hundred years, the last King of Burgundy having left his lands to the Empire in 1032. For the preceding century and a half it had been held by the Habsburg family, since 1555 the Spanish branch. It was, however, entirely French-speaking; this explains why Brun would have referred to 'Germania patria nostra carissima' in Latin.) It was Brun, too, who was the soul of the Spanish–Dutch negotiations.[47]

The Spaniards adopted this policy of relying on consensus notions because their military situation gave them cause for concern. The French were less sensitive to the appeal of consensus notions—because they were militarily in the ascendant. The main instruction for the French negotiators posited that, in order to

---

[45] See Dickmann (1985: 481).
[46] §3 IPM. On this issue, see also Ruppert (1979: 344 ff.).
[47] See Poelhekke (1948: 120 and *passim*).

prevent universal dominion by the House of Habsburg, France needed access to Italy and Germany so as to be able to come to the assistance of the local princes. It assumed that the German princes would support French claims in Germany from a wish to weaken the Emperor, and drew a parallel with the princes of Italy who had also adopted this position.[48] This instruction still dated from the days of Richelieu (who died in 1642, shortly after it had been agreed to hold the congress). But Mazarin, Richelieu's successor as French prime minister, fully shared the assumption that the German princes would, in their own interest, support the French desire for a foothold in Germany, and that, if they had so far kept a surprisingly low profile, it was only as a result of shyness or blindness about their own advantage. Speaking of the need to convince the reluctant German estates to attend the congress, Mazarin contended that there was no need to fool them—such tricks, he thought, the French could confidently leave to others— but merely to open their eyes.[49]

If it is assumed that actors will always seek to maximize their power, then the German princes really should have welcomed whatever would help them to become as independent as the princes of Italy. In reality, however, the consensus agenda on which their authority rested eliminated this option, as the French delegates were to learn to their surprise.

Even if the estates felt inclined to distrust the person of the Emperor, this did not mean that they rejected the Empire as such. Had not the eminent constitutional lawyer Althusius at the beginning of the century contended that the Empire was more important than the Emperor ('Imperator minor Imperio')?[50] And, even if the estates did take that view, it was ultimately impossible to separate the two and be loyal to the Empire but not to the Emperor. The estates could not, in practice, have the one without the other. The French did not realize at first that the German estates were attached to both, because both embodied the structures defining the community of which they felt part. An example of this failure of understanding is provided by the following account of a meeting

[48] APW I. i. 100 f.

[49] 'Pour cela il ne faut point user d'artifices ni de fausses suppositions, c'est une conduite qu'il faut laisser à ceux qui en ont besoin. Il ne faut seulement que faire ouvrir les yeux aux Allemands'. To d'Avaux, 30 Apr. 1644, APW II B. i. 157.

[50] Quoted Dickmann (1985: 135).

between a representative of the Mecklenburg ducal house, Dr Kayser, and the French negotiator d'Avaux. The meeting was reported by Kayser to the Imperial delegates at Osnabrück, who in turn reported it to the Emperor.

On the occasion of the said visit, he [Kayser] had paid to Monsieur d'Avaux the usual compliments and had, in particular, touched upon the *negotium pacis* [the peace business] . . . ; whereupon Monsieur d'Avaux embarked upon a discourse concerning the intention and eagerness of the King of France to preserve the liberty of the Germans, saying that necessity required the estates of the Roman Empire—as the ones who were principally concerned, on whose behalf the war was being fought—[to make every effort] once and for all to convert the servitude in which they had hitherto found themselves into a permanent freedom, whereby the crown of France would be the more encouraged to attend to their affairs with proper determination. On the subject of this discourse, he, the Mecklenburg envoy, pointed out that the purpose of this assembly was to negotiate so as to achieve peace, to put an end to the war and to talk about ways of removing the foreign troops from the soil of the Empire; for in this consisted above all the freedom of the estates, so that they might at some point be saved from the intolerable and cruel burden of the war . . . By means of the peace, the estates would be restored to their ancient freedom, but not by means of troops. As against which, d'Avaux retorted that the freedom of the estates consisted in [respect for the Empire's constitution—which guaranteed the rights of the estates], and as long as that had not been obtained the estates could not boast of any freedom. The Mecklenburg envoy said that this could not be brought about through the might of foreign troops, but as soon as they had been removed from the Empire, then the electors, princes, and estates could talk about those issues that concerned them and the Empire with Your Majesty . . . , *non oportere bella ex bellis serere* [roughly: one should not graft war upon war]. Whereupon d'Avaux attacked him in the following terms: *domine, tu non intelligis negotium, melius est bellum ex bello serere quam pacem servitute emere* ['Sir, you do not understand this business, it is better to graft war upon war than to buy peace with servitude'] . . .[51]

Mecklenburg had no reason to be unduly attached to the House of Habsburg. A Protestant, non-electoral principality, its ruling house had been deposed by the previous Emperor during the war. It owed its restoration to the Swedish intervention—which,

---

[51] The Imperial delegates at Osnabrück to Ferdinand III, 16 Feb. 1645, APW II A. ii. 189 f. The letter is in German; I have preserved the Latin passages of the original.

incidentally, did not prevent Kayser from being equally suspicious of the Swedes. He told the Imperial delegates that the Swedes wanted to achieve everything by force just like the French.

Kayser must have been keen to make a good impression on the Imperial delegates. Nevertheless, it is clear that the attitude that he took towards the French endeavours was quite typical of the German estates. Even before their encounter with Kayser, the French delegates reported to Mazarin that

we are obliged, by what little knowledge we have of the disposition of the princes of Germany, to represent to Your Eminence that it is very different from that of the princes of Italy, the latter, being very intelligent and well-advised, approving of, and wishing for, everything that may contribute to make them independent, and for this reason being quite happy for France to possess some strongholds in Italy to lend them a hand in case of necessity and to keep the Spaniards at bay, but these [the German princes] are much more affected by the love of their fatherland [*beaucoup plus touchés de l'amour de leur patrie*], and cannot approve of foreigners dismembering the Empire, no matter what hope of gain we hold out to them, preferring by a policy worthy of the climate [*par une politique digne du climat*] the substance of a body of which they are members to the advantage that each of them can obtain privately through the division of the Empire. But they do not want this good to be bestowed on them . . . , nor that, in order to have better means of assisting them, foreign princes should aggrandize themselves at their expense. We will not miss any opportunities to make it clear to the princes or their envoys that they must adopt a different maxim for their own good, but, whatever we may do, it will be difficult to win them over to what we desire, or to prevent them from preferring us at heart to give back all our conquests . . .[52]

In the German subsystem, there was no executive centre strong enough both to arbitrate differences between the participating actors and to enforce its decisions—which, as stated in Chapter 1, is the hallmark of an 'international' system. But in their allegiance to established institutions and procedures the estates of the Empire found sufficient common ground both to reach a peace and to conduct for the next century and a half their mutual relations with a high degree of stability. It is no accident that such internal warfare as did take place in Germany after 1648 can be traced almost exclusively to some of the strongest estates (especially Bavaria,

[52] D'Avaux and Servien to Mazarin, 14 Jan. 1645, APW II B. ii. 51.

Brandenburg, and Austria): these were also of weight in the less stable European system, but lacked any extra-German centre of gravity. (Conversely, Hanover and Saxony, with their British and Polish connections, favoured policies aimed at stabilizing the Empire.)

As long the Empire survived, that is to say until the turn of the nineteenth century, even the tiniest German princedom or free city was piously maintained in its rights and territorial integrity. During this period the peace was universally regarded with pride and as a masterpiece of statecraft. It was not until the nineteenth century, until the advent, not of nationalism (which has a much longer tradition), but of nation-state ideology, that the view prevailed in Germany that the peace was a disaster for the German nation, a triumph of particularism over unity. This interpretation is based on a projection back into the seventeenth century of the political ideas of a different age. It is linked to the absurd but widely held view that German national identity was somehow discovered around 1800, and that it played no role in German politics before that.[53]

On the European level, the two principles of loyalty and of structural inviolability of the given system, were much less effective. Who, on this level, was to be the recipient of loyalty? It could not be the Emperor, whose suzerainty had long ceased to be recognized by any European ruler outside the Empire. Neither, in an increasingly secular international environment, did the Pope retain much influence. He was to declare the treaties null and void—but, prophylactically, a clause had been inserted in the treaties to the effect that any Papal protest would not affect their validity.[54]

However, it is not the case that loyalty can only be shown to a superior. In the Empire, the estates felt loyalty to be owed, not only to the Emperor, but also to one another. On the European level, where the notion of a headship of the system was no longer accepted, this concept of reciprocal loyalty was the only one that could apply, and in practice it only applied with difficulty. There

---

[53] The changing evaluation of the peace is summarized in Dickmann (1985: introd.). The almost comically chauvinistic preface to Meiern (1734–6: vol. i) is representative of the earlier view, and illustrates the extent to which this, too, was impregnated with national feeling.

[54] Papal brief, *Zelo Domus Dei*, backdated 28 Nov. 1648; art. 17.3 IPO, §113 IPM. See Repgen (1956).

was no institutionalized cooperation on the European level similar to that operating within the German subsystem; therefore, in order to be effective, the loyalty principle had to merge in practice with the principle of structural inviolability. In other words, mutual loyalty was expressed by respecting the status quo. The extent to which this kind of loyalty was effective depended, first, on the strength of the actors' community feeling, and secondly, on the degree to which the existing structures had been defined.

In the case of the Empire, with its complex and largely written constitution, the degree of structural definition was high, and community (national) feeling, pervasive. As a result, the two principles could be operationalized in the treaties through a variety of procedural rules. Chief among these were the formal prohibition of war between the estates, with a parallel obligation to submit disputes to adjudication,[55] and the obligation, 'maioris concordiae inter status conservandae causa' ('so as to preserve greater unity among the estates'), for Catholic and Protestant estates not to try to convert one another's subjects, or to take up their cause against their rulers. This was offset by clauses enshrining, for example, the right to private exercise of the Protestant faith where it was not the official religion and vice versa, the faculty for subjects to emigrate to territories of their own faith without restrictions or economic penalties, and the prohibition of discrimination against subjects on religious grounds. It should also be emphasized that at the same time the sixteenth-century maxim of *cuius regio eius religio*, which had given princes the right to determine (and change) the official religion of their dominions as they pleased, was abandoned. It was agreed that every territory was to retain in perpetuity the official faith that it had had on 1 January 1624. If any ruler changed his personal faith after that date, as happened on a number of occasions, this could no longer affect the official faith of his dominions.[56]

On the European level, the two principles were to have been operationalized by means of Richelieu's grand scheme for a collective security system involving all the parties to the settlement.[57] Richelieu still envisaged that settlement as universal, covering

---

[55] Art. 17.7 IPO, §116 IPM.   [56] Art. 5 IPO, §47 IPM.

[57] The scheme was first put forward in 1629; see Dickmann (1985: 160 ff.), and the French main instruction, APW I. i. 70 ff. On this subject in general, see also Moser (1767: esp. 5 ff.)

Spain, Italy, and the Netherlands, as well as Germany. After Richelieu's death in 1642, his brief for the congress remained substantially unaltered. When the congress was finally assembling in 1644, Brienne, the French secretary of state, reaffirmed that the league project was still regarded by the French crown as the proper remedy against Spanish bad faith and against Habsburg megalomania in general.[58] But when the project was submitted, it was limited to its German leg, while the parallel Italian league envisaged by Richelieu was dropped:

they [the French] proposed, for the safeguarding of the peace, a general league between all those concerned in this pacification of the Empire and between all the princes and estates of Germany [*proposuerunt pro securitate pacis ligam generalem inter omnes interessentes in hac pacificatione Imperii omnesque principes ac status Germaniae*], with the reciprocal obligation for each and any of them to take up arms against him or those who might infringe the present treaty, provided that an attempt had previously been made to make good or halt the infringement by amicable agreement.[59]

After prolonged debate, the scheme was taken up in the final settlement:

and all the parties to the present transaction shall be obliged to defend and protect each and any of the provisions of this peace against anyone without respect of religion, and if there is any infringement of them by anyone, then the injured party shall first of all dissuade the offending party from the use of force, the matter itself having been submitted either to amicable agreement or to adjudication.

If, however, the matter has not been settled by either of these procedures within the space of three years, each and any party to the present transaction shall be obliged to join forces and counsel with the injured party and to take up arms to oppose the contravention, having been informed by the victim that neither amicable nor legal remedies had been of any avail . . .[60]

---

[58] 'pour nous, jusques à maintenant nous sommes persuadés que la ligue proposée dans vos instructions . . . est un remède assuré contre la mauvaise foi des Espagnols et contre la présomption qu'il sera malaisé de diminuer en eux et l'Empereur que leur maison peut et doit donner la loi à toute l'Europe.' To the French delegates, 14 Dec. 1644, APW II B. i. 756.

[59] Minutes taken by the Papal and Venetian envoys of an oral presentation by the French delegates, 7 Jan. 1646, Meiern (1734–6: ii. 202).

[60] Art. 17.5–6 IPO, §§115–16 IPM.

The scheme failed to acquire any European significance. Since no universal European peace was achieved, the project was reduced to a guarantee by France and Sweden of the Empire's constitution. In any case, it was only in the Empire, with its two supreme courts,[61] that adjudication was available and accepted as a means of peaceful settlement of disputes; there was, as yet, no question of similar institutions serving Europe as a whole.

On the European level, therefore, the two principles boiled down to a vague notion of good neighbourhood (the treaties call it 'loyal' neighbourhood, *fida vicinitas*).[62] Despite some lingering sense of obligation to the 'Christian commonwealth', this notion of good neighbourhood was too ill-defined to act as a real restraint on decision-makers comparable in effectiveness to nationalist community feeling in Germany.

When at the beginning of the congress the delegations exchanged their credentials (full powers to act for their respective sovereigns), the French produced a document of which the preamble uniquely combined ostensibly peaceful discourse with a vindication of war:

Since among all the goods that God . . . has imparted to mankind, peace is the one that is greatest, without doubt Christian kings and princes are the more obliged to procure it for their subjects, and to spare their blood and to see to it that the unavoidable evils of war may cease. Since they have been established for the purpose of defending their states, and of assisting their allies against invasion by those whose strength is superior, they sometimes find themselves obliged to take up arms; and he who does so for the sake of necessary and legitimate defence, and in order to bestow his protection on those to whom he owes it, acts righteously; so that, provided that he retains the intention of procuring peace, the disorder and the crimes that war brings about are in no way attributable to him. This was the maxim piously observed by the late Louis the Just [Louis XIII] of immortal memory . . . ; who, having been forced to take up arms for causes just, and manifest to all the world, and unwilling to desert the friends and allies of his crown for anything in the world, always nourished the desire for a general peace, welcoming every overture made to him to that end, and removing all the difficulties that could stand in the way.[63]

[61] The Reichshofrat at Vienna, controlled by the Emperor, and the Reichskammergericht at Speyer (later Wetzlar), controlled by the Reichstag.

[62] Art. 1 IPO, §1 IPM. The expression, rather German in flavour, seems to have originated with the Imperial delegates, who included it in their very first draft treaty of 6 May 1646 (Meiern 1734–6: iii. 66 ff.)

[63] French version in Le Clerc (1725–6: i. 151), Latin version in Meiern (1734–6: i. 202).

This document shows that the French were not particularly concerned with system-oriented cooperation at all. It refers, not to Christendom, with its connotation of commonwealth, but to Christian princes, in other words to individual actors. The text admits that these individual actors may be at odds with one another, and even implies that this is the normal situation, stating that the 'necessary and legitimate defence' of their territories is what princes are for. There is also an embryonic formulation of the concept of balance of power ('aid the weaker against the stronger') in justification of war. Loyalty, in this view, was due only to selected actors —the 'friends and allies'. It was not seen as something to be used to protect the stability of the system as a whole. All this implies an international system rather less static than that envisaged by the majority of the other participants at the congress.

On the European level, therefore, the solemn pledge at the beginning of the treaties ('And this peace shall be respected and upheld with all sincerity and dedication, in such a way that both parties shall promote the interest, honour, and advantage of the other')[64] could be no more than a hopeful assertion of goodwill. It could have been effective only in a system in which all the actors were content to 'know their place'; but France, for example, was not. Neither, in the end, were the Swedes—although, with less leverage, they posed less of a threat to the system as a whole.

4. A THIRD PRINCIPLE: LEGALITY

A further important principle, with perhaps a stronger influence on the shaping of the settlement than any other, was provided by the concept of legality, of conformity, that is, with written or customary law. Like the principle of structural inviolability, the legality principle was an outgrowth of that highly static conception of international politics that was common to the majority of actors at the congress. Their ideal was a settlement that would be definitive and final, restoring the public peace of the Empire and, if possible, extending it to Europe as a whole. It was this notion that the French and Swedish delegations stressed when, in the preparatory stages of the congress, they urged the reluctant estates to attend. The estates were warned that they would forever be bound by the

[64] Art. 1 IPO, §1 IPM.

results.[65] Restoring the Empire to its pre-war state, sanctioned by law and tradition ('Recht und Herkommen'), and untainted by autocratic tendencies on the part of the Emperor, was the official war aim of the two allied crowns. The Swedes took it particularly seriously—not only did they state it publicly themselves, but they urged the French, who were lukewarm about it, to do so, too.[66] The Stockholm government repeatedly reminded its delegates that

> although Her Royal Majesty, in her previous instruction, has, in particular, enjoined her representatives to reflect and endeavour with the mediators as well as with the French representatives and the estates to establish how the condition of the German princes and estates and of the Roman Empire itself might be restored to its previous state, yet Her Royal Majesty has nevertheless wished to repeat all this again, the stronger to impress on her representatives and enjoin them, that ... they should above all with all their strength press this point concerning the restoration of Germany and of the princes and estates of the Empire to their ancient liberty and condition as being the veritable main and fundamental cause of this war [*den rätta huvud- och fundamentalorsaken till detta kriget*] ... with such arguments and exhortations as its importance requires.[67]

The Peace of Westphalia is often considered to mark the beginning of a new era in European history, but the peacemakers far from regarded themselves as innovators. There was consensus among them that the settlement should bring a return to the *status quo ante bellum*, the main problem then being to define the *terminus ante quem*. The Emperor pressed for a date around 1630, but this would have introduced change with regard to the pre-war state. His opponents carried the day, essentially turning the clock back to 1618 in temporal and to 1624 in religious matters.

Any goal pursued by the participants at the congress was helped powerfully if they could show law and tradition to be on their side. For example, the French, in an attempt to prevent Habsburg from monopolizing the Imperial dignity, wished to outlaw the practice

[65] See e.g. the French circular to the estates of 6 Apr. 1644, Meiern (1734–6: i. 222), or the solemn exhortations in the Swedish safe conducts issued to the estates (ibid. i. 44, dated 14 Nov. 1643).

[66] The French circular was dispatched in response to a letter from Salvius to d'Avaux (11 Feb. 1644, APW II C. i. 163), and, indeed, used much of that letter verbatim.

[67] Memorandum for the Swedish plenipotentiaries, Aug. 1643, APW II C. i. 7 f. ('with the mediators': this was before the time when, for their part, the Swedes did away with the idea of mediation.)

of electing an emperor-designate during the lifetime and under the patronage of his predecessor. They claimed that this practice was against the 'laudable customs of the Empire'. What killed the attempt was the circumstance that this was precisely what it was not.[68] (In the Holy Roman Empire, as in several other European monarchies, the point of electing a ruler was not primarily to choose a candidate among several, but to ensure that the ruler respected the constitutional limitations on his power—as none other than Dr Volmar, of the Imperial delegation, explained to Longueville, the head of the French delegation.[69] Elective kingship was regarded as quite compatible with dynastic continuity. Indeed, barring such continuity would have weakened the system. The Council of Electors, with pained pomposity, therefore dismissed the French demand as manifestly contrary to law and tradition.[70])

The potential power of precedent was such that when the Imperial delegation proposed to reaffirm the rights of the Emperor (and of the electors) 'in accordance with the basic laws of the Empire and its laudable observances and usages, that is, custom as established of old',[71] the Swedes requested clarification as to whether the latter expression—'iuxta ... morem ab antiquo receptum'—referred to the ancients, covering the fullness of power enjoyed by a Tiberius.[72] They were assured by the Imperial delegation that, although tradition and unwritten rules were an important element of the Empire's constitution, it was the modern Empire that was being referred to.[73]

---

[68] See e.g. Meiern (1734–6: i. 444; ii. 201 f.).   [69] 26 Jan. 1646, ibid. ii. 216.
[70] Resolution of Apr. 1646, ibid. 920.
[71] Reply of 17 Sept. 1645 to the initial French peace proposal art. 7, ibid. i. 631; also in the reply to the parallel Swedish proposal art. 5, 17 Sept. 1645, ibid. 620. Version quoted here as in n. 75, below. Basic law (*lex fundamentalis* or *Grundgesetz*) was what the core texts of the German constitution were called.
[72] Swedish minutes of a meeting between the Imperial and Swedish delegations, dated 7 Jan. 1646, ibid. ii. 195. The French indicated to the Swedes that they intended to query the expression, but then apparently changed their minds; the Swedes went ahead. See J. Oxenstierna to Queen Kristina, 8 Jan. 1646, APW II C. ii. 43 f.; J. Oxenstierna and Salvius to Queen Kristina, 10 Jan. 1646, APW II C. ii. 63. Some, probably wrongly, appear to have interpreted the Swedish enquiry as merely polemical (see the statement by Brandenburg in the Council of Electors on 28 Aug. 1646: 'Die Krone Schweden hat in ihrer Replik schimpflich gesetzt, ob man den statum ad tempora Tiberii extendieren wolle,' APW III A. i. 651).
[73] Joint resolution of the estates at Münster and Osnabrück of 26 Mar. 1646, Meiern (1734–6: ii. 517 f.). The relevant passage was taken up almost literally by the Imperial delegation in a memorandum to the Swedes of 1 May 1646, ibid. iii. 59.

4.1. Legality Applied (I): Restoring the German Liberty

The episode just discussed took place in the context of the struggle for the rights of the estates—the so-called 'German liberty'.[74] At the same time that they gave the above-mentioned explanation, the Imperial delegates also included the expression in question almost unaltered in a draft treaty submitted to the Swedes. Article 5 of that document confirmed the participation of the estates in the legislation and foreign policy of the Empire, but it also confirmed the prerogatives of the Emperor and of the electors in the very words queried by the Swedes.[75] The Protestant princes, the free cities, and the Swedes all protested,[76] insisting that the controversial clause should either be omitted, or be made more specific by enumerating the Emperor's prerogatives exhaustively. The Imperial delegation eventually chose to drop it.

If the timid attempts to bolster the rights of the Emperor failed, the efforts made by the estates to vindicate theirs were much more successful. It was not that the estates had greater power. But they had the consensus agenda on their side, while the Emperor was fighting an uphill battle against it. If the success with which the estates defended their position at the congress had been exclusively due to the leverage afforded them by Swedish and French support, they might have exploited the opportunity to the full, and claimed new and more far-reaching rights for themselves. Instead, they chose only to reaffirm old rights, rights which they thought, or could at least acceptably claim, to have already possessed in the past. This was even true of the most important among these rights, that of alliance with foreign powers.

Article 8 of the Treaty of Osnabrück (which corresponds to paragraphs 62 to 66 of the Treaty of Münster) reaffirms the 'ancient rights, prerogatives, liberty, privileges,' etc. of the estates. It then makes specific mention of legislative activities as well as the declaration of war and the conclusion of treaties on the part of the Empire as a whole. In all of these activities the estates were to share. 'In particular,' the text then continues,

the right to conclude treaties with one another and with foreign powers, for the preservation and security of each, shall perpetually belong to each

---

[74] Mostly in the singular in the sources (whatever the language); also used in the plural: 'the German liberties'.

[75] Ibid. 67 f.   [76] See ibid. 77, 79, 91 f., 190.

of the estates; provided that such treaties are directed neither against the Emperor, nor against the Empire and its public peace, nor, in particular, against the present transaction, and that they are entirely compatible with the oath by which each is obligated to the Emperor and to the Empire.

Contrary to what is sometimes implied or asserted, this was really a clarification of the existing legal situation. The faculty for the estates to conclude alliances had been legally established since the Middle Ages. If the position expressed above had been an obvious innovation, the Emperor would undoubtedly have put up resistance. As it was, his delegates endorsed this position as soon as the need arose—in other words, they chose not to battle against the prevailing consensus.[77]

The Emperor's delegates were as concerned with legal forms as were those of the other estates. It was the Imperial delegates who modified an early Swedish proposal for a collective security system by introducing the obligation to submit disputes to amicable arrangement or adjudication before resorting to coercive measures, 'so as to prevent the shedding of Christian blood'.[78] This was endorsed by the estates.[79] The Council of Electors commented adversely that it had

noticed in the Swedish reply that the words, added by His Roman Imperial Majesty to article 17 of the Swedish proposal: *nec ea res intra spatium iam conveniendum possit amicabiliter componi vel iuris disceptatione terminari* [unless the matter can be settled amicably, or resolved by adjudication,

[77] Reply of 17 Sept. 1645 to art. 6 of the Swedish peace proposal of June, ibid. i. 620 f., and to art. 8 of the French proposal, ibid. 631. See also Ruppert (1979: 113 ff.), Dickmann (1985: 142 ff.). The stance taken by the Imperial delegates at Münster and Osnabrück contrasted with the much more restrictive 1635 Peace of Prague, of which Trauttmansdorff had been the chief architect. But the Peace of Prague had failed to win universal recognition, and ten years on, the tide had changed.

[78] Reply of 17 Sept. 1645, Meiern (1734–6: i. 622), to art. 17 of the Swedish peace proposal of June, ibid. 438. The idea of setting up a collective security system was French. However, the French delegates discovered that the Swedes seemed to dislike it. As a result, the French did not include it in their initial peace proposal to the Emperor. To their surprise, they found that the Swedes had, after all, taken it up in their parallel proposal, in a modified version apparently designed to create, in practice, a permanent alliance between the allied crowns and the estates, to be used against the Emperor if he infringed the settlement. Compare the unspecific corresponding art. 12 in the French proposal, ibid. 445. See also Lorenz (1969: 123 f.), Ruppert (1979: 107, 117).

[79] Draft resolution of the Protestant estates at Osnabrück, dated 27 Oct. 1645, Meiern (1734–6: i. 764); final draft (undated, Nov.), ibid. 830.

within a timespan to be agreed], and, more particularly, the little word *iuris*, are passed over and omitted.[80]

'das Wörtlein *iuris* präterieret und ausgelassen': nothing could be more typical of German legalism at the congress. 'They are all doctors', the Frenchman d'Avaux remarked of the delegates of the estates,[81] meaning that they were all lawyers, and this is reflected in their utterances. The conviction prevailed among the peacemakers that, provided the rights of each of the participating actors could be established definitively, no source of conflict would remain. Had not the present war been caused by the inadequacies of the 1555 religious settlement, which had not clarified the rights of Protestant and Catholic estates with sufficient precision?[82] A chief reason why the war had been so prolonged and acrimonious was that each party could convince itself that it was fighting for fundamental rights. Conversely, once agreement had at last been reached as to what exactly those rights were, the need to fight would be eliminated.

That belief was possible because of the status of legality as a consensus principle. For the purposes of international politics, law was not 'international law' in the modern sense, but the body of legal titles and privileges that, between them, the actors had accumulated over time. Where reverence for this corpus of individual actors' rights was sufficiently strong, it did indeed make an important contribution to the stability of the relations between the actors who shared it. This is exemplified by the German sub-system. Together with their sense of mutual obligation and their attachment to the existing political structures of the Empire, the legalism of the estates, and their satisfaction with the degree of protection of their rights achieved at the congress, largely preserved the Empire from further civil strife. In this respect, the Council of Electors was quite correct in its appreciation of the importance of 'the law'.

Coercive measures could be taken against local rulers to ensure respect for the Empire's constitution, including the 1648 treaties incorporated in it, and for individual rights of the estates. This was known as *Reichsexekution*. Such measures were ordered either by

---

[80] Resolution of the Council of Electors of Apr. 1646, Meiern (1734–6: ii. 928).
[81] Le Clerc (1725–6: iv. 62), quoted Dickmann (1985: 195).
[82] See Ruppert (1979: 229 f.).

the Emperor (usually acting on the advice of the Reichshofrat, one of the Empire's two supreme courts) or by the Reichskammergericht (the other supreme court). It was not the Emperor himself who normally carried out these measures, but, generally at circle level, the neighbouring estates, which were issued with a kind of execution warrant. *Reichsexekution* was not uncommon, and on quite a number of occasions successful.[83] But, obviously, it depended vitally on consensus, on a shared acceptance among the estates of the legitimacy of such measures. Of course, the system was power-less if any of the major actors decided to go against it, the most blatant example of which is Prussia's annexation of Habsburg Silesia in 1740 in total disregard of the Empire's constitution and its con-sensus agenda. But this was a rather exceptional occurrence. More-over, the 1740 act of aggression was between European rivals rather than between German co-estates, and it did not fundamentally upset the Empire's internal order. Significantly, between 1648 and the Empire's eventual disintegration in the 1790s, on the whole not even powerful Prussia threatened its weaker German neighbours—despite the fact that, from a purely power-political point of view, they presented much softer targets than Habsburg.

4.2. Legality Applied (II): Legitimizing Territorial Change

France and Sweden did seek to introduce change into the system, in the shape of territorial adjustments to be made in their favour. These territorial gains were supposed to serve as a 'satisfaction' or indemnity for services rendered to their German allies. But, although the territories that they coveted were already under their military control, their wish to appropriate them permanently faced stiff opposition. The opposition to the French and Swedish demands took strength from the fact that the two crowns had no *tituli legitimae possessionis*, that is legal titles, to the territories in ques-tion. Those actors who did were not easily convinced of the need to part with them. Interestingly, the right of conquest was admitted in theory as a means of legitimizing territorial change. But, con-trary to the popular perception of the period, it was universally rejected in practice.

One of the best-known thinkers of the so-called 'English School' of international-relations theory, Martin Wight, has claimed that

[83] Feine (1932: 110–11).

'prescription' was the cornerstone of 'pre-revolutionary' international legitimacy.[84] Wight thought that before the French Revolution, change in the international system could be legitimized by
the mere passage of time. This contention is not borne out by the
evidence that I have collected for this chapter, or, indeed, this
book. Logically, Wight's theory presupposes that, at the conclusion
of a peace, the victorious actors invoke, and the defeated ones,
though at first only under duress, acknowledge, a right of conquest.

At Münster and Osnabrück, the Council of Electors, in pro-
nouncing on the legal implications of the French and Swedish
territorial demands, dismissed the right of conquest as inapplicable.[85] No one, in fact, advanced the concept with any great conviction, preferring to rely on other notions instead.

The main French instruction for the congress, no monument to
coherence, claims that the French demands in Alsace and Lorraine
were justified by the *droit de la guerre*, that is, the right of conquest. Yet elsewhere it states that the French demands were based
on old and legitimate[!] rights (*droits anciens et légitimes*), whereas
those of the French allies were *only* based on the *droit de la guerre*.[86]

Servien, in a conversation with the Spanish envoy Saavedra,
agreed with the latter that sovereign rulers might rely on the right
of conquest, but was critical of 'usurpers' (meaning the Spaniards).
According to Servien, conquest was much more justified if it served
to re-establish pre-existing rights—a logically untenable position.[87]

The Spaniards, in their reply of April 1645 to a French peace
proposal of February, admitted that some past Spanish acquisitions
were perhaps based on a right of conquest and subsequent prescription ('habiéndolos [los derechos: not specified whose] prescrito
el tiempo por el spacio de muchos años'). But they warned against
such a conception as incompatible with stability. If France were to
keep the territories gained during the war, then the treaties to be

---

[84] Wight (1977: 158 f., 163).

[85] Resolution of Apr. 1646, Meiern (1734–6: ii. 921 ff.).

[86] Final draft 30 Sept. 1643, APW I. i. 75, 88, 69 ('[les prétensions françaises]
sont fondées en des droits anciens et légitimes, au lieu que la plupart de celles de
nos alliés n'ont autre fondement que le droit de la guerre').

[87] Saavedra said that 'le droit des souverains s'établissait et se conservait par les
armes. Je [Servien] repartis que si cette maxime est raisonnable en faveur de ceux
qui usurpent, elle l'est beaucoup davantage en faveur de ceux qui recouvrent ce
qui leur a appartenu.' The French delegates to Brienne, 8 Nov. 1645, APW II B.
ii. 823.

concluded could not be lasting, given that all princes had demands on their neighbours which the French example would encourage them to press by force of arms.[88]

The Spanish argument went to the heart of the matter, namely the problem of stability. The consensus agenda was bound up with the desire for a degree of stability, and the right of conquest therefore could not be part of it.

4.2.1. The Swedish 'Indemnity'

When Salvius discussed with some jealous German delegates the need to compensate the Elector of Brandenburg for his loss to Sweden of part of Pomerania, he rejected their argument that Sweden could claim Pomerania by right of conquest and that, therefore, compensation was not required. He emphasized the need to respect Brandenburg's established ancient rights in Pomerania.[89] Throughout the negotiations, the Swedes relied heavily on all three principles so far discussed—legality, loyalty, and structural inviolability—in order to justify and promote their demands. Indeed, these demands themselves, and the structural modifications of the system that they entailed, were shaped by the principles.

Sweden's demands were eventually reduced to claims on the Duchy of Pomerania, the Archbishopric of Bremen, the adjacent Bishopric of Verden, and the port of Wismar.

Wismar was owned by the Duke of Mecklenburg-Schwerin. He was in no position to make more than a very muted protest; his family had been dispossessed of its territories by the preceding Emperor, and it was to the Swedes that it owed their restitution.[90] However, since the duke's right to Wismar was uncontested, it followed that he had to be compensated. Had he pressed this point more forcefully, he might, with Swedish help, have obtained the Bishopric of Minden (one of a number of formerly Catholic ecclesiastical territories that the congress could dispose of, after the Catholic camp had finally agreed to their secularization). Instead, Minden was secured by Brandenburg. The Duke of

---

[88] Le Clerc (1725–6: i. 349 f.).

[89] J. Oxenstierna and Salvius to Queen Kristina, 18 Feb. 1647, APW II C. iii. 260.

[90] See the rambling but perfunctory protest (or rather plea) of the Mecklenburg representative at the congress, Dr Kayser, of 5 Feb. 1647, Meiern (1734–6: iv. 320 ff.), or J. Oxenstierna and Salvius to Queen Kristina, 26 Feb. 1646, APW II C. ii. 168; and 7 May 1646, APW II C. ii. 262.

Mecklenburg-Schwerin did receive the Bishoprics of Ratzeburg and Schwerin. These had, in fact, been administered (though not owned) by members of his family since the sixteenth century, so that the compensation was formal rather than substantial. Nevertheless, it is significant that it was felt to be necessary.[91]

The Archbishopric of Bremen and the Bishopric of Verden were governed by Prince Frederick of Denmark, the younger son of the Danish king. Frederick had been elected administrator in both bishoprics thanks to his father's influence (Protestant incumbents did not adopt the title 'bishop', but otherwise claimed the same status as catholic ecclesiastical princes).[92]

Frederick protested against his proposed deposition. He stressed his lawful election by the cathedral chapters, and his neutrality in the war.[93] He had, however, given up his neutrality after it had been violated by Sweden in 1644—indeed, the incident had prompted Frederick to take up a generalship in the Danish army and to fight in the Danish–Swedish war that had broken out in 1643, which had done nothing to endear him to the Swedes. But Frederick's greatest problem was his nationality. From the point of view of his German co-estates, there was not much difference between a Danish administrator and the proposed Swedish governor. (One difference—at least technically—was that Frederick had, by virtue of his election, only a lifetime entitlement to the bishoprics, while Sweden wanted them to be transformed into secular principalities in order to ensure their formal and perpetual appropriation by the Swedish crown. In practice, however, the firmly established pattern was that once a powerful princely house gained a foothold in one of the ecclesiastical territories, it was almost impossible to dislodge it.) Moreover, Frederick was expected shortly to mount the throne of his father, since his elder brother was childless and in bad health. For this reason, the German estates were even less likely to support him. Indeed, Frederick's brother died in June 1647, and Frederick was elected King of Denmark the following year.

For Sweden, he was therefore an ideal target. The Imperial delegation treated Frederick in a way that they would not have

---

[91] See Dickmann (1985: 384).

[92] The section on Bremen–Verden in this chapter owes much to Lorenz (1969).

[93] He repeatedly addressed himself to the congress in writing; see Meiern (1734–6: ii. 834 ff.; iii. 762 f.).

dared to treat a German prince—he complained that he was losing his possessions merely for being related to the Danish king ('bloß wegen der Verwandtnis mit der Krone Dänemark').[94] Indeed, the Imperial delegation adopted the extraordinary view that he had lost his lands to Sweden by right of conquest. It is difficult to see how this concept could be applicable in the Empire, because the possessions of each of the estates were supposed to be determined by inalienable vested rights, which could be ceded voluntarily but not taken from the estates against their will. But the Imperial delegation took the view that by participating in the Danish war, Frederick had forfeited any claim to protection by the Empire, and repeated pleading by his representative at the congress that he was being treated unfairly and less well than other princes availed him nothing. It is clear that the Imperial delegation was simply unwilling to treat him as one of the estates. If indemnifying the Swedes was unavoidable, it had better be at the expense of someone non-German.[95]

In secularizing the two Bishoprics of Bremen and Verden, the Emperor faced, and overrode, strong Catholic opposition. There was a rival Catholic claimant to the see of Verden, Franz Wilhelm von Wartenberg, and in 1645 the Pope also appointed Wartenberg apostolic vicar for Bremen. As it happened, Wartenberg was the vociferous mouthpiece of the Catholic radicals at the congress. They pressured the Emperor as much as they could in an attempt to prevent concessions to the Protestants. In March 1646 Wartenberg presented Trauttmansdorff (the Imperial plenipotentiary) with a memorandum severely criticizing the Emperor not only for abandoning Bremen and Verden to the Protestants, but also for allowing the bishoprics to be abolished. The Emperor, he warned, would have to answer for the perdition of a great many souls as a result. But, in his reply, Ferdinand III reminded Wartenberg that he, as Emperor, carried responsibility for a greater number of souls than the bishop did, and that failure to pacify Christendom would expose it to far greater danger: not from heretics, but from the infidels. This stance was supported by two of the most senior Catholic princes of the Empire, the Archbishop of Mainz and

[94] Memorandum by Frederick of 12 Nov. 1646, quoted Lorenz (1969: 154).
[95] Ibid. 151, 165, 168, 170, Ruppert (1979: 203 f.).

the Elector of Bavaria.[96] Initially, the Emperor tried to preserve
Bremen and Verden as bishoprics, but eventually he yielded. The
Imperial delegation merely stipulated that Frederick should
be given a pension and an adequate residence.[97]

Frederick himself, clearly regarding Bremen–Verden as *de facto*
part of the Danish royal patrimony, pressed for territorial compensation—which Queen Kristina was willing to help him get. But
Trauttmansdorff dismissed the idea and was unwilling to award
Frederick even financial compensation. When it became clear that
Frederick might succeed to the Danish throne, Trauttmansdorff
was able to point out, unanswerably in legal terms, that even if
Frederick were to keep the bishoprics he could not lawfully combine their tenure with occupancy of a royal throne. (Had the situation arisen, Frederick would presumably have circumvented this
problem by having another member of the Danish royal house
elected in his place.)

The knowledge that Frederick might become the most powerful
of Sweden's immediate neighbours induced Salvius to make a great
show of purporting to help him. Salvius reported to Queen Kristina
how, in the light of Imperial recalcitrance, the Swedish delegation
had 'brought up his compensation the more frequently, in order
to be excused the better and to show whose fault it is if he gets
nothing.'[98] Eventually, in June 1647, Trauttmansdorff offered
Frederick a golden handshake of 100,000 Reichstaler, to be paid
by Holsatia and Lübeck out of their dues to the Empire. However,
at the same time, Frederick became the official heir apparent to
the Danish throne, as a result of his brother's death, and this
caused Trauttmansdorff to waver again.[99]

In the end, it was Frederick himself who opposed being mentioned in the peace, because he did not wish to be seen to acquiesce
in the transfer. By the same token, he waived his compensation.
He was King of Denmark by that time and busy planning his
revenge on Sweden. The Swedes were unhappy about Frederick's

[96] Ruppert (1979: 207 f.).
[97] Draft treaty of May 1646, art. 22, Meiern (1734–6: iii. 71).
[98] J. Oxenstierna and Salvius to Queen Kristina, 27 May 1647, APW II C. iii.
427; also Salvius to Queen Kristina, 24 Dec. 1646, APW II C. iii. 149.
[99] J. Oxenstierna and Salvius to Rosenhane, 21 Mar. 1647, APW II C. iii. 338;
J. Oxenstierna and Salvius to Queen Kristina, 24 June 1647, APW II C. iii. 473;
Lorenz (1969: 174 f.). The administrator's yearly revenue from Bremen was esti-
mated at 60,000 Reichstaler in 1646, Lorenz (1969: 144). (Verden was much smaller.)

stance and would have preferred him to accept the deal formally. But they could not force him.[100]

Sweden received another serious setback when the Emperor created the city of Bremen a free city of the Empire in June 1646. This ingenious move gave Bremen-City the status that it had long been pressing for but never been able to obtain against the opposition of its archbishops. Free-city status meant that the city and the surrounding district under its direct jurisdiction were excluded from the deal with Stockholm, and as a result the Swedes did not gain control of this important port and the revenue that it generated. They were understandably aghast at being tricked in this fashion, but, at the same time, they were quite helpless to react. Bremen-City had, at a stroke, been converted into one of the Protestant estates of the Empire that Sweden claimed to be defending. As the Swedes depended on the Emperor for the legitimization of their acquisitions in Germany (proposing to receive them from the Emperor as their liege and to be admitted by him to the ranks of the estates), they were not very well placed to reject his authority to create other new estates as well; especially as his decision to make Bremen a free city had the sympathy of Sweden's Protestant German allies. Attacking the city would fatally undermine the patient attempts at legitimizing the Swedish position in north Germany without falling back on a right of conquest—put bluntly, it would blow the Swedish cover and make the Swedes much more vulnerable to opposition.

But Sweden's north German acquisitions were much diminished by the failure to gain Bremen-City. As a result, the Swedish attitude towards Bremen-City remained deeply ambiguous. The Swedes did not obstruct a passage in the final treaty that guaranteed the city's 'present' status both territorially and legally.[101] But they registered a reservation with the Imperial chancery to the effect that they understood 'present' to refer to the situation at the outset of the negotiations, thereby rejecting indirectly the 1646 Imperial decree. They requested the city to pay homage to the Swedish crown, which request was refused, and they also laid claim to some territory that the city insisted belonged to it, but which, according to the Swedes, had been under the direct jurisdiction of the

---

[100] Lorenz (1969: 185 ff.).
[101] Art. 10.8 IPO ('Civitati vero Bremensi eiusque territorio et subditis praesens suus status, iura et privilegia . . . sine impetitione relinquantur').

archbishops. However, for the time being they took no action. Only later did they resort to bullying. They laid siege to the city in 1653 and again in 1666, but, with the Emperor, Brandenburg, Hanover, Denmark, and the Dutch all poised to intervene, they refrained from capturing it. Eventually, a compromise was reached under which the city gave up the disputed territory but retained its status as a free city.

But of the prizes coveted by Sweden as a reward for its war effort, the most important was Pomerania. This was a very sizeable principality stretching along most of the German Baltic coast, not very distant from southern Sweden. Under a treaty dating from 1529, it should have passed to the Elector of Brandenburg on the death of its last native ruler in 1637. At that point, it was already under Swedish occupation. It was well known that Sweden had no intention of giving it up; however, as it turned out, neither did the Brandenburg elector, Frederick William.

The Swedes did not expect to be thanked for claiming Pomerania, but they were surprised at Frederick William's extreme tenacity. Their expectation was that, because he had never actually possessed the duchy, he would console himself for the loss, especially if given other territories in recompense. Not so. The Swedish negotiator Rosenhane, when describing to Johan Oxenstierna and Salvius an encounter with the head of the Brandenburg delegation Sayn-Wittgenstein, listed the numerous arguments heaped on him in order to persuade the Swedes to drop their claim. Wittgenstein seems to have saved the most effective argument until last. This was the fact that Sweden was supposed to be fighting *for* the Protestant estates, and relied on their support in Germany. Humiliating Brandenburg would demolish Sweden's standing with the estates. According to Wittgenstein, if Sweden insisted on claiming Pomerania then 'everything the crown of Sweden had so far built up and done to oblige the estates would, by pressing this claim, be torn down and transformed, as he explained at length and with a vehemence such that it took me aback'.[102]

The Imperial negotiator Trauttmansdorff also pointed out to Rosenhane the inconsistency of posing as the protector of the

---

[102] 'Ty eljest vad kronan Sverige härtill hade uppbyggt och gjort sig emot ständerna meriterad, skulle med denna begäran nederrivas och förändras, såsom han detta vidlyftigt och med en vehementia, att jag mig däröver förundrade, utförde'. 4 Nov. 1645, APW II C. i. 825.

estates while trying to deprive them of their possessions, warning against the ill-feeling and the desire for revenge that this would breed among them.[103] The Dutch, too, registered their opposition. They feared that their trade would suffer if Sweden controlled the mouths of the three great navigable rivers Weser, Elbe, and Oder, as well as most of the Baltic coastline. The Dutch intervention (at Münster, where the Dutch had their delegation) caused a great stir at the congress. Rosenhane, who reported it to his colleagues at Osnabrück, described Trauttmansdorff as basking in mildly ironic triumph at the Dutch stance: 'But if one desires too much for oneself,' Trauttmansdorff said, 'it is no wonder that one stirs up enemies in every quarter; that was not the way to achieve any sort of security. He who embraces too much may lose his grip! [*Chi troppo abbraccia poco stringe!*]' Trauttmansdorff then reiterated the need for 'equitable [*billiga*] terms'.[104]

In Stockholm, Chancellor Oxenstierna was undeterred by suggestions that the Swedish demands might go too far. He felt strongly that nothing that Sweden might do would win the acceptance of its neighbours anyway. In one of his letters to his son Johan, he complained of the jealousy even of 'our friends, whom we serve more than ourselves', and mused resignedly that '[i]t is our fatherland's innate misfortune [*vårt fäderneslands medfödda olycka*] that, no matter what we do and what benefit others derive from us, it is always interpreted maliciously.'[105] He remained faithful to the thinking of the late King Gustaf Adolf, who felt that the Swedish coastline was too long and equipped with too many natural harbours to be defensible. This made it necessary for Sweden to control the opposite shores as well.[106] 'We must', Axel Oxenstierna wrote to his son, 'look to what is right and to what the security of our state requires. We have no favours to expect from anyone involved in this matter. God and after him we ourselves must provide for our security.'[107]

But Salvius, Johan Oxenstierna's colleague at the congress, was convinced equally firmly of the need to find a compromise solution

[103] Rosenhane to J. Oxenstierna and Salvius, 8 Dec. 1645, APW II C. ii. 6.
[104] Rosenhane to J. Oxenstierna and Salvius, 2 Mar. 1646, APW II C. ii. 172.
[105] 8 June 1645, APW II C. i. 627.
[106] Gustaf Adolf to Axel Oxenstierna, dated 5 Mar. 1629, quoted Odhner (1877: 4 f.).
[107] Axel to Johan Oxenstierna, 21 July 1646, APW II C. ii. 370.

based on international consensus. Salvius was keenly aware that the Swedish war had been possible only because of the support of the German Protestants, that it had been fought with French money and German soldiers, and that delusions of grandeur were uncalled for. This is why he was so insistent that the Swedish position as defined by the peace should rest on general acceptance rather than on Swedish military strength. 'Our war in Germany', Salvius told Johan Oxenstierna in 1644, 'has up to now mostly rested on affection. Were we to lose that, a worse outcome would be imminent.'[108]

Commenting on the disastrous financial situation of the Swedish crown, Salvius observed that '[t]rue, there is the same complaint to be heard everywhere in Germany and France, and yet means are more easily found there owing to the size of these realms and their populous towns.'[109] The reference to size (*vidd*) is surprising if it is remembered that Sweden at that time was just as big on the map as France or the Empire—but, for all its expanse, it had only a fraction of the population of France or Germany, in proportion to which its war effort was enormous. With few towns to speak of and a lack of taxable wealth, Sweden could not be put in the same category as the French monarchy or the German lands.[110]

Salvius was, of course, not the only Swedish statesman to be aware of this. King Gustaf Adolf had hoped to marry his daughter and heir, the future Queen Kristina, to the Brandenburg elector, the result of which would have been to merge the Swedish dominions with those of the elector and to create a power that could maintain durable control of the Baltic. But while the elector was keen, Queen Kristina would not hear of marrying anyone. After the disastrous Swedish defeat at Nördlingen in 1634, the Swedish regency council urged Chancellor Oxenstierna to return home and

---

[108] 'Vårt krig i Tyskland haver härtill mäst bestått på affektion. Förlora vi den, så nalkas det till en värre utgång.' Salvius to J. Oxenstierna, 15 Feb. 1644, APW II C. i. 167.

[109] Salvius to Brahe, 19 Dec. 1646, APW II C. iii. 137.

[110] The number of troops in Swedish pay peaked at 120,000 during the period from autumn 1632 to autumn 1634. This level proved impossible to maintain, and by 1637 it had fallen to 45,000; Lundgren (1945: 167). On the Swedish war economy see ibid. 163 ff.; on the importance of French subsidies, ibid. 239 f. France, with a population that under Louis XIV approached 20 m., only fielded just under 500,000 troops even at the height of his campaigns; McKay and Scott (1983: 15). Germany probably had between 12 m. and 15 m. inhabitants when Salvius wrote, Sweden one-tenth of that figure.

reduce the Swedish overseas commitment, expressing their fear, as they put it, of seeing the fatherland wither at the root in proportion to the growth of the branches.[111] Even Axel Oxenstierna himself habitually commented on the political situation in a pessimistic vein. But his solution was to strengthen Sweden as much as possible in strategic and material terms, subordinating other considerations to this. From this point of view, the rationale for the Swedish demands was in part geo-strategic and in part economic; indeed, the Swedish war effort already relied heavily on revenue from tolls raised in and around the Baltic. Acquiring a sizeable part of the highly developed and commercially active German seaboards was one way of compensating for the backwardness of the Swedish economy.

Salvius, however, believed that any additional military and financial strength gained for Sweden was better not put to a serious test, even if, in order to avoid this, expansionism had to be curbed. He was careful to observe strictly the instruction that the Swedish delegation had received from the Council of State: 'And, in particular, you are to be mindful, that in promoting the interest of the [German] estates you see to it and ensure that affection for us is always preserved and on our side [*att lämpan alltid må vara hos oss och på vår sida*].' Swedish demands were therefore to be pressed 'as discreetly as you can [*på det diskreteste I kunna*].'[112]

The compromise solution favoured by Salvius was to award part of Pomerania—specifically, the eastern half (Hinterpommern)—to the Elector of Brandenburg in recognition of his legal claim, while compensating him elsewhere for the loss of the western half (Vorpommern), which would go to Sweden. There was a growing consensus at the congress on this proposal. However, two key players adamantly rejected the idea of a partition—the Swedish government and the Elector of Brandenburg.

Behind the scenes, Salvius embarked on a campaign of persuasion, writing to a variety of people in Sweden to promote his approach. Salvius pointed out, for example, that in the Swedish army there were many Brandenburg subjects, who could not be expected to make war on the elector. Indeed, the German officers in Swedish pay had indicated that they would no longer be available

---

[111] 15 Nov. 1634, quoted Lundgren (1945: 111).
[112] To J. Oxenstierna and Salvius, 11 July 1643, APW II C. i. 4.

after the current war. And how was a war over Pomerania to be fought without French subsidies? Further, it was to be expected that any attack on the Swedish presence in Pomerania would be launched in winter, when the Swedish coast was ice-bound and no reinforcements could be sent.[113]

Salvius argued that taking the territories in question without the consent of those concerned was tantamount to 'laying the foundations of a new war'.[114] His campaign culminated in the grand letter that he addressed to Queen Kristina on 17 September 1646.[115] Apologizing for expressing himself 'so forwardly [så dristigt]', but claiming that 'my duty and my conscience require it,' he conducted a complete tour d'horizon of the north European subsystem, listing the various actors and their objections to the Swedish scheme. 'Everybody', he said, 'is of opinion that Your Royal Majesty should rather take less with the consent and approval of all involved, than seek more without the approval of anyone. He who embraces too much may lose his grip!' (Trauttmansdorff had obviously hit home with his adage.) Salvius also reminded the queen that Swedish security had to rest on friendly relations with Brandenburg.

As for Johan Oxenstierna, he did not dare to express open disagreement with the hard line advocated by the queen and by his father. But passages in his letters make it clear that he, too, saw the need for Sweden to secure international consensus on its position.[116] Indeed, Johan Oxenstierna did not hesitate to tell the Pomeranian delegates, under a seal of secrecy and quite falsely, that he had 'never' approved of a policy of appropriating the whole duchy without the elector's consent, if that was not to be had. Incongruously, he attributed this policy to Salvius's influence on the Swedish government (of course, Salvius's campaign for the partition scheme was conducted privately, and Johan Oxenstierna may have had no knowledge of it). Johan Oxenstierna assured the Pomeranian delegates that, for his part, he felt that such an

---

[113] Salvius to Gyldenklou, 12 Feb. 1646, APW II C. ii. 139 f.; Salvius to Queen Kristina, 17 Sept. 1646, APW II C. ii. 448; Salvius to Brahe, 19 Dec. 1646, APW II C. iii. 138. Similar misgivings had already been voiced in the Riksråd in 1643, Odhner (1877: 86 f.).

[114] 'att taga all satisfaktionen utan intressenternas konsens, är intet annat än lägga grunden till ett nytt krig.' Salvius to Brahe, 19 Dec. 1646, APW II C. iii. 138.

[115] Salvius to Queen Kristina, 17 Sept. 1646, APW II C. ii. 446 ff.

[116] See J. Oxenstierna to Salvius, 28 Nov. 1646, APW II C. iii. 83; J. Oxenstierna to Queen Kristina, 31 Dec. 1646, APW II C. iii. 168 ff.

uncompromising stance would discredit Sweden and not bring lasting peace.[117]

Even the ordinary dispatches to Stockholm, written jointly by Salvius and Johan Oxenstierna, devoted a great deal of space to detailed reporting of all the opposition to the Swedish demands that the delegation encountered. In this way, the dispatches acted as a relay for the incessant propaganda and lobbying against the Swedish demands that emanated principally, but not exclusively, from the Brandenburg delegation.

One point raised by Brandenburg was that Sweden would need to maintain strong garrisons in Pomerania if the duchy was kept without the elector's consent. Garrisons would be a heavy economic burden on the inhabitants and induce them to rebel, in which case they could count on the support, not only of Brandenburg, but of Poland, Denmark, the Dutch, and anybody else who felt threatened by Swedish preponderance in the area.[118] The Pomeranian delegates themselves emphasized that there was no better safeguard for the Swedish possessions than the allegiance of the subjects and the consent of the neighbours.[119] They warned that the Pomeranians could not be 'treated as livestock [*inte kunna hållas likasom boskap*]'.[120] The Pomeranians felt under an obligation both to Sweden (which, during the war, had saved the duchy from Catholic occupation) and to the Elector of Brandenburg (who, in their eyes, was their rightful ruler). They were, in fact, open to any solution, including partition—but only if the elector agreed to it, and released them from their oath of allegiance if necessary, and provided also that the Pomeranian constitution, which gave the provincial estates a share in the administration of the duchy and which limited the power of the ruler, was maintained.

The Swedish government reluctantly accepted the partition scheme as a fall-back option if all else failed, but continued to instruct its plenipotentiaries to press for the cession of the entire duchy. Meanwhile, the elector came under pressure from just about

[117] Congress diary of the Pomeranian delegates, 9 Jan. 1647, *Baltische Studien*, 7/1 (1840), 165. Compare J. Oxenstierna to Queen Kristina, 31 Dec. 1646, APW II C. iii. 168 ff.

[118] J. Oxenstierna and Salvius to Queen Kristina, 19 Feb. 1646, APW II C. ii. 142; Salvius to Queen Kristina, 27 Aug. 1646, APW II C. ii. 426.

[119] Memorandum of 15 Dec. 1646, *Baltische Studien*, 7/1 (1840), 176 ff.

[120] Memorandum of 15 Dec. 1646, *Baltische Studien*, 7/1 (1840), 170; and J. Oxenstierna and Salvius to Queen Kristina, 2 July 1646, APW II C. ii. 348.

everybody at the congress, too. Despite the sympathy many of them had for the elector, the estates were not willing to postpone the peace indefinitely for his sake; neither were the Emperor or the French. At a time when sacrifices were being made by others, it was not regarded as fair that Brandenburg should be pursuing, with such intransigence, what was in practice its own aggrandizement, however well-founded its legal claim. Trauttmansdorff, who felt that, in the circumstances, the partition–compensation scheme was an excellent deal, was furious at the elector, and reminded his delegation 'with trembling hands and lips' that Brandenburg had never actually possessed the duchy—while the Emperor was ceding territories that Habsburg had owned for centuries.[121] By taking up one of the main Swedish reasons for claiming Pomerania in the first place (which the Swedes themselves stressed when talking to the Brandenburg envoys),[122] Trauttmansdorff leagued himself to some extent with his Swedish counterparts.

The French had their own reasons for supporting the partition scheme, probably little realizing that Salvius was happy for them to do so. They had already reached an agreement with the Emperor on what was to be ceded to them, and they had no desire to continue the war interminably because of the deadlock over Pomerania. If the war continued, the Habsburg armies might yet inflict a decisive defeat on them, and that would inevitably jeopardize the existing deal. In addition, the French felt a need to free resources for use against Spain, especially after the 1646 French campaigns against Spain in Italy, Catalonia, and Flanders had all failed.[123] Finally, it was annoying to them that Sweden should have secured such vast territories for free. What the French had got looked rather paltry in comparison, and they even had to pay cash for it (see further on). Sweden's expansion could only consolidate its influence in Germany further, of which the French were jealous as it was. Sweden could claim quite convincingly that it had come to the rescue of the Protestants, and that it needed a strong position in Germany to guard the Protestants against possible new undertakings on the part of the Catholics, who had all the weight of the House of Habsburg behind them. France, on the other hand, could count on the allegiance of neither the Catholics nor the Protestants

---

[121] Breucker (1879: 46).   [122] Ibid. 23, 40.   [123] Ruppert (1979: 185).

in the Empire.[124] For these reasons, despite the Franco-Swedish alliance, France had no wish to support Sweden in its claim to the whole of Pomerania.

Since the money for the Swedish war came in large part from the French, they had some leverage over Sweden. They embarked on a vigorous 'mediation' effort, bullying the Brandenburg delegation[125] and putting strong pressure on the Swedish delegation, too. D'Avaux was particularly active. 'We represented to him', the Swedish delegates reported to Stockholm, 'that he, d'Avaux, was almost our sole obstacle on the way to obtaining all of Pomerania. . . . we find that he has more scruples than even the Brandenburg delegates themselves . . . In sum, we parted this time in a bad mood and almost as enemies.'[126]

D'Avaux, no doubt much to Salvius's satisfaction, played the consensus card, urging the Swedes to claim only what could be had 'with the applause of the whole of Europe [*hela Europae applausu*]'.[127] France, he said,

did not begrudge Your Royal Majesty [Queen Kristina] a reasonable indemnity, and would do what it could to help obtain it, but at the same time he hoped that it would remain within the limits of the possible. To obtain the whole of Pomerania with the elector's consent was impossible, and to obtain it without consent . . . was hazardous and, for many reasons, disreputable [*hazardeust och för många orsaker disreputirligt*].[128]

D'Avaux also argued that if the elector refused to abandon even part of Pomerania, he would lose all his remaining support:

if he would still be obstinate, then Your Royal Majesty would have the entire congress on her side and could, in this fashion, obtain not only the elector's consent and consequently the provinces in question with better security . . . , but also the applause and affection, both of those here present and all others, especially if Your Royal Majesty, like France, which is almost buying its indemnity, gives up something and has regard for the present condition and interest of the entire Christian world.[129]

---

[124] See the French delegates to Mazarin, 3 Feb. 1646, Le Clerc (1725–6: iii. 70).
[125] Congress diary of the Pomeranian delegates, *Baltische Studien*, 6/1 (1839), 90 ff.
[126] J. Oxenstierna and Salvius to Queen Kristina, 4 Feb. 1647, APW II C. iii. 237.
[127] J. Oxenstierna and Salvius to Queen Kristina, 24 Sept. 1646, APW II C. ii. 464. See also APW II C. ii, nos. 197, 205; and iii, nos. 2, 5, 42, 43.
[128] J. Oxenstierna and Salvius to Queen Kristina, 21 Jan. 1647, APW II C. iii. 219.
[129] J. Oxenstierna and Salvius to Queen Kristina, 1 Oct. 1646, APW II C. ii. 479 f.

Finding himself increasingly isolated, the Elector of Brandenburg put his trust mainly in the Dutch. He stayed at The Hague in late 1646 and early 1647 to lobby them personally; and, having failed to marry Queen Kristina, he settled instead for a daughter of the Prince of Orange. The Dutch did register their displeasure over the Swedish demands and endorsed the Brandenburg case, but they would not commit themselves further.[130] Meanwhile, Trauttmansdorff toyed with the Swedish proposal that if the elector could not be brought to his senses, the Emperor, backed by the other estates, should make the whole of Pomerania over to Sweden under some special guarantee. He probably did not consider this proposal seriously. One suspects that he was really playing a double game, perhaps with the connivance of Salvius, in order to put pressure on the elector.[131]

Much disgruntled, the Elector of Brandenburg in August 1646 at last agreed to discuss a partition, but he instructed his delegates to publicize his emphatic protest and to make it very clear that he rejected any responsibility for the prejudice that might be caused to the Empire or anyone else as a result of 'this dismemberment'— in other words, the infringement of the structural-inviolability principle that he presented the partition as entailing.[132]

The partition scheme could then go ahead—provided that agreement was reached on the demarcation line (the elector was not easily brought to yield Szczecin and the Oder estuary, which for Stockholm was a *sine qua non* for accepting the partition at all); and provided also that the compensation issue was resolved. The elector had his own ideas about what was adequate. Eventually,

---

[130] See the States General to Queen Kristina, dated 15 May 1646, Meiern (1734–6: iii. 83 f.); J. Oxenstierna and Salvius to Queen Kristina, 24 Sept. 1646, APW II C. ii. 462; 14 Jan. 1647, APW II C. iii. 204 f.; 21 Jan. 1647, APW II C. iii. 215 f.; 4 Feb. 1647, APW II C. iii. 232.

[131] See notably J. Oxenstierna and Salvius to Queen Kristina, 2 July 1646, APW II C. ii. 348; 24 Sept. 1646, APW II C. ii. 458 f.; 21 Jan. 1647, APW II C. iii. 219; Salvius to Gyldenklou, 18 Mar. 1647, APW II C. iii. 335 f. The possibility of collusion between Salvius and Trauttmansdorff is suggested for example by J. Oxenstierna to Salvius, 23 Nov. 1646, APW II C. iii. 83 ff.

[132] 'wir wollten aber zuvörderst, und nochmalen bedungen haben, daß wir von Gott und der ganzen Welt, den benachbarten Königen, und unsers Hauses Verwandten, auch dem ganzen Römischen Reich gänzlich entschuldiget sein wollen, sofern durch diese Veräußerung dem Heiligen Römischen Reich künftig einige Gefahr zuwachsen und entstehen sollte, und die Verantwortung denen lassen, die diese Zergliederung mit gutheißen und billigen'. Instruction for the Brandenburg delegates of 18 Aug. 1646, *Baltische Studien*, 6/1 (1839) 111 f.

he secured the Bishopric of Halberstadt—which, in their draft treaty of May 1646, the Imperial delegates had considered enough of a compensation[133]—plus those of Minden and Kamień Pomorski (Cammin), and, above all, the Archbishopric of Magdeburg. This amounted to considerably more than he had lost, as Trauttmansdorff, figures to hand, proved to Wittgenstein, the Brandenburg plenipotentiary.[134] To put it differently, the elector's rights to Pomerania were so valuable that, in order to enable others not to have to rely on conquest, he could dispose of them at a profit.

In this way, the Swedes achieved their territorial aims 'cum totius Imperii omniumque interessatorum consensu' ('with the consent of the entire Empire and of all those concerned'), as they had publicly endeavoured.[135] To obtain this consent, they made a great show of deferring to the three principles of loyalty, structural inviolability, and legality. The Swedes received the territories in question as perpetual Imperial fiefs, so that their cession took the form, not of an amputation of the Empire, but of the substitution of the crown of Sweden for the original liegemen. Of these, only one, the administrator Frederick, was actually displaced—but, at least, he was not German, and by the time the peace was signed he had come into possession of a kingdom. The Swedes agreed to pay homage to the Emperor, and to perform loyally the duties that the Empire's constitution imposed on the estates. Further, they promised not to interfere with the ancient privileges and liberties hitherto enjoyed by their new subjects. In return, the Swedish crown was granted formal investiture by the Emperor, which automatically entailed a legal claim to protection by the Empire should the Swedish crown's new status or possessions be challenged. The Swedish crown also obtained seats in the Reichstag and in the assemblies (*Kreistage*) of the Upper Saxon, Lower Saxon, and Westphalian Circles (for Pomerania, Bremen, and Verden respectively).[136]

---

[133] Art. 29, Meiern (1734–6: iii. 72).

[134] Some German delegates protested both to Trauttmansdorff and to the Swedes over what they saw as excessive compensation for the Brandenburg elector. They calculated from the Reichsmatrikel (the Empire's tax register) that the compensation amounted to the triple value of the elector's losses. The Brandenburg delegates in turn contested their figures; Breucker (1879: 90 f.).

[135] Swedish memorandum to the Imperial delegation, dated 18 Nov. 1646, Meiern (1734–6: iii. 754).

[136] See n. 135, above, ibid. 754 f.; and art. 10 IPO.

4.2.2. The French 'Indemnity'

The French had a more aggressive attitude than the Swedes when it came to securing additional territories, as illustrated, for example, by the following memorandum. It was dispatched to Paris in December 1644 by Servien, one of the French plenipotentiaries:

Since it has pleased God to re-establish the ancient borders of France [a reference, it would appear, to Merovingian Austrasia, a full thousand years earlier] by allowing such important strongholds on the Rhine to fall into the hands of our kings, it seems hardly appropriate to part with them . . . Heaven having, by a visible justice, in a legitimate war . . . , compensated France at the expense of the Emperor and the King of Spain for the wrongs and injustices that it had earlier received from Charles V when he was Emperor and King of Spain all in one, it seems that reason does not wish us to forgo our present advantage, since in fairness [*selon la justice*] it must serve as a substitute for what has earlier been unjustly torn from the crown of France, when the fortune in war was favourable to its enemies, and since, by a secret counsel of Divine Providence, the two mighty bastions that the Emperor Charles V once boasted to have erected against France, Breisach and Perpignan, now serve France as bastions against Germany and Spain. . . . We have always believed that, given the condition that the affairs of Christendom are in, our enemies apparently not having the means to recover from their losses and France being united and, so far, short neither of prestige nor of money nor of powerful allies, all of whom are remaining faithful, we would be doing enough for the public repose by renouncing the new conquests that could be made by continuing the war . . .[137]

The key notions invoked here in justification of French policy are the recovery of former possessions, regard (of a sort) for the community (Christendom), a kind of manifest destiny defined in religious terms, retributive justice (i.e. reparation of wrongs suffered in the past), and security. French expansion is perceived as defensive ('bastions against'): France was strong, but so was its fear of Habsburg enmity.

It should be noted that Servien's text was not propaganda, that it was not aimed at a public; Servien was speaking, not to the congress, but to his own government. This was justification addressed to the self, made necessary by the French tendency to

---

[137] 16 Dec. 1644, APW II B. i. 777. That the 'ancient limits' were thought to be those of the Kingdom of Austrasia is shown by a memorandum by the French delegates of 28 Aug. 1645, APW II B. ii. 633.

disregard internationally accepted forms of behaviour. Given both its strength and its anxieties, France had a comparatively small stake in the creation and preservation of a stable international system. Nevertheless, the pull of the international-consensus agenda was still felt. Consensus notions did exert an influence on the decision-making.

Brienne, the French secretary of state, concurred with the memorandum. In his reply, he did not even bother with the *anciennes limites* but spoke of forthright expansion. He condemned the 'unjust wars' that were waged by France's enemies, and went on: 'But God's justice has confounded them, and Their Majesties' [Louis XIV and Anne of Austria, the queen mother and regent] victorious arms have taught them that France is a kingdom of sufficient power to preserve itself in its entirety, to defend its allies, and to extend its boundaries.'[138]

France could more easily afford to dispense with consensus than Sweden. Not only was Sweden a much poorer and less populous country, but, in addition, it faced two further problems: first, the territories that it coveted were owned by the very estates that it claimed to be defending; and secondly, these territories were separated from Sweden by the North and Baltic Seas. The first point created delicate political problems, and the second meant that, from a strategic perspective, the new possessions were in an exposed and vulnerable position. For these reasons, the need for consensus was perceived strongly, especially by the Swedish delegates at the congress. France, on the other hand, chose to demand territories owned by the House of Habsburg, which it could present as the sworn enemy of the liberty of the estates. Moreover, France only made claims in areas that were adjacent to its own borders—Alsace and Lorraine. Nevertheless, in pursuing these claims, France still deferred to the consensus agenda. For all its strength, it did not wish to incur the opprobrium of flouting it openly. Moreover, respecting the consensus agenda facilitated the negotiations.

The Bishoprics of Metz, Toul, and Verdun were legally part of the Empire. But they had been under French occupation since 1552,[139] and their populations were not German-speaking. In these circumstances, the protests of the affected rulers—especially the

---

[138] To the French delegates, 27 Dec. 1644, APW II B. i. 809.
[139] See APW I. i. 94 n. 2.

Duke of Lorraine, who had rights in the bishoprics, and the Bishop of Verdun—had little chance of success, despite their reliance on arguments such as their loyalty to the Empire or the illegal nature of a cession effected against the will of those concerned.[140] Nevertheless, the French delegates were worried that the Germans would make a fuss about the infringement or abrogation of ancient rights that the cession entailed. They concluded that they had to tread carefully lest the Germans woke up to the situation, and tried to re-establish their rights.[141]

All three bishoprics were grudgingly ceded to France. Alsace was a different matter—it was ethnically German and France had to be careful not to alienate the estates by threatening the rights of those among them that had possessions in Alsace. A sizeable part of Alsace was, however, part of the Habsburg dominions, and it was this part that France acquired with full sovereignty. The Emperor's military situation was increasingly desperate, and eventually he instructed his delegates to yield on all points. He relinquished not only Habsburg Alsace, but even the fortress of Breisach, a bridgehead on the eastern bank of the Rhine.[142]

Consensus considerations exerted a noticeable influence even here. France did not invoke publicly a right of conquest. In the end, the French agreed to *purchase* the Habsburg rights for substantial financial compensation. The Treaty of Münster fixed it at three million Livres, plus the obligation to take over Habsburg debts *pro rata*.[143] They did not know it, but the Imperial delegates could have obtained more: the French delegates had been given authority to pledge six million.[144]

Further, the French obtained legalization of the deal by the estates. This released the Emperor, in relation to Alsace and Lorraine, from the provision in his election oath that he was not to allow any territories to be alienated from the Empire.[145] It should

---

[140] e.g. memorandum by the Verdun envoy (who also represented Lorraine: the Bishop of Verdun was a member of the ducal family, while the duke himself was barred from sending an envoy by France) of 18 July 1646, Meiern (1734–6: iii. 572 ff.); memorandum by the Duke of Lorraine, May 1646, ibid. 528 f.

[141] 'il y a un grand sujet de craindre si l'affaire est agitée que tous les Allemands n'opinent à y établir les anciens droits de l'Empire.' Memorandum by the French delegates to Brienne, 22 July 1645, APW II B. ii. 540.

[142] For the successive proposals see Meiern (1734–6); for a detailed account of the negotiations Ruppert (1979: 144 ff.).   [143] IPM §§88–9.

[144] The French delegates to Anne d'Autriche, 17 Sept. 1646, Le Clerc (1725–6: iii. 300).   [145] §79 IPM.

be stressed that the French did not claim the whole of Alsace, but only the Habsburg rights there, and that they committed themselves formally (though quite probably insincerely) not to encroach on the rights of other estates in the area.[146] Significantly, the peace-makers spoke of 'rights' when they meant territories.

On one occasion, the French delegates did claim the whole of Alsace, as if to see what would happen. They chose the delegates of relatively pro-French Bavaria for this experiment. The reaction was one of disbelief; the French were warned that, even if the Emperor could be brought to abandon the Habsburg rights in Alsace, a French claim to the possessions of other Alsatian estates would lead to an outcry in the entire Empire, even among the French allies. The French thereupon declared that they would be content with the Habsburg possessions, even though 'for Alsace and for the other above-mentioned estates it would be quite appropriate [bien à propos] to be owned by the king in full sover-eignty, since they had formerly been part of the Kingdom of Austrasia, which belonged to our kings.'[147]

The French sought for some time to receive the territories in question as fiefs of the Empire (as the Swedes succeeded in do-ing), and they were ready to pay homage for them to the Em-peror. This would have involved an automatic guarantee of their possessions by the Empire, as well as admission to the Reichstag. In this way, France would have been enabled to intervene officially and directly in the affairs of the Empire. Moreover, the French delegates believed that, in the short term, this tactic would help overcome German resistance to the French demands.[148] Brienne, the secretary of state, agreed. He thought that, from a practical point of view, there would be little difference between this solu-tion and gaining full sovereignty.[149] But full sovereignty was what

[146] §87 IPM.

[147] 'ils [the Bavarian delegates] répondirent avec quelque étonnement ... que ce serait choquer tout l'Empire et nos propres alliés si nous y voulions prétendre plus de droit que n'y a eu la Maison d'Autriche.' Memorandum by the French del-egates, 28 Aug. 1645, APW II B. ii. 632 f.

[148] 'cela lèvera une partie des grandes difficultés qu'ils [the French delegates] prévoient devoir s'y rencontrer, non seulement de la part des ennemis mais des amis mêmes'. Memorandum by the French delegates to Brienne, 22 July 1645, APW II B. ii. 539.

[149] 'Celui qui est maître des murailles des villes en est bien le souverain bien qu'un autre en ait le titre'. To the French delegates, 9 Sept. 1645, APW II B. ii. 659.

the French did get. The Protestant estates, who were happy to have Sweden in the Reichstag, did not wish to see Catholic France represented there, too.[150] More importantly, neither did the Emperor.

Unlike Sweden, France could compete with Habsburg for the Catholic constituency in the Reichstag. Furthermore, granting Habsburg territories to France as fiefs rather than ceding them fully would, from a legal point of view, preclude the Emperor from attempting to retrieve them. Trauttmansdorff himself was reported to have said that the Emperor intended to do so. But the Emperor could not simply attack his own liegeman. In these circumstances, cession with full sovereignty recommended itself as the least damaging option.[151]

The negotiations involved a great deal of legal finesse. The Imperial negotiator Dr Volmar (a lawyer with first-hand knowledge of Alsatian affairs) ended up selling to the French a 'Landgraviate of the Upper and Lower Alsace'—something that not only did Habsburg not possess but which apparently did not even exist.[152] The French may or may not have seen through this. If they did, as a recent contribution suggests, they kept their insight to themselves.[153]

Not surprisingly, the imprecision of the terms of the *französische Satisfaktion*, or French indemnity, was watched with some alarm by the other estates in Alsace. A memorandum of April 1648 complained that '[t]o the Holy Roman Empire's Free City of Strassburg [Strasbourg] it appears quite preoccupying and grievous that in the peace treaty with France, in the paragraph *Teneatur Rex Christianissimus etc.* [subsequently to become §87 IPM], where several estates situated in the Upper and Lower Alsace are enumerated and mentioned by name, it has . . . been ignored and omitted.' Putting its trust in the legality principle, the memorandum urged a more specific wording,

---

[150] The French delegates to Mazarin, n.d. but probably Feb. 1646, Le Clerc (1725–6: iii. 70).

[151] See the Emperor's instruction for Trauttmansdorff of 16 Oct. 1645, APW I. i. 449; and J. Oxenstierna and Salvius to Queen Kristina, 24 Sept. 1646, APW II C. ii. 464.

[152] §75 IPM. See Ruppert (1979: 156, 167 ff.), and for a somewhat different account Dickmann (1985: 236 f.).   [153] Kraus (1984).

in order to ensure that any grounds for conflict, which ordinarily arise over questions of jurisdiction, and set neighbours one against the other, are as far as possible forestalled in time, no matters of dispute remain, and the Roman Empire is, thus, spared further dismemberment.[154]

Strasbourg obtained the requested confirmation of its separateness in the final wording of the paragraph (though that did not save it from eventual French annexation in 1681). But, in all likelihood, no amount of ransacking the archives could have clarified the legal position in Alsace fully. This legal position was both fearsomely complex and intrinsically confused, a criss-cross pattern of rights belonging to different estates that had been allowed to develop arbitrarily over the centuries. Not even Vienna had a clear idea of Habsburg or Imperial rights in the area.[155] The peace negotiations were not the best time to discover this, since, in the prevailing climate of distrust, attempts to clarify the situation by one side were bound to be challenged by the other. When the Imperial delegates tried to make the terms of the deal over Alsace less ambiguous, this immediately prompted a hostile French reaction.[156] While both Vienna and Paris undoubtedly exploited the situation to suit their own ends, it is difficult to see what else they could have done. Neither Habsburg nor France aimed at precision—that is, an arrangement stabilized by obvious and unquestionable legality—first, because precision could not, in practice, be had, and secondly, because neither party was happy to consider the settlement as quite the last word on the matter.[157]

The French offensive was soon resumed. Louis XIV did not neglect to surround it with a semblance of legitimacy. Lawyers were employed to fabricate *tituli possessionis* for the remaining territories in Alsace, in pursuit of Louis's policy of 'reunion' of these estates to France. But this was a transparent disguise, of course. 'Even though', the French philosopher Pierre Bayle commented later,

our invincible monarch only takes that which he proves to be rightfully his [*ne prenne que ce qu'il prouve lui appartenir légitimement*], imitating ... Joshua, who let his troops be preceded by the Ark of the Covenant,

---

[154] Meiern (1734–6: v. 168 f.). See also the parallel memorandum of the *Decapolis* (the other ten free cities of Alsace), ibid. 170 ff.
[155] Ruppert (1979: 152).   [156] Ibid. 175 ff.
[157] See Odhner (1877: 272 ff.), Ruppert (1979: 196), Dickmann (1985: 482 ff.).

containing the Law of God, our neighbours fail to relish the strength of our reasons. They say that it takes a mind assisted by one hundred thousand soldiers to discover in the treaties of Münster and Nijmegen [1678] the meaning that we discover in them ...[158]

5. INCHOATE AND INADEQUATE NATURE OF THE PRINCIPLES SO FAR DISCUSSED: THE ROLE OF CUSTOM

The three principles so far identified—loyalty, legality, and the inviolability of existing structures—are so closely bound up with one another that they are seldom easily distinguishable. In most instances in which the consensus agenda can be shown to have had an influence on the peacemaking process, all three principles were at work together. The low degree of differentiation of these principles, and the peculiarity that they could only protect existing structures, but could not shape the system in their own right, reflect the fact that the international system was largely the product of historical contingencies. This international system was a transitional set of structures on the threshold between the defunct medieval system and the new 'classical' European states system. It does seem appropriate to speak of structures in the plural, because, at the level of the system as a whole, the actors were considerably less integrated, in terms of the importance of their mutual relations, than was the case at subsystem level.

The three principles helped to preserve the existing structures of the system, but they could not determine any structures by themselves. They had no content of their own. Non-programmatic, they adapted easily to the manifold manifestations of what was the main source of the structures of the system—i.e. tradition or custom.

There was little or no analytical reflection on the nature and destiny of the international system. As a result, the only possible answer to the question of what that system ought to be like could be found in what, supposedly, it had always been like. I say 'supposedly' because, in reality, the system had of course undergone change over the preceding centuries—and, for all the peacemakers' professed conservatism, it underwent further change as a

---

[158] Bayle (1683: 100), quoted Meiern (1734–6: vol. v, pref. [not pagin.]).

result of the congress itself. But any recognition of this fact would have required a theoretical justification of why, at this particular point in time, the system was what it was, and a decision as to whether, at this important juncture in its evolution, it should not perhaps be transformed more actively. The 1648 peacemakers were not equipped with the analytical tools that would have enabled them to formulate, let alone tackle such problems.

For them, the only way to achieve a stable settlement was to leave things at least roughly as they had been, in other words, to remodel the system in accordance with what they saw as its own tradition. The one major source of consensus was therefore custom, which in turn presupposed consensus principles that could adapt to the manifold concrete manifestations of custom. Anticipating the remainder of this book, the evolution of the European states system from the seventeenth century onwards could be described as the gradual substitution of custom as the structurally determinant factor by a developing *programmatic* consensus agenda.

Non-programmatic consensus notions had only limited staying power in the face of violation. Actors did not identify with these notions as such, and were therefore roused to defend them from violation only if they were directly affected themselves. This meant that stability could be preserved only as long as a majority of the actors identified with some common goal or programme that gave a meaning to the otherwise empty principles.

This was the case in the German subsystem, where the consensus agenda was supplemented by national feeling—the fatherland ideology. An ideology works in the long run only if it serves the interests of those who share it. That it does so is not necessarily the reason why they subscribe to it—indeed, they may well be offended at the suggestion. But, in the long run, they will not support an ideology that actually hurts their interests. Regarding the German princes and cities in the seventeenth and eighteenth centuries, it is clear that, small as almost all of them were, they could not have survived unless they jointly respected and upheld the Empire and its constitution. This is entirely typical of what a stable international system involves—some realization that individual objectives (in this case, the very fundamental one of self-preservation) are more easily attained in a stable environment, so that maintaining such an environment becomes a collective goal.

If the collective goal (in this case, the preservation of the Empire) is itself the focus of a legitimizing ideology, so much the better for the individual objectives.

To illustrate these reflections, here is a statement by Bavaria in the Council of Electors of June 1648, urging the Emperor to give up his alliance with Spain (indirect speech because these are the minutes of the session):

To prostitute this magnificent realm any longer to foreigners would be daredevilry rather than wisdom. The Holy Roman Empire had hitherto been to all foreign kings, potentates, and republics an object of wonder, nay of imitation, and now it was being made into a spectacle and exposed to the ridicule of the world. All this could only have one outcome, with various kings and potentates agreeing among themselves on the division of the Empire as soon as all the electors, princes, and estates had finally perished. This extremity the electors, princes, and estates were in no mood to wait for, let alone to experience . . . This being the case, all electors, princes, and estates most obediently called on His Imperial Majesty . . . for the sake of the common fatherland and the salvation of the Roman Empire, not to allow anything to impede the German peace.[159]

In the European system at large, the equivalent to German nationalism consisted in Christian ideology, with a certain degree of consciousness of a common secular heritage as well. However, this common ideology did not have the same rallying power as German nationalism.

It is interesting to note what a small role even dynastic solidarity played at the time in maintaining community feeling between the actors or the stability of the system. Once again, this finding contrasts with the popular perception of the period. Seventeenth-century documents routinely employ the expression 'kings (or princes, or potentates) *and republics*' as a generic term for the actors in the system, drawing attention to the fact that a considerable number of these actors were not monarchies at all. And even between the monarchies there was little solidarity, however close their blood-ties.

This absence of dynastic solidarity came as a surprise even to some of the peacemakers. They marvelled, for example, at the fact that the Catholic crown of Spain found it relatively easy to reach an agreement with the Dutch States General, who were republican

[159] 6 June 1648, Meiern (1734–6: v. 901).

and Protestant as a result of having rebelled against the Spanish crown. At the same time, Spain found it impossible to make any progress with a Catholic France governed by a queen who was the Spanish king's sister.[160]

There was also virtually no coordination between the two Habsburg monarchies Spain and Austria at the congress.[161] Indeed, the peace even terminated their alliance, because the Emperor, in order to make peace with France, found it necessary to desert Spain. He took this step only at the last possible moment; Spain (whose ruler's late sister had been married to the Emperor) naturally enough pulled its full weight at Vienna in an attempt to prevent this desertion.[162] But pressure from France and the impatient German estates was more effective. Key Catholic estates (Bavaria and Mainz) reminded the Emperor that he must put his obligation to the Empire above his family ties, failing which their own obligation to the Empire ('die hohe und teure Pflicht, damit Kur- und Fürsten dem Heiligen Reich verwandt') would have to take precedence over their oath of allegiance to him. Indeed, the idea was mooted of the estates signing the peace in their own right even if the Emperor refused. He would have been free to accede subsequently, but, obviously, a grave constitutional crisis would have been created in the mean time.[163]

In fact, the Emperor had from an early date contemplated sacrificing Spain, as his instruction for Trauttmansdorff proves.[164] As early as November 1645 the Imperial negotiator Dr Volmar had indicated to the Frenchman Longueville that Spain would not be allowed to prevent the German peace.[165] The loyalty principle invoked by the estates was a more potent political factor than dynastic solidarity; disregarding the principle for the sake of family ties would have been too politically costly to be a serious possibility.

Nor were family ties effective in preventing actors from making demands on one another (while nationalist community feeling within the German subsystem on the whole did). When the

---

[160] 'Ammiravano alcuni la facilità degli Spagnuoli in tutto concedere a chi avev'altre volte riconosciuto la sovranità loro, e compiangevano altri, che altrettanto difficile riuscisse comporre le due corone [France and Spain], di religione non meno che di sangue congiunte.' Report to the Venetian Senate by an unnamed diplomat, Fiedler (1866: i. 370).
[161] Ruppert (1979: 350).   [162] Dickmann (1985: 488).
[163] Ibid. 485 ff.   [164] APW I. i. 450.
[165] The French delegates to Brienne, 18 Nov. 1645, APW II B. ii. 854.

Brandenburg delegation put forward the notion of dynastic solidarity (*Blutsfreundschaft*) and pointed out that Queen Kristina
and the Brandenburg elector were cousins and therefore should
not quarrel, the Swedes turned the argument round.

Their sarcastic riposte was to ask what compensation the elector
would offer the queen for Pomerania—showing himself as he did,
in his capacity as her blood-relative, to have her interest so much
at heart.[166] On another occasion, Salvius ironically remarked that,

[i]ndeed, the Queen of France is a sister of the empress and of the King
of Spain and they are all of one religion. But if the Emperor, for that
reason, is to relinquish Alsace, the patrimony of the House of Austria,
that is not thought to happen without some tears being shed.[167]

In other words, although dynastic ties might prevent demands
from being made, they might equally well encourage them to be
granted. The notion could work both ways, and was therefore
useless as an aid for decision-making or as a means of achieving
consensus.

The *ancien régime* was not particularly committed to dynasticism
on an ideological level—at least not as far as the international
sphere is concerned, which should be distinguished strictly here
from the domestic sphere. Ideological commitment to dynasticism
was a product of nineteenth-century *programmatic* conservatism,
as shown in greater detail in Chapter 4.

As a result, in part at least, of the weak solidarity between
them, the legitimacy of international actors was quite independent
of the nature of their regimes. The French delegates were informed
by a disapproving French queen mother in May 1644 that Spain
had recognized the insurgent English parliament 'pour un
parlement légitime'.[168] But soon they were told by Secretary of
State Brienne that the French resident in London had followed
suit, also recognizing the parliament as 'assemblée légitime'.[169] In
January 1645 Servien reported to Paris that Sweden was negotiating an alliance with the English parliament.[170] Everybody also

---

[166] J. Oxenstierna and Salvius to Queen Kristina, 5 Feb. 1646, APW II C. ii. 117.
See also Odhner (1877: 139 f.).
[167] 'det menas icke ske med torra ögonen'. Salvius to Queen Kristina, 4 Dec.
1645, APW II C. i. 864.
[168] 16 May 1644, APW II B. i. 224.   [169] 27 Aug. 1644, APW II B. i. 474.
[170] To Lionne, 15 Jan. 1645, APW II B. ii. 60.

recognized the Dutch Republic. Even Spain did so eventually, and in a most emphatic way.

The French prime minister Mazarin, in his instruction for the French delegates of November 1645, alluded to the impending victory of republicanism in England, and expressed his fear that, given 'the natural hatred and aversion that the English have for France,' they might wish to spread their republicanism and foment a Huguenot insurrection in France. He therefore thought that it was time to end the war against the Spanish crown, which might be needed as a counterpoise.[171] Mazarin did not, however, follow his own advice. France, in fact, made a *rapprochement* with Cromwell after the English republic had come into being in 1649, and it continued the war with Spain until 1659, all under the auspices of Mazarin. It is interesting to note, too, that in the same text Mazarin proposed to set up a new republic in Catalonia.[172]

In sum, given the looseness of the ties between the European actors, a consensus agenda based on custom-oriented principles and relying on a strong community feeling was not viable in the larger European system. Louis XIV's subsequent expansionism demonstrated of what little use this type of consensus agenda was against actors both discontented and powerful. Such actors pose a threat in any international system. But a consensus agenda with more abstract, programmatic notions, with some rallying power vested in the notions themselves rather than based only on community feeling, is more effective against them. A new, more programmatic, kind of consensus notions was required. And, indeed, an alternative consensus agenda was already in the making at Münster and Osnabrück.

6. THE AUTONOMY PRINCIPLE

Among the notions gathering momentum at the congress was one which I will call the autonomy principle. Unlike the other principles, this contained an abstract (though very simple) programme of its own. It stipulated that, whatever the historical particularities of their situation, any and all actors in the system were entitled to an autonomous existence, and that they alone were competent to define the extent of that autonomy.

[171] APW II B. ii. 888.   [172] APW II B. ii. 875.

The principle of autonomy was more than just another prop for custom. Although it was declared to be that (as a result of the peacemakers' determined traditionalism), it was, in fact, potentially a vehicle of change. Its abstract nature gave it greater force than that possessed by the other principles, so that it could prevail over them. In particular, there was nothing to prevent it being invoked by new actors, despite the fact that they might have come into being in violation of the other three principles.

It is significant that the notion of obedience played virtually no role in the negotiations (obedience, unlike loyalty, of necessity entails subordination). The autonomy principle, on the other hand, implicit for example in the frequent invocation of the 'German liberty', represented a leitmotiv of the congress. Before the war, the ancient principle of obedience to the Emperor had still, in an attenuated form, held sway. Later, the ascendance of autonomy over obedience was accepted in Germany, and subordination was largely replaced by coordination, or even by mere coexistence.

Neither the 1648 treaties nor the negotiations leading up to them were particularly concerned with the legal concept of sovereignty. That the Peace of Westphalia was a milestone on the road to a states system built around the concept of sovereignty is a popular view, especially with students of international relations— but it is a myth. Only in one case was there formal recognition of sovereignty at the congress—by the Spanish–Dutch treaty, which sanctioned Dutch independence from Spain. Contrary to what is often stated, there was no formal recognition at the congress of either Dutch or Swiss independence on the part of the Emperor or the Empire.[173] However, the non-legal concept of autonomy was very much at the core of the negotiations. This concept accommodates both the limited, distinctly non-sovereign self-determination defended by the estates of the Empire, and the full independence long enjoyed by other European actors.

Significantly, France and Sweden both identified their own 'security' (which really meant 'autonomy') with the autonomy of the German estates. Both took the view that the estates' autonomy, and that meant the Empire's constitution, should be upheld and protected. Otherwise, they argued, the Emperor would gain

---

[173] On the Dutch question, see Petri et al. (1991: 51); on the Swiss question Ruppert (1979: 304 ff.); also Dickmann (1985: 432 ff.).

absolute control over the whole of the Empire. If that happened, Habsburg might then gain control over the whole of Europe. Salvius, the Swedish negotiator, explained to the Pomeranian delegates

that the crown of Sweden had to pay close attention to Germany and protect itself, because it was a temperate and populous part of the world and a warlike people, that there was not a country under the sun in a better position to establish a universal monarchy and absolute dominion in Europe, than Germany; . . . now, if one potentate wielded absolute power in this realm, all the neighbouring realms would have to apprehend being subjugated . . .[174]

Salvius was the main propagator of this line of thinking at the congress. For example, in writing to the German princes, Salvius warned against attempts by the Emperor to deprive the estates of their constitutional rights and participation in the administration of the Empire. 'This course will lead straight to absolute domin-ion, and to the servitude of the estates,' he claimed. 'The crowns [i.e. France and Sweden] will oppose this as much as is in their power: their security consists in the liberty of the German estates.'[175]

Salvius's main aim, at this stage, was to persuade the reluctant estates to attend the congress. He also wrote to d'Avaux to urge the French to make a similar effort.[176] In response, d'Avaux composed a French circular addressed to the estates. He used Salvius's letter practically verbatim when he claimed it to be evident 'that the House of Austria is plotting a monarchy that is to cover all Europe; that, as a foundation for this vast edifice, it is establish-ing supreme dominion over the Roman Empire, so to speak, the centre of Europe;' that in the process the estates were being stripped of their constitutional rights, and that 'unless Your Highness, and all those with whom the Emperor shares his power, take timely action to prevent it, the German liberty is done with, the groundwork for an all-encompassing monarchy having been laid and consolidated.'[177]

[174] Congress diary of the Pomeranian delegates, 29 Oct. 1645, *Baltische Studien*, 4/2 (1837), 30.

[175] 'ihre Sekurität besteht in der deutschen Stände Libertät.' Salvius to the Margrave of Brandenburg-Kulmbach, dated 20 Jan. 1643, Meiern (1734–6: i. 12).

[176] 11 Feb. 1644, APW II C. i. 163.

[177] 6 Apr. 1644, Meiern (1734–6: i. 220). The text given by Meiern appears to be somewhat garbled; cf. the slightly different version and the French trans. given in

The Emperor would have preferred to make peace single-handedly, but in the prevailing consensus climate no strong case could be constructed against the participation of the estates. He tried some delaying tactics, but he never explicitly denied their entitlement to attend and offered no real resistance to their having a vote in the deliberations. The Emperor did not take the initiative in asserting the rights of the estates, but when they did so themselves he concurred—a study in 'I am their leader, therefore I must follow them.'[178]

Another illustration of the importance attached to the notion of autonomy is the equilibrist (balance-of-power) thinking found, not within the Empire (where the estates did not consider their security to rest on the distribution of forces between them), but in the less integrated larger European system. This mode of thinking eventually developed into the balance-of-power principle that was to be of such importance in European politics.

The notion that single actors should not be allowed to become too powerful is already encountered occasionally in documents of the period. Almost always, the notion of equilibrium was applied with regard only to these individual actors rather than being seen as a structural feature of the international system as a whole.

A couple of examples must suffice to illustrate this, since the balance-of-power concept did not as yet play a major role in international decision-making. In criticizing the anti-French bias of the mediators (the Papal and Venetian envoys at Münster), Mazarin alleged that they were motivated by 'the notion of the equilibrium in Christendom [*la raison de l'équilibre dans la chrétienté*], which is one of the chief maxims of these gentlemen [*ces messieurs*]', and on account of which 'they take the side of our enemies and wish to favour them as being the weaker party.'[179] In his instruction for the French delegates of November 1645, Mazarin warned that, in order not to provoke its neighbours, France should avoid becoming too powerful. Characteristically, in both cases, he appears concerned essentially with the position of France and the likely reactions of its neighbours, not with the system at large. In other

Le Clerc (1725–6: i. 247 ff.). Salvius was echoing his own letter to Mazarin of 10 Sept. 1643, APW II C. i. 25, as well as a letter addressed to him by the Riksråd, 8 Aug. 1643, APW II C. i. 5 ff.

[178] See Ruppert (1979: 86 ff., esp. 91); APW II B. ii. 215 n.; Becker (1973: 148 ff.).
[179] To Longueville, 19 Aug. 1645, APW II B. ii. 603 f.

words, he conceived of the notion of balance of power primarily in terms of a procedural rule, governing the *actions* of the actors, rather than in terms of a structural principle. Equilibrist utterances from other sources also show this characteristic.[180]

An exception to this pattern is provided by Salvius, who appears to have considered the problem in more developed and abstract terms than most. Salvius did take the conceptual step of applying the notion of equilibrium to the system as a whole. He used it in a near-structural sense, treating it as something permanently valid for the entire system and not just as a procedural rule to be invoked in a certain type of situation. He went so far as to declare the notion to be the mainstay of a stable system, writing to Queen Kristina that

The first principle of statecraft is that in the equilibrium of the single realms consists the security of the whole. When one of them begins to become too powerful and a threat to the others, they throw themselves by means of leagues and alliances into a scale against it, so as to create a counterweight and to preserve the balance.[181]

This is clearly *not* the formulation of a generally acknowledged principle. For one thing, the rather didactic tone indicates that Salvius thought that he was telling the queen something new—and she was famous for her erudition. Secondly, the passage constitutes a strange halfway house between a normative statement and an empirical one. In fact, Salvius casts as an empirical statement what he must have felt should have been a normative, or at any rate a speculative one.

There was, at that time, little empirical evidence that the notion of equilibrium, elevated to a general maxim, might provide for the security of a greater 'whole' or system. General security obviously implies a stable system. The only possible precedent that comes to

---

[180] APW II B. ii. 888. For other exx., see J. Oxenstierna and Salvius to Queen Kristina, 24 Sept. 1646, APW II C. ii. 458; J. Oxenstierna to Queen Kristina, 26 Nov. 1646, APW II C. iii. 74; Nassau and Volmar to Ferdinand III, 28 Nov. 1645, APW II A. ii. 601.

[181] 'Primum principium status är, att in aequilibrio singulorum imperiorum consistit securitas universi. När en begynner bliva för mäktig och formidabel hos de andra, så lägga de sig per uniones et foedera i en viktskål däremot, att väga upp honom igen och hålla balansen.' Salvius to Queen Kristina, 17 Sept. 1646, APW II C. ii. 447. This interesting passage seems to have been overlooked by balance-of-power historians, even though it was quoted for example by Odhner in his account of Swedish policy at the congress (1877: 163).

mind is the half century of pentarchy in the Italian subsystem after the 1454 Peace of Lodi. Apart from that, the international politics of Europe had been characterized at no time by stability based on the notion of equilibrium. In fact, Salvius's balance-of-power doctrine anticipates the European states system of the eighteenth and nineteenth centuries. At that time, the balance-of-power concept did become a major factor of stability—because the concept had by then become a consensus principle applicable to the structure of the system as a whole.

7. THE PROBLEM OF EQUALITY

The notion of autonomy, as an increasingly important ingredient of the consensus agenda, was in conflict with the fact that, whatever their specific constitutional arrangements, all the actors in the European states system represented societies organized on hierarchical, not egalitarian, lines. It is therefore not surprising to find similar, hierarchical tendencies in the relations between actors as well. In the case of the Empire, a rather complicated ranking of actors existed. On the European level, confusion reigned.

The nominal superiority of the Emperor was recognized at the congress in that his representatives enjoyed precedence over the other delegates, and in the two treaties, he was the party listed first. This had not been the case in the French and Swedish copies of the preliminary agreement to hold the congress concluded at Hamburg in 1641, as a result of which the Emperor almost refused to ratify that agreement.[182] When the peace treaties themselves were concluded, the Emperor was also obliged to concede that the French and Swedish monarchs were referred to in the text as 'Sacrae Maiestates' like himself.

But the peacemakers by no means regarded each other as equals. For example, the electors' envoys, whose masters traditionally thought of themselves as higher-ranking than other European rulers, fought a quarrel over precedence with the Venetian ambassador Alvise Contarini. In his defence, Contarini invoked four arguments: seniority (the republic was older than any of the electorates), independence (unlike the electors, it did not recognize

---

[182] Dickmann (1985: 105).

any suzerain), power (the electors were infinitely less mighty), and custom (traditional protocol at Rome and at the congress).[183]

In this instance, Contarini carried the day. But he was helpless against the snubs that he received from the French delegates. At the beginning of the congress, the Catholics at Münster held three full days of religious ceremonies to implore divine assistance for the negotiations. Although the French, in reporting these ceremonies, piously called the congress 'un si saint ouvrage', they nevertheless seized the opportunity to humiliate the Spaniards. Unable to prevent a public procession, the Spaniards eventually chose not to take part so as not to have to concede precedence to the French. The French, according to their own report, asserted their claim to equality with the Emperor in an unheard-of way.[184]

The Swedes did not succeed in their aim of establishing equality with the French, either. The instruction for the Swedish delegates insisted that they must ensure equal treatment for Sweden with other actors. It specified that, if speeches were to be made at Osnabrück for the opening of the congress, the delegates should allow the Imperial embassy to speak first, 'given that the ranking of the Emperor has not as yet been contested by the other kings of Christendom'. But the Swedish delegates were to see to it that they would speak next. Moreover, they were to ensure equality with the French envoys, and to insist that the same procedures were observed vis-à-vis the Swedish embassy as between the Emperor and France. The point was 'to preserve . . . the majesty and prestige of the realm and its equal status with other kingdoms.'[185]

The French opposed this Swedish objective vigorously. Brienne, the secretary of state, commented that

although the crowns, in regard of their sovereignty and independence, are equal, there is always pre-eminence, and, of necessity, one must give way to the other. . . . In so many places, all the crowns of Europe have yielded to us. Indeed, we are surprised that the Swedes should make those difficulties about which you have written to us.[186]

---

[183] Meiern (1734–6: i. 425 f.).

[184] The French delegates to Brienne, 16 Apr. 1644, APW II B. i. 93 ff.

[185] 'rikes höghet och respekt och likheten med andra kungariken.' Swedish main instruction of 15 Oct. 1641, APW I. i. 244 f.

[186] Meiern (1734–6: i. 197 f.). Meiern gives the date as 23 Apr. 1644. The same document is listed (though not printed) as APW II B. i, no. 78. There, the date is given as 30 Apr. 1644.

Salvius's suggestion to settle the question of precedence by lot was refused by Rorté, the French resident at Osnabrück, and the Swedes finally gave in.[187] The whole affair did place some further strain on the Franco-Swedish alliance. Salvius declared to Dr Volmar of the Imperial delegation that France only strove for the mastership of the Christian world ('arbitrium rerum christiani orbis'), and that it could not count on Swedish support for that.[188]

Yet it was the pretensions of the smaller actors that slowed down the peacemaking process most. These smaller actors caused almost unsurmountable difficulties to the French delegates, who complained of

their very unjust demands, which, in some way, are prejudicial to the dignity of the king, since, desiring to receive from us the same honours that they grant us, they establish by this means a certain equality between His Majesty and their masters. That, by the way, which is accorded to the one among them who holds the first rank undoubtedly has consequences for all right down to the last. The Dutch, for example, refuse to see us if we make any difference between them and the Venetian delegates. The envoy of Savoy intends to adopt the same stance if we do not treat him like the Dutch. And after that, the delegates of the electors, of Genoa, of Florence, and several others will feel entitled to break off all intercourse with us if we deny them that which we will have granted the Savoyard envoy.

The greatest problems were caused by the Dutch, who were particularly valuable allies to France because of their wealth and their hostility to Spain.

They [the Dutch] argue the decision of the late King [Henry IV], . . . the power of their republic, which is closely associated with France, which they see as creating an advantage for them over Venice, and the complete independence of their state, which, according to them, creates a very different situation from that of Savoy, which is under the suzerainty of the Emperor. When we ask them if, therefore, they mean to aspire to any equality with the king, they say no, but also that we would do them a greater injustice if we made any difference between them and Venice or

---

[187] 'Hier je conférai sur ce sujet toute l'après-dinée avec Monsieur Salvius et le priai de m'ouvrir son sentiment. Il mit de nouveau en avant qu'il en faudrait venir au sort, mais je lui fis connaître que la France ne mettrait jamais au sort une préférence qui lui est acquise par-dessus tous les autres rois'. Rorté to d'Avaux and Servien, 20 Apr. 1644, APW II B. i. 104. See also the French delegates to Brienne, 21 May 1644, APW II B. i. 208.
[188] Meiern (1734–6: i. 282 f.).

if we introduced any equality between them and a vassal of the Empire, who recognizes even the electors as his superiors.[189]

The French, as a rising but still insecure power, were clearly almost obsessed with their ranking in the system, craving acknowledgment of French pre-eminence and grandeur. Their problem was that they wanted to have their cake and eat it: they were keen to promote other actors' autonomy against the Emperor and Spain, but at the same time they would not accept the increasing equality of the actors that such an approach entailed. The Papal envoy, for once in tune with his time, put his finger on it when he remarked that, personally, he was happy to address everybody as 'Majesty' if that was what it took for them to make peace.[190]

French concessions were inevitable, however bravely the delegates dragged their feet. The pressure to grant more equal treatment to all actors was too great. For example, the Emperor instructed his delegates to treat the electors' delegates with the same honours that they awarded the Venetian, Spanish, and French ambassadors. This fulfilled a long-held ambition on the electors' part and left the French wringing their hands:

This makes it very difficult for us to decide what we should do. If we were to follow the example of the Imperial delegates . . . , then we find ourselves reduced to living on an equal footing with the ambassadors of princes who are vassals of the Empire . . . By the way, there is no doubt that the ambassadors of the [Dutch] and of Savoy will want to take advantage of what we will have done for those of the electors, which will lead to the ambassadors of the foremost crown of Christendom retaining precedence only over those of the smallest princes.

At the same time the French realized that if they wanted to boost the electors' autonomy against the Emperor, then they could not very well do less for the electors than the Emperor himself did.[191]

The French court fully shared the attitude of its delegates, but it also saw the dangers to which their zeal exposed it. The delegates were therefore told to moderate their stance.[192] Louis XIV himself

[189] To Anne d'Autriche, 29 Apr. 1644, APW II B. i. 140 f.
[190] Dickmann (1985: 207).
[191] The French delegates to Brienne, 14 Jan. 1645, APW II B. ii. 45 f.
[192] Anne d'Autriche to the French delegates, 9 Apr. 1644, APW II B. i. 54 f.; Mazarin to d'Avaux, 9 Apr. 1644, APW II B. i. 63 f.

(who was only 6 at the time) was made to write to them. He ordered the delegates to treat the representatives of the Dutch and of Savoy as 'Excellencies', and subsequently admonished them to accept the Dutch demands concerning protocol. In particular, he warned against attempts to break up the Franco-Dutch alliance.[193] But it was a case of too little too late.

The Spaniards, for their part, went out of their way to flatter the Dutch. Treating them with complete equality was part of Spain's strategy to decouple the Dutch from the French. The endeavour succeeded. In January 1647 d'Avaux informed the Swedes that a Spanish–Dutch agreement had been concluded. There were seventy-eight articles, 'of such regard for the States General that they could not have wished them to be better: the Dutch plenipotentiaries have, in the signature, the same rank and place as the Spaniards, each side disposing of half a page opposite one another, on an equal footing.'

It is interesting that this Swedish report does not waste a word on the actual content of the treaty, but seizes on what was clearly seen as its most interesting aspect. There was only the barest hint that the Spanish ambassador Peñaranda felt that the treaty quite literally implied a stepping-down for his king: 'When the signing had taken place,' the Swedish report continues, 'Peñaranda, it is said, approached [the Dutch] and took them aside, saying, "the king descends from his throne and now embraces you, no longer as subjects, but as his friends."'[194]

The agreement, signed provisionally on 8 January 1647, had still to be ratified by the Dutch States General. A few days later, Servien, the French plenipotentiary, appeared before the assembly of the States General at The Hague to deliver a remarkable speech seeking to dissuade them from ratification. The speech is

---

[193] Memorandum of 21 Jan. 1645, APW II B. ii. 73; Louis XIV to the French delegates, 18 Feb. 1645, APW II B. ii. 141 ('je continue l'ouvrage commencé par les rois mon aïeul et mon père de les [the Dutch] élever à la souveraineté et les égaler aux plus puissants princes de l'Europe').

[194] Seventy-eight articles, 'av den konsideration för Generalstaterna att de inte hava kunnat önska dem bättre: plenipotentiarii Batavici hava i underskrivandet lika rang och ställe med spanjorerna, hållandes var sin halv del av bladet mitt emot varannan, al pari. När subskriptionen var skedd, skall Peñaranda hava trätt till dem och framtagit holländerna, sägandes, Descendit de solio suo rex et vos nunc amplectitur non amplius ut subditos sed ut suos amicos.' J. Oxenstierna and Salvius to Queen Kristina, 21 Jan. 1647, APW II C. iii. 216 f.

characteristic of Servien's markedly power-political outlook. He warned the Dutch not to put their trust in written agreements, but in the protection that only French power could give them. According to him,

It is not what is written in a treaty, nor the diligence employed to conclude it today rather than tomorrow, nor the signatures or seals appended to it, which ensure that it is carried out, it is the continued ability, after it has been concluded, by virtue both of one's own strength and the number of one's friends, to ensure that the promise is honoured if the enemy decides to break his word, or to defend oneself in case of attack.[195]

But the Dutch did ratify eventually. Their decision was certainly facilitated by the fact that the deal offered by the Spaniards was very much in tune with the developing new consensus climate. The text places a strong emphasis on both autonomy and equality. Conspicuously, it omits to refer to the Spanish king as 'Majesty', although he was so described in all his dealings with other princes (apart from the Emperor).[196] Instead, the two contracting parties are both only given the title 'Seigneur'. The treaty refers to them uniformly as 'ledit Seigneur Roi' on the one side and 'lesdits Seigneurs États Généraux des Pays-Bas Unis' on the other. Furthermore, the opening paragraph recognizes Dutch sovereignty in the most solemn terms, in line with the autonomy principle.[197]

Equality was the unavoidable corollary of autonomy. The more there was of the one, the more there had to be of the other. In the German subsystem, where the autonomy of the estates fell short of complete independence, a hierarchical order was still practicable to some extent. In the European system at large, rejection of the universal authority formerly vested in Emperor and Pope logically implied complete equality for all the actors that recognized each

---

[195] 14 Jan. 1647, Le Clerc (1725–6: iv. 212).

[196] See the other treaties concluded by Spain around that time in Du Mont (1728).

[197] The opening paragraph declares the States General to be 'libres et souverains états, provinces et pays, sur lesquels, ni sur leurs pays, villes et terres associés . . . ledit Seigneur Roi ne prétend rien, et que présentement ou ci-après pour soi-même, ses hoirs et successeurs il ne prétendra jamais rien'. Spanish–Dutch Treaty of Münster of 30 Jan. 1648, ibid. vi. 1, 430. French and Dutch were the languages of the Spanish–Dutch negotiations; Dickmann (1985: 215). The Spanish envoy Antoine Brun, already mentioned, was a French-speaker; the Swedish report quoted earlier identifies him as the driving force behind the agreement ('Brun, en av dem spanska, som detta verket mäst drivit haver', APW II C. iii. 217).

other as such. In a system where the autonomy principle was accepted fully, the question could no longer be that of where in the system actors ranked, but merely whether or not they legitimately (that is, consensually) belonged to the system. We have already noted that no theoretical criterion had as yet evolved to determine this—apart from the basic religious qualification of adherence to Christianity.

In a system consisting of actors with greatly unequal resources, a principle calling for their total equality may, of course, face practical difficulties. In the nineteenth century this problem was resolved by introducing the concept of 'great powers', of actors that, because of their outstanding strength, enjoy certain prerogatives, but which are, at the same time, expected to maintain order in the system. Such actors are held, and hold themselves, answerable for their conduct to the other actors. In the seventeenth century this notion of great-power responsibility did not exist.

By 1648 France had become the biggest European power in terms of population and resources. But it was not comfortable with its position—indeed, if we look at French foreign-policy discourse of the period, its characteristic mixture of grandiloquence and latent insecurity suggests a parallel to Germany in the late nineteenth century. Such aggressive and overbearing behaviour is probably a natural reaction on the part of a newly risen power that is not exactly made welcome as such by the more established actors with which it enters into competition. The French fear of Habsburg enmity was real. It prompted the aggressive French expansionism that culminated in the reign of Louis XIV.

The aggressive policies of both France and Sweden during the remainder of the seventeenth century were not simply the result of any intrinsic strength or 'greatness'. They were prompted by insecurity. Of course, what was paraded, and catches the eye, is not that insecurity, but manifestations of strength, typical 'display behaviour' in other words. Neither power trusted for its own security in consensus on the legitimacy of its standing on the part of the other actors. With the notable exception of Salvius, decision-makers in both countries generally put their trust in expansionism, even to the point of attempting to eliminate hostile actors altogether—Louis XIV the Dutch Republic in the 1670s, Charles X the Danish crown in the 1650s. Such policies could only undermine further the consensus that, in the long run, was more important for security than additional territory or the weakening of potential rivals.

This vicious circle culminated in the decisive, almost tectonic, system-wide showdown that occurred early in the following century. This showdown saw both Sweden and the French dynasty, the House of Bourbon, involved in war against all of their neighbours simultaneously. Sweden succumbed. It had no chance against the awakening giant, Russia, and was reduced to a format more commensurate with its resources. The House of Bourbon, thanks to a remarkable combination of luck and diplomatic skill, scraped through. As the next chapter will show, it succeeded in consolidating and legitimizing both its gains and its standing in the European system.

3

The Peace of Utrecht

1. THE HISTORICAL BACKGROUND

At the beginning of the eighteenth century, two wars shook up the European states system—the Great Northern War (1700–21) and the War of the Spanish Succession (1701–14).

Despite the dazzling presence of the Swedish king Charles XII as the focus of the northern war, people tended to attribute greater significance to the Spanish one. Documents relating to the settlement that ended it talk of the *pacification de l'Europe* as if the northern quarrel were taking place on some other continent. The northern war was certainly significant: it destroyed the Swedish hegemony in north Europe and heralded the rise of Russia. But the Spanish war involved France, which, being more centrally located and far stronger, was seen to pose a more fundamental threat to the political organization of Europe. It is necessary to look at the situation in some detail to understand this.[1]

1.1. Antecedents

The Spanish king, the Habsburg Charles II, was an invalid and unable to produce an heir. Throughout his unexpectedly long reign, he regularly appeared to be at death's door. Both Habsburg and Bourbon relatives laid claim to his inheritance, due to a well-nigh intractable legal muddle. But a merger between the vast Spanish monarchy—comprising the Spanish mainland (minus Portugal), Belgium, large parts of Italy, and the overseas colonial empire— and either the possessions of the German Habsburgs or of the French (Bourbon) monarchy would fundamentally alter the character of the European states system. It would, it was feared, leave one actor in it in a position of disproportionate power in

[1] The main sources of the account that follows are Baudrillart (1890), Gaedeke (1877), Legrelle (1888–92), and Weber (1891).

relation to the rest. The prospect of this actor being Louis XIV was especially disagreeable to the rest of Europe. Louis XIV, given his past military successes and expansionism, stood accused of aspiring to a 'universal monarchy', the universal dominion over the European system that the Emperor was supposed to have been plotting during the Thirty Years War.

War over the Spanish issue would mean war on a scale not seen since 1648. The pressing of the French claim was likely to bring into being a grand anti-French coalition and force a decisive show-down. Given the way that the system was configured, the outbreak of war would inescapably lock it into a struggle for the mastership of Europe. Louis would have no choice but to try and secure that mastership—nothing else would save him. His opponents would not only seek to prevent French hegemony. If they were successful, they would be led by the logic of the struggle to reduce France to a position where it could not possibly become a threat again, and in doing so they would reverse Louis's past gains. For the French king, then, his life's work would be at stake.

Louis shrank from this prospect. He embarked on a vigorous, pertinacious, and skilful diplomatic campaign to forestall such an outcome. As his foreign minister was to put it in his memoirs, this was 'the resolution which His Majesty had judged most conducive to the good of the kingdom, and the general interest of Europe.'[2]

Louis entered into negotiations with William III of Britain, who, as Stadhouder, could also speak for the Dutch Republic. Because the Spanish monarchy was so large, a plan was eventually adopted by the three governments to split it up. This plan provided gener-ously for the Dauphin, somewhat optimistically expected Habsburg to make do with Milan (Lombardy), and gave the bulk of the Spanish possessions to a third party, the Wittelsbach dynasty of Bavaria, which also had some hereditary claim. Charles II of Spain, however, had enough vitality to resent both the attempt to dispose of his possessions while he was still alive and, especially, their proposed dispersal. The Franco-Anglo-Dutch scheme, not for long a secret, prompted him to make a will in favour of the Bavarian elector's only son, leaving him the whole of his dominions. This solution was accepted by France, Britain, and the Dutch. However, they put pressure on the elector to ensure that his son would cede

[2] Colbert [Marquis de Torcy] (1757: i. 23).

to the Dauphin what was due to him under the partition scheme. In this way, the scheme would effectively be maintained.

But this scheme did not command the support of the Emperor, Leopold. Moreover, the Wittelsbach heir unexpectedly died in February 1699. This destroyed the Bavarian claim, which derived from the elector's wife; personally, the elector had no entitlement.

A new partition scheme was worked out. But in October 1699 the Emperor rejected this one, too, despite Louis's efforts. France, Britain, and the Dutch went ahead with a new treaty, concluded in May 1700, which this time was made public. It awarded to the Dauphin the province of Guipúzcoa, the Spanish possessions in Italy except Milan, and the Duchies of Bar and Lorraine, whose ruler agreed to receive Milan in exchange. The Emperor was given time to adhere to this treaty. If he did so, his younger son the Archduke Charles was to receive the remainder of the Spanish monarchy. If the Emperor did not adhere to the treaty, then the other parties were to agree among themselves which prince should be substituted for the archduke as King of Spain.

But the Emperor remained unamenable. He told Louis that he was prepared to negotiate with France, but not with Britain and the Dutch. Indeed, the Emperor had negotiated with Louis on an earlier occasion, in the 1660s, but the Franco-Austrian partition treaty concluded at that time was superseded by events—because the Spanish king failed to die as quickly as expected. The Emperor signalled his agreement in principle to reopening the talks, but he objected to associating Britain and the Dutch on the grounds that they did not have any claim to the inheritance.

This may have been an excuse. The Emperor was reluctant to enter into an agreement while Charles II was still alive, partly at least because of fears that this would alienate the Spanish king and jeopardize his hoped-for commitment to an Austrian succession. In fact, the partition treaty contained a clause that the Emperor was to be given two more months from the date of the Spanish king's death to adhere to it. This was contained in a secret article, not in the published treaty, but the Emperor may well have had intelligence of it. This would obviously have encouraged him to maintain a wait-and-see attitude.[3]

Unfortunately for the peace of Europe, nobody had reckoned

[3] Legrelle (1888–92: iii. 318).

sufficiently with the Spanish king himself. Charles II, in line with Spanish popular sentiment, resented nothing as much as the prospect of a breakup of his monarchy. He made another will, this time kept strictly secret, under which his inheritance in its entirety was to go to the Duke of Anjou, the second son of the Dauphin, or to Anjou's younger brother, the Duke of Berry. The will explicitly ruled out any union of the French and Spanish dominions in the hands of a single ruler, but, of course, it provided the French king with a strong motive to defend the Spanish monarchy. Charles took this step because he thought that France, as Europe's strongest military power, was in a better position than the Emperor to defend his monarchy from division, and would do so once its king was given a sufficient incentive.

There was a positive as well as a negative incentive. The positive incentive was the addition of the entire Spanish dominions to the Bourbon sphere of influence. The negative one was that, if Louis chose to honour the partition treaty and reject Charles II's bequest, then, according to the will, the whole monarchy was to go to the Archduke Charles after all, because Vienna was not a party to that treaty. This would not only leave Vienna more powerful than Louis would really like; it also meant that the House of Bourbon would get nothing at all of the inheritance, at least not without a major war. And for that, Louis was unlikely to find allies.

It was a shrewd plan. It also destroyed the attempt to prevent a war of succession.

1.2. Crisis and War

The Spanish king died in November 1700. Having been informed of the will, Louis assembled his council and put before it the question of whether or not to accept the bequest. The memoirs of his foreign minister Torcy, who was present at the council, offer a reconstruction of the dilemma.

'It was easier to foresee than to prevent the consequences of the decision in question,' Torcy writes. By virtue of the partition treaty, the king 'had engaged himself to reject every disposition whatever, made by the King of Spain in favour of a prince of the line of France'. Therefore, if he failed to reject the bequest, that would not only be a breach of faith, a violation of the 'sacred word of a king', but 'the consequence of such a violation was inevitable war'.

Louis had concluded peace only three years earlier (at Rijswijk in the Netherlands), so as to allow a weakened France to recover from decades of warfare. But, if he went along with Charles II's will, another general war was unavoidable: 'there was not the least room to expect, that the neighbouring princes, who were so greatly alarmed at the power of France, would tamely suffer the king to extend his authority, so as to have the supreme direction, in the name of his grandson, of the dominions subject to the crown of Spain in the old and new world.'[4]

But, if Louis rejected the will, then he could no longer claim even part of the Spanish monarchy. This would then to go in its entirety to the archduke, who was not bound by the partition treaty and who would not hesitate to accept. Between father and son, the House of Austria would, once more, wield the power of Charles V (who had been both Emperor and King of Spain in the sixteenth century), 'heretofore so fatal to France'.[5]

Therefore, if Bourbon accepted the bequest, that would mean war with Austria. If Louis insisted on partition (to uphold both the partition treaty and the honour and security of the Bourbon dynasty), that would also mean war with Austria. But, in addition, respecting the treaty rather than the will would mean war with Spain.

Would it not be strange to make war on Spain as a result of the late king having left his dominions to a French prince—the more so as this decision also reflected the will of the Spanish people, who were fed up with German rule? Moreover, France would not be able to count on the support of the British and Dutch, who were not keen to enforce the partition scheme by military means. The point of that scheme had been to prevent a war of succession. If it could no longer do that it was obsolete.

Torcy's analysis is supported by other sources. For example, the British ambassador to Spain, Stanhope, reported in March 1698 that '[t]he general inclination as to the succession is altogether French, their [the Spaniards'] aversion to the queen [Maria Anna von Pfalz-Neuburg] having set them against all her [German] countrymen'.[6] And only weeks before the Spanish king's demise, William III of Britain had written to Holland that '[i]t would be

---

[4] Colbert (1757: i. 98 f.).   [5] Ibid. 99.
[6] Dated 14 Mar. 1698, quoted Legrelle (1888–92: ii. 161).

quite against my intention to be at present involved in a war for a treaty which I concluded only with a view to prevent it.'[7]

Since, clearly, war was inevitable in either case, the right thing for the French king to do was to accept the will.[8] As a result, the Duke of Anjou was proclaimed King of Spain as Philip V, and treated to an enthusiastic welcome in his new dominions.

Meanwhile, the Emperor occupied Milan (which was a fief of the Empire) and sought to rally Britain and the Dutch States General to his cause. In this, he was helped by Bourbon policy. News that Spanish ports would be closed to international shipping (French vessels excepted) caused British trade with these ports to collapse.[9] French troops occupied the Spanish Netherlands (Belgium) and virtually turned it into a French province. If this step was prompted by French security fears, any strategic advantage gained for France was offset by the impression of further expansionism that it created in the rest of Europe.

Moreover, on the death in France of the British ex-king, the deposed James II, Louis formally recognized James's son as King of Britain. The French king did not see this as rescinding his recognition of William III, extended at Rijswijk in 1697. In a circular to the European courts, he explained that his acknowledgement of the Stuart pretender was a mere act of courtesy, without practical relevance, and of which there were other examples in Europe. Louis politely omitted to cite the most applicable of these, the fact that William III himself, like his predecessors since the middle ages, laid claim to the title 'King of France'—a title which he had used, for example, in the 1697 Rijswijk peace itself.[10]

King William, however, was able to exploit the incident to whip up anti-French feeling in Britain. He broke off diplomatic relations. Earlier, he had demanded the cession of Ostend and Nieuwpoort as a pledge of France's good intentions, which Louis in turn interpreted as a gratuitous provocation. William felt that war against Bourbon preponderance was inevitable, and carried an initially reluctant public opinion, British as well as Dutch, with him.[11]

A few days before Louis's recognition of the Stuart pretender, in September 1701, the Emperor, Britain, and the Dutch States

[7] To Heinsius, dated 21 Aug. 1700, quoted Legrelle (1888–92: iii. 644).
[8] Colbert (1757: i. 101).   [9] Gaedeke (1877: ii. 128 f.).
[10] Legrelle (1888–92: iv. 250 ff.).   [11] Ibid. 110 ff., 120 f., 125 f.

General concluded an alliance at The Hague. It was a rather cautious document, which avoids taking sides as to the merits of either the Habsburg or the Bourbon claims. Article 2 merely stipulates for the Emperor a 'just and reasonable satisfaction concerning his claims to the succession in Spain'. Article 5 calls specifically for the conquest only of the Spanish possessions in Italy and the Mediterranean, and of Belgium. It does not spell out who was to rule these, but rather implies yet another partition scheme. The Archduke Charles is not mentioned at all.[12]

When Charles II's will became known, the Emperor had sought urgent negotiations with France about a compromise, indicating that he would be content with Milan, Naples, Sicily, and the Spanish Netherlands. This time, however, it was Louis who was unamenable.[13] He may have feared that any deal with Vienna at this stage would jeopardize his grandson's position in Spain. Philip had, after all, been recognized as king there on the understanding that France would protect the Spanish monarchy from partition. In addition, Louis seems to have overestimated the added resources that he would gain from the Spanish inheritance, underestimating the difficulty and cost of defending it.

In the spring of 1702 the signatories of the Hague Alliance declared war on France. France declared war on them in July. The estates of the German Empire adhered to the alliance and, in the autumn, the Empire in its own right also declared war. Two of the electors, however, in breach of the Empire's constitution, had joined the Bourbon camp. Both members of the Wittelsbach dynasty, they were the Elector of Bavaria and his younger brother, the Elector-Archbishop of Cologne. Savoy and Portugal, which had originally supported France, subsequently switched sides and joined the alliance.

Initially unsuccessful, the allies gained the upper hand after the battle of Höchstädt ('Blenheim') in 1704. From 1706 onwards, France repeatedly sued for peace, having put out feelers to that effect even earlier. In 1709 at The Hague and in 1710 at Geertruidenberg, Louis was prepared to make sweeping sacrifices for peace, but the allies, exorbitant in their demands, passed up the opportunity.

---

[12] Text in Freschot (1714–15: i. 1 ff.).   [13] Legrelle (1888–92: iv. 156, 168).

1.3. Towards Peace

The situation changed when the Whig ministry in Britain was
toppled by court intrigues and replaced with a Tory one. The
Tories then went on to win the 1710 parliamentary elections. The
Whigs were the war party; the Tories, for a variety of reasons,
favoured peace. The following year the Emperor Joseph—he had
succeeded his father Leopold in 1705—unexpectedly died, leaving
only his younger brother the Archduke Charles to succeed him as
Emperor. However, the archduke had already been proclaimed
King of Spain (calling himself Charles III), and his cause was
supported by the alliance. Charles's election to the Imperial throne
provided the perfect justification for the Tories' insistence on peace.
Bolingbroke, the new British foreign secretary,[14] was able to take
the view that the purpose of the Hague Alliance had been the
prevention of hegemony. Furthermore, as we saw earlier, the Hague
document had not made winning the entire Spanish monarchy for
Habsburg a war aim. It was only subsequently that the idea that
the entire Spanish inheritance should go to Charles had gained
acceptance.[15] As things stood, if Charles united all the old Habsburg
possessions in a single person, then this would create even more
of a hegemony than if Louis XIV and Philip V united their dominions in the same dynasty.

Naturally, Charles was anxious to continue the war. So, for the
time being, were many Dutch. Thinking in terms of their own
security as well as commercial advantage, they held that France
had not been weakened sufficiently, and that the French threat
should be eliminated once and for all. Furthermore, the Hague
government resented the fact that the Tories were putting out
feelers to the French and eventually even wrested from the Dutch
the leadership that they had exercised in the earlier, abortive
negotiations at The Hague and Geertruidenberg. And, most importantly perhaps, the Dutch government was afraid of Britain
obtaining concessions for itself at the expense of the Dutch, which
is precisely what happened.

---

[14] Henry St John. The title Viscount Bolingbroke was conferred on him during
the negotiations, but, for simplicity's sake, I have used it throughout. There were
two foreign secretaries in Britain at the time, but the other, Dartmouth, was much
less prominent in the negotiations leading up to the Utrecht peace.
[15] Weber (1891: 4 f.).

If Britain was to act as peace broker, it intended the Bourbon dynasty to pay for this service. Secretly, for the time being, but amidst much well-founded suspicion, Britain secured the promise of Gibraltar, Menorca, some French possessions in Canada, and the monopoly of the slave trade with the Spanish colonies.

In these circumstances, peace initiatives emanating from Britain inevitably met with a hostile reception from the Dutch and the Emperor. As a consequence, the new British government, unbending in its determination to stop or at least quit the war, resorted to a mixture of manipulation and bullying. The secret understanding worked out with France contained the essentials of the future settlement; there was no consultation with the allies. At length, a French peace offer was produced in October 1711, the London Preliminaries. Queen Anne declared this document to be an acceptable basis for negotiations—although the terms looked grotesquely vague and lenient in comparison with the harsh and detailed earlier preliminaries that France had been very close to accepting. The British ministers put pressure on the Dutch to agree to a general congress on the basis of these new preliminaries. They made it clear that, otherwise, Britain might sign a separate peace.

The congress opened at Utrecht in January 1712, in a climate of distrust among the allies. The Dutch rightly suspected double dealing on the part of the British, and the Emperor Charles sent a delegation instructed to try to scuttle the negotiations. For a long time Philip V, the Bourbon King of Spain, had no delegation, because he was not yet universally recognized. Louis XIV was happy to represent him. Initially much in awe of his grandfather, Philip was beginning to develop a mind more his own, much to the French king's annoyance.

The British and French originally hoped to hammer out a final settlement and obtain allied acquiescence by the spring, in time to prevent a new military campaign—which could only embarrass them, given that they were still officially enemies. But the scheme ran behind schedule. In May Bolingbroke was forced to order the British contingent not to participate in the new campaign, in other words, to desert the allied forces. Obligingly, the French commander was also informed of this as well as of the allied campaign plan. The allied reaction to this treachery, blatant at last and for everybody to see, is unnecessary to describe. Militarily, the French were in quite a desperate position, but the remaining allied troops managed to get themselves defeated at Denain. Demoralized, the Dutch abandoned the fight. In these circumstances, the Emperor eventually also resigned himself to peace, but a complication arose when the French, exploiting his isolation, tried to push through some rather injurious last-minute demands. Charles rejected these demands, and he and the Empire, on their own, embarked on another military campaign against France.

Technically, the Peace of Utrecht consists of a total of eleven bilateral treaties. On 11 April 1713 peace treaties were signed between France on the one hand and, respectively, Britain, Portugal, Prussia, and Savoy on the other. Peace between France and the Dutch followed on 4 November. Spain made peace with Britain and Savoy on 13 July 1713 and with the Dutch on 26 June 1714. The Emperor Charles eventually concluded his peace with France at Rastatt on 6 March 1714, on terms marginally better than what he would have obtained at Utrecht. The peace between the Empire and France, signed at Baden in Switzerland on 7 November of the same year, was essentially a copy of the Rastatt document. Finally, Spain belatedly made peace with Portugal at Utrecht on 6 February 1715.

It should be noted that, in this settlement, not much was actually decided at Utrecht itself. Bolingbroke later went so far as to speak of 'mock conferences'.[16] That does not mean, however, that the congress as such was unimportant. It was there that the bilateral Franco-British scheme was converted into a general European one, a scheme that became the object of a remarkable consensus despite the means employed to impose it. In spite of initial resentment, it was quickly accepted because, as we will see, it was in striking agreement with the international consensus agenda.

But the key negotiations took place between Bolingbroke and Torcy, the British and French foreign ministers, who appear as the principal framers of the peace. A record of these negotiations survives in their correspondence, published in 1798 along with other state papers.[17]

---

[16] St John [Viscount Bolingbroke] (1844: ii. 319).

[17] St John (1798). In this edn., an English trans. of all French documents is supplied. I have used it for quotations in this ch., but I have sometimes made changes. There is a parallel correspondence between Torcy and the British prime minister Oxford in the London Public Record Office. I have not consulted this

2. GENERAL REMARKS ON THE EUROPEAN STATES SYSTEM AT THE TIME OF THE UTRECHT CONGRESS

2.1. Differences from the Situation at Münster and Osnabrück: Implications

As we have seen in Chapter 2, the consensus agenda of the Peace of Westphalia was concerned predominantly with the German subsystem and its special conditions, and it was not really viable in the European states system at large. The three major consensus principles identified at Münster and Osnabrück (legality, loyalty, and structural inviolability) continued to function in the German subsystem, but they played virtually no role at Utrecht. On the other hand, the notions of autonomy, equality, security, and the balance of power, which we also encountered in the last chapter, enjoyed overwhelming prominence at Utrecht.

During the negotiations, none of the major actors tried to capitalize on treaties or custom; conversely, none was criticized for contravening these. Bolingbroke did remark later that the powers had no right to try to break up the Spanish monarchy, and that the Spanish nation and king had every right to dispose of the Spanish crown as they pleased. But he made this observation in passing and noted the disregard for right with a shrug of his shoulders: 'enough has been said concerning right, which was in truth little regarded by any of the parties concerned immediately or remotely in the whole course of these proceedings. Particular interests were alone regarded'.[18]

It did not occur to anyone to blame Louis XIV for failing to honour the partition treaty, or for accepting Charles II's will. And when Torcy pointed out that the British and Dutch had made it clear to the Emperor that they did not intend to enforce the partition, he did so without indignation.[19]

correspondence. Torcy had a closer rapport with Bolingbroke than with Oxford, and there is no indication that his correspondence with Oxford would yield any additional insight relevant to this book. Recent biographies of Oxford have stressed—not, to my mind, entirely conclusively—that he had a greater share in the peace than previous historiography (e.g. Trevelyan), captivated by the mercurial and splendidly articulate Bolingbroke, has given him credit for. But it is not relevant to the argument of this book to what extent Bolingbroke was the initiator or merely the mouthpiece of British policy. McInnes (1970: 131 ff.), Hill (1988: chs. 12 and 14).

[18] St John (1844: ii. 287).   [19] Colbert (1756: i. 153).

Like Bolingbroke in the passage quoted above, statesmen explained international politics quite straightforwardly as an interplay of interests—a key notion, which we will examine more closely later on. The heavy emphasis on 'interests' was by no means incompatible with adherence to consensus principles. But the notion of *pacta sunt servanda*, of the sanctity of treaties, was not a part of the Utrecht consensus agenda.

The principles of loyalty and of the inviolability of existing structures also played little or no role at Utrecht.

In the context of the Utrecht negotiations, the chief remnant of the notion of loyalty was the solemn pledge by the parties to the peace treaties to cooperate and seek their reciprocal good. For instance, article 1 of the peace between France and Britain stipulates that peace and friendship

shall be upheld and observed so sincerely and inviolately that they [the two monarchs] shall each promote the interest, honour, and advantage of the other; and in such a way that loyal neighbourhood, a secure peace, and the pursuit of friendship may on both sides be restored and continuously strengthened.[20]

A similar clause is found in most of the treaties. But these were ritual incantations rather than substantive statements of intent. The fact that they were formulas, and somewhat archaic formulas at that, is especially obvious in the case of the Franco-British document quoted above. It was unique in its use of the by then rather archaic-sounding *fida vicinitas*—loyal neighbourhood— reminiscent of the treaties of 1648.[21] It is also significant that these formulas were employed as a matter of course and did not have to be constantly repeated (as they were in the course of the negotiations at Münster and Osnabrück).

Early eighteenth-century Europe took international cooperation much more for granted than had been possible in the 1640s, when the international system had been much more regionalized and less closely integrated as a whole. At Münster and Osnabrück, a new international system was emerging, and all patterns of behaviour in it were necessarily somewhat tentative. Fear of the system

---

[20] Freschot (1714–15: ii. 466).
[21] The British had their copies of the treaties made out in Latin, which was also preferred by Prussia and by the Empire. The Spaniards and Portuguese used their own languages. Everybody else used French.

being severely disrupted was constant. Hence the frequent, sometimes anxious, protestations of readiness to cooperate. At Utrecht,
on the other hand, cooperation had become a matter of routine.
There was a confidence that it remained possible even in wartime,
when it was temporarily suspended.

In a similar way, it was because the structure of the international
system was so precarious that people in the 1640s were so concerned
to preserve what structure did exist. Hence the inviolability principle. Some decades later, the discarding of that principle and,
indeed, a lack of interest in the problem of structure as such were
symptomatic of an international system that had grown more secure
and self-confident, that could take itself much more for granted.
Structure at Utrecht was, of course, an issue in that the crucial
question was whether or not an actor in the system might be
allowed to attain a position of system-wide hegemony. But, as we
will see, the principles drawn on to deal with that question
were those of security and balance of power.

2.2. Identity of the International Actors and Structure of the System

Concerning the issue of membership in the system, this was no
more governed by some abstract criterion at Utrecht than it had
been at Münster and Osnabrück. As with other aspects of the
system's structure, it was still a concrete *situation* that was taken
for granted, providing a focus for consensus. This situation was
only to a low degree the result of, or in accordance with, abstract
principles. The reason was because, in its 'classical' version, the
European states system came into existence at a later point in
time than most of the actors that composed it. It was for this
reason that the legitimacy of these actors as such was, as yet,
unconnected to the system's structural principles. Only at a later
stage, when the system had evolved yet further, did it become
capable of including—indeed, obliged to include—the membership issue in its purview.

In early eighteenth-century Europe the legitimacy of the existing actors was still simply acknowledged, not deduced from any
abstract concept. The very notion of tradition or traditionality
itself, so prominent at Münster and Osnabrück, had by the beginning of the eighteenth century disappeared from mainstream

political discourse. The role of master concept had passed from tradition to reason. Rationality, not traditionality, was the main characteristic of that discourse.

In order to understand the identity of the system's actors, we must not be misled by the state-centric model that habitually underlies our conception of international relations. That model equates 'state' with 'nation state' and automatically assumes a state to be an autonomous entity. At Utrecht, the word 'state' was used in a different sense. Moreover, other expressions were also used to designate international actors.

The idiom in which the Utrecht statesmen conducted their policies refers not only to 'states', but also to 'monarchies', 'princes', 'peoples', and 'nations', without assuming that these should be interrelated in a given way. They sometimes coincided, but more frequently they did not. Furthermore, the way in which they were interrelated in concrete instances could change over time.

At Utrecht, the word 'state' was used ordinarily to designate an administrative unit with the potential to be an autonomous international actor, even though it might not, and in fact often did not, possess that quality at the moment. For instance, the French instruction for the congress refers to the Spanish dominions as 'a monarchy so vast and consisting of so many states'—so many that it should not be too difficult to transfer some of them to other rulers to procure general satisfaction.[22] Legrelle, the nineteenth-century historian, echoes this wording in a memorable formulation of his own: 'l'Espagne d'Europe, en 1697, avec ses vingt ou vingt-cinq couronnes juxtaposées, demeurait le plus vaste établissement monarchique du monde chrétien.'[23]

In the event, Sicily, one of the Spanish 'states' in Italy, was awarded to the Duke of Savoy, while the others, and Belgium, were given to the Emperor. Strictly speaking, there was not even a unified Spain as such; Aragón, Valencia, Murcia, etc. still subsisted as separate kingdoms.[24] The story was told at the time that, when the Spanish ambassador to France, Castelldosrius, went to inform Louis XIV of the Spanish king's will, and the initial response was evasive, the ambassador emerged from the audience

---

[22] Weber (1891: 425).   [23] Legrelle (1888–92: ii. 7).

[24] See the Imperial instruction for the congress, which contemplated a partition of the Spanish mainland along the borders between its various component kingdoms. Weber (1891: 454).

remarking to bystanding courtiers that 'I would never have believed it possible that I might make an offer of twenty-two kingdoms and be told in reply, I will see!'[25]

The Austrian monarchy was cast in a similar mould. Apart from the Austrian duchies, it comprised the Kingdoms of Bohemia, Hungary, Croatia, etc.—to name just some of its more important 'states'. In addition, its head was King of Germany and Roman Emperor. In the British Isles, the Kingdoms of England and Scotland had, with difficulty, been merged as recently as 1707, creating the United Kingdom of Great Britain, while Ireland remained separate until 1801. Bolingbroke still tended to refer to Britain as 'these kingdoms' in the plural.[26]

Unlike 'states', 'monarchies' were always autonomous, and acted through a prince. But they could do so in a concerted fashion if the prince agreed to subordinate his own interests to those of the dynasty. These interests might be at variance with those of the 'states', 'nations', or 'peoples' of which monarchies were made up. For example, when commenting on the dilemma in which Charles II's will placed Louis XIV, Bolingbroke wrote that 'adhering to the partitions seemed the cause of France, accepting the will that of the House of Bourbon'.[27]

Popular opinion and preference was monitored by decision-makers and referred to in foreign-policy discourse. In his memoirs, Torcy places a heavy emphasis on the will of the Spaniards to safeguard the integrity of their dominions, and to see them governed by a French prince rather than a Habsburg one. He mentions 'the almost general desire, which the nation expressed, of seeing a prince of the blood-royal of France called to the succession of King Charles'—even though he goes on to say in this particular passage (which deals with the situation prior to the will) that this was not enough to make a French bid for the succession advisable in the face of opposition from other international actors.[28]

Similarly, Bolingbroke acknowledged that the Duke of Anjou was called to the Spanish throne by Charles II's will, 'and by the

[25] The remark would have been made on 11 Nov. 1700. Legrelle (1888–92: iv. 41 f.).

[26] See e.g. St John (1798: i. 244, 248, 603). On other occasions, he did use the singular.

[27] St John (1844: ii. 288).   [28] Colbert (1757: i. 66, and *passim*).

voice of the Spanish nation'. Bolingbroke refers to the 'universal concurrence of the Spanish nation to the new settlement he [the late king] had made of that crown', pointing out that on the eve of the war '[t]he French were looked upon with esteem and kindness at Madrid; but the Germans were become, or growing to be, objects of contempt to the ministers, and of aversion to the people'.[29] As a practical result of this, hopes of mass support for the attempted allied conquest of the Spanish mainland proved unfounded. Except in Catalonia, local opinion strongly favoured Philip.[30]

As the war wore on, however, it was the turn of the French to become unpopular in Spain. The aristocracy resented the centralizing reforms championed by the new king's French advisers. There was also a general disenchantment as a result of the perceived failure of the French to act in Spain's best interest, which, it was felt, was being sacrificed to France's. Towards the end of the war, anti-French sentiment rose so high in Spain that French nationals there were insulted and even assassinated by the mob, while at night placards went up in the squares of Madrid, demanding 'in the name of the people' that the French should leave the city.[31]

Philip V himself seems to have been largely exempt from anti-French feeling, having come to be regarded by the masses as a Spaniard rather than a Frenchman.[32] He invoked the wishes of the Spanish 'nation' when, to the surprise of both Bolingbroke and Torcy, he rejected the plan proposed by Bolingbroke by which Philip was to exchange the Spanish monarchy for Savoy while retaining his rights of succession to the French throne. Instead, he chose to renounce these rights, declaring fulsomely that 'in order to remain united with the Spaniards, I would not only prefer Spain to all the monarchies in the world, but content myself with possessing but the tiniest part of it so as not to desert the nation.'[33]

Similarly, the German declaration of war of 1702 places a heavy emphasis on the insults which Louis XIV had inflicted on 'the German nation'. Adopting the nationalist discourse typical of the

[29] St John (1798: ii. 301, 286, 284, and *passim*).
[30] Bolingbroke to Drummond, dated 26 Dec. 1710, ibid. i. 34.
[31] Roussel de Courcy (1889: 63 ff., 203, 227 f., 248), Baudrillart (1890: 569 f.).
[32] Roussel de Courcy (1889: 63 f., 227); see, however, Baudrillart (1890: 569).
[33] 3 July 1712, Freschot (1714–15: ii. 55). The Archduke Charles had the same reaction with regard to the Catalans, who supported him.

politics of the Empire, the document also pays rhetorical homage
to the 'most cherished fatherland'. It accuses Louis of trying to
subjugate the Germans as a preliminary exercise to establishing
that horrible thing, a universal monarchy.[34]

Clearly, in early eighteenth-century foreign-policy talk, the
concept of 'nation' had considerable resonance. The 'bartering
peoples about' (Woodrow Wilson) that a later age would see as a
major vice of old-style European diplomacy was considered normal (i.e. it was covered by international consensus), but it was
admitted that the populations concerned might have their own
opinion in the matter. For instance, at one point during the negotiations, Torcy urged that the Duke of Savoy should stop trying to
obtain more French territory and make up his mind to accept
Sicily, which was being offered to him. If he hesitated any longer,
Torcy wrote,

he runs the risk of losing Sicily; for there is much disorder in that island,
and its inhabitants . . . declare openly it were better to choose a master,
and to give themselves up to the House of Austria, than to suffer themselves to be disposed of like a flock of sheep.[35]

But while it was regarded as admissible, and sometimes desirable, to switch certain 'states' from one actor to another, actors as
such could not be merged or suppressed at will. Torcy emphatically ruled out the possibility of a union between France and Spain
(the terms of the will forbade this, but towards the end of the war,
Philip V looked set to inherit the French crown, in addition to
being King of Spain). 'France', Torcy wrote, 'will never consent to
become a province of Spain; Spain says the same with respect
to France; the question then is, What well-founded means can be
used to prevent the union of the two monarchies?'[36]

The fluidity that the European states system was allowed to
retain stopped short of any alteration of the number or the identity of the actors. The nature of these actors is illustrated by the
request for recognition as a member of the system at large (rather
than just the German subsystem) put forward at Utrecht by the
Elector of Brandenburg in his new capacity as King of Prussia.
This title, already acknowledged by the allies, had not yet been

[34] Text in Lünig (1713: 286 ff.).
[35] Torcy to Bolingbroke, 17 Oct. 1712, St John (1798: ii. 95 f.).
[36] Réponse au mémoire apporté par le Sieur Gaultier, 23 Mar. 1712, ibid. i. 437.

recognized by the House of Bourbon. The Brandenburg dominions were a typical 'monarchy' of the type also represented by
the Austrian and Spanish ones: a conglomerate of 'states', still very
heterogeneous and in part not even contiguous, separately administered and sprawling all over the northern part of the Empire
into the Netherlands and beyond its eastern border into Poland.
What 'acted' in the international arena was not this plurality of
'states', but the prince that these states had in common and, in the
long run, the dynasty. It was not until later that this conglomerate
coalesced into one state, and that this single state as such took
over the role of international actor.

There is often continuity of a sort between 'states' in the sense
in which the word is understood now and previous international
actors of a different type (e.g. 'monarchies' in the sense in which
the word was used at Utrecht). This makes it easy to project
twentieth-century consensus notions back into earlier periods.
However, doing so interferes with a proper understanding of the
international system as it existed then.

By the early eighteenth century the antagonism and distrust
between actors that had been so marked at Münster and Osnabrück
had abated. The Prussian monarchy provides a good example. It
was an actor both in the European system at large and in the
German subsystem. At Utrecht, its ruler Frederick William I, in
his capacity as a European king in his own right, obtained recognition by France and Spain of his new royal title.[37] At the same
time, paradoxically enough, he remained a belligerent, at war with
France in his capacity as Elector of Brandenburg. It was agreed in
his peace treaty with France that, as long as the Emperor and the
Empire remained at war, the Brandenburg contingent in the
Reichsarmee would continue to take part in that war.[38]

This detail says a lot about the international system of the period. For one thing, only in a highly defined system, highly conscious
of, and attached to, its structure, was such an elaborately artificial
arrangement possible. Moreover, this is an illustration of how warfare at that time was not the result of any deep-seated antagonism
between the actors. In what strikes a more tormented age as almost
naïve or cavalier, warfare was treated as a surface disturbance,

[37] Peace treaty between Prussia and France, separate article, Freschot (1714–15:
ii. 593 ff.).   [38] Art. 2, ibid. 571 f.

something that did not affect the underlying fundamental consensus on which the structure of the system rested.

As a result of the Spanish imbroglio, Louis posed a threat to this structure. However, there is a sense in which he did so almost against his will and certainly not as a result of any sort of ideological commitment to subverting the system. Contrary to what many believed, he did not have a blueprint for 'universal monarchy'. At the same time, it is remarkable that the fundamental consensus on which the system rested was not destroyed by fears that he might; that, on the contrary, it could accommodate such fears.

The bond between actors in the system was underlined by the custom—not new, but certainly more emphatic than in the 1640s—for rulers to refer to each other as 'brother' or 'sister'. This is another manifestation of the strikingly benign and conciliatory tone of the foreign policy discourse of the period. Queen Anne's main instruction for the British plenipotentiaries at Utrecht speaks of 'our good brother the Emperor', 'our good brother the King of Prussia', 'our good brother the Duke of Savoy', and so on. Lesser, not quite autonomous, rulers are referred to as somewhat more distant relatives ('our good cousin the Landgrave of Hesse-Kassel').[39]

However, with cool correctness, the same document designates the King of France merely as 'His Most Christian Majesty', implying that, for the time being, he could not be considered 'part of the family'. All the less so because Louis had recognized the Catholic Stuart pretender. But, in his effort to conciliate Britain, the French king eventually went back on this. In June 1712 he sent Queen Anne a brief autograph letter, the chief purpose of which seems to have been to afford him the opportunity to address her as 'madame ma sœur', and to sign himself 'votre bon frère, Louis'.[40]

The increasing consolidation, integration, and self-assurance of the European system may have given dynastic ties greater importance as a factor of cohesion than had been the case previously. (Of course, it is also true that dynastic ties in a way caused the war of succession, but a contradiction is less apparent if we adopt the view that war in this period was a 'surface' phenomenon that did not affect the system's *overall* stability or structure.) Centralization of administrative structures within actors went in

---

[39] Text in St John (1798: i. 357 ff.).   [40] 22 June 1712, ibid. 544.

the same direction—in many cases, this enhanced the role of the 'crown' (the ruler and his or her circle) at the expense of other, more independent, political personnel. At least three European crowns that had been elective well into the seventeenth century—the Bohemian, the Hungarian, and the Danish—had become hereditary by the beginning of the eighteenth century. This is testimony to the growing strength of monarchism.

Nevertheless, as yet the prevalence of monarchies in the system in no way implied that republican actors were frowned upon. When Louis XIV was planning the partition of the Spanish dominions, he envisaged the creation of an independent Catholic Republic of the Southern Netherlands (Belgium) as a counterpart to its Protestant northern neighbour, with which it was to be allied.[41] And when the Catalans again took the opposite position to the rest of Spain in the war of succession (as they had also done during the Thirty Years War), this prompted the same response as in the 1640s. Then, it had been Mazarin who pressed for the transformation of Catalonia into a separate republic.[42] At Utrecht, it fell to the Emperor Charles, whom the Catalans were supporting, to revive that idea.[43] Nor were non-monarchical actors necessarily of secondary importance, even though their size, for reasons discussed in the next chapter, could not grow to match that of the larger monarchies. It was the Dutch Republic, rather than the Emperor or the British crown, that for several years assumed the leadership of the anti-French coalition.

To sum up, the international system of early eighteenth-century Europe is perhaps best described as having been subdivided at three levels. These can be called the administrative, the popular, and the dynastic levels. On the administrative level, the system was divided into states; on the popular level, into peoples or nations; on the dynastic level, that of the princes, into monarchies. International decision-making was generally concentrated at the third level, but might take place or be influenced at the other two. It certainly did in the case of the republics, where the third level did not exist.

---

[41] Legrelle (1888–92: iii. 18).   [42] See Ch. 2, sect. 5, above.
[43] Memorandum of the Habsburg representative in London, Hoffmann, for Queen Anne, 2 Nov. 1712; Lamberty (1728–30: vii. 356).

2.3. Self-awareness of the System: 'Public' and 'Private' Interest

That the sphere of international politics was a more sophisticated environment at Utrecht than it had been sixty years earlier is apparent not only from the sheer professionalism of the political personnel (which offers a striking contrast to the tentative dilettantism prevailing at Münster and Osnabrück). It is also apparent from the manner in which the system was conscious of itself. Whereas in the 1640s the self-awareness of the system had manifested itself as a noticeable but vague community feeling, at Utrecht statesmen were able to take a detached view of the international political environment.

With possible rare exceptions such as Salvius, the peacemakers at Münster and Osnabrück were conscious of the system only through their involvement in it. At Utrecht, there was an abstract consciousness of the system that was independent of participation. This abstract, analytical awareness is much apparent in the writings of Bolingbroke. He was fond of expressions which, expressly or implicitly, denoted the international system as a whole. In his correspondence during the negotiations, he referred to the 'système général des affaires de l'Europe' or to the 'system for a future settlement of Europe'.[44] In the eighth of his *Letters on History*, which deals with the Utrecht period, he speaks of the 'political system of Europe', the 'general system' or the 'general system of power in Europe', the 'constitution of Europe', the 'common cause of Europe', and the 'general interest of Europe'.[45]

In the documents relative to the negotiations, expressions denoting a sense of commonwealth are ubiquitous. The preambles of the treaties contain references to the *orbis christianus* and to the *respublica christiana* (as well as other religious phraseology) and are, in some cases, preceded by an invocation of the Trinity. But this type of rhetoric, familiar from the negotiations at Münster and Osnabrück, once again has a somewhat archaic ring here. At Utrecht, a common denominator was provided much more frequently by the concept of 'Europe', which had the advantage of being secular and neutral and therefore less likely to cause controversy. While the question of who or what could properly be regarded as Christian might always be a subject of dispute between

---

[44] St John (1798: ii. 443, 614).
[45] St John (1844: ii. 276 ff., e.g. 277, 285, 313, 302, 277, 293).

different denominations, there was less contention about who could be considered European. Moreover, tension could be created by actors seeing themselves as Christian in a superior way, even if they did not totally deny the Christian credentials of their peers. Europeanness did not admit of gradations so easily.

In foreign-policy discourse, the European states system was treated as a kind of imaginary super-actor with the same aspirations as the individual actors that made it up. The same key words were used both to refer to individual actors and, as frequently, to the system as a whole. The notion of 'interest', cited earlier, is an obvious case in point. The same applies to another key concept, that of 'repose' or 'tranquillity'. The desire for 'repose'—in other words, stability—could be manifested on behalf of individual actors as well as on behalf of the system.

Constructing consensus notions so as to bring the goals of the system as a whole and those of individual actors into line with one another provided an answer to the problem discussed in the last chapter of how to motivate the actors to defend these notions. They were more likely to defend the system's goals if—at least semantically—these were identical to their own.

In the parlance of the Utrecht statesmen, the system ('Europe') constituted a 'public' sphere in which whatever concerned only single individual actors was 'private'. 'Public' aspirations—pursued on behalf of the system as a whole—were more legitimate, that is, likely to engender international consensus, than mere 'private' ones. 'Private' aspirations were only legitimate if they were compatible with the 'public' interest. Actors were supposed to act in the 'interest' and for the 'good', not just of themselves individually, but of the 'public' or system, the 'public good' usually being identified with the 'repose' or stability of the system. For example, in Bolingbroke's remark quoted earlier concerning the problem of right, the emphasis in 'particular interests were alone regarded' is on the word 'particular'.[46] In the correspondence between the Dutch grand pensionary Heinsius and the British prime minister Oxford, both sides are supposed to work 'not only for their own good, but for that of all Europe', or 'for the good of the two nations, and the repose of all Europe'.[47] Torcy's memoirs abound with expressions

[46] See sect. 2.1, above.
[47] Heinsius to Oxford, 24 July 1711, Weber (1891: 402); 4 Oct. 1712, ibid. 420. The entire correspondence, ibid. 401 ff. Technically, Heinsius was grand pensionary

denoting the 'public' interest, such as 'bien de l'Europe', 'salut de l'Europe', 'repos public', 'repos général', 'repos de l'Europe', 'repos de la chrétienté', 'tranquillité publique', 'tranquillité générale', 'tranquillité de l'Europe', etc.[48] The expression 'pour le bien du royaume [de France] et de l'Europe entière', used in the memoirs and hence destined for publication,[49] appears in very similar form in Torcy's private journal, not published until 1884 ('pour ses affaires [i.e. those of Louis XIV] et pour le bien général de l'Europe').[50]

A similar terminology was used in the peace treaties themselves. For instance, in the preamble of the peace between Britain and France, the two monarchs (who are the contracting parties) are described as 'equally mindful of the interest of their subjects and concerned for the perpetual—inasmuch as this is granted to mortals—tranquillity of the whole Christian world'.[51]

The most emphatic invocations of the 'public' good emanated from the Spanish king Philip V. In the preamble of the peace between him and the Duke of Savoy, the Spanish king is described as 'Philip V . . . who has always assiduously sought the means to reestablish the general repose of Europe, and the tranquillity of Spain [*el reposo general de la Europa, y la tranquilidad en España*]'. Article 3 provides that if the new Spanish royal house should become extinct, its inheritance should go not to the French royal family but to Savoy, 'for the same reasons, and for the same motives, of the public good of the peace, the repose, and the equilibrium of Europe, and the tranquillity of the Kingdom of Spain in particular'.[52]

Article 4, which deals with the cession of Sicily to Savoy, again emphasizes the same 'reasons and motives'.[53] The details of the cession were laid down in a separate document, the preamble of

only of the Republic of Holland, not of the United Provinces as a whole, but in practice he acted as foreign minister for the entire confederation.
   [48] Colbert (1756: *passim*).   [49] Ibid. i. 35.   [50] Colbert (1884: 359).
   [51] 'tam consulentes utilitati subditorum suorum, quam perpetuae, quantum mortalibus permittitur, totius christiani orbis tranquillitati prospicientes'. French text, reversing the order: 'remplis du désir de procurer (autant qu'il est possible à la prudence humaine de le faire) une tranquillité perpétuelle à la chrétienté, et portés par la considération de l'intérêt de leurs sujets'. The French presumably thought that this would look more public-minded. Freschot (1714–15: ii. 458 f., 461 f.).
   [52] Ibid. vi. 725 f., 733.   [53] Ibid. 744 f.

which states it to be 'the duty of every Christian prince to desire
the repose and tranquillity of the world', with Spain not even
being mentioned.[54] In fact, when the interest of Spain is referred
to at all, it is always in the second place after the 'public' interest,
reflecting the weak position of the king in the system and his need
to reconcile it to him. To what extent this somewhat overemphatic
display of public-mindedness was sincere is another question, to
which we will return.

France was in a comparable position of relative weakness in
terms of integration in, and acceptance by, the international system. It is therefore not surprising that the concept of 'repos de
l'Europe', central to early eighteenth-century foreign-policy talk,
occurs nowhere more frequently than in French sources. For
example, the instruction for the French delegates at Utrecht contains this phrase, or a similar one, in at least twenty places.[55]
Moreover, Louis XIV's diplomatic correspondence of the period—
both before and after the outbreak of war—uses such expressions
frequently and routinely, despite the fact that this correspondence
was destined for internal French use and not—at least not directly
—for external propaganda.

A remarkable example of this kind of discourse is found in a
dispatch by Louis to his ambassador to Britain, Tallard, of August
1698. In this dispatch, Louis refers to a report from his ambassador to Spain, d'Harcourt, who had newly arrived in Madrid after
the Rijswijk peace had brought about the resumption of diplomatic
relations between Spain and France.

We have received a dispatch from the Marquis d'Harcourt . . . He informs
me of the attitudes that he has found in Spain in favour of one of my
grandsons. It is now not only the greater part of the peoples [des peuples],
but the most important persons in the kingdom who do justice to the
rights of the legitimate [i.e. French] heir . . . Thus, everything favours the
legitimate rights [les justes droits] of my son. In case the Catholic King

---

[54] 'Siendo tan de la obligación de todo príncipe cristiano desear el sosiego, y
tranquilidad del mundo'; 10 June 1713, ibid. 788 ff.

[55] The words 'repos de l'Europe' appear five times; the phrases 'repos général
de l'Europe', 'repos public', and 'repos fixe et constant' (sc. de l'Europe) once
each; and on four occasions reference is made to the 'tranquillité générale'. Other
expressions carrying the same meaning are 'bien général de l'Europe' (twice);
'bien public' (twice); 'intérêt public', 'pacifier la chrétienté' (twice); and 'bonheur
de la chrétienté'. Full text Weber (1891: 421–50).

[Charles II] were to die, I am in a position to uphold these rights by letting the troops that I have on the Spanish border enter the kingdom. I can forestall any undertakings on the part of the Emperor or of those who would assist him. But, in truth, I cannot do so without resuming a war as bloody as that from which Europe has just been delivered. The desire to preserve the general tranquillity is the foremost motive to have led me to take steps with the King of England to prevent the Spanish king's death from disturbing the peace. To be sure, when the first proposals were made to this effect [and they were made on Louis's own initiative] I did not know that it would be as easy as it appears now to have one of my grandsons recognized as the successor to that crown. But, since the repose of Christendom is always my principal objective [*le principal objet que je me propose*], the more it becomes apparent that I could secure the Spanish succession for one of my grandsons, the more I believe to be giving proof of moderation, and of this same desire for peace, by being content with but a part of that succession and by sacrificing such major interests [*d'aussi grands intérêts*] to the repose of my subjects and to the tranquillity of all Europe.

The orders for Tallard that follow make it clear how urgently Louis wished for the partition scheme to succeed.[56]

The tranquillity of Europe also figures prominently in the Hague Alliance of September 1701 ('Sa Sacrée Majesté Impériale, Sa Sacrée Royale Majesté de la Grande-Bretagne, et les Seigneurs États Généraux des Provinces-Unies, n'ayant rien tant à cœur que la paix et la tranquillité de toute l'Europe . . .').[57]

It is clear, then, that the preservation of the system, and the defence of its 'repose' against disruption, were an acknowledged official aim of the European actors. Its pursuit entailed what may be interpreted as one of the main consensus *rules* then current, namely the subordination of 'private' to 'public' interest.

In this context, it is worth noting the concordance of Bolingbroke's and Torcy's explanations for the failure of earlier peace initiatives. Torcy, in the instruction for the French plenipotentiaries at Utrecht, states that, in 1710 at Geertruidenberg, peace would have been obtained under great sacrifices for France 'if the influence and the ambition of certain private individuals interested in the continuation of the war had not prevailed in Holland over the public interest'.[58] Bolingbroke, in the eighth of his *Letters*

---

[56] 5 Aug. 1698, Legrelle (1888–92: ii. 459 f.).
[57] Art. 2, Freschot (1714–15: i. 7).   [58] Weber (1891: 421).

on History, observes that the goals of the Hague Alliance could have been achieved as early as 1706, after which the war

became a war of passion, of ambition, of avarice, and of private interest; the private interest of particular persons and particular states; to which the general interest of Europe was sacrificed so entirely, that if the terms insisted on by the confederates had been granted, nay if even those which France was reduced to grant [at Geertruidenberg], had been accepted, such a new system of power would have been created as might have exposed the balance of this power to deviations, and the peace of Europe to troubles, not inferior to those that the war was designed, when it began, to prevent.[59]

Bolingbroke, in the text from which this passage is taken, displays a tendency to reinvent the history that he had made. But comparison with his correspondence shows that, on this point, his analysis had not changed. Already in late 1711 he had written that 'we [in Britain] want a peace, and the sense of the nation is for it, whatever noise be made . . . by those who find their private account in the universal calamity.'[60] On a previous occasion, he had pointed out how the Dutch government was 'grown poor, whatever private men may be'.[61] The analysis in the latter two instances is on the domestic rather than the international level, but the approach is the same. Bolingbroke clearly regarded this approach as carrying persuasive force, and consequently affording political leverage.

Ideally, of course, 'public' and 'private' interest reinforced each other. Indeed, Bolingbroke held that further prolongation of the war against France was incompatible not only with the 'general interest of Europe' but, as (or more) importantly, with that of Britain.[62] This was echoed by Torcy who instructed the French plenipotentiaries that

The English were the first to recognize the futility of the war and the prejudice that they would suffer in prolonging it further, because its continuation would merely serve to satisfy the ambition and the advantage of certain private individuals whose ascendant would be terminated by

[59] St John (1844: ii. 298).
[60] To Strafford, dated 23 Oct. 1711, St John (1798: i. 264 f.).
[61] To Drummond, dated 30 Mar. 1711, ibid. 82.
[62] See e.g. Bolingbroke to Harrison, 2 Oct. 1711, ibid. 226; and 20 Oct. 1711, ibid. 242; the instruction for Strafford, ibid. 247 ff.; and the *Letter to Sir William Wyndham*, St John (1844: i. 116 ff.).

the peace [i.e. the Whig merchants and financiers who profited from the war, what Bolingbroke called the 'moneyed interest' as opposed to the 'landed interest']. . . . Private and public interest have happily come to coincide, and the truth has, as a result, been the more vigorously put forward, the interest of the state more clearly grasped, and the measures taken to procure it have been much more equitable than, perhaps, they would have been had the repose of Europe been the sole object of those applying themselves to this great task.[63]

These statements by Bolingbroke and by Torcy are examples of public or semi-public discourse calculated to impress an audience and rally it to a general consensus. Bolingbroke addressed the letters quoted to people who, he hoped, would spread the ideas contained in them in the Netherlands. Diplomatic instructions were also often semi-public documents. This is true for example of the main British instruction for Utrecht.[64] It contained what can only be called mock demands—demands that the British government had no intention of pressing, put forward for show in order to deflect allied criticism of British policies. The French instruction, unlike the British one, is perfectly honest, but at the same time it is a clever piece of propaganda—here, too, the ideas, though not the text itself, were addressed to a public. The remarkable unanimity between Bolingbroke and Torcy reflects a shared strategy on their part, which was to prove highly successful—that of promoting their political ends by heavy reliance on consensus notions.

If, unlike the example just given, 'private' and 'public' interest were at odds with each other, the former was supposed to give way to the latter. Actors might legitimately be coerced in order to ensure this. For example, Louis XIV, before the war, thought that the partition treaty could be imposed on Spain:

The Spaniards without strength or government are unable of themselves to hinder the execution of a treaty, which I shall have concluded with the Emperor, England, and Holland, when all these powers will be equally interested in the success of the measures taken for the tranquillity of Europe.[65]

King Charles, Louis thought, had little reason to complain ('I do nothing to his prejudice, when I enter into measures for securing the tranquillity of Europe after his demise').[66] Similarly, when the

[63] Weber (1891: 422).   [64] See ibid. 173.
[65] Louis XIV to d'Harcourt, 16 Aug. 1699, quoted Colbert (1757: i. 70).
[66] Ibid. 71.

Hague Alliance declared war on France and Spain, the paramount reason was that the interest of Europe should prevail over the Bourbon family interest.

This rule of putting the 'public' interest first was frequently invoked during the congress. With the settlement more or less in place, Bolingbroke urged Spain to bring the negotiations about the proposed treaty of commerce with Britain, and the peace with Portugal,

to a speedy issue; and not to hearken to the insinuations of those ministers, if any such there are, who, under the notion of saving a little on one hand, or of getting a little on the other, hazard the general tranquillity of Europe, and expose to ruin a scheme, which, by so much labour, and through so many dangers, is brought to the very point of accomplishment.[67]

In a similar vein, the French instruction for the negotiations chastised the Emperor, who was not keen on peace, for not heeding the interest of Europe: 'it is plain enough from his letters and from the complaints that he makes about the conduct of his allies that it is not the public interest but a boundless ambition that governs his conduct'. This may have been the pot calling the kettle black—but it was still good propaganda.[68]

The 'public interest first' rule was of great value as a face-saving device, in that it made sacrifices palatable to the participants in the negotiations. This is illustrated fascinatingly by the problem posed by the two Wittelsbach brothers, the Electors of Bavaria and Cologne, who had rallied to the French king in breach of the German constitution. Louis XIV tried everything in his power to obtain an advantageous settlement for them, especially for Max Emanuel of Bavaria. He stressed that he had pledged his word to this effect, and even addressed himself personally to Queen Anne in this matter.[69] Personal honour, in other words, a desire not to lose face, does seem to have been the king's main motive. The practical value of the Wittelsbach alliance had always been questionable,[70] and in the context of the peace negotiations the utility of dropping the two electors was obvious.

[67] Bolingbroke to Patricio Lawless (an Irishman in the service of Philip V), dated 21 Nov. 1713, St John (1798: ii. 546 f.).

[68] Weber (1891: 432 f.).

[69] Torcy to Bolingbroke, 28 July 1712, St John (1798: i. 589); Louis XIV to Queen Anne, 28 Oct. 1712, Lamberty (1728–30: vii. 533).

[70] See Legrelle (1888–92: iv. 278 f.), and Colbert (1756: ii. 215, 245 ff.).

Louis's British interlocutors were not in a mood to do much for the sake of French royal honour. They had no desire to risk their own reputation, already sufficiently compromised, by promoting the cause of minor protagonists, whom their allies, especially the Emperor and the other German estates, regarded as traitors for having fought against the Empire. Bolingbroke wrote to Torcy that

[t]he queen's ministers are far from wishing that the king should act contrary to his word and his honour; but, Sir, after having exerted himself for his ally, as much as he could reasonably expect, something must be done for the sake of the peace, and the interest of one individual must yield to the general interest of Europe.[71]

In his instruction for the congress, Torcy had said the same thing ('il faut dans cette extrémité que le bien public l'emporte sur l'intérêt particulier').[72] But he was not yet ready to acknowledge the extremity; instead, he continued insistently to press the Wittelsbach cause. The British eventually came round a little. Within a few months Bolingbroke wrote to the Bishop of Bristol (one of the British negotiators) commending to him 'the Elector of Bavaria, whose interests the old gentleman [Louis XIV] has I believe as much at heart as it is possible to imagine'.[73]

Louis had made Philip V cede Belgium to Max Emanuel days before the congress convened.[74] Louis would have liked to keep the elector there. However, he realized that the Dutch resented that idea strongly (for them, it was tantamount to bordering on France directly, which they wished to avoid). Louis was therefore prepared to use Belgium as a bargaining chip. The Dutch wanted to give it to the Emperor. Why should the Emperor not make some concession in return—such as agreeing that Max Emanuel become King of Sicily? It turned out that the British wanted Sicily for Savoy. The French then proposed Sardinia instead, and the British consented.

The Emperor, however, was very much opposed to this scheme. To bestow a royal crown on Max Emanuel as a reward for his felony seemed incompatible with Charles's dignity as Emperor and liege. But Charles's policy, due to his own inexperience and

---

[71] Dated 21 July 1712, St John (1798: i. 595).   [72] Weber (1891: 441).
[73] 8 Nov. 1712, quoted ibid. 341.
[74] *Acte de renonciation* of 2 Jan. 1712, Freschot (1714–15: i. 257 ff.).

a rather supine attitude on the part of his advisers, was quite ineffective. He showed little aptitude for putting his case persuasively, neglecting to couch it in the idiom of international consensus. This idiom could be compared to a language which Bolingbroke used well and understood better, in which Torcy was a past master, and which at Vienna was spoken only haltingly and with bad grace. Charles was quite literally unable to communicate on the international level. As a result, he found himself increasingly isolated. He was the last to bow to the inevitable and join the peace—at a time when his allies had already provided for themselves.

The Emperor's isolation seemed propitious to the French. The Wittelsbach brothers were sprung on Charles one final time, with new demands. Not only was Max Emanuel to be King of Sardinia, but also the Emperor was to indemnify him for all the damage done in Bavaria by the Habsburg troops that had occupied it since the beginning of the war. Queen Anne was to act as arbiter in this matter; moreover, for the time being, Max Emanuel would stay in possession of certain Habsburg territories in the Spanish Netherlands, to ensure that these demands were implemented. Further, the Emperor was to recognize Philip V immediately as King of Spain. On the other hand, France declined as yet to recognize Charles as Emperor. Louis had never done so (French documents consistently refer to him as 'l'archiduc'), on the grounds that Bavaria and Cologne had been barred from the election. However, Louis was willing to recognize Charles if the two electors were rehabilitated first.[75]

But the French had overplayed their hand, and even a hasty softening of their stance did not prevent Charles from breaking off the negotiations to continue the war on his own. This was an obstinacy which, it is true, nobody had expected. Shrewsbury, the new British ambassador to Paris, reported that the French court

is so very weary of the charge of a war, that they are truly sorry the Emperor gave them no opportunity, before his minister left Utrecht, to agree those trifling difficulties which remain between them, and repent they did not oblige the Elector of Bavaria to accept the propositions Mr Kirchner [of the Imperial delegation] last made.[76]

This illustrates how an inability, or an unwillingness, to communicate, and to take advantage of a potential for consensus, could

[75] Weber (1891: 370 f.).   [76] 23 June 1713, St John (1798: ii. 432).

be detrimental to the stability of the system. Eventually, both sides used the public interest rule to achieve consensus after all. Louis dropped his demands in line with the passage from the French instruction quoted earlier. The Emperor and the Empire consented, with regard to the renegade Wittelsbach siblings, to a return to the *status quo ante bellum*, restoring them to their dignities as princes of the Empire (but no more) 'par les motifs de la tranquillité publique'.[77]

3. CONSENSUS PRINCIPLES

3.1. Autonomy and Equality

The consensus principles that prevailed at Utrecht were based on a number of notions with which we are already acquainted from the last chapter. In every case, however, their impact was much greater than sixty years earlier.

This is true, for example, of the notions of autonomy and equality. To a much greater extent than the Peace of Westphalia, the Peace of Utrecht confirmed the fact that the European system was essentially made up of self-determining actors, none of which were entitled to dictate to the others.

At Münster and Osnabrück, the Emperor's claim to supreme authority had been contested and reduced largely to a matter of ceremonial, but the concept of *libertas Germanica*, despite being triumphant, had still accommodated itself to the notion of Imperial suzerainty. As to France, Sweden, and the other actors outside the Empire, their autonomy was, of course, an obvious and long-established fact, but not a formally recognized one.[78] At Utrecht, on the other hand, the status of the Emperor was simply not an issue any more. The concept of 'liberty of Europe' was used to cover each of the actors in exactly the same way.

The expression 'liberty of Europe' was much used in the context of both the War of the Spanish Succession and the subsequent peace (see various quotations in this chapter). It is a further

---

[77] Treaty of Rastatt, art. 15, Freschot (1714–15: v. 358); Treaty of Baden, art. 15, ibid. 461.

[78] Compare the way in which Spain, at Münster, formally recognized the autonomy of the Dutch Republic.

example of the tendency to attribute, via the idiom of international consensus, identical goals and interests both to each individual actor and to the system conceived as a kind of super-actor. To describe as the 'liberty of Europe' what was, in fact, the 'liberty' (autonomy) of each individual actor seems semantically dubious, but it indicates an awareness that individual goals were being achieved through a collective effort, and could therefore be treated as if the goals themselves were collective.

The safeguarding of the 'liberty of Europe' against Bourbon supremacy was the main justification for the Hague Alliance and the war against France and Spain. In this war, the position of the Emperor was not qualitatively different from that of any of his co-belligerents. This is reflected in the way in which he was designated. In enumerating the members of the alliance, the British declaration of war of 1702 refers simply to 'the Emperor of Germany'. This is an indication of the heightened consciousness of nationhood as an ingredient of the European system. At the same time, it implicitly denies the Emperor any wider competence, of which the more correct title of *Roman* Emperor (and *King* of Germany) was a historical reminder. In a similar vein, the French ambassador to Madrid spoke of his colleague, the Emperor's envoy, as 'l'ambassadeur d'Allemagne'.[79]

Unlike at Münster and Osnabrück, the Utrecht peacemakers generally accepted as self-evident that autonomy logically entailed equality, and that it was inconsistent to claim autonomy while denying equal rank to other actors, as, in particular, France had done in the 1640s and throughout the following decades. This acceptance is another illustration of the greater rationality and logical coherence that the European states system had acquired.

The triumph of equality is evident from the fact that, at Utrecht, the idea of a hierarchy of actors was discarded. There was none of the elaborate semiotic quarrels over questions of protocol that had characterized (and impeded) earlier negotiations, and which the French(!) instruction for the congress referred to disdainfully as 'les vains embarras causés ordinairement par le cérémonial'.[80] Instead, the delegates to the Utrecht congress speedily agreed on a *Règlement des conférences* designed to prevent such disputes. It

[79] The British declaration of war in Cobbett (1810: 16); d'Harcourt to Louis XIV, 18 Dec. 1698, Legrelle (1888–92: ii. 627).   [80] Weber (1891: 449).

was agreed that the delegates would enter the meeting rooms in no fixed order (*pêle-mêle*) and sit where they liked.[81]

These decisions were taken in the absence of representatives of the Emperor and the other estates of the Empire, because the Imperial delegation initially boycotted the negotiations in the hope of scuttling them. As long as the Emperor refused to take part, the estates would not participate either, despite British exhortations. In reply to Queen Anne's invitation to attend the congress, the Elector of Hanover—her designated successor—told the queen, with solemn pique, that he would willingly dispatch plenipotentiaries to the peace talks, 'as soon as His Sacred Imperial Majesty, from whom, as head of the Empire, Your Royal Majesty will easily grant it would not be proper for us to separate ourselves at this juncture, has given them licence to participate'.[82]

Eventually, the chief Imperial envoy Sinzendorf did appear at the conference table, together with the other German plenipotentiaries. No sooner had he done this than he claimed, first, precedence over everybody else, and secondly, the right to represent the estates of the Empire as well, allowing the estates' own representatives merely consultative status. On the latter point, he was defeated.[83] On the former point, the congress eventually made a concession by awarding him a place of honour in front of a large mirror (*sic*).[84]

In reality, Sinzendorf's manœuvres were just another attempt to obstruct the negotiations. If anything, the fact that they had so little effect proves how firmly entrenched the equality principle had become. This is also shown by the fact that the idea of simply listing the actors in the system in alphabetical order in preference

[81] 28 Jan. 1712, Freschot (1714–15: i. 298 ff.).

[82] Note the snub implied in the discrepancy between the titles given to the Emperor and to the queen (if the text given by Freschot is to be trusted), and compare the quotation from the text of the Hague Alliance in sect. 2.3, above. Dated 20 Jan. 1712, ibid. 276 ('nos plenipotentiarios ad supra dicta colloquia pacis ablegare numquam detrectabimus, quam primum iisdem intervenire a Sacra Caesarea Maiestate, a qua tamquam capite Imperii in hoc passu nobis non licere nos separare R. M. [Regia Maiestas] Vestra facile nobis concedet, decretum erit'). See also Weber (1891: 198, 202).   [83] Lamberty (1728–30: vii. 26).

[84] Weber (1891: 203). Lamberty relates that '[l]e Comte de Strafford [one of the British plenipotentiaries] alla trouver un ministre pour faire dire à celui de Sinzendorf, que le pêle-mêle ayant été arrêté, il ne trouvait pas bon qu'il se donnât ces airs de primauté'; but also remarks that 'quoique les têtes couronnées prétendent d'aller du pair avec l'Empereur, elles ne disconviennent cependant pas que Sa Majesté Impériale ne soit *primus inter pares*.' Lamberty (1728–30: vii. 25).

to any other criterion was already present at Utrecht—even though it was not formally adopted till the Congress of Aachen of 1818.[85] At Utrecht, then, despite the remnants of Imperial suzerainty, the equality principle was applied even though it was not officially proclaimed, and the reason why it had to be applied was because the autonomy principle was in operation. Due to respect for a longstanding hierarchical tradition, there was no slogan connected with the equality principle in the same way as the expression 'the liberty of Europe' was connected with the autonomy principle. Nevertheless, both notions had, at Utrecht, become mainstays of the system.

3.2. The Balance of Power

3.2.1. Bourbon and the Balance of Power

Equilibrist thinking, an outgrowth of a shared concern on the part of the actors in the system about their autonomy, was already much in vogue on the eve of the war of succession, and Louis XIV was at pains to reconcile his position in the European system with the concept of balance of power. His ideas for dividing the Spanish monarchy were informed by explicit adherence to what must at this stage be called the balance-of-power principle. The concept was no longer applied simply as a procedural rule ('counteract any power if and when it threatens to become dominant'), but as a device for controlling and planning—in advance, on this occasion— the structure of the system as a whole.

In February 1699 Louis wrote to Tallard, his ambassador to London, that

I know how much Europe would be alarmed at seeing my own power rise above that of the House of Austria, so that this equality of a sort [cette espèce d'égalité] on which it makes its repose depend would no longer obtain. But at the same time the Emperor's power is so much increased now, both on account of the submission of the princes of the Empire and of the advantageous peace that he has just concluded with the Porte [i.e. the Sultan], that it is in the general interest that, if it becomes even greater, my own power should still be such as to counterbalance it.[86]

In other words, Louis justified French aggrandizement under the partition scheme by the fact that the recent death of the

---

[85] See the list of the actors represented at the congress, Freschot (1714–15: i. 277 ff.).   [86] 13 Feb. 1699, Legrelle (1888–92: iii. 15).

Wittelsbach heir left no practical alternative to the Emperor acquiring control of much of the Spanish dominions on the reigning
king's imminent death. However, as we have seen, the partition
scheme that Louis had pressed with so much energy was effectively sabotaged by Charles II's will. Having accepted that, Louis
then argued, in a memorandum for London and The Hague, that,
since the terms of the will ruled out any merger between the French
and Spanish monarchies, it was actually more compatible with
the balance-of-power concept than the partition scheme. That
scheme would after all have resulted in augmenting the French
dominions.[87]

William III of Britain did not, however, think that the new-
found power of the House of Bourbon could be reconciled with
the liberty of Europe, and consequently opted for war. Indeed,
even before the Spanish king's death precipitated the crisis, and at
the same time as negotiating the partition treaties, the British king
had been conducting a Europe-wide campaign to alert actors to
the threat to their autonomy emanating from the House of Bourbon. He wrote, for example, to Charles XII of Sweden to exhort
the Swedes 'to adopt such policies as may rescue and preserve the
liberty of all Europe from the enormous power of the French,
aimed at establishing supreme dominion'.[88]

Given that this was the rationale of the British involvement in
the struggle, it is not surprising that the balance-of-power principle was invoked assiduously by the British government to win
support for its policies—at home as well as abroad, and for making
war and peace alike. Indeed, seizing on its rallying power, the new
Tory government used the concept to help bring about consensus
on its decision to end the war, and on its vision of a settlement.
For example, in an attempt to stress the (somewhat questionable)
continuity of British policies, Queen Anne told the Dutch States
General that '[n]otre conduite a toujours roulé sur le même principe
d'un désir sincère de conserver l'équilibre dans l'Europe'.[89] Speaking in parliament to defend what was almost a switching of sides

[87] Roussel de Courcy (1889: 9 f.).
[88] 'ut ea ineant consilia quibus universae Europae libertas ab immensa et summum
imperium ambiente Gallorum potentia vindicari atque immunis praestari possit'.
William III to Charles XII, n.d., but probably connected with the British–Dutch–
Swedish alliance of Jan. 1700. Quoted Legrelle (1888–92: iv. 150).
[89] 18 Jan. 1713, Freschot (1714–15: ii. 253).

in the war, the queen emphasized that '[i]t was the glory of the wisest and greatest of my predecessors to hold the balance of Europe, and to keep it equal, by casting in their weight as necessity required. . . . I have proceeded on the same principle'.[90]

The queen insisted that it was the peace project by means of which the European equilibrium would be upheld or, indeed, created ('And thus, by the blessing of God, will a real balance of power be fixed in Europe, and remain liable to as few accidents as human affairs can be exempted from').[91] She warned that if the negotiations were to be broken off, 'the present opportunity would be irrecoverably lost, of Britain's establishing a real balance of power in Europe'.[92]

The same expression—'a real balance of power'—was used by the British prime minister Oxford in his correspondence with the Dutch grand pensionary Heinsius. The redundant qualification 'real' emphasizes the importance attached to the concept. At the same time it suggested that the partisans of continued warfare were not, in fact, true to the principle.[93]

Louis XIV and Torcy also stressed the balance-of-power principle in their efforts to end the war. The London Preliminaries of October 1711, which stated the conditions on which Louis was prepared to make peace, declared that he would

consent willingly and in good faith that all just and reasonable measures be taken to prevent the crowns of France and Spain from ever being united in the person of a single prince; His Majesty being convinced that such an excessive power would be contrary to the good and the repose of Europe.[94]

It was this consensus on the necessity and legitimacy of a balance of power that enabled the peacemakers to overcome the objections of their opponents. This was the key to peace, not just in real terms, but, as much or more so, in public relations terms. Bolingbroke called this issue the 'great article' on which the whole

[90] *The Queen's Speech on Opening the Session*, dated 2 Mar. 1714, Cobbett (1810: vi. 1257).
[91] *The Queen's Speech containing the Plan of the Peace*, dated 6 June 1712, ibid. 1142.
[92] *The Queen's Speech at the Adjournment*, dated 21 June 1712, ibid. 1166.
[93] Oxford to Heinsius, 4 Aug. 1711, Weber (1891: 404).
[94] *Articles préliminaires de la part de la France, pour parvenir à une paix générale*, London 8 Oct. 1711, Freschot (1714–15: i. 162).

settlement hinged. He wrote to Strafford, one of the British plenipotentiaries at the congress, that 'if the French give the queen
satisfaction in that great article, of the union of the two crowns,
whatever *pli* [attitude] may be taken by the States [General, i.e.
the Dutch], the peace will be made and abundantly justified.'[95]
And he wrote to Torcy that

The expedient to prevent the union of the two monarchies of France and
Spain, is the most important point of our negotiation, and Her Majesty
[Queen Anne] would give up all those that have been agreed upon [such
as the rewards promised to Britain individually], rather than leave it
uncertain. She is responsible for it to her people, to her allies, to the
present age, and to posterity.[96]

The 'great article' was elaborated between Bolingbroke and
Torcy in a fascinating diplomatic exchange—which provided, as
Bolingbroke called it, the 'under-plot' to the whole peace business.[97] Luckily for our analysis, most of this exchange took place
by correspondence.

The death of the Emperor Joseph had brought peace closer by
undermining the Hague Alliance. In the face of the threat of the
Archduke Charles having control of both the Austrian and the
Spanish monarchies, gaining a potentially hegemonial position that
was counter to the spirit of the alliance, the British could invoke
equilibrist thinking to legitimize their decision to pull out of the
war. However, a series of fatalities in the French royal house
worked to make peace more remote again. Within less than a
year, in 1711–12, three successive heirs to the French throne died.
On 10 March 1712 Torcy informed Bolingbroke of the death two
days earlier of the little Duke of Brittany, which left only his
younger brother, who was 2 years old and suffering from the same
disease, between Philip V and the crown of France. This revived
the spectre of a French hegemony.

Torcy and Bolingbroke were in agreement that the possibility
of a merger between the French and Spanish monarchies had to
be eliminated, or, at least, to appear to have been eliminated, if
peace were to be achieved. This consensus was invoked relent-
lessly in the exchange that followed, to keep the negotiations on
track while each side tried to optimize its position.

---

[95] Dated 16 Apr. 1712, St John (1798: i. 461).   [96] 17 June 1712, ibid. 527.
[97] To Strafford, dated 29 Apr. 1712, ibid. 486.

Here is a sample. Bolingbroke to Torcy: 'one cannot have greater confidence than does the queen in the good faith of His Most Christian Majesty. She regards this reciprocal confidence between the two courts as the only means of re-establishing the repose of Europe.'[98] Torcy to Bolingbroke: 'I flatter myself . . . that the queen, who has experienced so many proofs of the king's good faith, will persist in her confidence, without urging demands that could only betoken a suspicion, of which I am convinced Her Britannic Majesty is incapable in her heart.'[99]

Note the veiled threats in these ostensibly conciliatory statements. Bolingbroke is saying, if you fail to do what we want in this matter we will stick with the alliance. Torcy is saying, beware of treating us as an enemy who has deserved punishment and whose hand needs to be forced because you cannot trust him—this scheme will only work if we have consented freely to the terms.

Bolingbroke made the opening move by suggesting that Philip should renounce his right of succession to the French crown. Torcy retorted that that would not do at all. In substance, he told Bolingbroke that the Bourbon family ruled by the will of God and that, the law of succession having been handed down practically from the Almighty, there was nothing anyone could do about it. To resort to renunciations, Torcy earnestly pointed out, would be 'bâtir sur le sable', building on sand.[100]

He therefore suggested that if Philip became King of France, he could be succeeded in Spain by his brother, the Duke of Berry, or by his uncle, the Duke of Orléans. When Bolingbroke did not warm to this suggestion, Torcy proposed a non-Bourbon replacement. How about the King of Portugal? Or the Duke of Savoy?

Bolingbroke was sceptical of arguments based on divine law. 'In case the Duke of Anjou's [Philip V's] right to the crown of France comes to take place, he is not to enjoy both [this and the crown of Spain]; how can he choose if he cannot renounce either? And can he renounce the crown of France, and not the right to it?' This was a 'gross absurdity', he told the British plenipotentiaries.[101] To Torcy he said much the same thing, albeit in different terms:

---

[98] 18 June 1712, ibid. 520.　　[99] 10 June 1712, ibid. 524 ff.
[100] To Bolingbroke, 28 Mar. 1712, ibid. 437.
[101] Dated 26 Mar. 1712, ibid. 445.

The queen has too much confidence in the equity of the king your master, and the sincere desire he has shown for peace, to be able to imagine that he should expect her to be content with such a feeble safeguard . . . , or that she will ever suffer that predicament to occur, in which he, who is in possession of the crown of Spain, shall have a right to succeed to that of France. Who then could assure us that this prince would not exert his power to preserve the one, and to acquire the other, rather than show an example of moderation which is without precedent?

We are happy to believe that you in France are persuaded that God alone can abolish the law upon which your right of succession is founded; but you will allow us to be persuaded in Great Britain that a prince can relinquish his right by a voluntary cession, and that he, in favour of whom this renunciation is made, may be justly supported in his pretensions by the powers who become guarantors of the treaty.[102]

Bolingbroke made it clear that he regarded the renunciation as a *sine qua non* for peace. Torcy then good-naturedly conceded that Philip should renounce one crown. It would be laid down that he would do so if and when he was called to the succession in France. In other words, he would *promise* to renounce *if the need arose*, but would not actually renounce yet. Bolingbroke probably took a deep breath before he composed his next letter.

You will say, all the powers are to be guarantors of this agreement; such a guarantee may really form a powerful alliance, to wage war against the prince who would violate this condition of the treaty; but our object is rather to find out the means to prevent, than to support, new wars. . . . the guarantee of the powers of Europe would be much more likely to prevent his [Philip's] return to France, contrary to the formal renunciation he will then have made of his right, than to force him to abandon a crown of which he is in possession, and to give up a claim which he has never renounced.

Surely, he thought, Torcy would concede this point; after all, 'Her Majesty only seeks the common security, the Most Christian King has the same aims.'[103]

So he did, Torcy assured him:

A *rapprochement* is easily brought about, Sir, if on both sides there is a sincere intention, and an equal desire to achieve the same goal. . . . Your observations, Sir, and your conclusions drawn from them, are equally just. The Catholic King [i.e. the King of Spain] must remove the

---

[102] 3 Apr. 1712, ibid. 439.   [103] 17 Apr. 1712, ibid. 453 ff.

disquietude of Europe, by an immediate declaration of the part he will take, should the succession be ever open to him.

In other words, Philip would still not actually renounce yet, although he would commit himself as to *which* crown he would renounce *if the need arose*. The assumption was that he would then choose to become King of France. To be sure, telling the Spaniards in advance that Philip would abandon them if he inherited the French crown might affect their loyalty to him. 'But this disadvantage must give way to the general good;' therefore, Louis would dispatch a courier to Spain to demand that his grandson make his choice immediately. The epitome of complaisance, Torcy even added,

I hope, Sir, the King of Spain will conform to the king's [Louis XIV's] advice; but, should it happen, which I can scarce suppose, that he will not comply, His Majesty will take all measures which the Queen of Great Britain may judge expedient to determine, even by force of arms, the choice of the Catholic King, and to secure to Europe a peace, which, at present, is so far advanced.[104]

One cannot help admiring Torcy's subtlety, the way in which he twists Bolingbroke's objections to make them mean something quite different from what Bolingbroke had in mind. In a letter to Strafford, the Utrecht negotiator, Bolingbroke acknowledged the possibility that he had been misunderstood (even though this is very unlikely), and restated the problem:

The French have undoubtedly a great advantage in treating in their own language, and I can easily believe that some of the expressions in my letters to Monsieur de Torcy, may have been either faint, improper, or ambiguous; but surely the whole tenor of them makes it plain, that we never intended to separate the option and the execution of the option.[105]

In other words, what was the point of Philip renouncing, or at any rate promising to renounce, the Spanish crown, if at the same time he still continued as King of Spain for the time being? The British government then resolved to make its intention easier to grasp for the French by holding out some promise of gain for France. Bolingbroke and Oxford put forward a scheme by which Philip would either renounce his right to the French crown immediately and stay King of Spain; should his line die out then the

---

[104] 26 Apr. 1712, ibid. 468 ff.   [105] Dated 3 May 1712, ibid. 492 f.

House of Savoy was to inherit, not a French prince. Alternatively, Philip would renounce the Spanish crown with immediate effect and become Duke of Savoy instead, as well as King of Sicily. The Duke of Savoy would then become King of Spain in his place. If the little Dauphin died, as everybody expected that he would, then Philip, on mounting the French throne, would cede Sicily to Habsburg. But Savoy and Piedmont would be united permanently to France. Louis XIV, the British thought, would welcome this. Therefore, he would do his utmost to induce Philip to choose the latter option.

Such an aggrandizement of France was, perhaps, a strange price to pay to end a war that had been fought against French preponderance. But it would not be in an area where it would affect the Netherlands or Germany, where concern about French expansionism was greatest. The balance of power would be improved, in that Spain and France would go to different dynasties. Most importantly, for the Tories, their diplomatic prowess would be seen to achieve the removal of Philip from Spain. They would bring about what the alliance and the Whig ministry in ten years of warfare had not. This would be a triumph. It would silence those troublesome allies, not to mention the Whig opposition, with their incessant propaganda campaign against Tory policy.

Bolingbroke confidently expressed his conviction that 'the interest of France and of the House of Bourbon will prevail, and that by consequence Philip will choose to evacuate Spain.'[106] It was a clever stratagem, bringing Bourbon and French 'private' interest into line with what could justifiably be declared the interest of Europe. Torcy rather feared that it would work. He actually advised Philip to renounce for the time being and invoke divine law later— albeit in a way that was a masterpiece of saying something without saying it while even saying that he did not want to say it.[107] It

[106] To Harley, dated 17 May 1712, ibid. 504. Oxford was of the same opinion; Hill (1988: 182).

[107] Torcy wrote to Mme des Ursins, who was very close to the Spanish royal couple, on 9 Apr. 1712 that '[s]i vous me demandez quel parti S. M. C. [Sa Majesté Catholique] peut prendre dans une conjecture aussi fâcheuse et aussi embarrassante, en vérité, Madame, je ne serais ni assez capable, ni assez hardi pour lui donner conseil. Un politique alerte lui dirait de tout promettre pour faire la paix, parce que les renonciations qu'il fera, étant contre les lois, ne pourront jamais subsister, mais je ne sais si ce conseil serait de son goût et j'aime beaucoup mieux que d'autres que moi le lui donnent.' Baudrillart (1890: 478).

appears from the French diplomatic correspondence that Torcy found the proposed renunciation genuinely distasteful.[108]

Louis XIV's attitude was much more straightforward and pragmatic. Even before the new British scheme was presented to him, he applied heavy pressure on his grandson to comply with the British demands that Philip either abandon his rights to the French throne or the Spanish crown which he was wearing. At this stage, Louis preferred the former alternative. He repeatedly expressed his anger at Philip's recalcitrance, probably unaware that it had some subtle backing from his own foreign minister.[109] After he learned of the British exchange scheme, Louis made a final effort to induce Philip to comply. This time, his strong preference was for Philip to give up Spain in order to permit the further aggrandizement of France (a reversion, in effect, to the old partition projects). This seemed a more solid advantage—for France and for the House of Bourbon—than Philip's still precarious hold on the Spanish throne.

'Should gratitude and affection for your subjects be strong inducements with you to adhere to them,' Louis admonished his grandson, 'I can tell you, that you owe those same sentiments to me, to your family, and to your country, preferably [i.e. rather than] to Spain. I now call upon you to show me their effects'.[110] At the same time Louis wrote to his ambassador to Madrid, Bonnac. He told Bonnac to exhort Philip to accept his replacement by the Duke of Savoy. Enclosed with this dispatch, there was another, sealed letter to the Spanish king, which Bonnac was to deliver only if Philip still failed to comply with the scheme.

In the event, this missive, which contained a threat to leave Spain to its own devices and make peace without it, remained unopened with the ambassador.[111] Philip accepted the scheme,

[108] Roussel de Courcy suggests that French insistence on the law of succession as an obstacle to the renunciation was a means of gaining much-needed time to convince a recalcitrant Philip to agree to giving up his French rights (1889: 59 f.). But there is much evidence to show that Torcy's dislike of the proposed renunciations was both sincere and profound, and that he was very keen to prevent them. See e.g. Torcy to Mme des Ursins, 4 Apr. 1712, ibid. 69 f., or Bergeyck to Philip V, 16 May 1712, Baudrillart (1890: 487).

[109] See the fascinating, detailed account—with abundant source-material—by Roussel de Courcy (1889).

[110] Louis XIV to Philip V, 18 May 1712, quoted Colbert (1757: ii. 299). See also Roussel de Courcy (1889: 109), Baudrillart (1890: 491).

[111] Roussel de Courcy (1889: 111 ff.), Baudrillart (1890: 492).

though he only met his grandfather halfway—he opted to keep the Spanish crown at the price of renouncing his French rights. The result was consensus between Britain, France, and—at least formally—Spain on the renunciation issue, on immediate renunciation in the name of the balance of power.

The Tory dream of removing Philip from Spain had evaporated. But even if, for the Tory cabinet, it was decidedly second-best, it was still a success. Torcy had artfully dragged his feet, but the British had carried him along. The British argument—the balance of power—was a consensus principle; Torcy's counter-case—whether based on divine law, dynastic right, or whatever—did not have the same quality. This is also made clear by the wording of the three renunciation documents that were eventually signed by members of the Bourbon family, in respect of their rights to either the Spanish or the French crown (as the case might be). These documents have the solemn ring of doctrinal pronouncements. The one signed by the Duke of Berry, for example, declared that

All the powers of Europe finding themselves almost ruined on account of the present wars, which have brought desolation to the frontiers, and several other parts of the richest monarchies and other states, it has been agreed, in the conferences and peace negotiations being held with Great Britain, to establish an equilibrium, and political limits [*des limites politiques*], between the kingdoms whose interests have been, and still are, the sad subject of a sanguinary dispute; and to consider it to be the basic principle [*la maxime fondamentale*] of the preservation of this peace that it must be ensured that the strength [*les forces*] of these kingdoms give reason neither for fear nor for any jealousies. It has been thought that the surest way of achieving this is to prevent them from expanding, and to maintain a certain proportion, in order that the weakest ones united might defend themselves against more powerful ones, and support one another against their equals.[112]

This text, incidentally, makes it clear that, although the consensus on the legitimacy of a balance of power was strong, a system officially based on that notion was still a novelty. It was seen to be a result of the peace, not something that had already existed in the past. The Peace of Utrecht did not simply highlight the existence of the balance-of-power principle; it also marked an important

---

[112] 24 Nov. 1712, Freschot (1714–15: ii. 199 f.). See also the renunciation of the Duke of Orléans, 19 Nov. 1712, ibid. 209 ff., and that of Philip V, 7 Nov. 1712, ibid. 164 ff.

stage in its development. It was at Utrecht that the balance-of-power principle started its two-hundred-year reign in the European states system. The desirability of an equilibrium was perceived and discussed before the Spanish war. But it was only at Utrecht that the system, as refashioned by the congress, was given the formal sanction of being officially regarded as embodying an acceptable equilibrium.

3.2.2. Habsburg and the Balance of Power

Faced with the crisis created by Charles II's will, the Emperor Leopold adopted a cautious attitude. He combined consideration for the balance of power and for security on the one hand with, on the other, an emphasis on the legal aspects of the problem that was not found with other European actors. This combination reflected the Emperor's double constituency—the European system at large on the one hand and the German subsystem with its special consensus agenda on the other. Which component was stressed depended on the addressee.

A typical example of this 'mixed' approach is found in an instructive exposé preparing the ground for Leopold's decision to wage war on France. This complex text, addressed to the Palatine elector, was calculated to appeal to a German audience. Leopold argued, among other things, that, for legal reasons, he could neither accept the Franco-Anglo-Dutch partition scheme nor the Spanish king's will. Both implied unlawful disposal of Imperial fiefs (such as Milan or Belgium) without Imperial consent. The Emperor could not give this consent because his election oath prohibited him from allowing any territories to be alienated—'torn' is the expression used—from the Empire, without the permission of the estates (such as the elector).

Having flattered the elector in this fashion, the document skilfully touched on, and invited sympathy for, the disregard for the Emperor's dignity that the partition scheme and the will entailed. This could be done all the more easily because Leopold enjoyed great personal prestige in the Empire. The elector was asked politely for his advice—probably not so much because it was really needed, but in order to secure his goodwill and support. Typically for this type of discourse addressed to a German public, the 'general freedom and security' and the need to prevent 'the

universal French dominion now threatening all Europe' are referred
to in this text, but they are not given pride of place.[113]

This document was written to support a mission by Count
Wratislaw, Leopold's close friend and adviser, who was to call on
the elector *en route* to the British court. In Britain, Wratislaw was
to seek negotiations for an anti-French alliance. For this latter
purpose, Leopold had instructed Wratislaw to use significantly
different, more pragmatic, language. In particular, the Emperor
was concerned about possible British objections that a war against
the united Bourbon dominions would drag on interminably and
that the proposed alliance stood little chance of achieving its aims.
In answer to this argument, Wratislaw was to stress the Emperor's
moderation and his willingness to accept any reasonable compromise. But what that might be, Leopold thought, was best decided
once it was seen how successfully the war went. Wratislaw was to
stress that what Vienna wanted above all was 'simply to preserve
some equilibrium in Europe': surely the King of England had the
same intention. On which basis—Wratislaw was to say—an agreement would no doubt be reached speedily once negotiations had
been opened.[114]

These texts display an obvious awareness of the need for consensus on the Emperor's policies, and the care taken by Leopold
to secure such a consensus. They also show that equilibrist discourse was used by Vienna, carefully dosed to suit different audiences. But the new Emperor, Charles VI, whose accession at the
age of 26 coincided with the convening of the Utrecht congress,
lacked his father's genial adroitness and patience. He was much
more impetuous, and so imbued with the righteousness of his cause
that he neglected the need to convince others of it. His instruction
for the congress made no concessions to the international consensus

---

[113] 30 Nov. 1700, Gaedeke (1877: ii. 96* f.) (in Gaedeke each of the 2 vols. is
separated into 2 sections, each of which is paginated separately, so '96' refers to p.
96 in the first section, and '96*' refers to p. 96 in the second section).

[114] 'so kannst Du dawider vorstellen, daß auch wir keinen Krieg ohne Ende
verlangen und billigmäßige Friedensconditiones nie ausschlagen würden,
welchergestalt aber dieselben einzurichten, dürfte sich ab dem Sukzeß der Waffen
am besten urteilen lassen, und ziele unsere Absicht hauptsächlich dahin, daß nur
einiges aequilibrium in Europa erhalten werden möge, und weil des Königs von
Engelland Intention zweifelsohne auch dahin gerichtet sei, so würden wir mit
Deroselben, wenn einmal die Tür zu den Traktaten eröffnet und denenselben vom
Gegenteil Platz gegeben werden wollte, darüber unschwer eines werden.' 6 Dec.
1700, ibid. 99* f.

agenda. From a public relations point of view, it was disastrously misconceived. Although it did, in fact, acknowledge as inevitable the partition of the Spanish monarchy, and, in a postscript, even countenanced the possibility that Charles might have to give up Spain proper, the Imperial delegation was not to say so publicly. Instead, it was told to try to block, or at least slow down, the negotiations by pressing the greatest possible demands.[115]

Insufficient consideration was given to the fact that this approach made the Emperor very vulnerable to attack on equilibrist grounds and that it was likely to leave him isolated. Sinzendorf, Charles's main envoy at the congress, found himself attacked in the following terms in a pamphlet of November 1712, a few months into the negotiations (and Lamberty records that this pamphlet caused a considerable stir):

what are we to think when, with so much passion, you oppose everything that might facilitate the conclusion of a general treaty of peace? We must necessarily believe that you will try to make us continue the war, until fate [or luck: *la fortune*] has put in the Emperor's hands all that the formidable Charles V possessed when he was at the peak of his power. Is this the equilibrium that you wish to bestow on Europe? Is an excess of power dangerous only when it is not in the hands of the House of Austria? But is this the object, are these the principles of our alliances, our treaties of association?[116]

This was somewhat ironic as Sinzendorf was, in fact, well versed in equilibrist discourse. As the Emperor's envoy to the French court just before the outbreak of the crisis, he had put forward Leopold's moderate two-track approach described above. He had assured Torcy that Leopold was prepared to go a long way to preserve the repose of Christendom, provided only that, first, it could be done in such a way that at least some respect for the Emperor's rights was maintained, and that, secondly, the increase of French power would not be such as to give the other European actors too much cause for concern.[117]

---

[115] Text Weber (1891: 450 ff.). See the demands made by the Imperial delegation at the congress, *Postulata nomine Sacra Caesareae et Catholicae Maiestatis atque Imperii*, 5 Mar. 1712, Freschot (1714–15: i. 314 ff.).

[116] *Remontrances d'un Hollandais à Monsieur le Comte de Sinzendorff Plénipotentiaire à Utrecht*, Amsterdam, dated Nov. 1712, Lamberty (1728–30: vii. 340).

[117] 'Wäre mir übrigens E. K. M. [Euer Kaiserlichen Majestät] allergerechteste Intention so nah bekannt,' Sinzendorf told Torcy, 'daß sie viel tun würden, um die

At that time Sinzendorf had also been eager to dispel the impression that the Emperor's power was itself growing excessively. This was a feeling voiced, for example, by Louis XIV in a passage already quoted ('the Emperor's power is so much increased now, both on account of the submission of the princes of the Empire and of the advantageous peace that he has just concluded with the Porte').[118] It is true that Leopold had succeeded, in his long reign, in reconsolidating the Emperor's authority in the Empire, after the low point reached at the end of the Thirty Years War. He achieved this by means of skilful policies and the great personal respect that he commanded. This derived in no small part from the prestige that he had gained through the campaigns that (jointly with the German princes) he led against the Turks and which resulted in extensive territorial gains for Vienna.

Before the war Louis had tried hard to win the favour and support of the German princes, offering alliances and subsidies to lure them away from Vienna. But his efforts came to nothing; all the princes rallied to the Emperor in the moment of crisis, with the exception only of the two Wittelsbach electors, and the Duke of Braunschweig-Wolfenbüttel, Anton Ulrich. The two electors were quickly driven into French exile and their lands occupied, while the duke was temporarily deposed by the Emperor in 1702.[119] A Hungarian rising during the war was suppressed, and Vienna also greatly increased its influence in Italy.

In 1699 Torcy had agreed with Sinzendorf that the expansion of Habsburg territory in east Europe need not worry other European actors. What had concerned Torcy was the possible union of the dominions of the Spanish Habsburgs with those of their German relatives, as had already happened under Charles V. Sinzendorf had replied that, even under Charles V, the other European princes had been strong enough to resist any threat to their own territories.[120]

Ruhe in der Christenheit zu erhalten, wenn es nur auf solche Weise geschehen könnte, daß es Ihro und Dero allerdurchlauchtigsten Erzhaus und Ihro vor Gott und der Welt zukommenden Rechten nicht gar zu nachteilig auch denen übrigen in Europa regierenden Potenzen durch die Vergrößerung der französischen Macht nicht allzu bedenklich wäre.' Sinzendorf to Leopold I, 27 Oct. 1699, Gaedeke (1877: ii. 138*).

[118] To Tallard, 13 Feb. 1699, Legrelle (1888–92: iii. 15).
[119] See ibid. iv. 272 ff.
[120] Sinzendorf to Leopold I, 27 Oct. 1699, Gaedeke (1877: ii. 138* f.).

In the context of the Utrecht negotiations, Torcy and Bolingbroke both took especial note of the Italian situation, one of the
main theatres of conflict in Charles V's day. They were once again
in unison when they declared that something ought to be done to
preserve the equilibrium there. But, ultimately, they washed their
hands of it. Torcy told Bolingbroke that

The public interest, justice, and the welfare of the peace really require
that His Majesty [Louis XIV], in concert with the queen [Anne], take
effectual measures to free the princes of Italy from the oppression they
labour under from the Germans. In truth, the conduct of those princes
merits little attention from France, but we must have compassion on their
weakness, and rescue them from the cupidity of those [i.e. Habsburg] who
want to swallow up everything.[121]

Bolingbroke in turn addressed to the British negotiators a
sublimely verbose and cryptic instruction on this point. He clearly
thought that, for all his official respect for the principle, there was
nothing to be done in practice. But he was keen to shift the blame
on to others:

Her Majesty desires, that the liberty of Italy may be preserved, and in
order thereunto that the balance of power may be equally sustained in
that country, she is sensible that the settlement, which is likely to be made
by the ensuing peace, may throw too much the scale on one side, and she
is very well apprised of the ill consequences which might follow from
hence . . . in respect to the general influence which the state of Italy must
have upon the affairs of Europe. The Italian ministers ought to be sensible in a particular manner of these truths, and as little as they have
deserved of the queen, her care of them has eminently appeared . . . [for
example] in the measures which she has taken to strengthen the House
of Savoy, which must be for the time to come the bulwark of that crowd
of indolent droning princes, and of those states, who with all the vices of
a commonwealth have not one republican virtue; after this they are not
to imagine, that the queen will suffer the negotiation of peace to be
embroiled or the conclusion of it retarded the sixtieth part of a second,
for the sake of those who have deserved so little of either side in the
course of the war; from all this it results, that Your Lordships are upon
every occasion to promote whatever may tend to prevent the exorbitance
of the Imperial power in Italy, but at the same time that you are to make
this principle give way, wherever the facilitating or quickening of the
general peace is concerned.[122]

[121] 10 Dec. 1712, St John (1798: ii. 132).
[122] 3 Mar. 1713, quoted Weber (1891: 375 n. 3).

In fact, the increase in Habsburg power at no time threatened the stability of the system. This shows that the balance-of-power principle may operate as a vehicle of international consensus, and thereby as a safeguard for international stability, quite independently of the actual distribution of forces (in fact, this is almost invariably the case, since an even distribution of forces between the actors is virtually impossible to achieve). It is only necessary that the existing distribution of forces is not regarded as illegitimate.

The inconsistency—from an equilibrist point of view—of French policy *vis-à-vis* Vienna shows how little worried statesmen were about the exact measure of other actors' strength, at least as long as no obvious hegemon emerged. France might claim to be alarmed at Habsburg's preponderance in Italy. But at the same time it was quite happy to allow Austria to absorb Bavaria if the Emperor consented to the Elector of Bavaria, Max Emanuel, retaining Belgium—an excellent bargain for Habsburg, as the French instruction itself pointed out.[123] The Emperor shared this view,[124] but he could not press the point against the opposition of his Dutch allies, who thought that it was too good a bargain for France, too. Much as equilibrism was an important part of political discourse and a main vehicle of consensus, in real terms it was not applied with much rigour.

3.3. Security

The peace treaty between Spain and Britain and that between Spain and Savoy both invoke the concept of balance of power explicitly. The former confirms the perpetual separation of Spain and France for the sake of a *iustum potentiae aequilibrium*.[125] The latter institutes the Duke of Savoy and his descendants as potential heirs of the new Spanish royal house, 'for the same reasons, and for the same motives, of the public good of the peace, the repose, and the equilibrium of Europe', and it cedes Sicily to Savoy 'for the same reasons, of the repose, and the equilibrium of Europe'.[126]

In the peace treaty concluded between France and the States

---

[123] Ibid. 430.   [124] Imperial instruction, ibid. 456.

[125] '(quod optimum et maxime solidum mutuae amicitiae et duraturae undiquaque concordiae fundamentum est)', art. 2, Freschot (1714–15: v. 146).

[126] Arts. 3 and 4, ibid. vi. 733, 744.

General, and the one between France and Britain, the renunciation documents (with their balance-of-power rhetoric) are declared
to be an integral part of the treaties. But, otherwise, the separation of the French and Spanish crowns is proclaimed to the accom-
paniment simply of invocations of the 'liberty' and the 'security' of
Europe.[127]

What may be called the security principle was connected with
the balance-of-power principle inasmuch as the maintenance of
a balance of power was seen as one form of protection for the
security of the actors. In consequence, the two concepts overlapped
to some extent. However, it is useful to discuss the security principle as distinct from the balance-of-power principle as a separate
ingredient of the consensus agenda of early eighteenth-century
Europe. This is justified to the extent to which the notion of
security influenced the structure of the international system beyond
the application of the balance-of-power concept (in accordance
with the terminology proposed in this book, which posits that
'principles' determine the structure of the system rather than the
day-to-day policies of the actors that make up the system).

The general preoccupation with security that characterized the
dealings of the congress can be explained to a large extent as a
reaction to the upheavals caused to the system by the expansionist
policies of Louis XIV. Systematic expansionism was clearly incompatible with a stable system. If a stable system was desired,
expansionism had to be proscribed. Minor adjustments alone might
in some cases be legitimate, if it could be demonstrated that their
purpose was to protect an actor against the potential expansionism of its neighbours. It was in this sense that the security principle had an impact on the changes made to the map of Europe at
Utrecht.

The Dutch case is a good illustration. The main war aim of the
Dutch was to provide security for their country against French
expansionism. This war aim was stated, for example, in a letter
which the States General addressed to Queen Anne during the
congress:

---

[127] 'D'autant que la guerre, que la présente paix doit éteindre, a été allumée
principalement, parce que la sûreté et la liberté de l'Europe ne pouvaient pas
absolument souffrir que les couronnes de France et d'Espagne fussent réunies sous
une même tête . . .'. Franco-British treaty of peace, art. 6, ibid. ii. 475. Compare art.
31 of the Franco-Dutch treaty, ibid. iii. 35 ff.

we only wish for peace, a peace such as to be enjoyed by the whole of Europe through the reestablishment and the assurance of its repose ... in this peace we desire nothing for our own state other than the safeguarding of our rights, and our security, and no other increase or aggrandizement than that which is necessary to us for this safeguarding and security.[128]

The Dutch wished to use Belgium as a buffer state for protection against France. They had no intention of acquiring Belgium for themselves—the idea of a common frontier with France was categorically rejected. In order to serve as a buffer between them and France, Belgium was to be administered by a friendly third power (the Emperor), but with the Belgian fortresses manned by Dutch garrisons under the control of The Hague (as they had been until 1700). This war aim of establishing a barrier between the French and the Dutch was spelled out in the Hague Alliance:

the allies, among other things, shall do everything in their power to recover and conquer the provinces of the Spanish Netherlands [i.e. Belgium], with a view to their serving as a dyke, rampart, and *barrier* to separate and remove France from the United Provinces; the said Provinces of the Spanish Netherlands having ensured the security of My Lords the States General until recently, when His Most Christian Majesty seized them and had them occupied by his troops.[129]

Like the balance-of-power principle, what is here called the security principle was a corollary of the autonomy principle, reflecting the latter's increased importance. Since the aspiration for security was universally acknowledged as legitimate, everybody felt entitled to claim a barrier somewhere in the context of the war of succession. The result was a somewhat indiscriminate use of the concept. Article 5 of the Hague Alliance invoked it to cover the conquests proposed on behalf of the Emperor:

Likewise, the allies shall do everything in their power to conquer the Duchy of Milan with all its dependencies, given that it is a fief of the Empire providing security for His Imperial Majesty's hereditary lands, and to conquer the Kingdoms of Naples and Sicily, and the islands of the

[128] Dated 23 Dec. 1712, ibid. ii. 248. See also Lamberty (1728–30: vii. 329), where the date is given as 29 Dec.

[129] Art. 5, Freschot (1714–15: i. 9). Emphasis in Freschot. On Dutch thinking on security in general and the barrier in particular, see e.g. the *Préambule de la pétition générale du Conseil d'Etat des Provinces Unies, présentée le 13 novembre 1711*, ibid. i. 170 ff., and the *Préface de l'Etat de Guerre pour l'année 1713, dressé par le Conseil d'Etat*, dated 16 Nov. 1712, Lamberty (1728–30: vii, esp. 292 ff.).

Mediterranean Sea with the dependent Spanish lands along the coast of Tuscany, which may serve the same purpose . . .[130]

In 1709, after a meeting with the Dutch grand pensionary Heinsius at The Hague, Torcy reported to Louis XIV that '[t]he term barrier is extended now to such a length, that he [Heinsius] told me, the Kingdoms of Naples and Sicily were a necessary barrier to Tyrol', adding that '[w]hen men reason on principles like these, it is difficult to come to any conclusion.'[131]

In the Empire, there were hopes of recovering the lost territories on the left bank of the Rhine, a concession which as late as 1710 France had been prepared to make.[132] Savoy, too, demanded various territories from France under the pretext of security.[133]

France, in seeking to regain the benefits of international stability, accepted the security principle as it accepted the others. The instruction for the French plenipotentiaries laid down that 'it will be necessary to agree on the safeguards [sûretés] that the king will provide to calm the genuine or affected alarm of his neighbours'.[134] In the instruction, the Dutch demands in particular were acknowledged:

For the interest of Holland, it is necessary that the [Spanish] Netherlands be in the possession of a prince who has no reason on every occasion to follow the interests of France, and who is sufficiently powerful to serve as a barrier against the undertakings that the king's enemies will always affect to be fearing on the part of His Majesty.[135]

---

[130] Freschot (1714–15: i. 9).

[131] Torcy to Louis XIV, 16 Aug. 1709, quoted Colbert (1757: i. 293).

[132] Note that the proposed return of these territories to the Empire was justified officially under the security principle and not because their annexation had violated the various treaties concluded with France since and including the Peace of Westphalia. See e.g. the demands on France put forward by the Assoziation der Vorderen Reichskreise (a league formed against France by several circles of the Empire adjacent to France): 'Quandoquidem tristis testatur experientia, quod circulis Galliae adiacentibus iam inde a tempore Pacis Monasteriensis, a Rege Christianissimo nullus pacis fructus relictus, sed ab ipso tam pacis, quam belli temporibus continua vel reunionum vexatione, vel apertis hostilitatibus afflicti fuerunt, hinc circulorum securitas vel maxime efflagitat, ut' etc., 5 Mar. 1712, Freschot (1714–15: i. 357 f.).

[133] Demandes de Son Altesse Royale de Savoye pour la paix générale à faire, 5 Mar. 1712, ibid. 351 ff.; Mémoire du Comte Maffei, envoyé extraordinaire de Son Altesse Royale de Savoye, dated 24 Dec. 1711, St John (1798: i. 375 f.).

[134] Weber (1891: 426).

[135] Ibid. Although the French pretended otherwise, they realized that the Elector of Bavaria did not fit this definition.

The plenipotentiaries were therefore authorized to give to the Dutch 'this so-called barrier which they want Europe to consider as an absolutely necessary rampart against the undertakings of France.'[136]

The Emperor's claims in Italy were also successful (except for the fact that Sicily, for the time being, went to Savoy—but it was exchanged for Sardinia in 1720). The Empire was less fortunate. By the time the congress got under way, Britain was keen to achieve a speedy compromise and was no longer willing to put pressure on France to comply with the demands of the allies. The Imperial government told its delegates to insist on the retrocession by France of all its conquests in Alsace and Lorraine since the Thirty Years War, including the Bishoprics of Metz, Toul, and Verdun—on the grounds, as the Imperial instruction put it, 'that, without this barrier, the Roman Empire would never be safe from France'.[137] But Louis XIV, safe in the knowledge of British connivance, withdrew only from the right bank of the Rhine, restoring Freiburg-im-Breisgau, Breisach, and Kehl.[138]

The skill of Torcy's statecraft is shown by the fact that not only did he concede the legitimacy of his adversaries' aspiration for security, whether it was 'genuine' or 'affected', but he also contrived to exploit this legitimacy for France's own benefit. Insisting to Bolingbroke that '[y]ou must allow, Sir, that no monarch ever did so much for the sake of peace, or ever extended so far his compliances for the restoration of the general repose of Europe,'[139] he proceeded on the assumption that the consensus notions that the French made such a point of respecting should be applied in France's favour as well. He declared, in his instruction for the congress, that Louis XIV had 'reason to claim barriers if all Europe demands barriers against France',[140] and took advantage of the consensus on the legitimacy of 'barriers' to retain territories claimed by the allies.

The German estates were militarily weak and hampered by Viennese ineptitude. They could therefore be dealt with relatively summarily. In dealing with the Empire, the French simply labelled the Rhine river itself a barrier, both for the Empire *and* for

---

[136] Ibid. 427.
[137] 'daβ ohne diese Barriere das Römische Reich gegen Frankreich niemal[s] sicher wäre'. Ibid. 455.   [138] See ibid. 433.
[139] 4 Aug. 1712, St John (1798: i. 605).   [140] Weber (1891: 431).

France—and that was the end of that.[141] The Dutch were more difficult, but Torcy knew what to do. The London Preliminaries had already declared that

As the king [Louis XIV] also intends scrupulously to ensure the observation of the peace after its conclusion; and the aim that the king is seeking being to safeguard the borders of his kingdom, without causing alarm, in any way whatsoever, to the states of his neighbours, His Majesty promises to consent, by the treaty to be concluded, that the Dutch be put in possession of the strongholds, therein to be specified, in the [Spanish] Netherlands, which will in future serve as a barrier against any sort of undertakings on the part of France.[142]

It should be noted how the unobtrusive phrase 'and the aim that the king' etc., almost drowns in the conciliatory noise that surrounds it. If the Dutch wanted a barrier, the French would let them have one. But Utrecht was not Geertruidenberg (the location of the 1709 peace talks, when France nearly accepted a dictated peace), so there was no question of allowing *all* the fortresses in Flanders to be garrisoned by the Dutch. For, in that case, northern France would be left exposed. France was also entitled to security, in other words, to some of the fortresses. The further south these fortresses were situated, the more France was entitled to them. Concerning the southernmost ones, Torcy was quite peremptory, stating that 'the restitution of the towns of Aire, Béthune, Saint-Venant, Douai, Bouchain, and of their dependent territories is necessary to safeguard the frontier of the kingdom. Therefore My Lords Plenipotentiaries shall demand it with the certitude that His Majesty will not on any account forego them.'[143]

This restitution had, in fact, already been agreed with Britain before the congress opened. The Dutch objected, and, indeed, the French demand looked rather arrogant when it was remembered that, although these places were French-speaking, they had been outside France's boundaries for centuries when Louis XIV came to the throne. But Torcy knew that, provided the Tories stayed in power, there was no longer any question of a punitive peace. The Utrecht peace was to be a peace of consensus, which meant that,

---

[141] French offer of peace to the Emperor and the Empire, Utrecht 11 Apr. 1713, Freschot (1714–15: ii. 353, 358).   [142] Ibid. i. 163 f.
[143] French instruction, Weber (1891: 439). See also ibid. 428.

under Torcy's direction, France would obtain all that the consensus agenda entitled it to.

The French were prepared to let the Dutch have the northern fortresses. Strong claims were made by both the Dutch and the French on the middle ones. But, since both sides claimed these fortresses on the strength of the same principle, that principle could not be used to settle the dispute—or, at any rate, it could not so easily be used *against* France. This in itself was a success for Torcy. What was at stake was the fate of two very important fortresses, Lille and Tournai. The French plenipotentiaries were authorized to accept the loss of these two places, but only if extreme necessity required it.[144]

The French secured Lille. Oxford, the British prime minister, insisted that, even though the Dutch were to be forced to accept the proposed settlement by a British ultimatum (take it, they were told, or leave it, in which case we will sign a separate peace), they had to be offered some reward—Tournai. Demoralized as they were, the Dutch accepted, fulfilling a cynical prophecy by Bolingbroke ('the Dutch, who, by the way, if this negotiation was broke, would give up Spain for a town more in their barrier, tomorrow').[145]

However, Torcy was prepared to do battle even with the British over the security principle. This was in connection with the claims of Savoy. At first, these claims received strong British backing, in line with the pro-Savoy policy of the Tories. Bolingbroke reminded the British plenipotentiaries 'of how great moment it is to the future repose of Europe that [the Duke of Savoy] be put in a condition of defending himself against any neighbour, who may hereafter attack him'.[146]

But, according to Torcy, Savoy was cheating:

After informing you [Bolingbroke] of what the king is willing to do to satisfy Her Britannic Majesty, I could wish to pass over in silence the article respecting the Duke of Savoy, since it is as disagreeable to refuse as to be refused. I assure you, Sir, the queen would not be so exposed, had not her demands, in favour of that prince, been directly adverse to the interest, the justice, and the honour of the king.

---

[144] Ibid. 437 f.
[145] To Peterborough, 19 Jan. 1712, St John (1798: i. 385).
[146] Letter dated 1 Jan. 1712, ibid. 370. See also Bolingbroke's instruction for his visit to France, ibid. ii. 2 f.

Were we to give up to the Duke of Savoy what he demands beyond the Rhône, Briançon, and Fort Barraux, we should lay open the kingdom to him, by giving him the keys thereof, and leave Dauphiny to his disposal. Take the trouble, Sir, to examine only the map of the country, and judge if His Majesty could, with any sort of security to his provinces, grant such pretensions?[147]

At this point, Bolingbroke resolved to travel to France in person. There, he found himself quite helpless in the face of Torcy's arguments concerning Savoy.

I wish I could have prevailed on the head of the barrier [for Savoy] . . . but it was impossible, at least it was so for me. Monsieur de Torcy represented that Exilles, Fenestrelle, and the Valley of Pragelas [Pragelato], besides the restitution of all which France is in possession of, was the utmost which the king would ever consent, or had ever consented, to give; that when the ministers of Savoy made, in Holland, the same ulterior demands which they now make, the pensionary laughed at them, and even at that time did not push him to comply with them; that, under pretence of security, His Royal Highness [the Duke of Savoy] really sought an aggrandizement at the expense of France, and out of the ancient domain of this crown; that though a king of France was a more powerful prince than a duke of Savoy, yet that the latter, backed by a confederacy, which is the only case wherein he will attempt anything, is a dreadful enemy to the former; that they have here a minority [i.e. regency] to expect, and therefore ought to be the more careful not to leave the frontiers of their kingdom exposed; in short, that Sicily was an ample recompense to His Royal Highness for all the services he has done the queen, and that if Her Majesty was easy, he was sure the Duke of Savoy would submit; he concluded by repeating, very earnestly, that the king never would grant him a larger barrier, and that His Majesty insisted to put this negative now, since he was resolved to do it at last, lest the duke should, by continuing in hopes, spin out the treaty and delay concluding the peace, for which reason he likewise insisted that the queen should concur in this negative.[148]

Torcy was undoubtedly helped by the knowledge (conveyed by his London agent Gaultier) that Bolingbroke's instruction in fact empowered him to yield on this point,[149] and it is possible that Bolingbroke actually colluded with Torcy. But, either way, Torcy

[147] To Bolingbroke, 28 July 1712, ibid. i. 588 f.
[148] Bolingbroke's report to Dartmouth, Fontainebleau 21 Aug. 1712, ibid. ii. 5 f.
[149] Weber (1891: 311).

succeeded because he had a good case, with the security principle and the concomitant rule of non-aggrandizement on his side; and because he pleaded it in such a way that Bolingbroke could 'sell' the French stance to his own government. 'It is needless to lengthen my dispatch', Bolingbroke continued his report,

by telling Your Lordship [Dartmouth, Bolingbroke's fellow foreign secretary], what answers I made to these representations. I replied in the best manner I was able and ended, as I am instructed, by letting the minister know, that the queen would consent to nothing which should foreclose His Royal Highness from obtaining what, for aught she knew, might be necessary; that this point must therefore not be now looked upon as determined, but must be left open for the ministers of Savoy to debate; that I did not understand Her Majesty's intentions to be to en-large the Duke of Savoy's dominions out of those of France, but that I was sure she would not sign a peace, unless this prince's security was really and effectually provided for, which France having promised in general terms to all the allies, could not refuse, in any particular, to the Duke of Savoy.[150]

This, of course, meant that Torcy had won. He lost no time in driving the advantage home. A protocol that he made Boling-broke sign laid down their respective positions, and pretended that the question of whether or not the demands of Savoy were in conformity with the security principle was as yet unresolved. Boling-broke again assured Torcy that the British government accepted the principle, as he had done on earlier occasions. Meanwhile, Britain retreated from supporting Savoy into neutrality—which, of course, left Savoy powerless to achieve its aims ('The queen, who cannot take upon her to decide this affair, desires His Royal Highness's [the Duke of Savoy's] reasons may be examined and decided, with those of His Most Christian Majesty, at Utrecht.')[151]

France did make a concession: it not only withdrew from Savoy proper and from Nice, both of which were under French occupa-tion, but also ceded Exilles and Fenestrelle, which Torcy had ordered the French negotiators to hang on to in his instruction.[152] But, having agreed with Savoy that, in order to form a proper

---

[150] St John (1798: ii. 6).
[151] Minutes taken by Bolingbroke and Torcy at Fontainebleau, 21 Aug. 1712, ibid. 7. See also Bolingbroke to Torcy, 1 Aug. 1712, ibid. i. 596.
[152] Weber (1891: 431, 439).

barrier, the boundary was to follow *la crête des Alpes*, France also made a substantial gain in the shape of the Valley of Barcelonnette.

4. THE UTRECHT CONSENSUS

4.1. The Temptations of Diktat

The dispute over the barrier for Savoy is a significant example of the way in which consensus notions were applied even in dealing with a succumbing actor. This even-handed application of consensus notions is all the more remarkable because, in the context of the negotiations, there was a strong tendency to point to Louis XIV's record of expansionism and to draw two conclusions: first, that it was necessary to continue the war until the power of France had been broken durably, and secondly, that France should be put in quarantine (so to speak), excluded from the company of 'peace-loving' actors because of its dangerous, militarist nature. These views, reminiscent of attitudes towards Germany in the wake of the First World War, were propounded especially by the Emperor, the Dutch, and the Whigs in England.

In an autograph letter to the States General three months before the opening of the congress, the new Emperor, Charles, dismissed the London Preliminaries as 'devised with great cunning and just what one would expect from the enemy [*magna arte concinnati et plane eiusmodi quales ab hoste expectare oportebat*]'. The Emperor argued that acceptance of these proposals would lead to the loss for Habsburg of the Spanish monarchy and therefore to an increase of French power that would be fatal to the liberty of Europe.

For who does not see that such an increase of power, added to what the enemy possesses already, would spell the most disgraceful servitude for each of the allies, a servitude which we have hitherto succeeded in avoiding [*a cervicibus nostris depulsimus*]? That it would place our liberty at the mercy of the enemy? and that, with intolerable arrogance, he proposes to lay down, in his turn, the law that only recently [e.g. at Geertruidenberg] we dictated to him?[153]

---

[153] Charles VI to the States General, 8 Nov. 1711, Lamberty (1728–30: vi. 705 f.) A similar letter was dispatched to London, but Charles's envoys there did not deliver it. They felt that it would be counterproductive; Weber (1891: 158). Charles also wrote to each of the electors; Freschot (1714–15: i. 213 ff.).

But, if the Spanish inheritance did not go to Philip, it would come to Charles himself, adding vastly to his own power. The Emperor cannot have expected his allies to overlook this—he seems to have counted on their preferring him to Philip because of their deep-seated distrust of France. This confidence, on the part of the Viennese court, that Europe would be more concerned about a further increase of French than of Habsburg power is found already before the war. For example, Leopold I's envoy Auersperg, in a meeting with Grand Pensionary Heinsius in March 1699, expressed his conviction that between 'the French slavery' on the one hand and 'Your Imperial Majesty's utterly just cause' on the other there was 'no longer any choice left', implying, by his choice of language, that nobody could possibly dissent.[154] After all, until 1700 Habsburg had already ruled at both Vienna and Madrid for a long time, without causing any undue worries to the rest of Europe. This was despite the fact that, under Charles II, policy at Madrid had been much influenced both by the pro-Austrian German queen (whose sister was married to the Emperor Leopold and who was surrounded at court by an active German coterie) and, until her death in 1696, by the queen mother (who was the Emperor Leopold's sister). Habsburg policy had always been opportunistic and less openly aggressive than France's. Indeed, had not the history of France, under Louis XIV and even before, been one of constant machinations against the stability of the international system? Were not the peace proposals just another proof of the French monarch's incurable and all-too-well-known disingenuousness?

'It is clear', the Emperor Charles continued his letter,

that the King of France, in submitting these nebulous peace preliminaries, is bent in his usual fashion [*pro more suo*] on separating the allies from one another and on dividing them once his goal of a peace congress has been achieved, by means of those well-known artifices [*solitis suis artibus*] by which he has always saved himself. Even if men failed to realize this, the sad recollection of the past [*tristis superiorum temporum recordatio*] would make it abundantly obvious.

---

[154] 'ich fragte, was denn Engelland und Holland für Mesuren nehmen wollten, sintemalen mich gedünket, daß keine Elektion mehr übrig und entweder die französische Sklaverei zu erwählen oder E. K. M. [Euer Kaiserlichen Majestät] gerechtsamste Sache mit allen Kräften zu soutenieren'. To Leopold I, 3 Mar. 1699, Gaedeke (1877: ii. 10*).

The letter concluded that the only way of coming to grips with the French was to treat them with all possible severity:

This is the main reason why all of us have always recognized that there is no better foundation for a future peace than so to tie down and hem in nimble France [*volubilem Galliam*] through preliminary articles that, in the peace negotiations themselves, it can no longer slip away.

What the Emperor and other hardliners had in mind was a dictated peace. They felt that, if negotiations were entered into, the unity of the allies might soon be destroyed. Another example of this view is found in a memorandum to Queen Anne delivered in London in December 1711 by an envoy of the Elector of Hanover, Bothmer. This memorandum was submitted on behalf, not only of the elector, but also the Emperor and the Dutch.

In this cogently worded document, Bothmer took the view that the 'liberty of Europe' (he uses the expression repeatedly) would always be under threat from France. There was little point in giving an enemy 'whose ways of behaving are sufficiently well known' the opportunity to discuss a settlement that would have to be harsh in order to be effective. Prolonged negotiations would only afford France another chance 'to employ its usual intrigues and ruses.' After the conclusion of the peace, the allies would still need to remain united, because France would again be a threat to them once it had recovered from the present war. The security of the allies could only be ensured by a system of mutual guarantees, of which Britain had to form part. Otherwise, first the continent and then Britain itself would ultimately be reduced to servitude. After all, in the present war, the combined strength of the allies had only just sufficed to defend them, and it was evident, therefore, that only by staying united could they hope, after the peace, to be 'safe from the undertakings of France.'[155]

The Dutch were similarly insistent that the wartime alliance should be carried over into the peace, and equally eloquent when it came to conjuring up the French peril. The preamble of the request by the Dutch Council of State for the military funds for the year 1713 dwelt at length on Louis XIV's continual aggressions since the Peace of Westphalia, and on the fact that the various peace treaties concluded with him had never lasted more than a

[155] 9 Dec. 1711, Freschot (1714–15: i. 224 ff.).

few years. It drew attention to 'the unruly nature of the [French] nation, its bellicose spirit, which for more than two hundred years already has made it the fear of its neighbours', and pointed out that the memory of three consecutive wars that the republic had had to wage against the French was too fresh for some mere ink and paper to 'restore the old friendship and trust to the heart of the peoples'.

This latter aim, the document suggested, could be achieved only by the passage of time; meanwhile, it was necessary to have more solid safeguards against a resurgence of the French danger. Three main safeguards were needed: first, the distance between the Dutch frontier and the French should be made as great as possible; secondly, there had to be a 'barrier' between the two countries, defined as 'a piece of territory equipped with several good fortresses'; and thirdly, there had to be a system of mutual guarantees between the allies, 'because the security of the [Dutch] state after the peace cannot consist in its own armaments and efforts'.[156]

The Tories could not remain impervious to these requests from Britain's allies, especially as they were amplified by the skilful propaganda campaign that the allies and the Whig opposition together orchestrated in Britain. This propaganda campaign, which involved much pamphleteering, leaks to the press, and the publication of memorials (such as Bothmer's) that were officially addressed to the British crown, was a source of some concern to the Tory government. Bolingbroke's reaction to it ranged from laconism to irritation and impotent fury ('You will probably', he wrote to a correspondent, 'have received a copy of the paper [containing the London Preliminaries] which the Earl of Strafford is to communicate to the foreign ministers, at The Hague, and which having been communicated to those who reside here [London], has been rendered as public as the *Daily Courant* can make it'[157]—'It is inconceivable how much mankind is alarmed at Bothmer's memorial'[158]—'Your Excellency [Strafford] will certainly do well to let Count Sinzendorf know, that the queen's ministers despise this correspondence with gazetteers, so much in fashion of late, yet that Her Majesty understands the indecency

---

[156] See n. 129, above.

[157] To Orrery, dated 15 Oct. 1711, St John (1798: i. 253). Italics added.

[158] To Strafford, dated 8 Dec. 1712, ibid. 331. On the stir that this document caused, see also Weber (1891: 137 ff.).

and disrespect which is shown to her, in printing memorials and other papers presented to her, and will in a proper time, show her resentment of this proceeding.'[159])

The Tory government did what it could to obscure its collaboration with France and to reassure the allies. Already in a letter to the Dutch grand pensionary some months before the opening of the Utrecht congress, Prime Minister Oxford wrote that, in order to dispel the malicious rumours concerning the state of Anglo-Dutch relations,

I take leave to offer you . . . a league offensive and defensive between the two nations to take place after the peace. I should be glad to have your thoughts for the making such a plan as may be agreeable to the present situation of affairs and may prove a lasting security to the whole and a real balance of power against France and anyone else . . .[160]

This initiative resulted in a British–Dutch agreement that confirmed existing bilateral agreements and committed the two countries yet again to working jointly towards an appropriate settlement. In addition, it pledged them to the upkeep of this settlement by all means, including military ones. Under the terms of the agreement, the two countries were required to intervene in defence of any right acquired as a result of the peace by any of the allies (but not France), in the event that the dispute could not be resolved amicably within two months, or within a shorter period if the danger was pressing. Moreover, an invitation was extended to all 'peace-loving Christian princes and states [*principes ac status christiani pacem amantes*], but especially His Sacred Imperial Majesty and the other allies', to accede to the agreement.[161]

This offers an interesting parallel with the League of Nations in the years immediately following the Treaty of Versailles (an association of states in principle universal but, in practice, perceived or even intended by many to be directed against a former foe considered an unfit member of international society). But the projected ostracism of France did not take place. By the time the agreement was signed in December 1711, the Anglo-French entente was not much of a secret any more, and the scheme turned out

---

[159] To Strafford, dated 7 Mar. 1712, St John (1798: i. 429).
[160] To Heinsius, 4 Aug. 1711, Weber (1891: 404). See also Bolingbroke to Strafford, dated 9 Nov. 1711, St John (1798: i. 290 ff.).
[161] Freschot (1714–15: i. 246 ff.).

to be merely a sop for The Hague. (Buys, the Dutch emissary who signed the agreement during a prolonged stay in London, seems to have been under no illusion about this. On the other hand, the Tory ministry was then in very serious danger from the Whig opposition in the Lords, which Buys seems to have fostered. If the ministry had fallen, things might have taken a different turn.)[162]

Bolingbroke did not then regard a 'Carthaginian' peace—which is how he describes the Geertruidenberg project[163]—as either desirable or possible. He did not want a peace that needed to be enforced (because that, if it were feasible at all, presupposed a continuation of the war), but a peace that France would freely consent to. In a letter written a few months into the congress, Bolingbroke told Torcy that the queen wished for a settlement that was 'reasonable' for France, which, however, was only possible if 'the interest of France is not made incompatible with general security'.[164]

In practice, for Bolingbroke, a peace based on reciprocal moderation was the only possible one. It was his declared opinion that neither side had the strength to lay down the law to the other. Years later he was to say that towards the end of the war the allies overestimated themselves just as the French had done at the beginning, and that the conditions that it would have been possible to impose in 1706 were no longer obtainable in 1712.[165] It is debatable whether this was, in fact, true before the change of government in London, but the Tory unwillingness to continue the war certainly made it so afterwards.

There was consensus on this point between Bolingbroke and Torcy. The instruction for the French plenipotentiaries was based on the assumption that both sides were either incapable of continuing the struggle, or, at least, reluctant to do so.[166] Torcy insisted that the only realistic peace was one based on mutual, and universal, consensus. Already the London Preliminaries had stated that '[i]t is the king's [Louis XIV's] intention that all the princes

[162] See Weber (1891: ch. 4, esp. p. 143 f.).

[163] *Letters on History VIII*, St John (1844: ii. 308).

[164] 'Sa Majesté souhaite sincèrement la paix; elle la souhaite raisonnable pour la France; mais pour parvenir à ce but, il faut que l'intérêt de la France ne soit pas rendu incompatible avec la sûreté générale.' Dated 29 Apr. 1712, St John (1798: i. 473).   [165] *Letters on History VIII*, St John (1844: ii. 293 ff.).

[166] Weber (1891: 438).

and states engaged in this war, without exception, may find a reasonable satisfaction in the treaty of peace to be concluded.'[167] Similarly, in the instruction for Utrecht, Torcy observed that 'the main aim of the treaty to be concluded is to find in the conditions of peace the satisfaction of all the parties involved in the war,' and that '[t]he new scheme for the forthcoming negotiation is drawn up with a view to satisfying, in accordance with the rules of reason, all the powers engaged in the present war'.[168]

It was because of Torcy's shrewd advocacy of a peace based on consensus, rather than on revenge, and of the Tory desire to go along with this, that consensus notions found such ready access to the negotiations. None of the rulings of the final settlement stood in opposition to the international consensus agenda. Otherwise, there would have been little chance of Britain 'selling' the scheme to the allies in the face of their recalcitrance and fears, and the Tories were keen to do this in order to salvage their reputation. Bolingbroke wrote to Strafford, one of the negotiators at Utrecht, that 'France must come to form such a project as the queen will accept, and can justify herself to her allies, to God, and to all the world'[169]—a project, in other words, that everyone could accept as legitimate. Britain's allies might protest, but, in the long run, they could not reject the settlement—unless they were willing to reject the very bases of the international system, which it had been the major purpose of the war to preserve.

Many years later Bolingbroke presented a very different view of the whole business. This was after he had been impeached for his part in the negotiations—although he evaded a trial by fleeing to France, where he had to wait nearly a decade for his pardon. In the eighth of his *Letters on History*, written in the 1730s, Bolingbroke claims that the settlement was flawed because it had not weakened France as it should have done: 'the low and exhausted state to which France was reduced, by the last great war, was but a momentary reduction of her power; and whatever real and more lasting reduction the Treaty of Utrecht brought about in some instances, it was not sufficient.'[170] Bolingbroke blames this failure on the opponents of the peace, who brought disunity into the alliance and prevented the other allies from following the British lead:

---

[167] Freschot (1714–15: i. 162). [168] Weber (1891: 436, 425).
[169] Dated 7 Mar. 1712, St John (1798: i. 429 f.). [170] St John (1844: ii. 316).

Thus the war ended, much more favourably to France than she [Queen Anne] expected, or they who put an end to it [such as himself] designed. The queen would have humbled and weakened this power. The allies who opposed her would have crushed it, and have raised another as exorbitant on the ruins of it. Neither one nor the other succeeded, and they who meant to ruin the French power, preserved it, by opposing those who meant to reduce it.[171]

This is a genuflection to the criticism, current dogma when Bolingbroke wrote his treatise, that the peace had been a sell-out. Like much else in the treatise, it is elegant nonsense. In fact, by the time that the Franco-British peace initiative was announced officially to the allies, by communicating the London Preliminaries, the settlement with France had already been worked out in its essentials. Bolingbroke had been instrumental in this. Neither he nor anyone else in the British cabinet ever intended to consult the allies about it, or to weaken France further with their help. Nevertheless, in later years Bolingbroke even paid homage to the idea that France ought to have been punished, although, clearly, he could not quite bring himself to like it. The following passage alludes to events that European opinion had found particularly gratuitous and shocking—the desecration by French troops of the tombs of the medieval Emperors in Speyer cathedral, and those of the Palatine electors in the Heidelberg Heilig-Geist-Kirche. Both cities were also burnt down. Bolingbroke wrote that

If the confederate army had broke into France, the campaign before this [i.e. that of 1712], or in any former campaign; and if the Germans and the Dutch had exercised then the same inhumanity, as the French had exercised in their provinces in former wars; if they had burned Versailles, and even Paris, and if they had disturbed the ashes of the dead princes that repose at St Denis, every good man would have felt the horror, that such cruelties inspire: no man could have said that the retaliation was unjust. But in 1712, it was too late, in every respect, to meditate such projects.[172]

Once again, this argument rests on the dubious assumption that the alliance would by 1712 have been too weak to continue the war even if Bolingbroke had not given (or transmitted) his notorious order to Ormonde, the British commander, to withdraw the British troops from it. This assumption is, incidentally, contradicted by an anecdote which Bolingbroke relates elsewhere in the

---

[171] Ibid. 320.   [172] Ibid. 324.

very same text. (Bolingbroke recalls a dinner party at the beginning of his exile in France in 1715, when the Duc de la Feuillade, referring to the military situation on the eve of the peace, said to him 'You could have crushed us in those days: why did you not do so?' Bolingbroke states himself to have replied, 'coolly': 'Because in those days we no longer feared your power.')[173]

To a reader who is unacquainted with the details of the negotiations, Bolingbroke's account makes convincing reading, but closer analysis essentially reveals one thing, and that is the opportunistic nature of Bolingbroke's utterances. In the 1730s treatise, he was paying homage to historical legend in an attempt to whitewash his personal reputation. At the time of the Utrecht congress, guided by personal ambition and a sure political instinct, he had been similarly opportunistic, conforming this time to the international consensus agenda. Bolingbroke wanted to appear as the great peacemaker in a bid to oust his hated rival Oxford and become the leader of the pro-peace Tory party.[174] Peace with France was, at that point in time, only to be had by consensus. There was no time to be lost by continuing the war, because the queen was seriously ill, and her designated successor, the Elector of Hanover, was pro-Emperor, pro-war, and pro-Whig. (Bolingbroke's nervousness on this account shines through on several occasions in his correspondence, for example in a letter to his friend and agent in France Matthew Prior, dated 19 September 1712: the queen 'had some slight feverish impression; however slight it was, you easily imagine our concern. Indeed, there is hardly an instance of any one life to be found in story [sic] so important as Her Majesty's.'[175]) With luck, the queen would live long enough for some grass to have grown over the whole business by the time the elector came to the throne (assuming that he did—for, once the peace was made, the idea of a Stuart succession rather than the Hanoverian one might conceivably be revived). In any case, speed was of the essence; the worst possible outcome for the Tories was for the queen to die while the peace was still being negotiated. As it happened, they just about had the time, before Anne's demise in August 1714, to clinch the settlement—which survived the elector's succession though the ministry did not.

---

[173] *Letters on History VIII*, ibid. 311.   [174] See Dickinson (1970).
[175] St John (1798: ii. 46).

This gives us a key reason why the Tory ministry offered the French a chance to play fair and to abide by the current consensus notions. The other allies took it for granted that the French, being French, could never be trusted. The Tories, because of the political circumstances in Britain, had a strong incentive to test the opposite assumption. It worked. The success of the Utrecht settlement in preserving and strengthening the international system of eighteenth-century Europe was undoubtedly due mainly to this reliance on consensus notions. Because it was so legitimate, the settlement proved lasting—especially with respect to the successful integration of the French monarchy into the system. I would suggest that this is the most important, and, at the same time, the least acknowledged, aspect of the Utrecht peace.

It is remarkable that so successful a peace should have come about in spite of strong initial opposition from many key players and the somewhat dubious motives of even those who wanted it. The allies did not want the peace at first, but eventually they accepted it. The Whig party in Britain left nothing untried to prevent it, but when it regained power after the death of Queen Anne in 1714 it did no more in the end than move the impeachment of Oxford and Bolingbroke. The Whig ministry then proceeded to conclude an alliance with France. Bolingbroke and Oxford themselves, as has been pointed out, were essentially opportunistic. What about the House of Bourbon?

4.2. The Problem of France

Torcy's disingenuous feet-dragging over the 'great article' and his discreet advice to Philip V to renounce his rights to the French throne for show have already been highlighted. That was not the end of the matter. The British went to some length to make the text of the renunciations legally watertight, at least in Philip's case. The ministry ostentatiously sought legal advice from a variety of sources, including the Faculty of Law of Oxford University. Torcy acknowledged all this gracefully ('Monsieur Prior m'a fait part des observations faites à Oxford, sur le projet de la renonciation')[176] and was totally complaisant.

But soon Shrewsbury, the new British ambassador to France, reported to Bolingbroke that it appeared that Orléans and Berry

---

[176] To Bolingbroke, 27 Sept. 1712, ibid. 51.

(Philip V's uncle and brother respectively) had not actually sworn an oath on their renunciations, even though the text of the documents stated it. 'I mentioned this the other day to Monsieur de Torcy, who seemed not to have remarked whether they had sworn or not, and is not versed in these forms'[177]—Torcy, who had lectured Bolingbroke on the law of succession!

Bolingbroke advised Shrewsbury not to make a fuss[178]—but he always judged the French soberly, despite a massive personal *offensive de charme* that Torcy made him the object of after Bolingbroke's visit to France. Bolingbroke wrote in December 1711 that the French court 'is not able to lay aside their habits of chicane, however unseasonable',[179] and a few months later that France was 'an enemy, who wants no inclination to take advantages, nor skill to manage them'.[180] One of his last acts in office was a stern letter to Torcy warning him not to tamper with the 'great article', i.e. the renunciations.[181]

An interesting comparison can be made between two passages from the pen of Torcy. He, whose public discourse was impregnated with consensus notions, had not hesitated to advise Louis XIV secretly in 1710 that an extortionate peace concluded under duress need not be accepted as final. In Torcy's private journal, not published until 1884, the following entry is found:

I told him [the king] that what was mainly necessary for his service was to divide his enemies and give his subjects time to recover; that, notwithstanding the cessions that he would make by the peace, France would still be the most powerful kingdom in Europe; that the repose of a few years would restore its strength, while that of his enemies would be on the wane; that disunity would come among them after the peace, that civil wars would break out in their states ... That it was then that France would find the happy opportunities to take revenge for a treaty imposed on it, that put it under an obligation which, in truth, to me seemed very similar to the promise made by a man to the thieves who would murder him at the corner of some forest, and that I did not believe for a moment that conscience required us to keep such promises when the time was come to shake them off; that it would be improper to speak thus to anyone other than His Majesty, but that I concluded from these maxims

---

[177] 23 Mar. 1713, ibid. 308.   [178] 4 Apr. 1713, ibid. 312 f.
[179] To Strafford, dated 4 Dec. 1711, ibid. i. 318 f.
[180] To Peterborough, dated 2 May 1712, ibid. 489.
[181] Dated 29 July 1714, ibid. ii. 676.

that, at the present juncture, it was necessary to concede everything to draw back from the precipice and to save one's hopes for the future.[182]

Torcy wrote this passage at the time of the Geertruidenberg conferences. He described these conferences somewhat differently in the French instruction for Utrecht:

If the conferences held at Geertruidenberg in 1710 proved futile with respect to the plan that the king had conceived of reestablishing the repose of Europe, at least they served the purpose of showing that His Majesty considered as his one claim to fame the pacification of Christendom, that he sacrificed his interest and that of the king his grandson to the desire of bestowing happiness on so many peoples that the burden of war had been oppressing for so many years.[183]

But there was an important difference between Geertruidenberg and Utrecht. The Utrecht peace was based on consensus, whereas the one proposed at Geertruidenberg was dictated. Bolingbroke, whatever his motives, took the right attitude with regard to the Bourbon machinations. Consciously or not, he acted on the correct assumption that to try to lay down the law to any actor in the European system was in contradiction with the very nature of that system. In an 'anarchical' society, the notion of punishment cannot be operative, and any attempt to impose punishment on an actor either presupposes that his autonomy, and consequently his very status as an actor, is taken away durably, or it will abort and be counterproductive. Therefore, whatever one might think of French behaviour, punishment was not the answer. As the passage from Torcy's journal shows, such a course would only exacerbate the French propensity to resort to those famous 'well-known artifices' or to those 'usual intrigues and ruses', referred to in the Emperor Charles's letter to the Dutch and in Bothmer's memorandum.

Bolingbroke refused to be blinded by exasperation. He did not lose sight of the fact that, despite all the French machinations, there was also a genuine desire for international stability in France, and, as a result, a genuine willingness to be conciliatory and abide by the consensus agenda. Indeed, that willingness far outweighed any contrary impulse, at least for the time being. In a letter to Shrewsbury, written already before the problem of the oaths arose,

---

[182] 21 June 1710, Colbert (1884: 206 f.).   [183] Weber (1891: 421).

Bolingbroke played down 'those little artifices, which they [the French] cannot abandon, which always fix a certain degree of infamy upon those who use them, and which seldom or never procure any advantage, equal to the constant disadvantage of a bad character.'[184] The French might be devious, but they were serious about peace, and they knew that a system-oriented, cooperative attitude was necessary to obtain a good peace. This is why they could be trusted sufficiently to get the settlement in place.

The French crown had been chastened and shown its limits in a war that had brought it very close to disaster, and this goes some way to explain its easy compliance with consensus notions (many of which it had persistently violated in the past). Furthermore, the conciliatory disposition that this engendered was no doubt enhanced by the *fin de règne* atmosphere at Versailles, which had already been noticeable prior to the war.[185] Later, there was the frightening *série noire* of royal deaths from 1711 onwards, which killed three Dauphins in succession and went on to claim the Duke of Berry, another of Louis's grandsons, all within the king's own lifetime. Not only must the king have been affected psychologically, but these events left him politically with only two options as an alternative to the settlement. Both options were equally unpalatable.

If the current heir to the throne, born in 1710, died too, as everybody assumed that he would, and if the set-up of the system were not modified, then the crown of France would pass to Philip of Spain, and the war of succession would start all over again. By this stage, however, France no longer had much hope of winning it (after all, it was not for nothing that Louis had tried to forestall it to begin with). France was almost certain to be defeated, and this would give its enemies the chance to take revenge for everything that Louis had done to them in his long reign and to unravel the achievements of his lifetime. Alternatively, if the present little Dauphin survived, there would be a long regency, since Louis himself was in his seventies and unlikely to live much longer (indeed, he died in 1715). A regency would make the country vulnerable, for a regency council was likely to be a disunited and weak government.

---

[184] Dated 18 Feb. 1713, St John (1798: ii. 273).
[185] See the memorable report by a German observer, Franz Melchior von Wiser, of 30 June 1698, written for Franz Ulrich von Kinsky, one of the Emperor Leopold's advisers. Gaedeke (1877: i. 152* ff.).

It was therefore better to accept the settlement. In the short term, this would stop the war before it was too late and before France was checkmated irrevocably. But at the same time the settlement had to be more than a glorified armistice in the manner of previous peace treaties. It had to be durable to provide for the possibility of a long regency with the predictable problems this would create—internal political squabbles and a concomitant loss of power abroad. These problems it was best not to compound by an unresolved international situation.[186]

Bolingbroke, after he had decided in the *Letters on History* that the settlement had not weakened France enough, needed to explain, of course, why then the French had failed to challenge the settlement, why, twenty years on, 'the last great war' was still the one that ended at Utrecht, with no major threat to the system in sight. This was a very different situation from what the preceding century had been used to. Why had the French stopped undermining the system? Bolingbroke attributed the stability of the settlement to want of ambition on the part of Louis XIV's successors.[187] But that is a superficial explanation. France could hardly have been unambitious if it had not felt the peace to be a good one, if it had perceived it as a humiliation calling to be remedied. Moreover, Bolingbroke's explanation overlooks the fact that the new regime in France did not just accept the settlement passively. In conjunction with Britain, it went to great lengths to uphold it against those who did try to overturn it.

4.3. The Problem of Spain

In particular, the settlement had to be defended against Philip of Spain. The Spanish king pursued extremely ambitious, indeed somewhat eccentric, plans to undo what he had agreed to at Utrecht. Why he, but not France? There were other factors, such as the aspirations of his Italian-born second wife and his own

---

[186] This reasoning (which is mine) is akin to Bolingbroke's in the eighth of the *Letters on History*: 'Such family misfortunes, following a long series of national misfortunes, made the old king . . . desirous to get out of the war at any tolerable rate, that he might not run the risk of leaving a child of five years old, the present king, engaged in it'. St John (1844: ii. 319). Exactly the same point as Bolingbroke's is also made in Torcy's memoirs; Colbert (1756: iii. 419 f.).

[187] *Letters on History VIII*, St John (1844: ii. 328).

increasing mental instability. In the main, however, his attitude sprung from the fact that France had participated in the making of the peace, but had imposed it ruthlessly on Philip without giving him much say about it. There was much resentment in Spain at the fact that Louis had bought peace for himself by allowing the Spanish monarchy to be dismembered after all. This was the more painful as it had been precisely in order to prevent this outcome that Charles II had put his monarchy under Louis's protection.

This explains why Philip V was extremely reluctant to accede to the British peace proposals, thereby causing much friction between him and his grandfather. Louis complained bitterly that the Spaniards pursued unrealistic aims and then expected him to bail them out, which he could no longer do. For example, Philip tried to 'sell' his consent to renounce his French rights by insisting, vainly, that the British should restore Gibraltar and Spain's Italian possessions in return.[188] Louis repeatedly used the big stick—the threat of concluding a separate peace, which would leave Spain in the lurch. He wrote to his ambassador at Madrid that Philip had better take notice of the *benefits* that the British proposals entailed.

More than anyone, the Catholic King is aware that these advantages are real; but, if that has no effect on him, he must at last be made to realize that it is absolutely impossible for me to continue the war any longer. . . . peace being an absolute necessity, my intention is to make it as quickly as can be done, whatever reply I receive from the King of Spain.[189]

Philip submitted—at least as far as the Utrecht peace was concerned (exasperated, Louis eventually made his peace with the Emperor and the Empire at Rastatt and Baden without him). But no sooner was Louis dead than Philip was found plotting the overthrow of the French regent to put himself in his place. He also tried to reconquer Sicily and Sardinia and even, for good measure, to invade Britain.

To be sure, there had been warnings. There is a curious phrase in all the renunciations that were signed by members of the Bourbon family, and in Philip's cession of Sicily, pledging the signatories to what they had agreed to despite the 'obvious, enormous, even very enormous prejudice' to them that these acts

[188] Philip V to Louis XIV, 22 Apr. 1712, Roussel de Courcy (1889: 83 ff., esp. 86 f.).   [189] To Bonnac, 18 Apr. 1712, Baudrillart (1890: 480 f.).

constituted.[190] This strange wording rather looks like a reservation in disguise, suggesting that the transaction was inherently vitiated. Moreover, in ceding Sicily, Philip came close to spelling out that he was acting under duress.[191] If these documents had been drafted in France, their tone would almost certainly have been different. But Louis, in order to avoid the impression that they had been imposed on Spain, had them drawn up in Madrid.[192]

Seen in this light, the emphatic expressions of the Spanish willingness to put 'public' before 'private' interest on which we commented earlier may have been, not only a means of winning acceptance abroad, but also a face-saving device for the Spaniards themselves.

In their approach to the legal aspects of the problem, Louis XIV and his British interlocutors seem to have shared a pragmatic and, indeed, a secretly dismissive attitude. For example, the president of the Parlement de Paris represented to Louis that the renunciations were contrary to the 'lois fondamentales de l'état', only to be told by the king that such concerns had to give way to the 'bien de l'état'.[193] The Spanish ambassador to France, Cornejo, reported at the same time that the general opinion in France held the renunciations to be invalid.[194]

But Louis, clearly quite rightly, judged that what mattered to the British government was not the legal value of the renunciations but their public-relations value, their role as a vehicle of national and international consensus. As Louis saw it, the ostentatious

[190] e.g. Philip renounced the crown of France despite 'la lesión evidente, enorme, y enormísima, que se pueda considerar haber intervenido en la desistencia y renunciación de poder en algún tiempo suceder en la referida corona', Freschot (1714–15: ii. 186). An almost identical formulation is found in the document by which he ceded Sicily, art. 10, ibid. vi. 826. Compare the renunciation of the Duke of Berry ('l'évidente, énorme et très énorme lésion qui se peut trouver en ladite renonciation à la succession de la couronne d'Espagne', ibid. ii. 206) and that of the Duke of Orléans, ibid. ii. 214.

[191] The preamble of the *Instrumento de cesión* blames the transaction on Queen Anne and the Duke of Savoy, discreetly omitting to mention Louis XIV: 'habiéndose considerado por la Reina de la Gran Bretaña, por uno de los medios necesarios para establecer, y asegurar la paz universal entre otras ventajas al Duque de Saboya, que yo le ceda el Reino de Sicilia, y instándome a ello repetidamente, y convenido con Su Maj. Británica por concurrir por mi parte aunque tan costosamente, a que se consiga este importante, y deseado bien universal'. Ibid. vi. 789 f.

[192] Baudrillart (1890: 503).

[193] The president related this exchange publicly in a speech which he made during the renunciation ceremony held for Orléans and Berry in the Paris Parlement, on 15 Mar. 1713. Ibid. 531.   [194] Dispatch of 20 Mar. 1713, ibid. 534.

consultation of legal experts in this matter was really for public-relations purposes, as a shield against attacks on the government's policies. 'A university as famous as Oxford', Louis told his ambassador to Madrid, 'having been consulted, those who are favourably disposed towards peace will be less vulnerable to the accusations that their enemies might aim at them in the future, and the opinion of that university is a sort of warranty for their conduct.'[195] Previously, Louis had grown quite impatient when Philip justified his reluctance to declare himself on the renunciation issue with the need to consult his lawyers, whose views, Louis felt, were only useful if one had the military strength to enforce them.[196]

However, notwithstanding this pragmatism in legal matters, both Louis's and Bolingbroke's patience snapped when the *Instrumento de cesión* by which Philip made over Sicily to Savoy was found to go back on stipulations contained in the Spanish peace treaty with Savoy, signed at Utrecht. Bolingbroke threatened that Britain would not ratify its own peace with Spain, or the treaty of commerce with Spain that was still being negotiated, unless this was rectified. Subsequently, he was able to note that it had been.[197] But it is likely that this was brought about not so much by his own intervention as by the explosion that Philip's tactic caused at Versailles, and which is reflected in a dispatch by Louis to his ambassador at Madrid:

No sooner does the Spanish court perceive some semblance of good fortune than it wants to do everything insolently and without consultation [*avec hauteur et sans concert*], but the moment that it finds itself in the slightest difficulty, its strength fails it, and it can think of no other expedient than to ask me to make war for it at my expense. If it considers my assistance necessary, the King of Spain must at least implement the treaties by which I have in some way committed myself on his behalf. The modification that he has introduced in the one with Savoy is beginning to harm

---

[195] 'Une université aussi célèbre que celle d'Oxford ayant été consultée, les bien intentionnés, pour la paix, seront moins exposés aux reproches que leurs ennemis pourraient leur faire à l'avenir, et le sentiment de cette université est une espèce de garantie de leur conduite.' To Bonnac, 26 Sept. 1712, Roussel de Courcy (1889: 180).

[196] 'Ces ouvrages de gens habiles sont bons lorsqu'on peut les soutenir par la force des armes.' Louis XIV to Bonnac, 25 Apr. 1712, Baudrillart (1890: 481).

[197] Bolingbroke to Lexington, dated 1 Aug. 1713, St John (1798: ii. 457); Bolingbroke to Trivié, 19 Sept. 1713, ibid. 489 f.

his reputation, and if I fail to complain myself about this deviation, all Europe will believe that it was decided in consultation with me and that I approve of the king my grandson not keeping his promises.[198]

Bolingbroke, for his part, wrote to the British ambassador at Madrid that

The French are sufficiently convinced, that they ought to close with all those who will close with them . . . The same maxim Your Excellency will instil into the minds of the Spaniards: if they are fond of disputes, and hope to repair the losses their monarchy has sustained, by new struggles, the ordinary course of affairs will hereafter produce enough; let them, in the meanwhile, perfect the great work of peace, before they begin a new plan. Let all Europe acknowledge King Philip, even his rival, and let the settlement of the two monarchies be universally received. On this foundation, the Catholic King may build what designs he pleases, but before this is laid, he runs a great risk if he ventures to disoblige those who have owned him, or to make those desperate who have not.[199]

This is much the same reasoning that he had used with Torcy concerning the 'great article':[200] first create a settlement that is universally acknowledged, then let people try to subvert it if they absolutely must. If they have to oppose an existing and recognized settlement, then in challenging it they will attract the opprobrium of flouting the general consensus inherent in the system, which will reduce their chances of success. The validity of this reasoning was demonstrated by the relative ease with which France and Britain, in the years following the Utrecht peace, jointly defended the settlement against Philip.

The Spanish reaction is, of course, understandable. Philip's plenipotentiary Bergeyck wrote to him in September 1712 that

there surely was nothing so sad as seeing oneself being stripped of such great and beautiful states without having any part in the negotiation, unable to indicate and declare [insinuer et dire] one's arguments in order to make those who demanded this cession understand that it was not even in their interest. It seems to me that Your Majesty should attribute the blame for this not so much to England as to France.

Somewhat unrealistically, Bergeyck went on to suggest that Philip should begin new talks from scratch as soon as he was recognized

---

[198] To Bonnac, 28 Aug. 1713, Baudrillart (1890: 539).
[199] To Lexington, dated 1 Aug. 1713, St John (1798: ii. 458 f.).
[200] See sect. 3.2.1, above.

and able to have his own delegation admitted to the congress.[201] Subsequently, another Spanish diplomat, the Duke of Osuna, expressed his opinion that France should cede all its own territory south of the Garonne to Spain in compensation for the latter's losses.[202] Unfortunately for Spain, however, it was virtually the only actor that was aggrieved lastingly by the settlement—the only one that did not come to share the Utrecht consensus. This meant that it had little chance of finding allies in Europe for its endeavour to overturn the settlement—apart from the unhappy and increasingly pathetic Charles XII of Sweden, who had seen Swedish power crumble in his hands and who was killed in action before he could send the promised reinforcements for Spain. Even the Emperor soon concluded an alliance with France and Britain, in order to prevent Spain from recovering its former Italian territories from him.[203] Despite the Spanish attempts (which eventually did have some success in Italy), the Utrecht settlement essentially remained in place.

[201] 12 Sept. 1712, Baudrillart (1890: 507).
[202] Torcy to Mme des Ursins, 3 June 1713, ibid. 540.
[203] See Sturgill (1987).

4

The Congress of Vienna

1. INTRODUCTION

We know what to think of the political scaffolding upon which the turbulence and incapacity [*nullité*] of European cabinets have struggled so long and so ostentatiously, at the expense of the interest of the peoples. We have at last learned that the only real profitable and reasonable leadership [*primatie*]—the only one to befit free and enlightened men—consists in being master at home, and in never entertaining the ridiculous pretension of being the master of other peoples. We have at last learned—rather late, perhaps—that for states, as for individuals, real wealth is acquired, not by conquering and invading foreign countries, but on the contrary by improving one's own. We have learned that all increase of territory, all the usurpations of force and cunning, long associated by time-honoured prejudices with the idea of rank, leadership, inner cohesion, and superiority in the hierarchy of the powers, are but the cruel mockery of political folly [*des jeux cruels de la déraison politique*], false estimates of political strength, which increase the expense and complications of government and diminish the wellbeing and safety of the governed, for the sake of the transient advantage or vanity of those who govern.

The reign of illusions is, then, over in France. In her maturity she will not be seduced by the grand political considerations which so long and so deplorably led astray and prolonged her childhood. Circumstances, which no human sagacity could foresee, have placed her in a position without example in the history of peoples.

Charles-Maurice de Talleyrand, Bishop of Autun, entered politics as a representative of the French clergy in the États-Généraux, whose meeting in 1789 precipitated the French Revolution. The memorandum quoted above contains the creed to which Talleyrand adhered throughout his political career, tortuous as that was to be (as Joseph Chambon aptly said of him, Talleyrand frequently changed party, but never changed his mind). The document is dated 25 November 1792.[1]

It did not have any impact. Talleyrand abandoned the ecclesiastical office forced on him by his family, temporarily became *persona non grata* in France, and spent some years in Britain and the United States as an exile. Meanwhile, revolutionary France embarked on a policy of expansion. After his return to France, Talleyrand was foreign minister under the Directoire from 1797 to 1799, and again under Napoleon before resigning in 1807. Napoleon did not, however, allow Talleyrand to resign from his council.

Having tried, unsuccessfully, to restrain Napoleon's excesses, Talleyrand was instrumental in toppling the dictator, and it was he who recalled the Bourbon pretender, Louis XVIII. Thereupon he resumed office as foreign minister. In September 1814 he was dispatched to Vienna, to represent France at a congress convened to complete the reconstruction of the European states system. It was here that, more than twenty years after his 1792 memorandum, Talleyrand found himself in a position to act on it.

The anti-Napoleonic coalition had already made peace with France at Paris on 30 May 1814. By this First Peace of Paris (so called to distinguish it from the Second, concluded after Napoleon's temporary return from his exile in Elba), France secured boundaries somewhat in excess of what it had possessed in 1792. It was neither required to pay reparations nor to restore the substantial treasure of works of art looted from the countries that had come under its sway. The latter decision in particular caused much indignation, because it was so conspicuous a manifestation of the failure to punish France for what had happened. The leniency of the peace terms was justified in the treaty's preamble by the change of government in France and the restoration of the pre-revolutionary dynasty.[2]

---

[1] Quoted Talleyrand (1881*b*: ii. 253 f. [1881*a*: 438 f.]). Talleyrand's correspondence during the congress was published in 1881 both in French and in an English trans. Unfortunately, this trans. is not always quite precise or adequate. I have therefore made some changes in line with the original French. Where changes have been made, page numbers in the French edn. 1881*a* are given in square brackets.

[2] The full text of this treaty is found e.g. in Chodźko (published under the pseudonym 'Comte d'Angeberg') (1864: i. 161 ff.). References to this treaty will not be footnoted further in this ch.

But the dislocation of the European states system, brought about by French expansion and hegemony and by the struggle against it, had been such that the Peace of Paris alone could not deal with it. Vast territories in the system were without recognized rulers. As someone put it, they were *sub judice*, pending redistribution, or confirmation of the arrangements arisen from the war. Hence the need for a pan-European assembly, the decision to hold which had been written into the Treaty of Paris (article 32). As a result, representatives of some 200 states, cities, associations, and individuals converged on Vienna in the autumn of 1814. The Emperor of Austria was the official host. Other monarchs, such as Czar Alexander of Russia, or the Kings of Bavaria, Denmark, Prussia, and Württemberg, were also present.

How was this vast gathering to be structured and to reach any decision? It was difficult to see how this question could be solved other than by those actors—increasingly known as 'the great powers'—that had borne the brunt of the struggle against Napoleon.

In the end, the actual 'congress' consisted of two groups. The larger committee, which comprised the representatives of the eight original signatories of the Treaty of Paris (Austria, Britain, France, Portugal, Prussia, Russia, Spain, Sweden) played only a very limited role. The more select group, which invested itself with the real authority for decision-making, consisted at first only of representatives of the four major erstwhile allies[3]—Austria, Britain, Prussia, and Russia. These four were determined to keep the initiative in their own hands. France and even more so Spain, also restored to its Bourbon ruler, were to be allowed to intervene only when the Four had reached a decision among themselves.

The great powers were shy of asking the assembled plenipotentiaries to ratify this set-up officially. From a strictly formal point of view, the proposed congress never actually opened. Protest against this outcome, while present, was relatively feeble.

As a consequence, most of the delegates remained quite idle. The delegates of the great powers worked behind closed doors. They appointed various subgroups among themselves to help them with specific problems—the notorious statistical committee, for example, whose task was to establish reliable estimates of population figures for the territories to be disposed of.

---

[3] Technically they were still allied, as the Treaty of Chaumont of March 1814 between them against France had been concluded for twenty years.

The most serious issue with which the great powers had to deal was that of Poland and Saxony. The Czar, inspired by his close friend Adam Czartoryski, who was Polish, dreamt of a reconstituted Poland of which he would be king. This meant that Prussia and Austria would not recover all the territory that they had acquired when Poland was partitioned at the end of the preceding century. Prussia accepted this but in recompense wanted to annex Saxony, whose monarch, it was argued, had forfeited his dominions by remaining loyal to Napoleon a little longer than everybody else. Initially, Castlereagh, the British foreign minister, who wanted to strengthen Prussia, wholeheartedly supported it over Saxony; his Austrian colleague Metternich did so with great reluctance. Yet neither was prepared to countenance the massive extension of Russian influence in east Europe that the Czar's ideas entailed. Metternich, in particular, was prepared to sacrifice Saxony only in order to induce Prussia to give up its pro-Russian policy and help prevent Russian expansion. Furthermore, the proposed annihilation of Saxony caused an ever-growing popular uproar, including in Austria and Britain. In the end, the Russian and Prussian designs were not realized fully. Poland was repartitioned, much against the will of the Czar. His relations—and Prussia's—with Austria and Britain deteriorated to the point where it was feared that war would break out between them.

The key question in the event of war between the allies was what France would do. Talleyrand, who from the start had championed Saxony, was not the man to miss this opportunity. He concluded a secret alliance with Britain and Austria, and in early January 1815 he was brought into the inner committee. As a consequence, the final settlement was, in fact, worked out in the name of the Five Powers that for the following few decades were to preside over the system.

The Czar gave way, allowing substantial parts of Poland to be repossessed by Austria and Prussia. Prussia grudgingly consented to absorb Saxony only in part. In addition, Prussia gained substantial territories elsewhere, notably in the Rhineland. Austria had already renounced Belgium, which became part of the new 'Kingdom of the United Netherlands'. By way of compensation, Austria expanded into Dalmatia and northern Italy, acquiring or regaining Lombardy and the former possessions of the Venetian Republic. The principalities of Parma, Modena, and Tuscany were allotted (or re-allotted) to collateral branches of the House of Habsburg.

The German subsystem was restored and reorganized as a confederation under the presidency of Austria. Switzerland was consolidated with a new constitution and declared perpetually neutral. Russia gained Finland from Sweden, while Sweden, in return, acquired Norway from Denmark. The issue of Naples had not yet been dealt with by the congress when Joachim Murat, an erstwhile follower of Napoleon and still King of Naples, rejoined Napoleon on the latter's surprise return from exile in March 1815— only to follow the dictator into his final defeat. This enabled Naples to be reunited with Sicily under its 'legitimate' Bourbon ruler. Finally, the Papal States were re-established. This is a rough summary of the settlement, most of the details of which were written into a document called the Final Act (for simplicity's sake, I have also included some changes here that were not actually decided at Vienna).[4]

The deliberations continued even when, unexpectedly, the campaign against Napoleon had to be resumed, and they closed ten days before the final battle at Waterloo. Drawn up by the Five Powers, the Final Act was signed by the Eight Powers (except Spain) on 9 June 1815. The plenipotentiaries of the other actors assembled at Vienna were then invited to accede.

When Napoleon returned from Elba, Louis XVIII fled to Belgium, subsequently to be restored a second time. The interlude of the Hundred Days necessitated a new peace with France, which many people thought should be more punitive than the first one. Talleyrand, who was French prime minister in the summer of 1815, strenuously fought these schemes. He argued that the war had been against Napoleon, not against France, and that it was a violation of the principles acted on at Vienna to hold the Bourbon monarchy responsible for the transgressions of the usurper. Nevertheless, France was, this time, reduced to the frontiers of 1790. It had to agree a 700-million-franc indemnity, a temporary allied occupation of part of its territory, and the surrender of foreign works of art. This Second Peace of Paris was concluded on 20 November 1815. It explicitly reconfirmed the Final Act of Vienna.[5]

---

[4] Text e.g. in Klüber (1815–18: vi. 1 ff.).
[5] Text e.g. in Chodźko (1864: iv. 1595 ff.).

The allied occupation of France was lifted at the Congress of Aachen (Aix-la-Chapelle) in the autumn of 1818. This sequel to the Congress of Vienna completed the post-Napoleonic rebuilding of the European states system.

In the rest of this chapter, I will examine, first, the attitudes and outlook of the main peacemakers; second, the general political and intellectual climate at the time of the congress; and third, those notions operating at Vienna that can be interpreted as consensus principles.

Since the Holy Roman Empire no longer existed, and since in this chapter three men are mentioned that laid claim to the title 'emperor' (Napoleon of France, Alexander of Russia, and Francis of Austria), the title is no longer capitalized when used on its own.

2. ATTITUDES; 'PRINCIPLES'

2.1. Talleyrand

Talleyrand left a wealth of material concerning his political thinking. His 1792 memorandum has already been quoted. He elaborated on his ideas in documents that he produced as head of the French delegation at Vienna, beginning with his instruction.[6]

Talleyrand's point of departure was the urgent need for international stability. This led him to adopt a determinedly system-oriented outlook. Talleyrand spent a great deal of his time at Vienna and afterwards persuading both European and French statesmen and public opinion that the true interest of France coincided with that of Europe as a whole. 'I have never', he wrote in the preface to his memoirs, 'considered the interests of any party, my own, or those of my friends, before the *true* interests of France, which besides are never, in my opinion, contrary to the *true* interests of Europe.'[7]

In his instruction, Talleyrand only posited a community of interest between France and the smaller states of Europe, not

---

[6] Ibid. i. 215 ff. Talleyrand (1891–2: ii. 152) allows the reader to think that he drew up this instruction himself. Pallain and Webster also ascribe it to him; Talleyrand (1881*b*: i. xvii), Webster (1934: 51). According to Gulick, however, it was conceived by Talleyrand but drawn up by La Besnardière (Gulick 1982: 227). Talleyrand (1891–2: ii. 157 ff.) contains a rather clumsy English trans. of the instruction. Quotations from the instruction in this ch. appear in my own trans.

[7] Talleyrand (1891–2: vol. i, p. x). Emphasis in original.

between France and the other 'great powers'.[8] This was because he did not think that the victorious great powers were prepared to treat France as one of them, which made it seem expedient to appear as the spokesmen of the weaker actors against them. Soon, however, Talleyrand was writing to Metternich that, with regard to the Saxon question, 'the interest of Austria and the interest of Germany' coincided with 'the general interest of Europe'.[9] In the same vein, Talleyrand informed Castlereagh that Britain's and France's interest was the same, and that it coincided with the interest of Europe.[10]

For Talleyrand, divergence of interest was a short-term, transitory phenomenon. In his final report from the congress, written for Louis XVIII, he reiterated that '[a]lthough the French interest might differ from the current and temporary interest [*l'intérêt actuel et momentané*] of some of the powers, it was fortunately in accordance with the interests of the majority, and even with the permanent interests of all.'[11]

Not long afterwards in July 1815, the *Moniteur universel*, a government periodical that Talleyrand used as a mouthpiece to influence public opinion, exhorted its readers to regard Europe

in its entirety and in the general system of its fundamental relations, as a society, a family, a republic of princes and peoples. From this point of view, we perceive that there is, in the midst of so many apparently conflicting and opposing interests, some fixed and indisputable principle capable of solving more than one political problem.[12]

This reference to principle, both emphatic and vague, is typical of the idiom of the Vienna negotiators. Talleyrand, in particular, championed 'principle' and 'principles'. For example, in a letter to Castlereagh he analysed the destabilization of the European system by the French Revolution in terms of a lack of consensus on principles:

[8] Chodźko (1864: i. 217).
[9] 19 Dec. 1814, Metternich (1880–2: ii. 598). This (partial) English trans. of Metternich's papers was published simultaneously with the German edn. Once again, the trans. is not very conscientious. Where I have made changes, page numbers in the German edn. (Metternich 1880–4) are given in square brackets. Metternich (1880–2) gives the date as 12 Dec. 1814, but Klüber (1815–18: vii. 48) has 19 Dec., probably rightly.
[10] 26 Dec. 1814, Klüber (1815–18: vii. 61).
[11] Talleyrand (1881*b*: ii. 220 [1881*a*: 444]).
[12] 27 July 1815, quoted Talleyrand (1881*b*: ii. 259 f. [1881*a*: 457]).

The great and final goal to which Europe must aspire, and the only goal guiding France, is to terminate the revolution, and thus to establish a genuine peace. The revolution has been a struggle between opposing principles. Terminating the revolution means terminating that struggle, which is only possible by ensuring fully the triumph of the principles in defence of which Europe has taken up arms.[13]

In other words, in order to end the turmoil to which the French Revolution had subjected the European system it was necessary to re-establish some system-wide consensus, a consensus which the settlement had to express. Elsewhere in his correspondence, Talleyrand refers variously to 'those principles without which there can be nothing stable in Europe, nor in any state, because they alone can guarantee the security of each and the tranquillity of all',[14] to 'those principles which are the foundation of public order and security',[15] or to 'principles on which rests the security of every throne'.[16]

Especially that of the French throne. 'You and I, My Lord,' Talleyrand told Castlereagh,

desire equally the wellbeing and the repose of Europe, we are striving for the same goal, and our intentions are the same. Our views only differ on the method. Believe me that, if I adhere to mine, the reason is not at all obstinacy but my conviction and my duty not to deviate from principles [*de ne point dévier des principes*: it is not made clear which], not only out of respect for them, and in order to act as I am instructed; but also because the House of Bourbon, if it is to strengthen its hold on the throne that once more it has mounted, has no surer means than to surround itself with that esteem which can only derive from unshakeable attachment to what is just [i.e. in accordance with prevailing consensus notions].[17]

Principles, for Talleyrand, would restore to France the rank that was due to it in Europe,[18] not least by winning over both the smaller actors, less interested in power-political stratagems, and public opinion.

---

[13] 26 Dec. 1814, Klüber (1815–18: vii. 62).
[14] To Louis XVIII, 6 Jan. 1815, Talleyrand (1881b: i. 251).
[15] To Louis XVIII, 17 Nov. 1814, ibid. 140.
[16] To Louis XVIII, 19 Oct. 1814, ibid. 75.
[17] 5 Oct. 1814, Klüber (1815–18: viii. 69).
[18] To Louis XVIII, 9 Oct. 1814, Talleyrand (1881b: i. 30 f.).

Talleyrand employed demonstrative adherence to principles to dispel the widespread suspicion that, as he put it in his final report from the congress,

France was still hankering after the left bank of the Rhine and Belgium, and would never rest until she had recovered them; . . . that therefore the utmost precaution should be taken against France; that barriers through which she could not break must be opposed to her; that the arrangements of Europe must be coordinated to that end; and that all should hold themselves vigilantly on their guard against her negotiators, who would not fail to do everything to defeat it.

Talleyrand went on to state that he 'felt that trust in him was renewed; it was perceived that he was arguing not more in the interest of France than in that of Europe in general, and of each individual state'.[19] Talleyrand did not omit to contrast his own noble behaviour with the other great powers' undignified tussle over the redistribution of territories:

The sovereigns, by their language and their present principles, look like having forsaken the goal for which they armed themselves. They had embarked on a crusade for principles and already they admit to abandoning them. They seem to have detested nothing in Bonaparte other than his success.[20]

It could be argued that France had, in some ways, an easier part to play than other actors. As Friedrich von Gentz, secretary both to Metternich and, for the time being, the congress, expressed it,

The part of the French ministers at this congress was in fact the most simple and agreeable of all. Everything relating to France having been regulated by the Treaty of Paris, they had nothing to demand for themselves, and could confine themselves to watching the conduct of others.[21]

But this is perhaps too negative a formulation, suggesting as it does that France was not in a position to ask for more. Talleyrand, in line with his 1792 memorandum, was adamant that it did not want more. Apart from stability for the European system, that is—and that was no minor desideratum, of course. 'By the [First Peace of Paris]', Talleyrand wrote,

[19] Ibid. ii. 225.
[20] Talleyrand to Jaucourt, 13 Oct. 1814, Jaucourt (1905: 33).
[21] 12 Feb. 1815, Metternich (1880–2: ii. 559 [1880–4: ii. 479]).

France ... was deprived of nothing that was essential to her safety, and she lost only the power of domineering, which had not conduced either to her happiness or to her prosperity, and which was incompatible with the advantages of a durable peace.[22]

2.2. Castlereagh

Britain was represented at Vienna throughout the main part of the negotiations by its foreign minister Castlereagh (until in February 1815 he was replaced by Wellington, later replaced in turn by Clancarty). Castlereagh, too, believed in the virtue of 'principle' or 'principles', however ill-defined. Talleyrand, although he habitually spoke of principles without specifying what he meant, made some effort to define them (as we will see further on). As far as Castlereagh was concerned, the balance of power was the only thing in the way of principles that he was sure he believed in.

Castlereagh distrusted and misread Talleyrand, suspecting him of using his much-flaunted 'principles', in particular that of dynastic legitimacy (on which more later), to enhance the position of France without regard for the cause of Europe. Early on during the congress, Castlereagh wrote to Wellington that

the difference in principle between Monsieur Talleyrand and me is chiefly that I wish to direct my main efforts to secure an equilibrium in Europe, to which object, as far as principle will permit, I wish to make all local points subordinate. M. de Talleyrand appears to me, on the contrary, more intent upon particular points of influence than upon the general balance to be established . . .[23]

But, in fact, for Castlereagh this was not just true of Talleyrand, although the Frenchman was the worst offender. 'Our misfortune is, that the powers *all* look to points instead of the general system of Europe,' Castlereagh told Wellington.[24] Castlereagh's conviction that the British alone were acting responsibly at the congress, a conviction as deeply and, indeed, sorrowfully held as it was patronizing and of questionable justification, did not facilitate relations with his continental interlocutors. They respected Castlereagh's uprightness and his strong sense of duty, but they were amused and exasperated by his obstinacy and bigotry.

[22] Final report to Louis XVIII, Talleyrand (1881b: ii. 216).
[23] 25 Oct. 1814, Webster (1921: 217 ff.).
[24] 20 Oct. 1814, Wellesley [Duke of Wellington] (1861–5: ix. 357). Emphasis added.

Castlereagh seems to have felt that only he knew what Europe needed in terms of a balance of power. Gentz complained that, impervious to other considerations, the British minister aimed too exclusively 'at what he called (often very gratuitously) a just division of forces'.[25] The need to supplement equilibrism by other principles was felt even by the British. However, what was proposed as a content for such principles was not consensus notions but empty moralizing.

Some time before Napoleon's downfall, Charles Stewart, Castlereagh's half-brother and a member of Britain's delegation at Vienna, wrote that '[a] despot without character may do anything. The powers of Europe, on the other hand, must in some degree uphold themselves by the great principles of faith, justice, and moderation.'[26] Castlereagh was much in favour of such high-sounding 'principles'. Already at the abortive peace talks of Châtillon in February 1814, he had told the allies that 'now that [Britain] might look forward to a return to ancient principles, she was ready to make the necessary sacrifices on her part'.[27] And, in a document drafted for the deliberations at Vienna, he spoke of the 'principles recognized as being the necessary basis for the general system of Europe' and to which the leading powers had to adapt their proposals.[28]

But, like Stewart, instead of defining the principles that he had in mind Castlereagh fell back on moralism, insensitive to the fact that moderation was a more attractive precept to an established and satiated power like Britain (by virtue not least of its huge overseas empire) than it was to more marginal and ambitious players such as Russia and Prussia. In the dispute with the Czar over Poland, Castlereagh exhorted the Czar to 'inspire the councils of Europe at the present conjuncture with that spirit of forbearance, moderation, and generosity which can alone secure to Europe the repose for which Your Imperial Majesty has contended', he admonished the Czar to adhere to 'just principles' and not to disregard 'public opinion', and he warned against a 'lawless

---

[25] Memorandum of 12 Feb. 1815, Metternich (1880–2: ii. 574 f.).
[26] To Castlereagh, 10 Jan. 1814, Wellesley (1861–5: viii. 498 f.).
[27] Castlereagh to Liverpool, 6 Feb. 1814, Webster (1921: 146).
[28] *Projet de déclaration... proposé par Lord Castlereagh*, 3 Oct. 1814, Klüber (1815–18: viii. 64).

scramble for power' (which, in the French version, became 'une lutte sans frein pour acquérir du pouvoir au dépens des[!] principes').[29] (Castlereagh drew up his communications in English, and gave them to Gentz to translate into French. Gentz remained faithful to the content, but tended to transform the sober tone of the original into something rather more rhetorical and rousing. It was in this version, of course, that the communications reached their addressees.)[30]

In a subsequent memorandum to the Czar, Castlereagh preached 'liberality', 'indulgence', 'moderation', 'justice'. He reminded the Czar of the 'duty which [the powers, more specifically Russia, Prussia, and Austria] owe to Europe not to aggrandize themselves unduly, either to the subversion of its just equilibrium, or to the unnecessary prejudice of its weaker states.' Castlereagh declared that '[t]he principle [advanced by Russia] . . . of territorial compensation for expenses incurred in war, unless qualified in the strictest sense by its bearing upon the general system of Europe, cannot be too strongly condemned.' Indeed, Castlereagh asserted, '[t]he peace of the world cannot coexist with such doctrines.'[31]

The one concrete concept that can be discerned here is the balance of power; the rest is incriminating rhetoric that had no very positive effect on the relations between the two countries. Indeed, none of the actors at the congress wished to appear as ruthless and selfish. But at the same time it was difficult to reach agreement on anything without a consensus on what exactly was understood by the term 'principles'. Moralizing reliance on 'duty' could not replace this consensus, especially if it appeared as an indignant call on actors who saw themselves as underprivileged not, please, to rock the boat. In international affairs, 'forbearance', 'moderation', and the like cannot create consensus, they presuppose it.

The intrinsic inadequacy of his approach meant that Castlereagh was easily wrongfooted. As a result, he appeared wavering and uncertain despite his stubbornness. He would vehemently defend his views even in the face of increasing opposition, and then change

[29] 12 Oct. 1814. English text: Wellesley (1861–5: ix. 329, 331); French text: Chodźko (1864: ii. 280, 282).
[30] Webster (1950: 331), Gentz (1873: 320, 327).
[31] 4 Nov. 1814. English text: Wellesley (1861–5: ix. 415 f.); French text: Chodźko (1864: ii. 400 f.).

his mind after all while still arguing that he had not. Gentz described Castlereagh as '[g]uided by the purest intentions, but with some radically false views', and as muddled and vacillating.[32] Talleyrand regretted that 'Lord Castlereagh . . . has such imperfect, and I may say foolish notions about everything . . . that, while it is necessary to convince him in even the smallest things, he is extremely difficult to be convinced.' More specifically, Talleyrand deplored Castlereagh's lack of understanding of German politics.[33]

Castlereagh's permanent occupation of the moral high ground was irritating to the peacemakers because, implicitly, it called on them to bow to personal rather than abstract virtue, in contrast to the equally obstinate Talleyrand. At bottom, Castlereagh, in criticizing the peacemakers, told them to be ashamed. This was the more unnerving because the moral standard to which Castlereagh held them seemed arbitrary and vague, while, at the same time, it fostered British interests. In contrast, when Talleyrand criticized the peacemakers, he pointed out not sin, but error.

2.3. Russia

Although Castlereagh went as far as to tell the Czar that his policies were not in the interest of his subjects, the Czar did not lose his temper. He delegated the rebuttal of the detailed points made by Castlereagh to his advisers, and responded personally with dignified restraint. 'Concerning the care that I owe to my own subjects,' he told Castlereagh, 'and my duties to them, it is for me to know what they are, and the uprightness of your motives alone enabled me to go back on the original impression which reading that passage of your letter produced in me. For the rest, my answer and my confidence in you on this occasion bear witness, My Lord, that my sincere feelings for you have not changed.'[34]

The Czar's forgiveness was helped by the knowledge that he depended on British goodwill. He had gained immense admiration as Europe's liberator from the Napoleonic yoke, and he intended to build on this admiration to make Russia a respected, permanent key player in European politics. If he allowed himself to be drawn into a war with 'established' major actors, such as,

---

[32] Memorandum of 12 Feb. 1815, as n. 25, above.
[33] To Louis XVIII, 19 Jan. 1815, Talleyrand (1881*b*: i. 270 f.).
[34] Chodźko (1864: ii. 352).

above all, Britain and Austria, then Russia might be pushed once again to the periphery of the European system. Moreover, such an outcome would squander the prestige gained in the fight against Napoleon. This explains the Czar's keen desire not to destroy the wartime entente. In an effort to optimize Russia's position, that entente might be stretched almost to breaking point, but it was not allowed to suffer lasting damage. Meanwhile, it was good policy to humour the British as much as possible.

In January 1815 Castlereagh, in a note to the three eastern great powers,[35] registered the British desire that Poland, short of regaining its independence, should be granted a measure of national autonomy by the three powers among which it remained divided. Castlereagh saw this as a safeguard for the stability of the partition. He feared that Russia would use preferential treatment of its own section of Poland to incite rebellion in Prussian and Austrian Poland if Berlin and Vienna did not adopt a similar line.[36] But the main purpose of brandishing this note was as a sop for pro-Polish popular opinion in Britain.

Russia, Prussia, and Austria hastened to reassure Castlereagh of their good intentions. By insisting on what they all chose to call the 'principles' laid down by Castlereagh, they exploited to the full this opportunity to highlight their unselfishness and their willingness to cooperate. This was despite the fact that, in this instance, Castlereagh himself had not used the term 'principles' at all, and that the content of the note, moralizing and vague, scarcely warranted it.

Castlereagh's note explained that

Experience has proved, that it is not by counteracting all their habits and usages as a people that . . . the happiness of the Poles . . . can be preserved. A fruitless attempt, too long persevered in by institutions foreign to their manners and sentiments, to make them forget . . . their existence and even language as a people, has been sufficiently tried and failed. It has only tended to excite a sentiment of discontent and self-degradation, and can never operate otherwise, than to provoke commotion, and to awaken them to a recollection of past misfortunes.[37]

---

[35] English text: Webster (1921: 287 f.); French text: Chodźko (1864: ii. 795 ff.).
[36] Castlereagh to Liverpool, 11 Jan. 1815, Webster (1921: 287).
[37] Webster (1921: 288); compare Chodźko (1864: ii. 796).

Such noble sentiments were a little unconvincing if it occurred to anybody to replace the expression 'the Poles' in this text with 'the Irish'. The Kingdom of Ireland, having been granted self-government only in 1782, was suppressed after an anti-British rising and annexed by the United Kingdom in 1801. Castlereagh himself had been one of the authors of this measure. The three east European great powers could consider themselves quite safe from actual British complaints over their treatment of the Poles as long as, in order to answer such complaints, it was enough to mention the word 'Ireland'.[38]

Even prior to Castlereagh's note, Russia had advocated some measure of national autonomy for the Poles to be granted by all three eastern powers.[39] Razumovsky and Nesselrode, the Russian ministers who replied to Castlereagh on behalf of the Czar, declared that '[t]he fairness [*justice*] and liberality of the principles enshrined in the English note have been welcomed by His Imperial Majesty with the utmost satisfaction.' They added that 'His Imperial Majesty is pleased by the conformity of intentions and sentiments manifested on this occasion by His Royal Highness the Prince Regent of England, and by the spirit of conciliation by which Viscount Castlereagh is constantly animated'—the latter remark presumably being somewhat tongue-in-cheek.[40]

Czar Alexander wanted Russia to be recognized as a full member of the European system, on an equal footing with such established powers as Austria, Britain, or France. For all its size and resources, Russia suffered from a strong inferiority complex. It was regarded as a semi-barbarous country both abroad and by its own leadership, a conspicuous portion of which had been recruited from other nations (among the Czar's principal advisers at Vienna, Nesselrode, Stackelberg, and vom Stein were German, Anstett was Alsatian, Czartoryski Polish, Laharpe Swiss, Pozzo di Borgo Corsican, and Kapodistrias Greek). As the Czar and his advisers saw it, Russia needed to control east Europe in order to be taken seriously in the counsels of Europe. Its planned westward expansion would increase its interface with west Europe.

By this scheme, Sweden acquired Norway in return for Russia's acquisition of Finland. Prussia was to receive Saxony and the

[38] Treitschke (1879: i. 659).
[39] See e.g. the note by Nesselrode to Austria, Britain, and Prussia, 31 Dec. 1814, Klüber (1815–18: vii. 69 ff.).   [40] Chodźko (1864: ii. 797, 799).

Rhineland, and Austria parts of Italy, in return for which the Czar would become king of all Poland. The Nordic transaction was clinched before the congress convened. At the same time Britain and Austria were worried by Russia's expansion at the expense of Turkey and Persia, about which they could do little. However, they *were* able to intervene in the settlement of the Polish issue, because that was on the agenda of the Vienna congress. As a result, at Vienna, the Czar's designs on Poland met with strong opposition from Castlereagh and Metternich.

This opposition to the Czar's Polish plans was all the more galling because he attached special importance to Poland—a Slavic country like Russia itself, but one that was seen as more 'civilized' and developed, more 'European' than Russia. Poland would be Russia's foot in the European door. Already in his first letter from Vienna, Talleyrand had reported to Louis XVIII that '[o]ne of the Russian ministers said to us [the French delegation] yesterday: "They wanted to make an Asiatic power of us; Poland will make us European." '[41]

In fact, this desire to be European naturally predisposed Russia to go along with what it could be persuaded were to be the accepted guidelines of European politics in the future. But it would have required a lot of faith to consider 'generosity', 'liberality', and the like as plausible candidates for these guidelines. That kind of discourse could only appear as a disingenuous way of keeping Russia down and out. The old concept of balance of power or the new great-power concept were a different matter.

The desire to play a leading role in the European system also prompted the Czar to adopt a markedly ideological stance. This proved somewhat counterproductive, because it aroused the irritation or even amusement of the other leading powers. At first, the Czar posed as the champion of political modernity, and inveighed against any return to pre-revolutionary ideas. Later, he exchanged this stance for an emphatic, missionizing espousal of Christianity, to the point of making his fellow negotiators question his sanity. No doubt a present-day psychologist would have diagnosed an image neurosis. This will be illustrated more fully as the chapter progresses.

[41] 25 Sept. 1814, Talleyrand (1881*b*: i. 2).

2.4. Prussia

Prussia also signalled allegiance to 'principles' over the Polish issue. Its reply to Castlereagh's note stated that

The undersigned [Hardenberg, the Prussian chancellor and head of the Prussian delegation] having taken the orders of the king his august master concerning the note of H.E. Lord Castlereagh on the arrangements for the affairs of Poland hastens to assure His Eminency that the principles therein developed concerning the manner of administering the Polish provinces placed under the dominion of the various powers are very much in accordance with the sentiments of His Majesty.... The undersigned feels great satisfaction to have been able to outline, on behalf of his court, ... principles so much in accordance with those of the British government.[42]

Of the five great powers at Vienna, Prussia was the pushiest and most blatantly 'selfish', that is, the least system-oriented in its policies. This is explained by the fact that it was by far the weakest among the great powers and that the disastrous humiliation that it had received at the hands of Napoleon had deeply traumatized it. Moreover, Napoleon had left it with a very odd, sprawling geographical shape, which meant that the length of its frontiers was disproportionate to its size and that its possessions were practically undefendable. As a consequence, Prussia put forward only such 'principles'—for example, the right of conquest—as were likely to abet its goal of expansion and of becoming the equal of the other great powers. The importance of the system as a whole, let alone of any kind of obligation to it, was played down.

This is shown, for example, by two memoranda composed by Wilhelm von Humboldt, one of the Prussian plenipotentiaries, in September 1814. In these memoranda, Humboldt stated that 'Europe does not form a constitutional body [*un ensemble constitutionnel*]', which was something that he regarded as 'forever and intrinsically impossible'. For Humboldt, Europe was merely a 'theoretical entity [*un ensemble idéal*]' that was not 'subject to constitutional norms'. The congress was 'not just *one* negotiation, not even one group of negotiations closely linked by a common goal, but simply a bundle of different negotiations leading to as

---

[42] Chodźko (1864: ii. 801).

many separate treaties, and with no other link between them than the general interest of Europe.'[43]

The way in which Humboldt dwelt on this issue indicates that Prussia felt under pressure from 'Europe' to conform to a more system-oriented outlook, to show greater solidarity with the other powers, and that it resented this as likely to perpetuate its own relative fragility. Gentz wrote indignantly that 'Prussia only brought to the congress an immoderate desire for extending her possessions at the expense of all the world, and without regard to any principle of justice or even of decency.' He noted that, because only Russia could be expected to support Prussia wholeheartedly over its efforts at aggrandizing itself, the Berlin government 'had made the first principle of its policy a blind submission to the will of that power [Russia].'[44]

Even the nineteenth-century historian Treitschke, that inveterate apologist of Prussia, admits that 'Prussia's diplomacy [at the congress] was not of the same standard as its military achievements'.[45] However, Prussia's stance was not as machiavellian and dismissive of the 'general interest' as the brashness with which it was sometimes presented made it appear. As Prussia saw it, showing the restraint that was demanded of it would not optimize the interest of Prussia and that of the system alike. On the contrary, such restraint would amount to a subordination of Prussia's interest to that of the system, which was something that none of the other great powers was under any necessity or prepared to do. Humboldt wrote to Hardenberg, the head of Prussia's delegation at Vienna, that

Frankly it is very doubtful whether we would merely sacrifice our momentary advantage to the real and permanent interest of Prussia, if in the Polish affair we went along with Austria. Rather it has to be admitted that, in this case, Prussia would give up its personal interest [daß Preußen dann sein persönliches Interesse aufgibt] to espouse the cause of Europe. Nevertheless, Prussia will always act in accordance with principles, and never seek mere expediency [Dennoch wird Preußen immer den Weg der Grundsätze und niemals den der reinen Konvenienz einschlagen].[46]

---

[43] Webster (1934: 156, 164). Compare Humboldt (1903: 164 f.). Emphasis in original.
[44] Memorandum of 12 Feb. 1815, Metternich (1880–2: ii. 557 [1880–4: ii. 478]).
[45] Treitschke (1875: 658).
[46] Memorandum of 25 Oct. 1814, quoted Treitschke (1879: i. 632).

2.5. Metternich

Metternich, in replying for Austria, told Castlereagh that

At no time did Austria see a free and independent Poland as a rival and hostile power, and the principles that had guided the emperor's august predecessors as well as His Imperial Majesty himself, until the time of the partitions of 1773 and 1797, were only abandoned owing to a combination of pressing circumstances, over which the sovereigns of Austria had no control.[47]

Once again, the 'principles' to which this text alludes can only be guessed at. There may be a reference here to the autonomy principle and the concomitant implicit rule barring the gratuitous elimination of actors from the system—a rule that also came into play in the case of Saxony. Metternich, even though or because he knew that this was not a real option, may have been sincere in wishing for a restored independent Poland, which, from an equilibrist point of view, would have served as a counterweight against Russia. But he may equally well have acted in the knowledge that such discourse cost him nothing.

At any rate, Metternich was in charge of a political entity that was as large as it could reasonably expect to be. Indeed, given its size and heterogeneity, keeping it together presented difficulties as it was. The populist aspirations that had provided the momentum for revolution in France and elsewhere had already shown their proclivity to react and combine with that other potent factor, nationalism. This mixture proved an excellent fuel for revolution, capable as it was of mobilizing the masses when an abstract, maybe complicated, political programme alone would not have performed as well. Contrary to what is often assumed, nationalism was nothing new. But previously it had either not been associated with any political programme at all, or, as in the case of the old German Empire, it had actually been harnessed to a conservative programme. Those days were over. The flirtation between radical politics and nationalism that became characteristic of post-1789 Europe thenceforth posed a mortal threat to the old order.

---

[47] Chodźko (1864: ii. 799 f.). The note is co-signed by Wessenberg. The dates as well as the facts are wrong. The partitions took place in 1772, 1793, and 1795. Austria was reluctant to agree to the first of these and not a party to the second. It was, however, instrumental to the third, by which Poland disappeared from the map as an independent country.

Of none of the actors was this more true than Austria—a motley bunch of territories and nationalities held together exclusively by the dynasty, which for its legitimacy relied on secular tradition. In post-1789 Europe, this set-up put it in a difficult position. If the populist thinking that was behind the recent upheavals, and which people at the time often referred to simply as 'the revolution', triumphed, other actors might survive in one form or another, but the Habsburg monarchy would be finished. Indeed, Metternich was determined to fight 'the revolution' regardless of the chances of success, even 'to my last breath'.[48] The new political ideas might be a timebomb, but at least he would ensure that it was ticking away as slowly as possible.

The rule of non-destruction of autonomous actors, which had lapsed so fatefully during the Napoleonic era, must have appealed to Metternich:

The course that the emperor [of Austria] has followed . . . can leave the powers with no doubt, not only that the re-establishment of a Kingdom of Poland, independent and handed back to a national Polish government, would have given utter satisfaction to His Imperial Majesty, but that he would have been prepared to make greater sacrifices to achieve the salutary restoration of this ancient order of things.[49]

As it was, Metternich was in agreement with Castlereagh that it was necessary for a government to have 'just regards [de justes égards]' for 'the nationality and the habits' of its subjects, and he assured his British colleague how much the intentions of the Austrian emperor were 'in accordance with these principles'.[50]

In looking at Metternich's utterances, it is noteworthy that any principles referred to in them are always other people's, and if Metternich agreed with them, he preferred to do so in someone else's name. He did not put forward principles himself, and it may be doubted whether he had any. Henry Kissinger suggests that this shows a supreme insight and logic.[51] Faced with the challenge of 'the revolution', the conservatives, in order to defend their position, resorted to abstract principle—because abstract principle

---

[48] 'Wird die Frage gestellt, ob die Revolution ganz Europa überschwemmen wird, so möchte ich nicht dagegen wetten, aber fest entschlossen bin ich, bis zu meinem letzten Atemzuge gegen dieselbe zu kämpfen.' 10 Apr. 1820, Metternich (1880–4: iii. 323).
[49] Chodźko (1864: ii. 799).   [50] Ibid. 800.   [51] Kissinger (1957: ch. 11).

was what 'the revolution' used against them. Metternich understood (at least intuitively) that not only was this battle over principle difficult, even impossible, for the conservatives to win, but that the very act of joining it amounted to a defeat. The strength of the old order was its spontaneity, its being taken for granted. Once it was destroyed by being discussed, that spontaneity was lost irretrievably and then *had* to be replaced by principle, or, failing that, violence. Metternich acted on the premiss that by preventing and eschewing debate on, let alone concessions to, abstract principle in any form, this erosion of spontaneity could be slowed down, and the staying power of the old order, increased.

3. THE POLITICAL CLIMATE AT THE CONGRESS

3.1. System-consciousness

One strong bond between the negotiators was their awareness of a common responsibility for the future destiny of Europe, and of the *need* for consensus if the political condition of Europe was to improve from what it had been in the preceding two-and-a-half decades. The peacemakers also knew that the destiny of each of the actors that they represented was intertwined with the destiny of the others, and that whatever policies were adopted by one of them would have repercussions on all the others and elicit strong responses from them. As a result, the peacemakers approached the congress with a very high degree of 'system-consciousness'. This is reflected in the widespread use of the term 'system' itself in the foreign-policy discourse of the period.

Gentz, for example, in a draft final declaration of the Eight Powers dating from February 1815, referred to the 'social order', the 'general system', and the 'political edifice' of Europe, and emphasized the need for a 'political system endowed with a universal sanction [*revêtu de la sanction universelle*]'.[52] Castlereagh, too, on numerous occasions spoke of the 'general system of Europe'.[53] The Russian delegation insisted on a 'system of genuine political

---

[52] Klüber (1835: 191 f.).
[53] See e.g. the *Projet de déclaration . . . proposé par Lord Castlereagh*, 3 Oct. 1814, Klüber (1815–18: viii. 64), or his memorandum to the Czar of 4 Nov. 1814, Chodźko (1864: ii. 400).

equilibrium',[54] and Nesselrode, one of the Russian ministers, spoke of the 'system of pacification with France'.[55] Talleyrand was planning a 'permanent system of common guarantee and general equilibrium',[56] and the *Moniteur universel* held forth on the 'general system of [the] fundamental relations' of Europe.[57] It would appear that the very word 'system', and by extension the system-oriented approach that it implied, had positive connotations, and that it was used eagerly because of the political credibility that, it was hoped, it would bestow. It shared this quality with the word 'principle(s)'.

The general acceptance of the desirability of a system-oriented approach is also apparent from other expressions. In a declaration to the Poles of May 1815, the Czar spoke of admitting his new kingdom to the *cercle des nations*, calling it 'this new link in the chain of European interests'. In fact, the Czar told the Poles that, if their national hopes had been realized only in part, this was because the interest of Europe as a whole had to take precedence over their own.[58]

The expression employed in the declaration is *l'intérêt général*. Numerous other references to the 'interest of Europe', the 'common good of Europe', etc. could be adduced. Sometimes, the importance attached to the system as a whole was emphasized by a term with a stronger emotive appeal, such as the expression 'the European family' employed by the Duke of Saxe-Coburg when he appealed to Castlereagh to preserve Saxony.[59]

Also worthy of note is the assiduous use of religious phraseology. Every treaty signed in the context of the congress is headed by an invocation of the Trinity, a habit that was observed more strictly on this occasion than at the two congresses discussed in the earlier chapters. Indeed, it is probable that the habit was clung to so painstakingly precisely because it was felt to have outlived itself. It was deemed indispensable because no substitute seemed available.

It is true that attempts were made in some quarters to revive religious community feeling. The most famous of these attempts

[54] Russian memorandum to Castlereagh, 21 Nov. 1814, Chodźko (1864: ii. 453).
[55] Nesselrode to Castlereagh, 7 Sept. 1815, in Stewart [Viscount Castlereagh] (1853: iii. 11).
[56] Final report to Louis XVIII, Talleyrand (1881b: ii. 232 [1881a: 457]).
[57] Quoted Talleyrand (1881b: ii. 259 n. 21).
[58] Chodźko (1864: iii. 1224).   [59] 14 Oct. 1814, Klüber (1815–18: vii. 16).

was the 'Holy Alliance', thought up by the Czar during the negotiations for the Second Peace of Paris in the summer and autumn
of 1815. The Holy Alliance was not a treaty but a declaration of
intent, to be signed by all the sovereigns of Europe. It pledged
them to a *fraternité véritable et indissoluble*, by virtue of which they
would all 'consider themselves exclusively as members of the single
Christian nation [*d'une même nation chrétienne*]', their various
dominions being but 'branches of the same family'.[60]

The Holy Alliance was derided by Castlereagh, who, in a famous
passage, spoke of it as 'this piece of sublime mysticism and nonsense'. The Czar paid a personal visit to Castlereagh to introduce
him to his project:

The Duke of Wellington happened to be with me when [the Czar] called,
and it was not without difficulty that we went through the interview with
becoming gravity.... Upon the whole this is what may be called a
scrape ... The fact is, the emperor's mind is not completely sound.[61]

The original document called, not for a return to, or the preservation of, any old or existing order, but for a visionary new
departure, suggesting that never yet had international dealings
lived up to the Czar's lofty aspirations. Since, rather infelicitously,
this implicitly condemned the Vienna congress, Metternich undertook a rewriting that made the settlement appear as part of what
the Czar had in mind.[62] Metternich subsequently dismissed the
project as a 'philanthropic aspiration clothed in religious garb'
and as a 'useless scheme' liked neither by the Emperor of Austria
nor even by the pro-Russian King of Prussia.[63] Metternich insisted
that '[t]he Holy Alliance was not an institution to keep down the
rights of the people, to promote absolutism or any other tyranny.
It was only the overflow of the pietistic feeling of the Emperor
Alexander'.[64] In fact, Castlereagh, Metternich, and Talleyrand all
favoured the full integration of the Islamic Ottoman Empire into
the European system. But this pro-Ottoman policy was hindered
by Russian claims on Ottoman territory, the acceptance of which
was the Czar's condition for allowing the Ottoman Empire to be

[60] 26 Sept. 1815, Chodźko (1864: iv. 1547 ff.).
[61] Castlereagh to Liverpool, 28 Sept. 1815, Webster (1921: 383 f.).
[62] See e.g. Kissinger (1957: 188 f.).
[63] Metternich (1880–2: i. 260 ff.).   [64] Ibid. 262.

covered by the Vienna settlement. The scheme eventually came to nothing.

I suspect that, for the Czar, the exaltation of the Christian commonwealth of Europe served a subconscious motive—that of enhancing the club of which the Czar was not only so keen to be a full member, but of which, as a result of this initiative, he might flatter himself to be the spiritual leader. Indeed, his earlier liberalism was hardly 'the latest' any more, while Christian romanticism was becoming the fashion all over Europe. The Czar obviously looked rather grotesque in his endeavours to keep abreast of philosophical fashion. But it is significant that, despite the scorn and hilarity of his fellow negotiators, their criticisms were not voiced publicly. All the Christian European actors subscribed to the 'alliance' (except the Pope, for whom it was too ecumenical). And although the text was completely innocuous and contained no programme for action, it came to be regarded widely as a veritable conspiracy of monarchs and as a sinister instrument of counter-revolutionary oppression. To statesmen whose thinking was still grounded in eighteenth-century rationalism and the doctrines of the enlightenment, the effusive religious terminology that the document contained might seem absurd. However, the need for some kind of unifying ideology was evidently admitted by them.

3.2. Public Opinion and the Problem of Populism

3.2.1. General Remarks

Observers are often inclined to dismiss the effect of public opinion on international decision-making because it is difficult to demonstrate. Frequently, public opinion is too diffuse and unfocused, as well as, in the short term, too ill-informed, to exert pressure on politicians to do (or not do) specific things. Instead, public opinion influences decision-makers because they anticipate the way in which their actions will be judged retrospectively in the eyes of the public.

Public opinion often acts as an amplifier for consensus notions. It has done that during the entire period considered in this book. Reasons of space make it impractical to look at this phenomenon in greater detail. Concerning the Vienna congress, however, what made it different in this respect from the earlier ones was the self-conscious way that public opinion was monitored by the peacemakers. The serene self-awareness of the Utrecht system was replaced at Vienna by anxious self-consciousness.

The difference from the situation before 1789 was that, in future, order could only rest on principle or on oppression, that it could never again be quite spontaneous. If this was not yet fully the case, the tendency was, nevertheless, inescapable. Whatever violent upheavals the old Europe had experienced, it had always been able to fall back on custom as a source of consensus. In the nineteenth century custom, already dealt a severe blow by 'the revolution', continued to be eroded whatever anyone might do to slow the process down.

As a result, despite all the endless festivities celebrating the post-Napoleonic restoration, the peacemakers were in a precarious position. Napoleon was gone, but 'the revolution' had only gone underground. Dance as they might, the political order that the plenipotentiaries represented was under mortal threat from current and ultimately unstoppable social developments. The genie of populism was out of the bottle and nothing could put it back in. All of the main negotiators sensed this.

There were two possible ways of dealing with the new political climate, the threat of revolution: one could either face the storm or try to ride it. But, in any event, it was necessary to watch the masses carefully, even anxiously. They had flexed their muscles, and ignoring them would have been madness.

During his stay in Paris as Austrian envoy under Napoleon, Metternich had complained in 1808 to his chief, Foreign Minister Stadion, about the lack of any attempts by the government in Vienna to feed the right sort of information to the German press. 'Public opinion', Metternich wrote,

is the most powerful of all means; like religion, it penetrates the most hidden recesses, where administrative measures have no influence. To despise public opinion is as dangerous as to despise moral principles . . . Posterity will hardly believe that we have regarded silence as an efficacious weapon to oppose to the clamours of our opponents, and that in a century of words! . . . The newspapers are worth to Napoleon an army of three hundred thousand men, for such a force would not control the interior better, or frighten foreign powers less, than half a dozen of his paid pamphleteers.[65]

---

[65] 23 June 1808, ibid. ii. 226 f. [1880–4: ii. 192 f.].

Having taken over from Stadion as foreign minister, Metternich saw to it that, at the congress, the German press wrote what the Vienna government wanted it to write; Gentz was in charge of ensuring this.

Gentz predicted that deference to public opinion would prevent the break between the allies that many thought the dissension over Poland and Saxony made inevitable. Gentz explained to a correspondent that

in the whole course of the latest events, the sovereigns federated [*coalisés*] to destroy the ascendancy of Napoleon have regarded public opinion as one of their main supports, and . . . far from neglecting this opinion, they have rather laid themselves open to the accusation (if it is one) to have listened to it too much on some occasions. The Emperor Alexander, in particular, attaches the utmost importance to it; whatever his political or personal ambitions, I am sure that he would rather sacrifice them than to be seen in the eyes of the public as unjust, ungrateful, or a disturber of the public peace [*la tranquillité générale*] . . .[66]

Talleyrand also attached great importance to public opinion, instructing his deputy in Paris, Jaucourt, what to insert in the *Moniteur universel* and why.[67] Talleyrand also kept up a propaganda offensive at Vienna. This reached a climax in the solemn requiem that in January 1815, on the anniversary of the execution of Louis XVI, he arranged in St Stephen's cathedral. 'I do not yet know what it will cost,' he told Louis XVIII, 'but the expense is a necessary one.'[68] It was a monumental celebration of his cherished principle of dynastic legitimacy, which he made the entire congress attend (only the Czar, who did not like the principle, refused).

The religious occasion was only a pretext for what nowadays would be termed a media event. Talleyrand did not have much faith in organized Christianity. 'Formerly', he told the French king,

the secular power could derive support from the authority of religion; it can no longer do this, because religious indifference has penetrated all classes and become universal. The sovereign power, therefore, can only rely upon public opinion for support, and to obtain that it must seek to be at one with that opinion.[69]

---

[66] To Karadja, 9 July 1814, Gentz (1876: 87 f.).
[67] See e.g. Talleyrand to Jaucourt, 13 Oct. 1814, Jaucourt (1905: 33).
[68] 4 Jan. 1815, Talleyrand (1881*b*: i. 240 f.).
[69] Final report to Louis XVIII, ibid. ii. 242 f. [1881*a*: 469].

Therefore, Talleyrand urged, the king ought immediately to grant the democratic rights that the French people demanded, and to give up any outmoded pretence to absolutism. The passage dates from June 1815 and is informed by the shock of the return of Napoleon and the realization of how shaky the Bourbon cause actually was. By this time, it seems, Talleyrand's earlier confidence in the malleability of public opinion had given way to a more resigned belief that it was too strong a force to be manipulated and had therefore to be humoured.

Talleyrand had observed with some gloating the discomfiture suffered by the Czar in his own endeavour to appear as the champion of public opinion. At first, the Czar distinguished himself by his ostentatious flirtation with political radicalism. He emphasized his solidarity with popular aspirations and supported them against his fellow sovereigns. As Gentz explains, the Czar was 'an adherent of modern political ideas, great admirer of the famous [French] constitution of 1791, and, above all, anxious to please all parties, all sects, and all individuals'.[70] But, at the congress, the energetic backing that the Czar gave to Prussia's designs on Saxony cost him dearly in public relations terms—even though he appears to have claimed, somewhat feebly, that the annexation of the whole of Saxony (rather than just some of it) by Prussia would really be in line with the will of the Saxon people, which was keen to remain undivided.[71]

Talleyrand was highly critical of the Czar abetting, as he saw it, a revival of the revolutionary convulsions that the congress was supposed to terminate. He was pleased to find that both the Czar's stance on the Saxon question and his progressive rhetoric met with increasing disapproval (though which was most responsible for the public's disenchantment with him is hard to tell). In October 1814 Talleyrand noted that 'public opinion becomes day by day more favourable to the cause of the King of Saxony',[72] and in January 1815 he observed that '[t]he Emperor Alexander, with his liberal ideas, has made so little way here, that it has been found necessary to triple the police force in order to prevent his being insulted by the people in his daily walks.'[73] (This took place before

---

[70] To Karadja, 11 Apr. 1814, Gentz (1876: 76 f.).
[71] Talleyrand to Louis XVIII, 7 Dec. 1814, Talleyrand (1881b: i. 192 f. [1881a: 167 f.]).
[72] 25 Oct. 1814, Talleyrand (1881b: i. 92 f.).   [73] 25 Jan. 1815, ibid. 278.

the Czar gave up being a liberal and became a Christian romantic instead—although his conversion was already under way, helped, in all likelihood, by his waning appeal as a liberal.)

Castlereagh reported to Liverpool, the British prime minister, his own impression that '[t]he general sentiment of dissatisfaction and alarm occasioned by his [the Czar's] conduct is becoming too strong and too universal to be any longer a secret from him. . . . Under these circumstances . . . perhaps His Imperial Majesty may moderate his pretensions'.[74] Indeed, Castlereagh had personally warned the Czar that '[i]f Your Imperial Majesty should leave public opinion behind you . . . I should despair of witnessing any just and stable order of things in Europe'.[75]

Metternich in November 1814 told Castlereagh that, in an interview with Hardenberg, he had argued 'the impolicy of attempting to extinguish totally that monarchy [Saxony], against the declared purpose of France and the prevailing feeling of Germany.'[76] A little later he told Castlereagh that,

however desirous of bending, as far as possible, for the sake of an adjustment, he [Metternich] did not feel that he could venture to run counter, on the Saxon question, to the moral feeling of Germany, to the sentiments of his own cabinet, and to the declared opinion of the French government . . .

To do so would deprive Austria of the necessary support in Europe against the St Petersburg–Berlin axis.[77]

The Czar eventually changed his mind; but so had Castlereagh, who, at the beginning of the congress, had been more than ready to hand Saxony over to Prussia. Public opinion in Britain was opposed to the annexation,[78] and in a letter to Cooke, a member of the British delegation, Prime Minister Liverpool expressed his hope that Saxony would be saved at least in part. 'I do not like the annihilation of ancient independent states,' Liverpool wrote. 'I am persuaded the annihilation of Saxony would produce the worst moral effects in Germany and throughout Europe.'[79] To Castlereagh, he wrote that '[i]t is just that the King of Prussia

[74] 25 Nov. 1814, Webster (1921: 243).
[75] 12 Oct. 1814, Wellesley (1861–5: ix. 331).
[76] Castlereagh to Liverpool, 21 Nov. 1814, Webster (1921: 240).
[77] Castlereagh to Liverpool, 5 Dec. 1814, ibid. 250.
[78] Gentz to Karadja, 20 Dec. 1814, Gentz (1876: 127).
[79] 9 Dec. 1814, Wellesley (1861–5: ix. 468).

should gain, but the total and unnecessary annihilation of one of the oldest powers of Europe would revolt the feelings of all mankind.'[80]

It is true that public opinion in Britain was at least as favourable to an independent Poland as it was to preserving Saxony ('we shall have a hard battle to fight against public opinion in defence of any arrangement of which the independence of Poland does not now form a part', Liverpool informed Castlereagh).[81] However, no structural principle could be harnessed to the cause of Poland. Balance-of-power considerations could, and were, satisfied by keeping Poland divided, while dynastic legitimacy was not applicable. Poland had been an elective monarchy—the belated attempt to make it hereditary in 1791 failed. It had lapsed two decades earlier, an event that was not directly connected with the struggle against the French Revolution and Napoleon. In these circumstances, the re-establishment of Poland had to wait for the advent of the nationality principle a hundred years later. Saxony was different. Here, both the balance-of-power principle and the principle of dynastic legitimacy provided powerful focuses for public opinion, making it virtually impossible to ignore.

3.2.2. Analysing the Polish–Saxon Issue: A Critique of Webster, Gulick, and Kissinger

There is substantial evidence, then, to suggest that public opinion did enter into the thinking of the Vienna negotiators. This section is given over to a critique, in the light of this fact, of some approaches to the Polish–Saxon imbroglio by authors writing in English. The problem is, indeed, rather complex, and it is little wonder that both the decision-makers in charge and subsequent scholars have had a hard time with it.

Webster, having noted the 'attempts to influence the decisions of the congress through public opinion', concludes that

[i]t cannot, however, be said that they affected the decisions of the statesmen in any material degree. The Polish–Saxon question was settled purely on grounds of expediency; and the populations of Germany were transferred from one monarch to another, with scarcely the slightest reference to their wishes.[82]

---

[80] 6 Jan. 1815, ibid. 531.   [81] 25 Nov. 1814, Webster (1921: 246).
[82] Webster (1934: 93 f.).

This invites the general objection put forward earlier—the difficulty of measuring, even of establishing, the impact of public opinion on political decision-making is no reason to dismiss that impact. The fact remains incontrovertible that, on the Saxon question (over which public debate became most heated, producing a strong consensus opposing the annexation), four out of the five great-power delegations reversed their stance, while Talleyrand, who was in line with public opinion on this point, triumphed.

The 'expediency' argument put forward by Webster and elaborated upon by Gulick is empty. Webster does not make it clear quite what he actually means by 'expediency'—he uses the term as if it were self-explanatory, which it is not. Gulick, on the other hand, seeks to prove that Metternich and Castlereagh acted in accordance with the precepts of Gulick's own balance-of-power theory. This has resulted in a book that contrives to account for the peacemakers' every act in terms of some Gulick theorem.

For Gulick, the position was as follows: Russia wanted the bulk of Poland, and it wanted Saxony to go to Prussia in recompense. Metternich, the argument continues, could accept either half of this scheme, but not both, because that would have given Austria a too-long and too-hard-to-defend common frontier with the other two actors. When the attempt to induce Prussia to oppose Russia by promising it Saxony had failed, both Metternich and Castlereagh therefore opposed the absorption of *all* of Saxony by Prussia— logically so, as Gulick would have it, in terms of the desirability of a strategic equilibrium between the three actors concerned. In short, according to Gulick, the balance of power was only compatible *either* with Russia obtaining Poland *or* with Prussia obtaining Saxony.

This raises the following points. Hardenberg, the Prussian chancellor, accepted Castlereagh's and Metternich's offer of Saxony in return for Prussian help in the rollback of Russia; but he was disavowed by the Prussian king after the Czar, on hearing of this scheme, threw a memorable scene. If Hardenberg had had his way, and if Russia had been deprived of most of Poland as a result, would this not have left Prussia, increased by Saxony *and* a substantial share of Poland, in a position in which it could be dangerous to Austria? Would, in this event, the common border between Prussia and Russia on the one hand, and Austria on the other, have been any shorter? If it was any more defendable, how much would that really have mattered, in what is essentially flat country?

Given that the King of Prussia refused to implement the scheme, what was the logic of denying him all of Saxony, unless it was to 'punish' him for being uncooperative? Hardenberg certainly took the view that that was what it was, as Gulick himself admits in passing.[83] From a purely equilibrist point of view, Prussia should have been given Saxony more than ever at this point! Castlereagh had originally advocated the absorption of all of Saxony by Prussia because, as the weakest and territorially by far the smallest of the major actors, Prussia needed strengthening in order to play its proper part in the balance of Europe as a whole. If denying *all* of Saxony to Prussia was intended as a means of inciting it to seek a greater share of Poland, then once again this was merely political bribery and not, as Gulick would have it, applied equilibrism—since Metternich and Castlereagh had, after all, been prepared to give Prussia the bigger share of Poland *and* Saxony in return for 'good behaviour'.

Kissinger, in his somewhat different analysis of the Polish–Saxon dispute, rightly emphasizes that Metternich had both the European and the German level to concern himself with, that Castlereagh neglected the latter, and that, on the German level, the problem of ensuring the acceptance of the settlement was of special significance.[84] Kissinger reached this view despite a somewhat careless reading of the sources, which is discussed in the Appendix.

Territories were, of course, important, but not as much in themselves as is often supposed. For Metternich, more than anything, the outcome of the redistribution talks mattered as an indicator of how successful Austria was at *asserting itself*. Austria was anxious to confirm its role as a principal international player, after its inglorious record during the Napoleonic period. If, on the European level, Russia could be held at bay, and the threat that the Czar's plans posed to Austria's *European* position (in terms of prestige and credibility as much as anything else) could be averted, the sacrifice of Saxony would be worthwhile—albeit under protest to minimize the resulting damage to Austria's standing in Germany. But if Russia could not be thwarted, Austria certainly could not afford to fail on this front *and* lose face in the German

---

[83] Gulick (1982: 222 f.).   [84] Kissinger (1957: ch. 9, esp. pp. 155 ff.).

Confederation as well. If Austria bowed to Prussia, which was much smaller than itself but backed by an overpowering Russia, and a member of the Confederation of the size and standing of Saxony was gobbled up as a result, it would make a mockery of the Austrian emperor's credibility as the Confederation's head. Hence the absolute necessity, in this event, for a substantial portion of Saxony to be preserved as an independent state. (In his correspondence with Hardenberg, Metternich had been careful from the start to stress the illegitimacy of suppressing Saxony—a clever reinsurance tactic, which gave him something to fall back on, and which was in marked contrast with Castlereagh's stubborn insistence on an allied right of conquest.) This was not simply a matter of 'expediency', and it *was* important, vitally important, to Austria what German and European opinion thought of it.

In this situation, Castlereagh had the choice only between supporting either Hardenberg or Metternich. He opted, of course, for Metternich, if nothing else because Prussia had antagonized him. It would have been foolish to offend Metternich for having been willing to cooperate, and to reward Prussia for failing to do so. But this means that, however reluctantly, Castlereagh went along with the Metternich–Talleyrand line. He even emphasized this himself—for example, in his Commons speech of 20 March 1815.

In this speech, Castlereagh insisted that there was no question of simply restoring the old international system of Europe. He inveighed against the 'principle of imbecility' of wanting to rebuild 'those rude and shapeless fabrics . . . those scattered fragments . . . those antiquated and ruinous institutions . . . those very governments [that] had tended to produce the calamities by which Europe had been so long and so severely visited'—and he insisted that Prussia, by virtue of some allied right of conquest, was entitled to Saxony. This was his defence against the criticism that he should never have advocated the elimination of Saxony from the map of Europe at all.

But, in another part of the speech, Castlereagh affirmed explicitly that he was

persuaded that the public feeling not merely of the people of Germany, but of other countries, would have been wounded by so great and complete a sacrifice of an ancient family; that the general opinion of mankind would have revolted at such a proceeding, and that Prussia would be prejudiced in the general estimation of Europe by the annexation.[85]

As to Webster's remark suggesting that the wishes of the German populations were not heeded in the redistribution of territories, it is misleading. Like so many historians, Webster falls into the trap of projecting back into the past the consensus notions of a different age. His remark effectively presupposes the principle of national self-determination that became generally accepted only at the end of the First World War (which is when Webster was writing). At the time of the Vienna congress, national self-determination was present as an idea held by some, but it was not a consensus principle of the international system. In reality, while the redistribution of territories by the congress may not always have been welcomed, ill-feeling, such as in Saxony, was restrained. In any case, the political climate in early nineteenth-century Germany was resolutely pan-German, leaving little room for particularism.

In conclusion, we should discard the popular image of the Vienna decision-makers cutting up Poland and Saxony with only strategic considerations in mind, sheltered from, and with utter disregard for, the international consensus agenda and the clamours of public opinion. Strategic considerations (or whatever else is meant by 'expediency' to the exclusion of consensus notions) had their part in the proceedings, but they were by no means solely responsible for the final result.

3.2.3. Populism Resisted

It is true that the negotiators sometimes disregarded public opinion. Talleyrand pointed out to Louis XVIII how strongly the leniency of the First Peace of Paris went against public opinion in Prussia and Russia.[86] And when the Second Peace of Paris was in the making, Castlereagh noted that, in proposing further dismemberment of France, a policy not eventually implemented, Austria and Prussia were under strong pressure from German public opinion. 'Their politics', he wrote to Liverpool from Paris in August 1815,

---

[85] Webster (1921: 396; 401 f.).
[86] Final report, Talleyrand (1881b: ii. 216).

at this moment, receive an extraordinary impulse from the public sentiment of Germany, from the temper of the smaller powers, and from the
desire they each feel not to yield to the other the influence in Germany
which belongs to what is most popular. No doubt, the prevailing sentiment throughout Germany is in favour of territorially reducing France.
After all the people have suffered, and with the ordinary inducements of
some fresh acquisitions, it is not wonderful that it should be so . . .[87]

But it is important to note that, in each case, public opinion was
unsupported by any consensus principle. This lack of focus took
away much of its thrust.

Kissinger makes it clear that the leniency even of the Second
Peace of Paris was mainly due to the fact that Castlereagh stub-
bornly resisted the clamour for revenge and for territorial safeguards against any future resurgence of the 'French danger'.[88] In
doing so, Castlereagh not only braved German public opinion and
the resulting pressure from Prussia, Austria, and the 'smaller
powers', but the prevailing mood in Britain and, indeed, the London
cabinet. This is reminiscent of Oxford and Bolingbroke doggedly
pushing through their controversial peace, which, nevertheless,
proved successful because of its scrupulous respect for the international consensus agenda. The autonomy and self-esteem even
of the vanquished were preserved. Indignation and a rash desire
to punish might be running high, but they were not fired by violation of a consensus principle. This was a temporary effervescence,
which it would have been dangerous to allow to affect the shaping
of a settlement built to last. In 1815 as in 1714, indignation sub-
sided quickly and the settlement became accepted.

The validity of this reasoning is demonstrated *ex contrario* by the
infelicitous peace treaties of 1919–20, which will be discussed in
the next chapter. At Paris in 1919–20, the peacemakers very much
allowed themselves to be influenced by a 'public sentiment' or
'temper' which they shared without detachment, at the expense of
the consensus agenda. The result was protracted disaster, only
eventually remedied at horrendous cost.

It is particularly interesting to observe the debate on the conditions of the Second Peace of Paris from a post-Versailles perspective. Prime Minister Liverpool, writing in early August 1815,
formulated the dilemma:

---

[87] 17 Aug. 1815, Stewart (1853: ii. 488).   [88] (1957: 178 ff.).

we are involved with our allies in this very embarrassing alternative: By demanding considerable sacrifices from France for the security of Europe, we unavoidably lower the character of the government, which it is our wish to uphold. On the other hand, the stability of that government, after the allies shall have evacuated France, is so very problematical, that we should not do our duty by Europe if we looked to no other security than that which the legitimate government of the King of France could in itself hold out to us.[89]

As can be seen, Liverpool was aware of the fundamental problem but wavering. A week later he insisted that '[h]owever desirous we may be of seeing the government of Louis XVIII popular in France', this objective should not be achieved at the expense of 'everything which is judged important for the general security of Europe'.[90] In other words, he did now separate international 'security' and the reaction of France to the way in which it would be treated: the emphasis on 'security' rather than stability indicates the lack of any solid awareness that security was better served by consensus than by fortresses.

Prussia was the most vociferous, among the great powers, in demanding the punishment of France (it is true that it was also the only one to share a—short—border with France, as a result of its new Rhenish possessions). 'France', the Prussian chancellor Hardenberg wrote,

has again disturbed [the peace]; Europe has generously pardoned France last year. Experience has shown that this generous trust in the loyalty of the French nation has failed to achieve the desired aim. Once more to entertain such generosity would be impardonable. Europe therefore owes it to itself, and every power owes it to its peoples, to take such safety precautions as will protect them from being easily disturbed by France. Europe has the right to demand such guarantees, since France has not proved itself worthy of its trust and its generosity.[91]

Metternich, in the run-up to the First Peace of Paris, had been an eager advocate of conciliation, to the point that he 'desired to reserve the consideration of some concession to France, neither extensive nor important in itself, beyond the ancient limits', as a gesture of allied goodwill towards France.[92] Both in 1814 and in

[89] To Canning, 4 Aug. 1815, Wellesley (1861–5: xi. 95).
[90] 11 Aug. 1815, Stewart (1853: ii. 479).
[91] 4 Aug. 1815, Chodźko (1864: iv. 1479 f.).
[92] Castlereagh to Liverpool, 29 Jan. 1814, Webster (1921: 143).

1815, there was pressure on Habsburg, from Prussia, Russia, and others, to repossess Alsace, but Metternich would not hear of it. Metternich was not guided by a narrowly conceived 'national' interest. He knew that international stability—which presupposed conciliation—was crucial above all else if the erosion of the old order was to be retarded. If the seeds of further war were sown by allowing irredentism to be generated in France, then that would obviously afford 'the revolution' fresh opportunities. 'This war', Metternich declared in August 1815,

must not degenerate into a war of conquest . . . . because any considerable alteration in the distribution of territories such as it has been established by the Congress of Vienna would result in a general shift, in which the aim of the war, *the urgent necessity to put a stop to [mettre un frein à] the principles subversive of the social order, on which Bonaparte has founded his usurpation* . . . , would be lost straight away . . .

Under pressure, however, from public opinion and his cabinet, he went on to point out that French aggression was not something that the French Revolution had invented, but something that had also been visited on Europe by royal France, and that the idea should be destroyed among the French that such aggression, even if it failed, would never produce any unpleasant consequences for France itself. He therefore called for the cession or at least the dismantling of the outer line of French border fortresses.[93]

Russia, helped by the fact that it was neither under any direct threat from France nor in a position to obtain additional territory there, was adamant that there ought to be no punishment of France. Kapodistrias, one of the Czar's ministers, wrote that

We would undo from its inception the restoration of that monarchy if we oblige the king to consent to concessions that would indicate to the French people the extent of the distrust with which the allied powers view the stability of their own work. To reduce directly the strength of the French nation, in order to oblige it to respect the government that Europe is prepared to recognize as legitimate, would be saying to France that such a government is a disaster for it . . .[94]

In this situation, the stance taken by Britain was decisive. Wellington, fresh from his victory at Waterloo, laid down his views in an important letter to Castlereagh.

[93] Chodźko (1864: iv. 1482 ff.) (exact date not given). Emphasis in original.
[94] 28 July 1815, ibid. 1472.

My opinion is, that the French Revolution and the [First] Treaty of Paris have left France in too great strength for the rest of Europe, weakened as all the powers of Europe have been by the wars in which they have been engaged with France . . . Notwithstanding that this opinion is as strongly, if not more strongly, impressed upon my mind than upon that of any of those whose papers have lately come under my consideration, I doubt its being in our power now to make such an alteration in the relations of France with other powers as will be of material benefit.

Wellington argued that, if France was to be reduced territorially, another war was pre-programmed. Nor would territorial safeguards then matter decisively:

We must . . . , if we take this large cession, consider the operations of the war as deferred till France shall find a suitable opportunity of endeavouring to regain what she has lost; and, after having wasted our resources in the maintenance of overgrown military establishments in time of peace, we shall find how little useful the cessions we have acquired will be against a national effort to regain them. . . . Revolutionary France is more likely to distress the world than France, however strong in her frontier, under a regular government; and that is the situation in which we ought to endeavour to place her.[95]

Castlereagh also felt that '[t]hese arguments about . . . strategic boundaries are pushed too far. Real defence and security comes from the guarantee which is given by the fact that they cannot touch you without declaring war on all those interested in maintaining things as they are.'[96] He, too, pointed out that, concerning a territorial diminution of France, 'it is one thing to wish the thing done and another to maintain it when done'. In a passage that one wishes the Versailles peacemakers had borne in mind, Castlereagh argued that, if only the French king's authority could be established firmly, then this would be

valuable beyond all other securities we can acquire. . . . If on the contrary, we push things now to an extremity, we leave the king no resource in the eyes of his own people but to disavow us; and, once committed against us in sentiment, he will be obliged soon either to lead the nation into war himself, or possibly be set aside to make way for some more bold and enterprising competitor.

[95] 11 Aug. 1815, Wellesley (1838: 596 ff.).
[96] Webster (1950: 268) (n.d. given).

Castlereagh insisted that 'it is not our business to collect trophies, but to try if we can bring back the world to peaceful habits.
I do not believe this to be compatible with any attempt . . . to
affect the territorial character of France'. And given the threat to
Europe that, in Castlereagh's view, the expansion of Russia posed,
he wondered whether France, 'even within her existing dimen-
sions, may not be found a useful rather than a dangerous member
of the European system.'[97]

No revenge was taken on France, even though the Second Peace
of Paris was less lenient than the First. Reparations were exacted,
but the French were allowed to bargain about the sum, which was
much reduced eventually from the initial proposals. France was
deprived of some peripheral territories that had not been within
its 'ancient limits', as well as of the fortress of Landau in the
Palatinate and the looted works of art. However, France still made
a gain, compared to what it had possessed before the French
Revolution. It was allowed to retain without compensation all the
territorial enclaves previously owned by foreign rulers, and which
it had annexed in the 1790s (Avignon and the Venaissin, which
had belonged to the Holy See, and the remaining possessions of
some German princes in Alsace).

Though the French were indignant, the Second Peace of Paris
did not violate any part of the international consensus agenda, nor
was it seriously humiliating. As a result, Prime Minister Richelieu
was able to lay it before the Chamber of Deputies and the Chamber
of Peers with an impressive and clever speech (written by
d'Hauterive), urging acceptance and reconciliation:

Far from us, gentlemen, the unwise idea of forming for the present or of
sowing for the future the seed of impolitic and dangerous discontent! . . .
    France, pitted against all the nations, has deployed extraordinary
energy; all states have suffered from its efforts; almost everywhere, France
has carried its victorious arms; but, it must be said, wherever it has conquered, it has given rise to fears, provoked vengeance, and inspired
resentment, which only time, only a great moderation, only a persevering
and invariant prudence offer the means of allaying. . . .
    We have enough sought, we have enough obtained the fatal glory won
by the courage of armies and the bloodstained trophies of their victories:
there remains a better glory for us to obtain; let us force the peoples,
in spite of the suffering that the usurper has inflicted upon them, to be

----

[97] To Liverpool, 17 Aug. 1815, Stewart (1853: ii. 488 ff.).

dismayed at the suffering that they are causing to us; let us force them to trust us, to come to know us, to be frankly and forever reconciled with us.[98]

4. CONSENSUS PRINCIPLES AT VIENNA

The purpose of the remainder of this chapter is to identify the main consensus notions current at the time of the Vienna congress. They will be considered in ascending order of importance and effectiveness.

4.1. The Right of Conquest

The notion of right of conquest was at the centre of much debate at the congress. It was put forward determinedly by some parties as a way of legitimizing changes to the map of Europe—in other words, attempts to employ this notion as a consensus principle were certainly made. But the notion of right of conquest failed the test of public opinion and therefore did not acquire the status of a consensus principle.

Initially, the victorious great powers were inclined, and, in some cases, determined, to uphold the right of conquest. A protocol drawn up by the Four Powers in June 1814 and adding Belgium to the Dutch state declared bluntly that the powers took this step 'by virtue of their right of conquest of Belgium'.[99] But a few months later such language had become difficult to hold, even though Prussia continued to defend the right of conquest until the issue of Saxony was settled. Castlereagh was equally stubborn at first, and heatedly supported Prussia on this point. Metternich avoided committing himself, although he was by no means sympathetic to Prussia's designs on Saxony.

Public opinion generally turned against the right of conquest, and invoking it proved to be a strategy that was both costly in public relations terms and ineffective. After all, it was rather poignant for the victors to be reminded by the French delegation, of all people, that conquest had been the very basis of the Napoleonic hegemony, and an outgrowth of that revolutionary spirit

[98] 25 Nov. 1815, Chodźko (1864: iv. 1644 ff.).
[99] 14 June 1814, ibid. i. 182.

which the congress was there to exorcize. To ignore this contradiction was impossible.

Gentz commented in early October 1814 that '[t]he measure to be inflicted on [Saxony] is blatantly unjust [*d'une injustice criante*]. The Prussian ministers themselves cannot conceal it, and feel very keenly the difficulty of defending it.'[100] And in early November 1814 the French delegation reported to Paris that 'Prince von Hardenberg has admitted to one of his friends that he believes that this incorporation of Saxony is very distasteful to Germany, and that Prussia would perhaps consent to leave a nucleus of it.'[101]

Castlereagh, in two notes of October 1814, had given Prussia full support over Saxony. He elaborated at length on why the Saxon dynasty deserved no better, even claiming that, had the Saxon king been an officer in command of a fortress, the language that he had employed to defend his 'criminal conduct' would make him liable to execution by firing squad.[102] Gentz, who translated at least one of these notes into French, told Metternich that he had done so 'with a feeling of shame'; that he could not understand how anyone with a reputation to lose could lend his name to such spurious arguments; that he did not want to believe that a cause defended in such a way could succeed, and that he had a premonition that it would not; that 'the voice of the world' was against it; and that the British might yet come to regret the role that they had played in this issue.[103]

Indeed, as early as 25 October Castlereagh himself confided his hope to Liverpool that, with regard to Saxony, public opinion would have a moderating effect on Prussia. Castlereagh expressed his opinion that the French strategy of defending Saxony by stressing the illegitimacy of its extinction was wrong—implying that, by this stage, he had in fact come to sympathize with France's objective of preserving Saxony. Indeed, Castlereagh eventually advised Hardenberg not to press the claim to all of Saxony 'against the general sentiment of Europe'. He even urged Prussia to take greater account of the German subsystem, pointing out that

in proportion as he [Hardenberg] had failed to bring forward his king upon the Polish question, he ought to be accommodating on that of

[100] To Karadja, 6 Oct. 1814, Gentz (1876: 114); see also 20 Dec. 1814, ibid. 125.
[101] 6 Nov. 1814, Talleyrand (1891–2: ii. 296).
[102] Wellesley (1861–5: ix. 339 f.), Klüber (1815–18: vii. 10 ff.).
[103] 13 Oct. 1814, Gentz (1913: 303).

Germany, if he wished to be respected among his co-estates, and not to build his authority amongst them upon an external influence [i.e. Russia's].[104]

As can be seen, Castlereagh had, at this stage, espoused the Metternich line fully in practice, whatever he might say in public.

One factor contributing to the failure of the concept of right of conquest to be included in the international consensus agenda was that nobody adopted a logically consistent stance on this point. Quite the contrary. When Napoleon had returned from Elba and regained office, the plenipotentiaries of all the allied powers put their signature to a text denying that his uncontested military control of France could ever provide him with a title to representing his country.[105] Castlereagh, who had so ardently defended the right of conquest over Saxony, denied that it was applicable to Poland, so as to be able to resist the Russian claim to that country. When the Czar pointed out that he was in control of Poland, occupied by the Russian troops that had captured it, Castlereagh actually replied that

it was very true, His Imperial Majesty was in possession and he must know that no one was less disposed than myself hostilely to dispute that possession, but I was sure His Imperial Majesty would not feel satisfied to rest his pretensions on a title of conquest in opposition to the general sentiment of Europe.[106]

In September 1815, in defending the further territorial demands made on France in the run-up to the Second Peace of Paris, Castlereagh assured Louis XVIII that the allies 'founded their claims in no degree upon the right of conquest'.[107] And in his Commons speech of 20 March 1815, Castlereagh rejected allegations by the opposition 'that Austria and Prussia were endeavouring to seize and appropriate to themselves, as if by right of conquest, territories to which they have no right, upon any principles of moderation or fair repartition.'

Castlereagh could not bring himself to admit to having been wrong over Saxony, and he still reiterated in the same speech

---

[104] To Liverpool, 7 Dec. 1814, Webster (1921: 255 f.).
[105] This text was submitted for approval by the signatories of the Peace of Paris on 12 May 1815. Klüber (1815–18: vi. 290 ff.; see esp. 293 f).
[106] To Liverpool, 14 Oct. 1814, Webster (1921: 208).
[107] To Liverpool, 25 Sept. 1815, ibid. 380.

that 'I must be allowed to argue, and I do it with perfect confidence, that never was the principle of conquest more legitimately applicable, or more justifiably exerciseable than in the case of Saxony.'[108] But a concept over which it was possible to adopt such a contradictory approach obviously did not qualify as a consensus notion.

4.2. Dynastic Legitimacy

4.2.1. The Role of Kingship in Europe

Together with the balance of power, the concept of dynastic legitimacy is the best known of the political ideas dominating the congress. Talleyrand, who simply referred to it as 'legitimacy' without further specification, saw this principle as a major safeguard of stability in Europe. But in order to put it into context, it is necessary, before proceeding, to look at the role of kingship in general, in pre- as well as post-revolutionary Europe. What deserves emphasizing here is the fact that dynastic legitimacy had played little role in European international politics before the late eighteenth century.

What distinguishes the traditional concept of kingship, even absolutist kingship, from dictatorship is its being rooted in a strictly hierarchical social order. In this social order, rank was largely determined by birth, and there was little social mobility. The social hierarchy was pyramid-shaped, with the number of individuals at each social level declining the closer one moved to the top. For as long as the notion prevailed that political authority presupposed high social rank (which, in practice, meant high birth), such an order tended naturally towards supreme authority being vested in the few or, indeed, in a single person. To wear a crown it was not always necessary to inherit it—but it *was* necessary to make sure that one had the right sort of ancestors, and enough of them. Indeed, the number of elected rulers in pre-revolutionary Europe was higher than is generally realized, comprising the (German) Emperor, the Kings of Poland, Bohemia (until 1628), Denmark (until 1660), and Hungary (until 1687), a number of Swedish rulers (elections for the Swedish throne were held in 1650, 1719, 1720, 1743, and again in 1810), the German and Swiss ecclesiastical

---

[108] 20 Mar. 1815, ibid. 400, 401.

princes, and, of course, the Pope himself. The degree of dynastic continuity in these elective monarchies was quite variable.

Another explanation for the prevalence of kingship in early modern Europe is suggested by the fact that purely republican regimes were only found in relatively small communities, most of which were highly urbanized. In a republic, it was necessary to have supreme decision-making units comprising more than one person. These units had to be both small enough to work efficiently, yet at the same time they had to be considered representative of the community's political élite (which, to put it very simply, was virtually always made up of the more important property-owners). The domestic political legitimacy of republican government could not be 'borrowed' from the monarch (who for his or her legitimacy could rely simply on his or her social background and the legality of his or her accession: he or she did not have to be representative or efficient). But representativeness required that the decision-making units kept in close touch with the class that they represented. Given the slowness of the available means of communication, this was obviously much easier if the distances over which communication was necessary were short. This is one reason why the republics of the *ancien régime* were small compared to the larger monarchies.

There were some self-governing farming communities, notably within the German Empire (the most famous example perhaps being the 'peasants' republic' of Dithmarschen) and in Switzerland. But this phenomenon required that the soil was owned by those who cultivated it, and not mostly in the hands of a non-farming, higher social class. Since the latter was the normal situation in pre-revolutionary Europe, republican spirit was usually found in cities. Unlike the land-owning class in the countryside, the members of the urban propertied classes dwelt in close proximity, which made collective decision-making easier. In addition, country estates were often quite autarchic. Urban political élites, on the other hand, were mostly made up of merchants and craftsmen, who shared between them a much closer network of mutual relations and dependencies than existed in the countryside. This made collective decision-making desirable.

As a result, territorially more sizeable, predominantly agrarian communities where ownership of the land was concentrated in the higher strata of society—a description that fitted most of Europe—

were sociologically unlikely to support republicanism. Interestingly, the territorially large actors that, prior to the French Revolution, developed quasi-republican regimes of some permanence also still retained the institution of kingship—the Polish Republic (1572–1795) and the Sweden of the so-called 'age of liberty' (*frihetstid*, 1718–72), during which power lay with the Riksdag estates. On the other hand, the Doge in Venice and Genoa or the Dutch Stadhouders were really semi-monarchical figures, too.

We are led to conclude, therefore, that, in fact, there was no clear-cut division between the various constitutional categories, but a continuum, a spectrum of forms of government. This ranged from the strictly hereditary, absolutist kingship of the French type to the more purely collective forms of decision-making found, for example, in the city republics of the German Empire. Various kinds of hereditary or elective rulers, who wielded greater or lesser power and bore variegated secular or ecclesiastical titles, populated the space in between.

Sometimes, these forms of state defied the learned attempts at putting them into abstract categories, most notoriously in the case of the German Empire. On the other hand, eighteenth-century France and Sweden, for example, are both conventionally described as monarchies, but they could hardly have been more different in their constitutional arrangements—the one concentrating all power in the hands of the ruler, the other leaving him or her virtually none. If they had one thing in common, it was what they also had in common with all the other international actors—their hierarchical social order.

The prevalence of monarchical regimes was linked, then, to notions of legitimacy, but it was not necessarily or primarily dynastic legitimacy that came into play here. What mattered most was the legitimacy of the hierarchical social set-up, of which kingship was simply the outgrowth. The legitimacy of the highest political office-holder, whatever his or her description, was derived from the twin sources of social standing and legality of accession, and, of the latter, heredity was only one form.

The first French republic, in the 1790s, still underwent a similar historical experience to the English Commonwealth in the 1650s or the Roman republic in the first century BC—when a polity was too large for collective government by the ruling élite, kingship returned through the back door in the adulterated form of military dictatorship. But around the turn of the nineteenth century conditions were changing. The French Revolution had begun to experiment with the concept of *representative democracy*, of *mandated* assemblies representative of the people as a whole. For the first time in Europe, this made republicanism a serious possibility not confined to small communities. Representative democracy provided a source of political legitimacy that was relatively easy to handle even in a larger polity. Moreover, from the rationalist point of view, this type of legitimacy was attractively independent of the arbitrary qualification of social standing.

The new concept of political equality of all men was incompatible with power being wielded by someone who owed his or her position to birth. Although the concept could and does cohabit with a great deal of inequality in practice, a hereditary monarch with real power had by the early nineteenth century become too conspicuous a symbol of inequality to be legitimate in the eyes of progressive opinion.

For conservative opinion, however, both among the nobility and among the bourgeoisie, kingship was the most conspicuous symbol of the old order, which, at least to some degree, it wished to retain. (True, the bourgeoisie tried to wrest the nobility's political power from it—but, at the same time, it sought to imitate the nobility's lifestyle, and was keen to keep the lower social strata excluded from power.) But the old order could only be defended if the higher social classes closed ranks against possible intruders and usurpers. Applied to the concept of kingship, this meant, under the conditions of the new era, that the crown could not possibly be elective any more. At the same time, however, anyone who wielded power in the new era was expected somehow to be 'representative'. In these circumstances, in order to survive as a politically meaningful institution kingship had to square the circle.

It failed, of course. In France, the constitutional monarchy of Louis XVIII was followed in turn by the aristocratic neo-absolutism of Charles X and the 'democratic' kingship of Louis-Philippe ('le roi citoyen'). Then came a republic replaced by a dictatorship soon converted into an imitation monarchy, and ultimately a republic again. The alternative to such upheavals was the British model—discreetly stripping the monarchy of all power, while retaining it as a legitimizing agent for domestic arrangements that also evolved towards greater populism.

4.2.2. The Position at Vienna and the Ideas of Talleyrand

At the time of the Vienna congress, revolutionary innovation had resulted in a potential for choice, even for erratic switching between forms of government. To defend themselves—their authority as well as the social order of which they were the outgrowth—the princes waged war on 'the revolution' (as 'the revolution' waged war on them). But some people, like Talleyrand, also realized that rulers had to do more: they had to enhance their legitimacy.

The heightened concern with dynastic legitimacy was a defensive reflex on the part of that section of the European political classes—the nobility and, increasingly, the upper bourgeoisie—that had hitherto been in control of most politics, domestic or international (or, at any rate, that aspired to such control, as in the case of the bourgeoisie). For the first time, the princes and their followers were faced with a serious challenge. It was Talleyrand who, at the congress, elaborated the concept of dynastic legitimacy and defended it with some success. But, obviously, he could not have done so if the concept had not already been 'in the air'. It was the longing for political repose that had found a focus in dynasticism, erroneously credited with having been, not merely the hallmark of the old order, but the cause of its stability.

Because the fixation with dynasticism was so much based on wishful thinking, the underlying fallacy went unchallenged. Talleyrand believed, or wanted to believe, that dynastic legitimacy was an essential safeguard for stability. In his view, stability could only be ensured in the long run if, in each state, power was transferred from one individual to the next in a manner that did not give rise to internal quarrels.

The French instruction posited that '[t]he usual and almost inevitable consequence of an uncertain right of succession is to cause domestic or foreign wars, and often both simultaneously'.[109] Talleyrand elaborated on this idea in his final report from the congress and in his memoirs. Both in the instruction and the final report, 'legitimate' government is taken to mean the reign of an ancient dynasty. In his memoirs, Talleyrand specified that

I speak of the legitimacy of governments in general, whatsoever be their form, and not only of those of kings, because it applies to all governments. A lawful government, be it monarchical or republican, hereditary or

---

[109] Chodźko (1864: i. 222).

elective, aristocratic or democratic, is always one whose existence, form, and mode of action, have been consolidated and consecrated by a long succession of years, and I should say almost, by a secular prescription. The legitimacy of the sovereign power results from the ancient status of possession, just as, for private individuals, does the right of property.[110]

But Talleyrand, in the memoirs, went on to explain that he still considered monarchical regimes to be superior. This was because monarchical (hereditary) succession offered the least opportunity for a contest between personalities in which the claimants had to demonstrate their suitability for leadership—an obligation which would incline them to embark on foreign-policy adventures. This attitude was obviously informed by the experience of instability in revolutionary and Napoleonic France. Successive revolutionary regimes sought to forestall their overthrow, forever imminent, by seeking success in foreign wars and expansion. The only one to retain power for a relatively long period did so owing to the military genius of Napoleon—at the price of relentless and, as Talleyrand well foresaw, eventually self-destructive aggrandizement.

Talleyrand justified the concept of dynastic legitimacy in purely pragmatic terms, and explicitly rejected any admixture of mysticism.[111] However, he did so against a background of widespread, almost neurotic, fascination with monarchism and its trappings, and it is difficult to avoid the impression that his whole theory of dynastic legitimacy was really a rationalization of subconscious atavistic yearnings.

It is a remarkable fact that in the early years of the nineteenth century republican actors became what looked like an endangered species in the European states system. Poland, Venice, and Genoa vanished as independent states—they could be allowed to vanish because there was no dynasty to uphold there. By 1815 the autonomous city republics found themselves reduced to four, all in Germany (Bremen, Frankfurt, Hamburg, and Lübeck)—though as a spin-off of the Polish imbroglio the congress set up a new one in Poland, the Free City of Cracow.

Meanwhile, among rulers there was a scramble for grander titles. Napoleon started it by adopting the hereditary title of

---

[110] Talleyrand (1891–2: ii. 120).

[111] This is made very clear in Talleyrand's summary of his thinking on the subject of 29 July 1815, in Griewank (1954: 395).

'Emperor of the French' in 1804. Not to be outshone, the head of the House of Habsburg promptly became the self-styled hereditary 'Emperor of Austria'. Since he was still the elected Emperor of Germany (until Napoleon forced him to relinquish that post two years later), he was left with two imperial titles to be worn simultaneously. The rulers of Bavaria, Saxony, and Württemberg decided to upgrade themselves, too, each adopting the appellation 'king'. After the defeat of Napoleon, they were joined by the Prince of Orange, who became King of the Netherlands, and by the Elector of Hanover (who already wore the British crown).

Following a fashion set under Napoleon by the Margrave of Baden and the Landgrave of Hesse-Darmstadt, the rulers of Holstein-Oldenburg, Mecklenburg-Schwerin, Mecklenburg-Strelitz, and Saxe-Weimar were elevated by the Final Act of the congress to the rank of 'grand-dukes'. They were addressed thenceforth as royal highnesses. So was the Landgrave of Hesse-Kassel. In 1803 he had become an elector, and he kept that title even though the dissolution of the Holy Roman Empire in 1806 rendered it obsolete. During a stay at the Vienna congress in October 1814, and again in 1818 in time for the Congress of Aachen, he applied for a royal title, too. Metternich, however, turned him down on the grounds that he was not grand enough. In order both to invalidate this objection and to allay the jealousy of his relative, the Landgrave of Hesse-Darmstadt, the elector put forward the idea of a collective Hessian kingship. The two branches of his house were to take turns wearing the crown. But Metternich drew the line at this firmly, expressing his conviction that such a kingship would lack all dignity. Clearly, the impression was to be avoided that royal titles had by then come within reach of more or less any potentate.[112]

Apart from the five free cities (four German and one Polish) and minuscule San Marino, the only remaining republic was Switzerland; the only remaining elective monarchy, for reasons of its own, the Holy See.

4.2.3. Dynastic Legitimacy and the Framing of the Settlement: Ambiguities and Apparent Triumph

Having engineered the overthrow of Napoleon, Talleyrand set to work to restore the 'rightful' ruler (according to the principle of

---

[112] Metternich to the Emperor Francis, 19 Mar. 1818, Metternich (1880–4: iii. 154); Treitschke (1882: 479).

dynastic legitimacy) to the French throne. He made his point forcefully to the Czar, whom he invited to stay at his townhouse when the allies entered Paris. 'Neither you, sire,' he claims to have told the Czar,

nor the allied powers, nor I, whom you believe to possess some influence, not one of us, could give a king to France. France is conquered—and by your arms, and yet even today, you have not that power. To *force* a king upon France, would require both intrigue and force; one or the other alone would not be sufficient. In order to establish a durable state of things, and one which could be accepted without protest, one must act upon a principle. With a principle we are strong. We shall experience no resistance; opposition will, at any rate, vanish soon; and there is only one principle. Louis XVIII is a principle: he is the legitimate king of France.[113]

It was the Czar who needed most persuading in this respect. Some time before the allied victory, Castlereagh had sounded out his allies about their views on the future government of France. He reported that the Czar had little sympathy for the Bourbon cause.[114] Although the Czar eventually accepted the recall of Louis XVIII by Talleyrand, he continued on many occasions to voice his opposition to the principle of dynastic legitimacy. Many people were shocked by his views (which meant that, at least, he achieved the objective of getting their attention). For example, Ernst von Münster, who represented Hanover (at that time part of the British dominions) at the congress, indignantly reported to London in December 1814 that the Czar 'said . . . to the Duke of Saxe-Coburg, that he counted dynasties and so-called hereditary rights as nothing when the interest of states was in dependence. This overthrows one of the strongest guarantees of the tranquillity of states.'[115]

Metternich thought that a Bourbon restoration was desirable, though he was not inclined to intervene in French domestic affairs to bring it about. Castlereagh shared this attitude.[116] Both were unwilling to subscribe to any *principle* in this respect. As we have seen, Castlereagh would have been happy to sacrifice the Saxon crown, while Metternich was prepared to do so as a last resort. Neither at this stage nor, more surprisingly perhaps, after Louis

[113] Talleyrand (1891–2: ii. 124). Emphasis in original.
[114] To Liverpool, 29 Jan. 1814, Webster (1921: 139).
[115] 17 Dec. 1814, Münster (1868: 206).
[116] Castlereagh to Liverpool, 22 Jan. 1814, Webster (1921: 137 f.).

XVIII had already been restored once, did the allies commit themselves publicly to the cause of dynastic legitimacy. After Napoleon's return from Elba, which drove Louis XVIII into exile once more, the British government made an official declaration stating that the renewed alliance of March 1815

must not be regarded as an undertaking pledging His Britannic Majesty to pursue the war with a view to forcing any particular government upon France. Whatever may be the prince regent's desire to see His Most Christian Majesty restored to the throne, and whatever his eagerness to contribute, in concert with the allies, to that happy outcome, he nevertheless feels obliged to make this declaration . . . , as much out of regard for the interests of His Most Christian Majesty in France, as in order to conform to the principles [once again undefined here] upon which the British government has invariably acted.[117]

Russia, Prussia, and Austria subsequently made an identical declaration using almost the same terms as the British.[118]

Talleyrand was aghast at this prudent refusal to endorse his principle. Others were dissatisfied, too. Clancarty, then head of the British delegation at Vienna, and Münster, the Hanoverian representative, deplored the British government's official attitude, although they could not say so in public.[119]

In fact, Castlereagh made quite an effort to help reinstate Louis XVIII—but he did so behind the scenes. He secretly agreed with Talleyrand that Louis XVIII provided the only option salient enough to hold any promise of stability.[120] Wellington was unsure whether Louis XVIII could be restored a second time, and wondered whether the allies should not rather back the Duke of Orléans. Castlereagh took Wellington's point, but disagreed. 'Various circumstances', he wrote, 'have come to our knowledge tending to confirm Your Grace's [Wellington's] information that the Duke of Orléans has a very considerable party . . . in his favour . . . Our hands must not be tied, however cordially we may

---

[117] British reservation, included in the minutes of the Council of Five, 25 Apr. 1815, Klüber (1835: 143 f.). See Talleyrand (1881b: ii. 186 [ed.'s n.]) and the dispatch by the British ambassador in Paris to Jaucourt, quoted ibid. 271 f. n. See also Talleyrand to Louis XVIII, 23 Apr. 1815, ibid. 176.

[118] Klüber (1835: 144).

[119] Webster (1950: 442); see also e.g. Clancarty to Castlereagh, 19 May 1815, Webster (1921: 335 n.), and Stewart (1853: ii. 355).

[120] See Webster (1950: e.g. 446 ff.).

desire to employ them in support of the legitimate monarch'. However, Castlereagh thought,

were the Duke of Orléans in power, more especially if brought forward improvidently, his authority probably would soon prove incompetent to repress the factions of the country, and it is not the interest of the allies, if obliged to enter upon war, to encourage an early and hollow compromise.[121]

This was really what Talleyrand meant. The problem, for Talleyrand, was that it was not enough just to preserve the same family in power. The Duke of Orléans would not do. For Talleyrand, the case for dynastic legitimacy rested on the need to remove any element of arbitrariness or competition from the order of succession. Louis XVIII had no children. At best, he could have abdicated in favour of his brother, a stubborn reactionary of whom Talleyrand expected the worst. When this brother eventually succeeded to the throne as Charles X, he did cause another revolution and was replaced by the Duke of Orléans after all. But that was in 1830, when the new international system had solidified and was reasonably stable again. In 1815 the situation was much more fluid, and Talleyrand may well have been right in thinking that, if the international system in general and France in particular were to be stabilized, there was no alternative to Louis XVIII. As Talleyrand correctly foresaw, the restoration of Louis XVIII caused surprisingly little opposition either in 1814 or at the repeat performance in 1815—even though it was hardly greeted with enthusiasm. The principle that Louis XVIII represented was indeed accepted, if only because any conceivable alternative would have smacked of prolonging the French Revolution and the concomitant instability at home and abroad. Few people, at the time, were in the mood for that.

Concerning Joachim Murat, the British rather agreed with Talleyrand that to allow the 'illegitimate' King of Naples to continue on his throne was likely to have a destabilizing effect, in particular on France. But, once again, they did not say so openly enough for Talleyrand's liking. Talleyrand complained to Louis XVIII that

---

[121] To Wellington, 16 Apr. 1815, Webster (1921: 330 f.). See also Wellington to Castlereagh, 24 Apr. 1815, Wellesley (1861–5: x. 146 f.).

Your Majesty will probably learn, not without surprise, that attachment to the principle of [dynastic] legitimacy enters little into the calculations of Lord Castlereagh, or even of the Duke of Wellington with regard to Murat; it touches them very feebly; they do not even seem quite to take it in.

Yet Talleyrand indicates that Castlereagh was by no means impervious to his argument, for the letter just quoted goes on: 'Nothing has made so much impression on Lord Castlereagh . . . as my declaring to him that peace would be impossible if Murat were not driven out, for that his occupation of the throne of Naples was incompatible with the existence of the House of Bourbon' (the 'rightful' pretender to the throne of Naples, the King of Sicily, was also a Bourbon).[122] Moreover, Talleyrand clearly did not know that Wellington, in a letter to Prime Minister Liverpool written from Paris just a few weeks earlier, had explicitly subscribed to this point of view.[123]

When Napoleon returned from Elba, Murat gave up his uneasy alliance with the agents of restoration, which had taken the shape of a treaty with Austria. He thereby freed Vienna from a considerable source of embarrassment. Talleyrand confided to his deputy Jaucourt his hope that, as a result, Murat would

shortly be overthrown. The triumph that, on this point, the principle of [dynastic] legitimacy will achieve . . . will, I hope, be the presage of a greater and more complete triumph [i.e. the second restoration of Louis XVIII]. It will promote it both through the forces that are at present employed against Murat and which it will be possible to use against Bonaparte, and through the demonstration that it will afford of everybody's firm resolve to destroy these new dominions, founded on violence and injustice, the existence of which is incompatible with the repose of Europe.[124]

Castlereagh, as we have seen, eventually relinquished his obstinate support for Prussia's and Russia's desire to do away with the Saxon monarchy. Even Prussia felt that it could not simply ignore the principle, as is shown by the fact that, eventually, it proposed to give the King of Saxony a new kingdom somewhere else, for example in the Rhenish territories that Prussia looked set to

[122] 15 Feb. 1815, Talleyrand (1881b: ii. 22 f.).
[123] 25 Dec. 1814, Wellesley (1861–5: ix. 503).
[124] 1 May 1815, Jaucourt (1905: 316).

acquire but did not particularly want.[125] There, the Electorates of Cologne and Trier, former ecclesiastical principalities, could be disposed of without having to displace an established dynasty. Prussia therefore suggested that the Saxon king should be transplanted from Dresden to Bonn, the ex-capital of electoral Cologne. Metternich feared that because of the proximity of this proposed new kingdom to France, and because France had supported the Saxon dynasty all along, the result would inevitably be a French client state that would allow France to exert excessive influence in Germany.[126] Castlereagh had the same fear.[127] However, Talleyrand also rejected the proposal—on the grounds that it was incompatible with his strict interpretation of dynastic legitimacy, and that it was dangerous to imperil the equilibrium both of Germany and of Europe by too much aggrandizing Prussia.[128]

As a result, in January 1815 Talleyrand was able to write that

Austria, England, Bavaria, Holland, Hanover, and almost the whole of Germany are agreed with us upon the maintenance of the King and of a Kingdom of Saxony. A Saxony will therefore be maintained ... All that concerns the principle of [dynastic] legitimacy has been agreed upon between Lord Castlereagh, M. de Metternich, and me.[129]

By the early summer of 1815, then, in spite of all the ambiguities that went before, the triumph of dynastic legitimacy seemed complete: Louis XVIII was back in Paris, Naples had been restored to the Bourbon Ferdinand IV, and 'a Saxony' had been preserved. In a proclamation co-signed by Talleyrand, Louis XVIII declared that

My subjects have learned through cruel trials that the principle of the legitimacy of sovereigns is one of the fundamental bases of the social order, the only one on which a prudent and orderly freedom can be

---

[125] Hardenberg to Metternich, 29 Oct. 1814, Chodźko (1864: iv. 1865). See also Hardenberg to the Czar, 16 Dec. 1814, Klüber (1815–18: vii. 44). Saxony was contiguous with Prussia, German-speaking, and Protestant; Poland was contiguous but non-German-speaking and Catholic; the Rhineland was German-speaking, but non-contiguous and Catholic.

[126] Note by Metternich, submitted in the session of the representatives of the Five Powers, 28 Jan. 1815, Klüber (1815–18: vii. 87).

[127] To Liverpool, 8 Jan. 1815, Webster (1921: 283 f.).

[128] Talleyrand to Louis XVIII, 6 Jan. 1815, Talleyrand (1881b: i. 250 f.); French instruction, Chodźko (1864: 232 f.); Talleyrand to Metternich, 12 [19] Dec. 1814, Metternich (1880–2: ii. 593 ff.).

[129] To Louis XVIII, 19 Jan. 1815, Talleyrand (1881b: i. 269 [1881a: 231 f.]).

established amid a great people. This doctrine has just been proclaimed to be that of the whole of Europe.[130]

To keep it that way, Liverpool, speaking for the British cabinet, repeatedly told Castlereagh to make the return of the French fortresses placed under allied occupation conditional on respect for the principle of dynastic legitimacy:

We are . . . of opinion that it cannot be too clearly expressed that the fortresses are not in any case to revert to France, except it shall be under the government of Louis XVIII, or his successors by rightful inheritance. The explicit recognition of this principle, whilst it explains the motives which have actuated the councils of the allies, affords one of the best securities for the continuance of the king's authority.[131]

4.2.4. The Aftermath: Inherent Weakness and Decline of the Principle; Democracy versus Monarchism

It was, alas, a somewhat specious triumph. Talleyrand was blind to the fact that, in spite of all the temporary attention that he managed to draw to it, his pet principle was not very solid. It might be a good way of ensuring a stable order of succession, but this was increasingly irrelevant in proportion as the rise of democratic aspirations challenged the concept of a hereditary executive. Talleyrand himself became enmeshed in a contradiction here— on the one hand, he defended dynasticism, but, on the other, he also fought absolutism, which he thought would make dynasticism unacceptable to the people. His French opponents, the right-wing royalist 'ultras', did not see the point of restoring the king if his power was to be given to the people—a more logical position, although it was indeed politically suicidal.

As we have seen, in the pre-revolutionary era kingship did not have to be absolute in order to survive, because it was rooted in a hierarchical social order. But with the notions of popular sovereignty and political equality of all citizens unleashed, political agents mandated in some form by the people encroached inexorably and increasingly on the function of the crown. This left three choices: imitation kingship to disguise what was really a populist dictatorship (as practised in France by Napoleon and again by Napoleon III), a kingship that was increasingly ornamental, and

---

[130] 28 June 1815, Wellesley (1861–5: x. 615).
[131] To Castlereagh, 28 Aug. 1815, Webster (1921: 373).

absolutist reaction. For the conservatives, only the last was a real option.

Talleyrand tampered with the life-blood of kingship by insisting that 'the recall of the princes of the House of Bourbon was not the acknowledgment of pre-existing rights. If they so construed it, it was neither on my advice, nor with my assent'.[132] He had forced Louis XVIII to grant a representative constitution (the Charte). Not content with that, in his final report from the congress he urged further democratic reforms.

Indeed, it was the turn of republicanism to return through the back door. Mandated parliamentary assemblies sprang up everywhere, more ambitious and more effective than their precursors in pre-revolutionary Europe. Many people thought that kingship had to live with these democratic assemblies in order to survive, and actively urged their creation in the interest of kingship—in a way, a compromise with republicanism. Talleyrand expressed this when he wrote that

However legitimate a power may be, its exercise nevertheless must vary according to the objects to which it is applied, and according to time and place. Now, the spirit of the present age in great civilized states demands that supreme authority shall not be exercised except with the concurrence of representatives chosen by the people subject to it. . . . These opinions are no longer peculiar to any one country; they are shared by almost all. Accordingly, we see that the cry for constitutions is universal; everywhere the establishment of a constitution adapted to the more or less advanced state of society has become a necessity, and everywhere preparations for this purpose are in progress.[133]

The Czar originally wanted representative constitutions in all states,[134] and Hardenberg and Humboldt, the Prussian plenipotentiaries, insisted on including in the German Act of Confederation an obligation for all member states to enact representative (*landständisch*) constitutions.[135] But many of the German states—among them, ironically, Prussia—evaded this obligation for decades, and Metternich, at a pan-German conference convened in Vienna in 1820, had the relevant article 'interpreted' in a non-democratic sense.

[132] Talleyrand (1891–2: vol. i, p. ix) (from a declaration dated 1 Oct. 1836, which Talleyrand added to his will).
[133] Final report to Louis XVIII, Talleyrand (1881b: ii. 238, 244 f.).
[134] Treitschke (1879: 604).   [135] Art. 13; text e.g. in Huber (1961: 78).

The basic reason was as follows. The principle of dynastic legit-imacy as conceived by Talleyrand was actually inoperative. The new political forces had no reason to be particularly attached to it, while the princes realized that it would not ensure their sal-vation. A different, simpler concept soon prevailed, namely that only monarchical rule was legitimate. This came to be called the 'monarchical principle'. With it went a concomitant rule of mon-archical solidarity—meaning that, if kingship was in danger any-where, all rulers had a duty to intervene to uphold it.

This new reactionary conception was one that all the great powers rallied to. Somewhat in contradiction with their earlier maxim of non-intervention, the allies decided after the final defeat of Napoleon to impose a temporary occupation on France. The occupation troops were to be commanded by Wellington, who was instructed by the allies to use these troops to maintain Louis XVIII on the throne, and to protect him against any revolutionary undertakings.[136]

At the Congress of Aachen in 1818, the French request that the occupation troops should be withdrawn was granted. The French king seemed safe again and the impression was to be avoided that he was being imposed on France. An agreement to lift the occu-pation was signed on 9 October. The foreign ministers of all five great powers stated in a joint final declaration that that agreement

is regarded by the sovereigns who have concluded it as the finishing touch of the peace settlement, and as a complement of the political system destined to ensure its stability. The intimate union established between the monarchs associated with this system, by their principles no less than by the interest of their peoples, affords Europe the most sacred warrant of its future tranquillity.[137]

The tenor of this passage shows that the post-1815 European system came perilously close to a conspiracy of princes—note the expressions 'intimate union' and above all 'sacred'. This kind of rhetoric became increasingly common in the aftermath of the Vienna congress, with the Czar, of all people, as its principal pro-moter. Recovered from his infatuation with radicalism, he set

[136] Memorandum of the ministers of the four allied courts (Castlereagh, Hardenberg, Kapodistrias, and Metternich) to Wellington on his appointment as commander of the allied troops in France, 20 Nov. 1815, Wellesley (1861–5: xi. 241).
[137] 15 Nov. 1818, Chodźko (1864: iv. 1760).

the tone with his Holy Alliance scheme, which we have discussed already. It was so imbued with the 'sacredness' of monarchical solidarity as to provoke the distaste or even the hidden amusement of the other negotiators, but it had a powerful impact on people's minds. As pointed out already, it was simply a declaration of intent with no practical applications. Nevertheless, it came to be seen as the covenant of a conspiracy of rulers against their subjects. (It was backed up, in a sense, by the renewed Quadruple Alliance against France, supplemented by a Quintuple Alliance against no one in particular and comprehending France in 1818, but there is no real connection between the two schemes.) The Russian government took the Holy Alliance very seriously in the years following the settlement. When in 1820–1 a spate of revolutions threatened the rulers of Spain, Sicily–Naples, and Sardinia–Piedmont, it offered armed support, and Russian troops salvaged the Habsburg Imperial crown as late as 1849.

The reformulation of the principle of dynastic legitimacy as the 'monarchical principle' resulted logically from the realization that if it were to survive monarchism had to be defended as such, as a symbol of the old non-egalitarian order, and not because it made an intrinsic functional contribution to the cause of political stability. What consensus the monarchical principle generated resulted from common adherence to a conservative political creed, not from the pragmatic considerations that Talleyrand had in mind. Even so the consensus was weak.

4.2.5. Assessment

Perhaps, then, the concept of dynastic legitimacy is best described as a rather impressive red herring. Talleyrand was fooling himself (but he was not the only one). Dynastic legitimacy could not be a factor of stability. The premiss was wrong: it was not because there were dynasties that the pre-revolutionary order had been stable, it was the existence of a stable, hierarchical social order, in which political authority presupposed high rank owed to birth, that encouraged the development of dynasties.

Talleyrand with his principle of dynastic legitimacy illustrates the validity of the stance adopted by Metternich, of eschewing reliance on principle as a source of legitimacy for what had been saved or restored of the old order. Louis XVIII might be declared a principle, but, even with the democratic packaging insisted on by Talleyrand, he was in essence a reactionary principle fighting a losing battle against 'the revolution', which had the better rational arguments. Metternich was careful not to invoke dynastic legitimacy in too programmatic a fashion even over Saxony, where he was happy to let Talleyrand do it for him. As to the Habsburg monarchy, rather than putting it at the mercy of any principle he preferred to place his trust in what Kissinger calls a 'spontaneous pattern of obligation'.[138] This was possible, of course, because the Habsburg monarchy, unlike the French one, had not been swept away by 'the revolution'. It still subsisted entirely by inertia, by the sheer weight of secular habit reinforced by a little repression. It was the skilful management of the peacemakers, their success in stabilizing the European system, more than its dynastic legitimacy, that gave the Habsburg monarchy a new lease of life—until the next general war swept it away, too.

There is another aspect of the concept of dynastic legitimacy, however, that deserves emphasizing. Apart from the fact that a number of them had failed to survive the period of troubles, the actors in the European system remained to a considerable extent the same as before and as sanctioned by custom. Nevertheless, what Talleyrand had come up with is important in that it was the first attempt in the history of the states system of Europe to provide an abstract criterion for membership of that system—the earlier criterion of Christianity had only been a necessary, not a sufficient, condition for membership. It was in this capacity that, at Vienna, the concept did have a certain impact: the prominence given to it contributed, perhaps decisively, to the non-re-establishment of earlier non-dynastic actors (Genoa, Venice, Poland). At the same time, it helped to prevent the destruction of another (Saxony).

4.3. The Balance of Power

4.3.1. The Balance of Power as a Programme for the Vienna Congress

At Vienna as at Utrecht, in the utterances of the peacemakers the concept of balance of power enjoyed pride of place among the components of the consensus agenda. The re-establishment of a

---

[138] Kissinger (1957: e.g. 200).

European balance of power was the declared main aim both of the wartime coalition and of the congress. For example, the Declaration of Frankfurt of 1 December 1813, drawn up by Metternich as a statement of allied policy towards France, was a reminder that

> The allied powers are not waging war against France, but against that loudly proclaimed preponderance, against that preponderance which, unhappily both for Europe and France, the Emperor Napoleon has for too long exercised outside the limits of his empire.
> ... The allied sovereigns desire France to be great, strong, and happy
> .... But the powers also want to be free, happy, and tranquil. They want a state of peace that, through a wise distribution of forces, through a just equilibrium, will henceforth preserve their peoples from the numberless calamities that, for twenty years now, have burdened Europe.[139]

The preamble of the Treaty of Chaumont of 1 March 1814, which renewed the anti-Napoleonic alliance, again pronounced the war to have been 'undertaken with the salutary intention of ending the plight of Europe, of assuring its future repose by re-establishing a just equilibrium of powers'.[140] The First Peace of Paris stated, also in the preamble, the desire of all parties for a 'solid peace, founded on a just distribution of forces between the powers'.

The great powers were all committed to this principle. Gentz declared that 'the preservation of a just equilibrium between the powers will constantly be the fundamental principle, the compass, and the northern star of the Austrian government.'[141] Utterances by Metternich (which may have been drafted by Gentz) support this contention.[142]

Prussia, too, expressly acknowledged the principle, though it subordinated it to considerations of 'national' interest. The King of Prussia, Hardenberg maintained,

> is by no means bent on aggrandizement, but he cannot but insist on what is essential for the interest of the [Prussian] monarchy, and in accordance

---

[139] Chodźko (1864: i. 78 f.). For the authorship of the declaration, see Gulick (1982: 140 n.).
[140] Klüber (1815–18: i(1). 1).
[141] To Karadja, 5 Feb. 1814, Gentz (1876: 54).
[142] e.g. Metternich to Hardenberg, 22 Oct. 1814, Chodźko (1864: ii. 316 ff.).; note by Metternich, submitted in the session of the representatives of the Five Powers, 28 Jan. 1815, Klüber (1815–18: vii. 83 ff.).

with the treaties [promising the re-establishment of Prussia on its pre-Napoleonic scale]. He holds himself to be giving the most incontrovertible proof of his attachment to the solid establishment of an equilibrium of repose and of good harmony between the different states of Europe, by yielding on all points that are not indispensably necessary to the reconstruction of Prussia, such as it is entitled to by virtue of the treaties.[143]

The Russian delegation, also keen on aggrandizement, protested against the charge that it was disregarding the balance-of-power principle. It invoked a 'rule of conduct which the emperor [Alexander] has imposed on himself, in order to attain the great aim of delivering Europe from the yoke that oppressed it, and of consequently re-establishing a political system founded on justice and on a solidly built equilibrium'. Of these two notions, 'justice', according to this document, meant that the victors were entitled to an aggrandizement proportionate to their war effort, and 'equilibrium' made it necessary 'to give to each state a cohesion [*consistance*] and a relative strength sufficient to make the guarantee of political agreements inherent in the means of which it disposes to ensure their respect.'

The same document argued that the other allies,

being in a position to obtain considerable increases of power, from a territorial, military, commercial, and political point of view, cannot legitimately refuse that which Russia is claiming, not with a view to augment its resources, but as a necessary weight in the balance of the European system.

The point was to make sure that 'the law of equilibrium will not be violated at its [Russia's] expense'.[144]

Talleyrand, as usual, had the most developed ideas on the European equilibrium. For any theorist of the balance of power, the most difficult problem is, of course, that a real equality of the actors, in respect of their size, resources, etc. is impossible to establish in practice. In elaborating on this point, the French instruction for Vienna stated that

An absolute equality of strength between all states, apart from the fact that it is forever out of the question, is by no means the prerequisite of political equilibrium, and might even . . . be harmful to it. This equilibrium

[143] Note by Hardenberg, submitted in the session of the representatives of the Five Powers, 8 Feb. 1815, Klüber (1815–18: vii. 96).

[144] Russian memorandum to Castlereagh, 11 Nov. 1814, Chodźko (1864: ii. 452 ff.).

consists in a relationship between the power of resistance and the power of aggression of each political entity respectively. If Europe were made up of states linked by a relationship such that the minimum power of resistance of the smallest were equal to the maximum power of aggression of the biggest, then there would exist a real equilibrium . . . But the situation of Europe is not such, and cannot become such. Adjacent to large territories belonging to a single power, there are territories of similar or of smaller size, divided up among a greater or lesser number of states of often dissimilar character. To establish a federal link between these states is sometimes impossible, and it is always impossible to give to states between which such a link does exist the same unity of purpose and the same capacity for action that they would possess if they were but one body. Therefore, they will contribute to the establishment of a general equilibrium only as imperfect elements, in their quality as composite bodies; they possess their own balance, susceptible of a thousand modifications that necessarily affect the one of which it forms part. Such a situation only admits of a very artificial and precarious equilibrium, which can only last for as long as some large states continue to be animated by a spirit of moderation and justice that will preserve it.[145]

Put differently, the concept of equilibrium is refined here by introducing the notion of subsystems. These are defined in two different ways: by the geographical or ethnic affiliation of the actors, and by their relative strength. While Italy and Germany, for example, each constituted a subsystem defined by the actors belonging to the same geographical area and ethnic group, the five actors with the greatest relative strength formed what could be called the great power subsystem, invested with a supervisory function—we will look at this phenomenon in greater detail shortly.

To return to the French instruction, a European equilibrium was, as it noted elsewhere, to be the 'main and final aim' of the proceedings of the congress.[146] The balance-of-power principle was to be the main criterion for the redistribution of territories.

Castlereagh, in a letter to Liverpool, stated that he considered it his duty '[i]n the first place, so to conduct the arrangements to be framed for congress, as to make the establishment of a just equilibrium in Europe the first object of my attention, and to consider the assertion of minor points of interest as subordinate to this great end.'[147] Gulick has shown how Castlereagh envisaged

---

[145] Ibid. i. 228 f.   [146] Ibid. 222.
[147] 11 Nov. 1814, Webster (1921: 232).

the reorganization of Europe from an equilibrist perspective.[148] In line with these ideas, in west Europe, the states surrounding France were strengthened to contain it, for example by uniting Belgium with the Netherlands and by firmly implanting Prussia in the Rhineland. Here, Castlereagh was at one with the other allies. In the east, he strongly championed the aggrandizement of Prussia as a counterweight to Russia; to his dismay, Prussia in turn was not keen to oppose the aggrandizement pursued by the Czar. On the other hand, Talleyrand, as already noted, was adamant that to strengthen Prussia was highly dangerous, because that would give it too much weight in Germany.[149]

It soon became clear that, as a guideline for the decision-making, the balance-of-power concept was in fact inadequate—despite such refinements as the congress's statistical committee, which established mutually acceptable estimates of 'souls' or inhabitants for the various territories to be disposed of. The prominence given to apparently mechanical redistribution of 'souls' in such documents as the congress's Final Act should not lead us to the wrong conclusions—things were not as simple as the way in which the outcome was presented might suggest.

4.3.2. Difficulties with the Balance-of-Power Principle: A Vehicle for Consensus, or an Obstacle?

Talleyrand, in his final report from the congress, reiterated that

It was laid down in the Treaty of Paris that the distribution of territories should be such as to establish in Europe a real and permanent balance of power. . . . On the other hand, the balance of power would be established to no purpose if the congress did not adopt, as one of the foundations of the future tranquillity of Europe, those principles which alone can secure internal tranquillity in individual states, and at the same time protect them from being subject in their mutual relations to the influence of force only.

The French king's aim, Talleyrand informed him, was 'to bring back with you the purest political morality as the rule of your government. Your Majesty felt that it was necessary that a similar desire should be shared by other cabinets, and that it should appear in the relations of states with each other.'[150]

---

[148] Gulick (1982: esp. 204 ff.).
[149] See the French instruction, Chodźko (1864: i. 231 ff.).
[150] Talleyrand (1881b: ii. 222).

Talleyrand may be paraphrased as saying that consensus was more important for the stability of Europe than the actual distribution of material strength among the actors. It seems that, like Castlereagh, Talleyrand did not understand the concept of balance of power as a source of consensus in itself. Instead he, too, was inclined to regard it as a purely mechanical safeguard against disruptive expansionism.

When, at the time of the Utrecht congress, Bolingbroke and Torcy debated the 'great article', the prevention of a union between France and Spain, or when the 'barrier' concept was used to decide the location of borders, it was for show as much as it was dictated by genuine strategic considerations. There was an intuitive awareness that, in order to reach consensus, what was needed above all was an abstract concept to which both sides could rally without loss of face. Whatever unilateral advantage was forgone in doing so was, at least ostensibly, compensated for by a mutually acknowledged reciprocal or common advantage. For the same reason, there was no undue concern at Utrecht over the actual material distribution of forces. The fact that the Habsburg dominions were vast even without the addition of Spain was addressed only in passing—and, in the end, Austria had much of Italy, plus Belgium, thrown in, as a consolation prize for failing to obtain Spain. Similarly, no one can have believed seriously that the safety of Germany from French attack was increased materially by putting the Rhine between the two countries. After all, the river had not stopped the French in the past. The importance of such 'strategic' boundaries was psychological as much as anything else. The Utrecht peacemakers used principles as a tool to attain consensus at least as much as they observed them for their own sake. Adhering to principles in too much of a crusading spirit is obviously likely to create discord rather than consensus.

By 1814, for a hundred years statesmen had been telling one another that the balance of power was the be-all and end-all of Europe's international politics. Moreover, in the climate of abstract political discussion created by the French Revolution—the intellectual climate that led people to be so concerned with 'principle(s)' and 'systems'—it was less easy to be simply pragmatic than it had been at Utrecht. It is not surprising, then, that the statesmen in charge at Vienna were so obsessed with the balance of power that there was a tendency to put the need to re-establish it *above* the need for consensus, to the point of seriously contemplating resumption of the war over the Polish issue.

Talleyrand did, however, explicitly place the need for consensus above principles seen as absolute in their own right. He pointed out in his final report that 'the idea even of perfect political institutions, and of a perfect balance of power, had to be made subservient to the establishment of a lasting peace.'[151] And the Czar, whose designs on Poland created the problem, protested his adherence to the principle all along. When he finally backed down it was, at least ostensibly, the balance-of-power concept that provided the necessary, face-saving basis for consensus. The Russian delegation confirmed the Czar's commitment to maintaining

that system of equilibrium which, placed henceforth under the protection of the powers of the first order and shielded from all preponderance, will have acquired through the loyal policy of Russia the means of resisting, if necessary, the very force [i.e. Russia itself] that has the most contributed to establishing it.[152]

Note that the concept of equilibrium is, once again, supplemented here by the great power concept, with the expression 'henceforth [*désormais*]' indicating the novelty of this approach.

Finally, Metternich, least given to programmatic adherence to any principles, was most alive to the need for conciliation. While he wished to prevent any exorbitant aggrandizement of Russia, his behaviour in the Polish–Saxon crisis makes it clear how much he was concerned about consensus rather than the mere distribution of forces. As we have seen, he vetoed the annihilation of Saxony so as not to destroy the consensus on which was to rest the German Confederation—quite apart from equilibrist considerations. Metternich also offered the Czar the sizeable district of Tarnopol (first acquired by Austria in the 1772 partition of Poland) if, in return, Russia gave more Polish territory to Prussia. The aim was to reconcile Prussia with Austria. It was Metternich who, in the run-up to the First Peace of Paris and before Napoleon was quite beaten, insisted that France should not be reduced to its pre-revolution borders, but that it should be granted some symbolical

---

[151] Ibid. 231 f.
[152] Reply by Russia to Castlereagh's circular note of 12 Jan. 1815, 19 Jan. 1815, Chodźko (1864: ii. 799).

augmentation (though, as we have seen, he went back on this when the Second Peace of Paris was negotiated).

The skill with which Metternich avoided antagonizing other actors is illustrated fascinatingly by his handling of the Saxon question. After it had been agreed that 'a Saxony' would be maintained, but that Prussia should have part of Saxony's existing territory, Metternich at first dug in his heels in order, ostensibly, to save the fortresses of Torgau and Erfurt for Saxony. Castlereagh reacted by trying to prove to Metternich, solemnly and not altogether plausibly, that these fortresses were of little strategic value to Austria (as a forward defence against Prussia in Saxony), but of great strategic value to Prussia against the French (of all people).[153] Clearly, Castlereagh felt that, in order to reaffirm his impartiality, it was time to do something for Prussia again, and this enabled Metternich to place the blame for the dismemberment of Saxony on him. In this way, Austria would be seen as trying to save as much of Saxony as possible (indeed, it really was trying to do that, but being seen to do so was at least as important as the fact of doing it). Castlereagh himself describes the situation without any apparent awareness of being used:

There was a good deal of rather warm discussion upon the impossibility of conceding largely to Prussia in Saxony. Prince Metternich's *projet* did not go to one third of the whole contents [of Saxony]. I stated that it was a little hard the British minister, who had no other possible interest in the question than to save the continental powers, and especially Austria, from war, should have the odious task thrown upon him of urging severe measures towards Saxony . . .[154]

Castlereagh reaffirmed, however, that he would not 'sacrifice the peace of Europe' to the interest of the Saxon dynasty. Metternich's next move was to trade in Torgau and Erfurt for the much more important, populous city of Leipzig:

The following morning Prince Metternich acquainted me, that notwithstanding the military advice the emperor [of Austria] had received, His Imperial Majesty was ready to acquiesce in both Torgau and Erfurt being Prussian, if the British minister pronounced it necessary [!] . . . , but that he expected Prussia to be proportionally moderate and conciliatory on other points, and especially not to press the cession of Leipzig.[155]

---

[153] To Liverpool, 22 Jan. 1815, Webster (1921: 293).
[154] To Liverpool, 29 Jan. 1815, ibid. 295 f.   [155] Ibid. 296 ff.

Castlereagh duly did the dirty work for Metternich by inducing the King of Prussia to consent to this:

> I was directed to attend the King of Prussia..., and I had with His Majesty an audience of an hour and a half, the most painful in all respects, that it has been my fate to undergo since I have been upon the continent. It is inconceivable to what a degree His Majesty had been worked upon on the point of Leipzig...

But Castlereagh had some help from the Czar, who offered to give Toruń to Prussia to placate it. Castlereagh himself threw in some of the territory earmarked for Hanover and the Netherlands, taking up a suggestion devised earlier by the British government to save Saxony.[156]

It ought also to be pointed out that, in terms of the distribution of territories and populations, the Vienna settlement fell far short of the theoretical goal of rough equality at least between the major actors. For example, Prussia, the smallest of the great powers, was less than half the size of the Habsburg dominions, with, according to Castlereagh, some ten million inhabitants in 1815 as opposed to twenty-five million for Habsburg.[157] Moreover, Prussia consisted of two separate pieces, situated in the west and east of Germany. This oddity meant that Prussia was still impossible to defend in the event of a system-wide war. It could not hope to weather a major conflict other than as a client state supported by at least one of the other major actors, such as Russia—or else (the only alternative) it had to be firmly in control of Germany. It was this logic that later prompted Bismarck to annex Hanover and parts of Hesse in the 1860s, linking up the two halves of Prussia. He then went on to unite the remainder of the German actors, save Austria, around Prussia in 1871.

However much it was talked about and thought of as paramount, and although it did have a strong influence on the shaping of post-Napoleonic Europe, the balance-of-power principle was, nevertheless, no longer the chief source of consensus that it had provided at Utrecht. Indeed, the need for some other concept to play that role, and to supplement the balance-of-power principle, is in fact apparent from the very ubiquity of the expression '*just* equilibrium'.

---

[156] To Liverpool, 6 Feb. 1815, ibid. 300 ff.
[157] To Liverpool, 22 Jan. 1815, ibid. 293.

4.4. The Great-Power Principle

4.4.1. The Need for a New Master Principle

Why was it that in the early eighteenth century the European states system could make do with the balance-of-power principle as a chief source of consensus for what (relatively little) restructuring the system needed? The reason was because the set-up of the system was still to a substantial degree determined by custom. For example, both the identity of the actors and, to a considerable extent, their dominions had been determined centuries ago, long before anything like the current system had existed. As a result, these things were not really at the disposal of the peacemakers—nor, for that matter, of concern to them. There was consensus that the general set-up of the system would be maintained. This (literally) went without saying. What the Utrecht peace did was repair those portions of the system that had been affected by the recent controversies, and reintegrate the Bourbon dynasty into the system. The rest it left untouched. No sweeping reforms were either needed or contemplated, only consolidation. For this, the balance-of-power principle, together with the autonomy and security principles to which it was organically related, provided both a sufficient source of overall consensus and the means for fine tuning, for example of frontiers.

At Vienna, the situation was different. If the thinking that had triumphed in the French Revolution had a basic message, it was that every custom, every social construct could be challenged. The international system, just as much as the domestic organization of the actors that made it up, was such a construct. Moreover, revolutionary upheaval and, in particular, Napoleon had in fact succeeded in changing the system almost beyond recognition; which was something that Louis XIV had not done.

The old set-up was not entirely destroyed, of course, either domestically or internationally. It showed considerable staying power, and much that was done away with resurfaced. Both domestically and internationally, the post-Napoleonic restoration followed the natural reflex of using the state of affairs before the recent transformations as a guide for the decision-making. But, as far as eliminating custom as a prop for consensus was concerned, the French Revolution had created a situation that was impossible to reverse. Even if the old set-up was partially retained or restored, it could not be simply for the sake of custom. In order to have consensus on, or legitimacy for, anything, thenceforth it had to be in the name of some abstract concept.

This is a chief reason why by 1815 the variegated pattern of pre-revolutionary constitutional forms had given way to a considerably more standardized international landscape, which was shaped to a much greater extent than before by abstract theorizing. It is the *abstract* nature of this thinking that is its most striking feature, and if this is borne in mind the apparent dichotomy between its two competing branches, the conservative and the populist, is rather reduced. This also explains why everybody was constantly talking about 'principle(s)', and why people were so fond of the equally abstract expression 'system'.

As far as the international sphere was concerned, the balance-of-power concept alone could not satisfy this need for principles. Talleyrand went to the heart of the matter in reminding the other peacemakers that it was not enough simply to look at the redistribution of territories. Two other points imperatively required attention. Who were to be the actors entitled to territories, and hence participation in the system, in the first place? What were to be the relations between them?

It was not enough to pretend that the French Revolution had not happened and to carry on as before to the extent to which that was possible and desirable. It was also necessary to find new, and that necessarily meant abstract, consensus notions if the restored system was to be stable. Talleyrand's principle of dynastic legitimacy was designed to furnish an answer to the first of the two points mentioned above, while, regarding the second, such hazy notions as 'political morality' were the most that even he could muster.

None of these notions provided a sufficient safeguard for stability. Both at Münster and Osnabrück and at Utrecht, collective security schemes had been elaborated to defend the newly restored system (though, in practice, they proved irrelevant). At Vienna, too, there was a felt need for some form of guarantee. Who was to preserve the work of restoration? The answer seemed self-evident: the powers that had, or so it could appear, vanquished 'the revolution', the powers increasingly known as the great powers.

They as much as everybody else sensed that there was no going back to a system without great powers—if only because this would have required the five of them to step back *jointly* from the responsibility for the system that, without even realizing it fully, they had already assumed, by deciding the Napoleonic struggle between them. (This was, in fact, a case of the prisoner's dilemma.) They had to cooperate precisely *because* they could not trust one another. As a result, the great-power principle was born.

4.4.2. The Great-Power Principle Establishes Itself

The great-power principle provided the missing concept needed to stabilize the system. It was suitably abstract and totally new, concerning as it did the status of the actors and their relations with one another without any reference to custom. It was more abstract than the balance-of-power principle, which was concerned with structure in a more material sense—the distribution of territories. At the same time, it dealt with the vexing problem of equality in a system where all actors were supposed to be autonomous despite great disparities of strength, disparities that had increased significantly in the recent past. The great-power principle respected the principle of autonomy of the actors while modifying the concomitant principle of equality—by introducing two classes of actors.

In practice, there was no alternative to the great powers keeping both the proceedings of the congress and, afterwards, the running of the system firmly under control. At least intuitively, both they and the other actors were aware of that. Despite the fact that their emerging privileged role generated some discontent, the great powers were, in a sense, mandated by the expectations placed in them. They were also helped by the military prestige gained during the recent struggle—by France no less than by the coalition. None the less, this tacit legitimation of their special status required that the great powers understood themselves to be answerable to the other actors, as well as to one another, and that they conducted themselves accordingly.

The need felt by the great powers to explain their conduct is apparent, for example, in Castlereagh's draft declaration justifying the (as it happened, indefinite) postponement of the official opening of the congress—the very measure, in other words, that left the great powers solely in charge of the decision-making. Castlereagh stated that the courts parties to the Treaty of Paris, by which the present congress has been set up, *hold themselves to be obliged* to submit for its consideration and approval the project of settlement which they judge to be most in accordance with the principles recognized as the necessary basis for the general system of Europe.

At the same time, the opening of the congress was to be suspended 'until . . . it has been possible to bring to the knowledge and approval of the congress a proposal capable of satisfying the common ideal [*le vœu général*]'.[158]

The declaration as published stated, somewhat more tersely, that the formal opening of the congress was adjourned because of the conviction of the parties to the Paris treaty that

it will be in the common interest of all the participants to postpone a general convocation of their plenipotentiaries until such time as the questions to be decided by them will have reached the degree of maturity without which a result as much as possible in accordance with . . . the just expectations of the contemporaries would not be attainable.[159]

The 'just expectations of the contemporaries' were also addressed in a draft final declaration for the congress dating from February 1815 and composed by Gentz at Castlereagh's instigation. This text was not officially adopted, but it was circulated by the press.[160] It emphasizes the difficulties facing the negotiators, and then defends their achievements in the following terms:

If the congress has not fulfilled the exaggerated expectations of the contemporaries [*ce qu'il y avait d'exagéré dans l'attente des contemporains*], if it has not been able to satisfy every desire, meet every need, heal every ill that burdens nations and individuals, if, in a word, it has not been able to attain that ideal perfection of the social order to which the enlightened minds and the benevolent souls of all ages have aspired in vain, it has accomplished at least that which its immediate mission demanded, that which the limits of its duration, the extent and the diversity of its tasks, and the difficult conditions in which it found itself placed, made it possible to accomplish.[161]

At the two congresses that we examined earlier, the stronger actors had, of course, had a larger share in the proceedings than

---

[158] 3 Oct. 1814, Klüber (1815–18: viii. 64 f.). My emphasis.
[159] 8 Oct. 1814, ibid. i(1) 34 f.
[160] See Webster (1950: 428 f., 431), and Gentz (1873: 356).
[161] Klüber (1835: 192). The same document in Gentz (1873: 443 ff.).

the smaller ones. But it had not occurred to them to constitute themselves into a distinct subgroup, into what was, in fact, a dominant subsystem. Until the latter part of the eighteenth century, even the largest actors had not been in a position to dominate militarily, or even merely to disrupt, the system as a whole. The new great powers, however, constituted a subset of actors of sufficient potential military strength, not perhaps, in each case, to dominate the system, but certainly to cause tremendous damage both to it and to one another should they clash. Napoleon had demonstrated this.

The source of this change lies, once again, in the social transformations taking place in Europe, in the increasing importance of the masses. For example, the *levée en masse*, the introduction by France of conscription, multiplied the size of armies needed for successful warfare. This accentuated the disparities between the power potential of the more populous actors and that of the less populous ones.[162] In pre-revolutionary days, relatively small but rich communities, such as the Dutch or Venetian republics, could be quite formidable in military terms, because the size of armies depended more on how many mercenaries actors could pay for than on the size of their population. But the rise of nationalist populism transformed this situation completely.

Responsibility for keeping the system stable came to rest with the most populous actors, for the simple reason that they were capable of doing the most damage—both to each other and to the lesser actors.

4.4.3. The Great-Power Principle in Practice: The Problem of France

The French instruction, which contains very developed theoretical reflections on Europe's international politics, urged the admission of all European states to the congress. But it does dwell on the disparities between them, not just of size, but, significantly, of population. Out of a total of 170 million inhabitants of Christian Europe, it says, more than two-thirds are subjects of the eight signatories of the Peace of Paris; another sixth are in conquered territories; and the last sixth make up the forty-something remaining states, which therefore even combined would not be equal to

[162] See Webster (1921: p. xliv).

'the big powers of Europe' (*les grandes puissances*: the expression seems to refer simply to size and not to status).

Giving the small states the same weight at the congress as the big ones, the French instruction continues, is out of the question. But then the 'general equilibrium of Europe ... is necessarily composed of partial systems of equilibrium': therefore, the 'small and medium states' should only take part 'in what is of concern to the particular system to which they belong'. Here, then, the great-power concept is introduced indirectly, by establishing the notion of subsystems (the ones specifically mentioned are Germany and Italy).[163]

Originally, the victorious Big Four intended to give both France and Spain a sort of associate great-power status without any real say in the shaping of the settlement. But Talleyrand succeeded in securing a different outcome—through a combination of diplomatic skill, perseverance, and luck, and helped potently by the fact that France commanded considerably greater resources than Spain.

Article 1 of the First Peace of Paris provided that '[t]he high contracting parties shall make every effort to preserve, *not only among themselves, but also, as far as depends on them, among all the states of Europe*, the good harmony and understanding that is so necessary for its repose.' (My emphasis.) The treaty was signed by the Eight Powers (Austria, Britain, France, Portugal, Prussia, Russia, Spain, Sweden). However, the first of the secret articles stipulated that the disposition of the territories ceded by France, 'and the relations of which a system of real and durable equilibrium in Europe is to be the result, will be decided at the congress along the lines laid down by the allied powers among themselves'.

'The allied powers': that did not include France. But, because of its size and population, France could not logically be excluded from the great powers. If it had been, they could not have kept the system stable, because then France, presiding over a faction of malcontent smaller actors, would have contested both the legitimacy of the allied great powers' supervisory role and the settlement that they would have elaborated.

Indeed, the French instruction emphasized the need for France to support the smaller actors,[164] and this strategy was implemented

---

[163] Chodźko (1864: i. 227).   [164] Ibid. 217.

by Talleyrand to put pressure on the allied great powers in the initial phases of the congress. Castlereagh reported that, as a result, there was

a meeting of 13 of the smaller German powers who applied to Bavaria to join them, and to support France in resisting what they called, the usurpation of the great powers. This gave a most unpleasant complexion to our discussions, and produced an impression, that the object of the French minister was to sow dissension in Germany, and to put himself at the head of the discontented states.

Castlereagh proceeded to lecture Talleyrand on the shamefulness of such behaviour. 'I had a long interview with him, in which I took the liberty of representing to him without reserve the errors into which he appeared to me to have fallen, since his arrival here'. Talleyrand was all sweetness and light ('Prince Talleyrand received with perfect good humour my remonstrances'), but Castlereagh, prudently, concluded nevertheless on a resigned note ('I left him in a temper apparently to be of use; but I have lived now long enough with my foreign colleagues not to rely . . . upon any appearances').[165]

Some observers, like Ernst von Münster, who represented Hanover for the British prince regent, feared that the leadership of the great powers would not be accepted by the smaller actors. Münster warned 'that several courts will refuse to accede to arrangements in which they have formerly had no part.'[166] But the event was to prove him wrong—only Spain refused to accede (until 1817) out of dissatisfaction with the settlement. Although it had been considered for great-power status originally, Spain, unlike France, failed to pull sufficient weight at the congress to achieve its inclusion in the inner committee. Among the smaller actors, grumblings were certainly heard; but whatever objection there was to the new principle was evidently less operative than the principle itself.

Full recognition of the great-power status of France came in January 1815, when the intransigence of the Czar produced a secret alliance against him and Prussia between the other three great powers—including France. That Austria and Britain turned to

---

[165] To Liverpool, 9 Oct. 1814, Webster (1921: 203 ff.).
[166] To the prince regent, 14 June 1814, Münster (1868: 286). See also 11 June 1814, ibid. 277.

France is in itself a clear indication of France's indispensability to the proper functioning of the European system. There was a further complication when the temporary return of Napoleon led to the renewal of the old quadruple alliance of Chaumont (despite the fact that Talleyrand also signed the treaty renewing the alliance, in the name of the deposed Louis XVIII, in practice the alliance was, once again, only between Austria, Britain, Prussia, and Russia). The renewed quadruple alliance was to remain valid even after the Second Peace of Paris of November 1815. But, unlike the projected exclusion of France from full participation in the framing of the peace settlement, this was not contrary to the great-power principle. When three of the great powers combined against the other two, this was certainly not seen as detracting from the status enjoyed by the latter. Similarly, the renewal of the quadruple alliance did not permanently detract from the status of France, which ostensibly joined the alliance at the Congress of Aachen in 1818.

The fact that the original quadruple alliance against France was not actually dissolved—despite the new quintuple alliance being concluded with France—was communicated confidentially to the French government without being publicized. But this curious arrangement proved to be of little practical relevance, because the quadruple/quintuple alliance was no more called upon in practice to defend the settlement than the collective security schemes set up in 1648 and 1711. Its interest lies rather in the fact that this alliance, not between all actors but between the major ones, once again throws into relief the new great-power concept. Moreover, the Second Peace of Paris made only minor changes to the Final Act of June 1815. The new international system essentially remained as reformulated under the auspices of all the great powers, including France.

4.4.4. The Great-Power Principle as a Consensus-inducing Constraint

Interestingly, the great-power principle displayed an inbuilt capacity to generate consensus among the members of the great-power club. This is one functional reason why it proved so successful.

The best illustration of the consensus-inducing nature of the great-power principle is furnished by the behaviour of the Czar. The Czar was understandably keen on the new great-power concept—after all, it enhanced Russia's status. As a result, significantly, he sacrificed his more far-reaching desiderata at the congress to the new principle. Witness a conversation which he had with Talleyrand, and which is reported here by the latter:

'each [the Czar said] must find what suits it here [i.e. at the congress].' 'And what is right [Talleyrand replied].' 'I shall keep what I hold.' 'Your Majesty would only wish to keep that which will be legitimately yours.' '*I am in accord with the great powers.*' 'I do not know whether Your Majesty reckons France among those powers.' '*Yes certainly*; but if you will not have each have its advantages [*convenances*], what do you propose?' 'I place right first, and advantages after.' 'The advantages of Europe are the right.' . . . I turned towards the wall near which I was standing, leaned my head against the panelling, and, hitting the woodwork, exclaimed, 'Europe, unhappy Europe!'[167]

Talleyrand's exercise in political histrionics may be unverifiable. But, psychologically, his report rings true. The Czar was by no means as sure of himself as his bellicose and deliberately ruthless discourse was intended to suggest. He knew that he had little chance of enjoying the 'advantages' accruing to him from his war effort in the face of great-power opposition. Hence his somewhat bewildered 'but . . . what do you propose?'

Striving to prove himself unimpressed by Talleyrand, the Czar obstinately repeated that he would go to war again rather than renounce his booty, and rushed off ('Then, lifting up his arms, waving his hands as I had never seen him do previously . . . , he cried rather than said, "It is time for the play, I must go. I promised the emperor [Francis]; they are waiting for me." ') But he did not go without a conciliatory gesture for Talleyrand ('He then withdrew, but returned from the open door, put his two hands on my sides, gave me a squeeze, and said, in a voice quite unlike his own, "Adieu, adieu . . ." ').

What had lost him—and even if this account of the interview is not entirely accurate, it does capture the general situation—was, of course, that he fell into the trap tended by Talleyrand, and admitted that France, as one of the great powers, had a right to object to his designs.

Look at the Russian answer to the vituperation launched at the Czar by Castlereagh. Although it is presented as forbearing

[167] Talleyrand (1881*b*: i. 23 [1881*a*: 21 f.]). My emphasis.

altruism, the eagerness for approval by the other major actors is evident:

It was for the purpose of recreating a system of real political equilibrium, of reaching in legitimate and orderly ways the provisions from which it must spring, of making it rest on the solid base of the real and intrinsic strength of each power, that Russia has taken it upon itself not to anticipate on the dispositions of a general settlement, when it would have been at liberty to put forward its rights over a country [Poland] conquered by its arms, without any foreign assistance. Russia, on the contrary, . . . adjourned every project of legitimate aggrandizement until the time when its allies would have taken the true measure of the power falling to their lot, and when all the states of Europe, restored to their full independence, would convene to discuss their interests, and to contribute by casting their votes to the just conciliation of those of the allies.[168]

What came into play here was an important rule flowing from the great-power principle, and which could be called the rule of coordination. A joint hegemony exercised in the name of the great-power principle would work only if a minimum of coordination was preserved between the actors sharing that hegemony. At the same time, the higher the stakes, the greater the degree of coordination required. In other words, the more responsibility the privileged actors had, the more they depended on maintaining agreement between them. It stands to reason that, faced with the task of reconstructing the international system, the great powers found that agreement between them was absolutely crucial. Later on, when the system had been firmly established, their cooperation could gradually become looser. There was even room for strictly limited conflict between them (such as the Crimean War and, following that, the Austro-Italian, Austro-Prussian, and Franco-Prussian clashes), until, eventually, the basis for great-power co-ordination was eroded to the point where the system collapsed in 1914.

Because Russia was a relative outsider among the great powers, it was particularly anxious to preserve the 'concert' between them. If the other great powers combined against Russia, and even if only three of them did so, Russia could not play the role in Europe to which it aspired, but would be relegated yet again to the sidelines. This, at least as much as fear of war as such, determined

---

[168] Memorandum to Castlereagh, 21 Nov. 1814, Chodźko (1864: ii. 453).

the success of the secret alliance of Austria, Britain, and France in inducing Russia to back down over Poland. Significantly, when the Polish crisis reached its climax at the end of 1814, Russia appealed repeatedly for respect for the rule of coordination and emphatically pledged itself to observe that rule. For example, one of the Russian ministers, Razumovsky, in a note sent to Metternich at the very height of the crisis, began by saying that

His Imperial Majesty [the Czar], penetrated by the conviction that the principle of union and harmony, which has ensured the success of the combined efforts of the allied powers during the recent war, must be applied with equal success to the present negotiations, has ordered me to let you know, *mon prince*, his firm resolution never to separate, in the discussion of the questions to be decided, the interests of his empire from those of his allies. As a consequence of this principle, to which His Imperial Majesty is happy to adhere invariably, he desires . . .[169]

A few days later, a colleague of Razumovsky, Nesselrode, launched another, rather ardent, appeal for unity, emphasizing that only a common front of the great powers could preserve the social order of Europe from further revolutionary upheaval.[170]

However arduous, coordination within a subsystem of only five actors was considerably easier than maintaining consensus in a larger system with many more players. The important thing to note here is that, given the small number of players involved, coordination was possible even in the absence of any far-reaching consensus between them—as long as such coordination was seen to be imperative to avoid a potentially catastrophic breakdown of the system. From this perspective, the exact territorial extent of Russia–Poland or of Prussia, for example, was not as fundamental an issue standing in the way of coordination as the heat that it generated led many to believe—not in comparison with the prospect of another system breakdown, which would reopen the floodgates of revolution.

While Castlereagh was busy rattling the British sabre over Poland, the British prime minister Liverpool was as alarmed at this as was the Czar, and equally prepared to back down. Liverpool was dismayed that the Polish problem had become 'a question

---

[169] 27 Dec. 1814, ibid. iv. 1861.
[170] Note by Nesselrode to Austria, Britain, and Prussia (France was not yet included in the inner circle), 31 Dec. 1814, Klüber (1815–18: vii. 69 ff.).

of serious embarrassment, and it is very material that we should lose no character by the part we take in it. I am inclined to think that the less we have to do with it . . . the better.'[171] When Castlereagh remained stubborn, this prompted Liverpool to explain himself more fully. 'It may be quite true', he wrote,

that if the Emperor of Russia does not relax in his present demands, the peace of Europe may not be of long continuance; but for however short a time that peace may last, I should consider it of great advantage. . . . if war should be renewed at present, I fear that we should lose all we have gained, that the revolutionary spirit would break forth again in full force . . . A war some time hence, though an evil, need not be different in its character and its effects from any of those wars which occurred in the seventeenth and eighteenth centuries, before the commencement of the French Revolution.

Liverpool was unhappy about the language that Castlereagh employed with the Czar, his deadpan comment being that it was 'quite triumphant'.[172]

One sees his point: it was sound policy (a policy also employed, as we have seen, by Bolingbroke) to allow the system to settle down again and solidify before dealing with any fresh challenges— because anyone trying to upset it again would then have to overcome the moment of inertia created by the consensus that it embodied. Even Castlereagh, who was unwilling to concede this point with regard to Russia, had actually made it himself with regard to France, as we saw in an earlier quotation.[173] The future was to prove Liverpool right. Revolutionary attempts against the settlement occurred continually in the decades following the congress. But they could not threaten it seriously as long as the great powers, short of remaining united, at least did not checkmate one another. What warfare occurred was limited and quite non-revolutionary.

Kissinger contends that, if Castlereagh had followed Liverpool's preferred line of signalling British indifference over Poland, that would have made war, and the defeat of Austria, more likely, and that Castlereagh, by indicating Britain's readiness for war, successfully implemented a policy of deterrence.[174] This analysis is

---

[171] To Castlereagh, 14 Oct. 1814, Webster (1921: 210).
[172] To Castlereagh, 25 Nov. 1814, ibid. 244 f.
[173] Above, sect. 3.2.3.   [174] (1957: 165).

typical of the distortion created by too exclusive a focus on power politics, simplistically assuming as it does that to secure more territory, if necessary by military means, was the Czar's only aim. In fact, Kissinger misunderstands the Russian position in the same way that Castlereagh did. The Czar's paramount goal was the acceptance of Russia's role as one of the leading actors in the European system; Poland was a means to that end. Had it been an end in itself he might have gone to war over it. As it was, the larger ambition that Poland symbolized would have been defeated even if Russia had won that war. A victorious war over Poland might have increased Russia's resources, but would have destroyed its prestige and influence in the European system for a long time to come.

Castlereagh was surprised at the ease with which the contentious issues were eventually resolved ('the leading territorial arrangements have been wound up with a degree of good humour which I certainly did not expect to witness among the powers, from what had passed in the earlier stages of our proceedings'). Contentedly, he attributed this outcome to his own policy ('the course of our policy has been conciliatory and unvaried, and it has been marked with enough of [sic] impartiality on the part of Great Britain . . . to give the whole the character of a sincere but commanding effort to execute with justice and fidelity the engagements taken at Paris').[175] Castlereagh overestimated himself a little: what had resolved the issue was not primarily his own diplomatic ability, but the operation of the great power principle.

A further illustration of the rule of coordination is that when Austria, Britain, and Prussia formulated their ultimatum to the Czar over Poland (before the King of Prussia backed out), they offered Russia the choice between two options. Either they could settle the matter privately among the great powers, that is by compromise, or, if Russia refused, they would appeal to Europe as a whole by actually opening the congress officially. They proposed

to make another attempt to settle this question amicably and confidentially with him [the Czar]; in the event of succeeding in which they flatter themselves to be enabled very speedily to bring to a satisfactory arrangement the other affairs of Europe, and would for that purpose desire a further adjournment of the congress.

[175] To Liverpool, 13 Feb. 1815, Webster (1921: 304).

If, on the contrary, they should unfortunately fail in arriving at the conclusion which they so much desire, they will in that case feel it their duty to suffer the congress to meet as now fixed [1 November 1814], before whom the subject must be entered upon formally and officially.

The memorandum went on to state that, if Russia agreed to the former alternative, Austria and Prussia would be satisfied with less—a clear indication that the great-power principle took precedence over the balance-of-power one.[176]

As for Prussia, it was as keen to belong to the great powers as Russia. As a result, for all its obstinacy, Prussia also bowed to pressure from the other great powers, rather than risk a break. Its king declared that Prussia did not possess a village other than with the consent of all Europe.[177] In the same vein, Chancellor Hardenberg abandoned the demand for a territorial diminution of France after Waterloo in the face of strong opposition from Russia and Britain. He stated that the King of Prussia would forgo his opinion 'so as to preserve, above all other things, the happy union between the four courts.'[178] Austria, which on this point was in sympathy with Prussia, took the same attitude.

4.4.5. Results

Since, in spite of the friction between them, the great powers ultimately remained united, and since their leadership role was, on the whole, acknowledged as legitimate by the other actors, they could reconstruct the system quite successfully. They appointed a committee to sort out the affairs of Switzerland; the Swiss, awarded some additional territory in the process, enthused and spoke of eternal gratitude.[179] The Saxon issue was eventually resolved between the great powers, without consulting the Saxon king. An embassy consisting of Metternich, Talleyrand, and Wellington was dispatched to Bratislava to acquaint the exiled king

---

[176] English text of a memorandum to the King of Prussia and the Emperor of Austria, transmitted by Castlereagh to Liverpool on 24 Oct. 1814, ibid. 213 f.; French version: Chodźko (1864: ii. 291).

[177] Quoted Treitschke (1879: 671) (n.d. given).

[178] Memorandum of 8 Sept. 1815, quoted Griewank (1954: 333).

[179] 'La diète de la Confédération Helvétique ... exprime par les présentes la reconnaissance éternelle de la nation suisse, envers les hautes puissances qui ..., établissant une ligne de démarcation plus favorable qui lui rend d'anciennes et importantes frontières, réunissent trois nouveaux cantons à la confédération' etc. 27 May 1815, Klüber (1815–18: v. 323 f.).

with the dispositions agreed on concerning him. When he dared to make representations, it was put to him that the three had come, not to have his opinion, but his consent.[180]

The great powers drew all the new borders. They guaranteed the Saxon acquisitions of Prussia. They declared Switzerland perpetually neutral, and guaranteed both this neutrality and Switzerland's territorial integrity—'in the true interest of the politics of all Europe', and in the name, this time, of the Eight Powers (though Sweden and Spain did not sign that declaration).[181] In a treaty with the Dutch king, incorporated in the Final Act, the four victorious great powers confirmed his possession of Belgium while imposing conditions—political equality of the new subjects with the Dutch and, in particular, religious freedom.[182]

Utterances prompted by changes that the great powers made to the map of Italy illustrate the attitude of smaller actors towards the great powers. The Kingdom of Sardinia–Piedmont, for example, ceded some of its territory to Switzerland at the great powers' request, and invoked its respect for them—in other words, the great power principle—as a face-saving device:

The undersigned minister of state and plenipotentiary of His Majesty the King of Sardinia has laid before his sovereign the desire of the allied powers that Savoy [which belonged to the kingdom] cede some portions of territory to the Canton of Geneva, and has submitted to him the proposal formulated to this effect. His Majesty, always eager to give his powerful allies a proof of his gratitude, and of his desire to do what may be agreeable to them, has overcome the very natural repugnance with which the thought of parting with good, ancient, and faithful subjects inspired him, and has authorized the undersigned to consent to a cession of territory in favour of the Canton of Geneva . . .[183]

The king had little reason to complain—he received handsome compensation from the same great powers, notably the former Republic of Genoa. More remarkable is the fact that the provisional government of Genoa itself, in a solemn protest against the

[180] Minutes of the session of the representatives of the Five Powers, 12 Mar. 1815, ibid. vii. 145 ff.   [181] 20 Nov. 1815, Chodźko (1864: iv. 1640 f.).
[182] Treaty of 31 May 1815, Klüber (1815–18: vi. 167 ff.) (esp. art. 8 and the annexed protocol).
[183] 26 Mar. 1815, ibid. v. 328 f. '[T]he allied powers': Italy was dealt with by the congress after the return of Napoleon in early Mar., which caused the Chaumont treaty to be revived against him. But this new treaty was co-signed by Talleyrand in the name of the exiled Louis XVIII.

absorption of the republic by Sardinia, also paid homage to the great powers. After a long enumeration of all the arguments against the suppression of Genoa's independence, and after insisting that the rights of the Genoese could be ignored but not extinguished, the document proceeded to point out that all this was 'in no way at odds with the profound and inviolable respect with which we are imbued for the high contracting powers in the Austrian capital'. The document then declared that the provisional government abdicated 'without regret', and went so far as to predict that 'the people will remain calm, and they will deserve, by an attitude worthy of these great events, the esteem of the prince that will govern them, and the attention [*l'intérêt*] of the powers that take part in our destinies.'[184]

'Les puissances qui prennent part à nos destinées': probably not a euphemism, but an expression of genuine confidence in the great powers—and which subsequent decades were to prove justified. Great-power relations had their ups and downs. But the international system enjoyed an unprecedented degree of stability for the next hundred years, warranting a general presumption throughout the system that the great powers—or simply 'the powers' in the parlance of the later nineteenth century—knew best and would act wisely. Witness the cartoon published in 1914 in *Punch*, with the old lady, informed of the imminence of war, exclaiming, 'oh no, the powers will intervene!'

[184] 26 Dec. 1814, ibid. vii. 433 ff.

5

The Peace Conference of Paris, 1919–1920

1. INTRODUCTION

The interior of all European countries, without exception, is tormented by a burning fever, the companion or forerunner of the most violent convulsions which the civilized world has seen since the fall of the Roman Empire. It is a struggle, it is war to the death between the old and the new principles, and between the old and a new social order.... All the elements are in fermentation; ... the most solid institutions are shaken to their foundations, like the buildings in a city trembling from the first shocks of an earthquake which in a few instants will destroy everything.

These words were written precisely a century before the end of the First World War. They are taken from a memorandum by Friedrich von Gentz, whom we encountered in the last chapter. He composed it on the occasion of the Congress of Aachen in 1818.

'If in this dreadful crisis', Gentz consoled himself at the time,

the principal sovereigns of Europe were disunited in principles and intentions; ... if ... the eyes of all were not open to the revolutions which are preparing, and the means which remain to them for preventing or retarding the explosion, we should be all carried away in a very few years. But, happily, such are not the dispositions of the princes who are protectors and preservers of public order; their intimate union ... is the counterpoise to the disorder which turbulent spirits try to bring into human affairs; the nucleus of organized strength which this union presents is the barrier which providence itself appears to have raised to preserve the old order of society, or at least to moderate and soften the changes which are indispensable.

Elsewhere in the same text, Gentz elaborated on this point:

The whole of the European powers have since 1813 been united, not by an alliance properly so called, but by a system of cohesion founded on generally recognized principles, and on treaties in which every state, great or small, has found its proper place. One might deny that this state of things is what, according to the old political ideas, characterized a federative or well-balanced system. But it is not the less certain that, in the present circumstances of Europe—circumstances which she will not quickly get rid of—this system is the one most suited to her needs, and that the destruction of that system would be a dreadful calamity; for, as not one of the states comprehended in it could remain isolated, all of them would enter into new political combinations, and adopt new measures for their safety; consequently new alliances, dislocations, reconciliations, intrigues, incalculable complications, by a thousand different chances, all equally fatal, would bring us to another general war—that is to say (for the two terms are almost synonymous), to the definitive overthrow of all social order in Europe.[1]

With hindsight, Gentz's words take on the character of a prophecy. If 1789 is a key date for domestic political culture in Europe, then 1914 must be seen as a key date in the history of international society. Fittingly triggered by the assassination of a Habsburg heir, the first general war for a century turned Gentz's nightmare scenario into reality; this time, the old order did not recover. The war brought revolution in the domestic sphere, as illustrated by the abolition of kingship in Russia, Germany, Austria, Hungary, and Turkey, and by the triumph of Bolshevism. The idea that the masses should participate in the political process gained fresh and unstoppable momentum, shown for example by the widespread lifting of voting restrictions and the introduction of female suffrage. The map of Europe changed. Numerous new actors emerged (or re-emerged): Finland, the three Baltic states, Poland, Czechoslovakia, Yugoslavia, Iceland, and Ireland. The peace conference had little to do with this—in their essentials, the new states were in place before the conference convened. (Ireland, which gained independence in 1922, is the exception. In any case, however, it should be remembered that, while the war facilitated change, *pressure* for change existed quite independently of it. It is worth noting, for example, that Norway seceded from Sweden as early as 1905, that kingship was overthrown in Portugal and China in 1910 and 1911 respectively, and that female suffrage was introduced in some countries even before the First World War.)

---

[1] Memorandum of Nov. 1818, Metternich (1880–2: iii. 193 f., 191). I have made some changes to the trans.; see the original in Metternich (1880–4: iii. 168 f., 166).

The war was, indeed, the cataclysm that the Vienna peacemakers lived in fear of, the result of those powerful populist currents to which they referred simply as 'the revolution'. In 1919 many believed that it was the system put in place in 1814–15 that was ultimately responsible for the calamities brought by the Great War. But it was not the system of Vienna, with its reliance on a great-power 'concert', its concern with the distribution of territories, and its ephemeral focus on dynastic issues, that had caused the Great War. Rather, the cause was the deterioration of that system, its being undermined by the very currents that the Vienna statesmen had combated.

In saying this, I am not making a judgement about the intrinsic moral value of either the conservatism practised at Vienna or the populist aspirations that it sought to hold down. There can be no doubt that those aspirations really were 'the revolution'. They subverted what order existed, and they were incapable of producing stability either domestically or internationally until that order had been displaced. The Vienna peacemakers understood this to their disquiet, and were confirmed in their conservatism. Having just had a foretaste, they knew what 'the revolution' had in store—cataclysm.

But as the nineteenth century wore on, and Europe enjoyed the stability the groundwork for which had been laid at Vienna, the spectre of cataclysm gradually receded, or it was deliberately ignored, even by the statesmen themselves. They eventually chose to ride the storm rather than face it, in the hope of being able to bridle it. To do so, they actually *espoused* populism, in the form of nationalism, so as to divorce it from ideological currents that were subversive of the existing order. Bismarck showed what could be achieved by marrying the Vienna system on the one hand with populism in the guise of nationalism on the other. (Indeed, his motto, or one of them, was *fert unda nec regitur*—one can ride a wave, but one cannot steer it.)[2]

'The revolution' was not of its nature 'democratic' or 'liberal'. What really defined it was its populism. It was their populism that brought leaders like Napoleon or Hitler, among others, to power. The French Revolution and Napoleon, even in their worst excesses, remained committed in theory to the liberal thinking of the Enlightenment. But it would be wrong to believe that the French

---

[2] Srbik (1925: ii. 317).

Revolution was archetypal because of this particular ideology. Indeed, by promoting the emancipation of the individual from ossified social convention, it helped to uproot and set adrift vast portions of the population that were then left in search of an identity—in other words, the revolution contributed to their 'alienation'. This paved the way for a different type of ideology, a type that was increasingly anti-individualist so as to provide the masses with the new identity that they were lacking.

Nineteenth-century socialism, which was strongly communitarian, provides early examples of this. Socialism, however, made the crucial mistake of *discounting* the importance of national feeling. Socialist theory assumed that the decay of traditional identities would also affect the virulence of national feeling. It did—but in the opposite sense to what was posited in the 1848 *Communist Manifesto*. Far from weakening national feeling, the decay of traditional identities exacerbated it, as the one thing that the masses could cling to in the face of depersonalization. Industrialization did away with many traditional social structures, but language and shared mentality remained as a vehicle, even *the* vehicle, of belonging. The failure to recognize properly the importance of national feeling was an error which socialism has never fully come to grips with.

Anti-individualist ideology did not develop fully in Europe until the twentieth century, receiving a strong impetus from the unprecedented social and spiritual dislocation brought about by the Great War and then worsened by the Great Depression. The new type of ideology was exemplified by Leninism, Stalinism, and the various brands of Fascism and National Socialism.

It is significant that Fascism and National Socialism, in a sense the most modern of these ideologies, used nationalism as a built-in feature, integral to the ideology itself, rather than as a helpful co-factor. No less than their left-wing counterparts, Fascism and National Socialism were eminently revolutionary in outlook. All of these ideologies placed a strong emphasis on eliminating the old class distinctions and on fusing the nation into a single community, at one in its loyalty to a Messianic leader.

In the nineteenth century populism, in the guise of nationalism, gradually converted the Vienna system into a minefield. It set the actors against one another. In order to enhance their domestic legitimacy, increasingly governments gave up the solidarity with one another on which the Vienna system had been based. Instead, the ruling élites played the card of competitive nationalism—a form of populism that could rally the ruled to the rulers. It could be said, in effect, that governments were trying to harness 'the revolution' to prevent it from happening. (This is what put the Habsburg monarchy in such a particularly difficult position, especially after Bismarck deprived its German or Germanized ruling class of much of its strength and self-confidence by separating it from the rest of Germany. The result was the *Ausgleich* or compromise with Hungary, designed to prop up the monarchy by committing to it the vigorous nationalism of the Magyars. Nevertheless, the new Austria-Hungary was a distinctly rickety structure, whose days were felt by many to be numbered.)

The effectiveness of this patriotic solidarity between rulers and ruled even in the face of social tension between them was shown by the surprise collapse of the Second Socialist International in August 1914 (when the major socialist parties in the belligerent countries rallied to their respective governments, despite their earlier opposition both to those governments and to the concept of warfare in general). But the price paid for this domestic solidarity was growing international tension, resulting eventually in a general breakdown of international stability. In particular, the great-power principle and the concomitant rule of coordination, both crucial to the stability of the Vienna system, proved increasingly inoperative in the years preceding the World War.

The antecedents of the 1914 eruption are not dissimilar to those of the Thirty Years War in Germany. In 1914 the European states system was split into two camps, just as the German subsystem was split between Protestants and Catholics three hundred years earlier. In 1914 one camp consisted of the Triple Alliance between Germany and Austria-Hungary (known as the 'central powers'), plus Italy, and the other camp consisted of the Triple Entente between Britain, France, and Russia.

Just as the German war that broke out in 1618 had consequences for, and in part involved, the rest of Europe, so the European war that broke out in 1914 affected, and in part involved, the rest of the world. In both cases, a new international system emerged and was sanctioned at the peace talks, although it remained distinctly unstable for some time afterwards.

The cessation of hostilities in 1918 was not easy to bring about. Locked in combat, the two camps proved roughly equal for almost three years; then domestic revolution in Russia, which began in

February 1917, gave Germany a chance of victory. But in April of the same year the United States entered the war and decided it for the entente. The armistice with Germany was signed in November 1918, and a peace conference convened in Paris the following January.

On what principles was the international system to be rebuilt? Populist political thinking had by this stage become so strong that any return to the past was out of the question. A majority of people felt strongly that the recipes of the past, of the age of conservatism, had failed. Something new was needed, and it was hailed enthusiastically when it appeared. The United States of America, personified by President Woodrow Wilson, was identified as the saviour. The United States, it seemed, had the military, economic, and ideological means to sort out the mess that Europe had got itself into.

This had indisputable logic in the sense that it was in America that a forerunner of 'the revolution' had first appeared (in the 1770s), preceding and encouraging what was to happen in France. The United States owed its existence to that proto-revolution. It was therefore not unnatural that the United States should be called in to relieve the final bankruptcy of the old order in Europe.

It failed dismally. But at the same time it bestowed a legacy that lived on and, eventually, prevailed. The peace conference was unable to remove the fundamental cause of the war: the fact that the European governments relied on populism domestically to such a degree as to leave them incapable of lasting international consensus. Even the governments of the victorious actors were faced with the threat of revolution, or at the very least electoral defeat. This alone would have induced them to pander to domestic chauvinism, but, in addition, statesmen themselves were conditioned by this chauvinism and they lacked detachment. This situation was ill-understood, and instead of building consensus the peacemakers ended up by creating a situation that was soon to prove no more stable than that of 1914.

2. CONSENSUS NOTIONS: WHAT THE PEACEMAKERS SAID

In order to understand the peacemakers' peculiar frame of mind, it is necessary to listen closely to their utterances. This section does not attempt to do exhaustive justice to the peacemakers' thinking or to the manifold theoretical issues raised by their ideas. It is merely intended to highlight and clarify some of the more important aspects of the intellectual input into the negotiations.

2.1. Wilson

The new consensus agenda was expounded by President Woodrow Wilson in the speeches that he made after the United States had entered the war. By the time the peace conference convened, Wilson had acquired the status of prophet of a new age, propagating a creed which he and many others saw as the ultimate answer to disorder and violence in international relations.[3] His influence was immense, not least because he was preaching to audiences that held themselves to be converted already. The principles that Wilson defended were not of his own invention. The importance of his thought did not lie in any originality but in his peculiar ability to interpret and formulate what was 'in the air'.

'We believe', Wilson declared on 11 February 1918, 'that our [i.e. the United States'] own desire for new international order, under which reason and justice and the common interests of mankind shall prevail, is the desire of enlightened men everywhere.'[4]

Indeed, the famous *Fourteen Points* of 8 January 1918 came several days after the Bolshevist statement of war aims, as well as after Lloyd George's great address to the British trade unions, both of which expressed ideas very similar to Wilson's.[5] The fact that basic assumptions about international relations were held in common by Trotsky and Wilson shows how pervasive these assumptions were. So also does the ready acceptance of 'Wilsonism' by republican Germany, whose delegation at the conference later rejected the draft treaty proposed to it on the grounds that that document violated the principles on which Germany had been assured that the peace would be made.

The legal basis for this was the exchange of notes between Berlin and Washington that preceded the November 1918 armistice. In these notes, it was agreed that Wilson's programmatic speeches of

---

[3] See e.g. Nicolson (1934: 35 ff.), Keynes (1920: 34 f.).

[4] Temperley (1920–4: i. 439). In quotations from original sources the original spelling has been maintained in this ch. Capitalization has been changed in accordance with the rules followed earlier.

[5] See Bailey (1963: 25), McCallum (1944: 28).

1918 would constitute a *pactum de contrahendo*, pledging the parties to the peace negotiations to the principles that Wilson in his speeches had set forth.[6]

But despite Wilson's obvious didactic intentions, the five great speeches that he delivered between January and September 1918 were beset with vagueness and inconsistencies, a fact that was to have unhappy consequences at the conference table. The speeches contain a mixture of consensus notions, concrete proposals, and moralizing harangue. Consensus principles and rules are not set apart from the other elements, nor are they confined to the central cores of the speeches, labelled respectively the *Fourteen Points*, the *Four Principles*, the *Four Ends*, and the *Five Particulars*. These do not add up to twenty-seven separate items, because of overlaps and repetitions. For example, three of the *Four Principles* are elaborations on the idea of national self-determination, which also underlies many of the *Fourteen Points* and which is restated in the second of the *Four Ends*. Self-determination is also frequently referred to in the remainder of the speeches.

Indeed, among the principles advocated by Wilson, national self-determination was by far the most prominent. It was to be the new master principle, and it is not difficult to see why. Self-determination was the application of populism on the international level. It was a principle with enormous rallying power, because it harnessed the force of national feeling. This was something that no international consensus principle had done before. Moreover, the principle of national self-determination had enormous scope, greater than that of the great-power principle or the balance-of-power principle, in that it was potentially capable of doing two very important things at once. It could determine who would be a recognized actor in the international system—roughly speaking, any ethnic group that was coherent enough to invoke the principle. And it could determine the boundaries between international actors —these would now follow, as far as possible, the ethnic divides.

Furthermore, national self-determination was perfectly compatible with, and, in fact, almost subsumed, other consensus notions that had traditionally been of great importance, in particular autonomy and equality.

'Self-determination', Wilson proclaimed on 11 February 1918,

---

[6] Text of the notes in Temperley (1920–4: i. 448 ff.).

'is not a mere phrase. It is an imperative principle of action which statesmen will henceforth ignore at their peril.'[7] The eventual triumph of this principle was probably inevitable, given the historical momentum of populism and the fact that the functional strength of the principle enables it to determine the structure of the international system largely by itself. But the qualification 'largely' is nevertheless important here.

Indeed, Wilson himself anticipated problems. In the same speech, he explained that 'each part of the final settlement must be based upon the essential justice of that particular case and upon such adjustments as are most likely to bring a peace that will be permanent'.[8] This was a covert reservation and, indeed, an obscure one. What could be meant by 'the essential justice' of a 'particular case'? Wilson never gave a satisfactory answer to this, nor did anyone else. In the event, the settlement applied the principle in a haphazard and arbitrary manner.

On 8 January 1918, in the eleventh of the *Fourteen Points*, Wilson spoke of 'historically established lines of allegiance and nationality'[9] as a guiding criterion for the settlement (he was referring specifically to the Balkans). This appears to be the only reference in his speeches to history as a possible source of consensus. But how could historical considerations be a criterion for implementing 'the revolution'?

The somewhat unsystematic nature of Wilson's thinking is also illustrated by his treatment of the (crucial) question of the German constitution. Unless it is modified by some other concept, self-determination implies total autonomy, and consequently the freedom for each people to choose its form of government. Accordingly, Wilson declared on 8 January 1918 that the United States did not 'presume to suggest to [Germany] any alteration or modification of her institutions.' But, without any apparent awareness of the inconsistency, Wilson immediately qualified this stance: 'But it is necessary . . . that we should know whom her spokesmen speak for when they speak to us, whether for the Reichstag majority or for the military party and the men whose creed is imperial domination.'[10]

When in October 1918 the German government approached Wilson to seek an armistice, Wilson made it clear in the ensuing

---

[7] Ibid., app. iii, p. 437.   [8] Ibid. 439.   [9] Ibid. 434.   [10] Ibid. 435.

exchange of notes that, unless Germany became a thoroughly democratic state, the war would continue until it capitulated:

the President deems it his duty to say, without any attempt to soften what may seem harsh words, that the nations of the world do not and cannot trust the word of those who have hitherto been the masters of German policy, and to point out once more that in concluding peace and attempting to undo the infinite injuries and injustices of this war the government of the United States cannot deal with any but veritable representatives of the German people who have been assured of a genuine constitutional standing as the real rulers of Germany. If it must deal with the military masters and the monarchical autocrats of Germany now, or if it is likely to have to deal with them later in regard to the international obligations of the German Empire, it must demand not peace negotiations but surrender.[11]

The president assumed that self-determination automatically implied a democratic form of government. But there could be no doubt that, despite the relative powerlessness of the electorate, most of the German population accepted the pre-1914 German state as legitimate. The military failure of the old regime brought about the revolution of November 1918, a development which the allies might have welcomed more enthusiastically than they did but which officially could be none of their business. Wilson's suggestion, prior to that revolution, that Germany only had a choice between democracy and capitulation was, in fact, from an international point of view, an act of interventionism at odds with the principle of self-determination.

Wilson saw the struggle against the central powers as a 'war of emancipation—emancipation from the threat and attempted mastery of selfish groups of autocratic rulers'.[12] What he was referring to was the threat to the autonomy of parts of Europe that the central powers posed. Germany's violation of Belgian neutrality, and the subsequent German ambition, laid down for example in the September 1914 war aims, to establish hegemonial dominion over Belgium had come to symbolize the threat to the autonomy principle. The seventh of the *Fourteen Points* demanded that

Belgium ... must be evacuated and restored without any attempt to limit the sovereignty which she enjoys in common with all other free nations. No other single act will serve as this will serve to restore confidence

[11] Note to the German government of 23 Oct. 1918, ibid. 456.
[12] Ibid. 439 (11 Feb. 1918).

among the nations in the laws which they have themselves set and determined for the government of their relations with one another.[13]

The notion of equality, with its more democratic overtones, was
dearer to Wilson than sovereignty (autonomy), and equality had
greater prominence in his pronouncements. But, as we have seen
in earlier chapters, conceptually the two notions were inseparably
connected. 'This war had its roots', Wilson declared on 11 February 1918, 'in the disregard of the rights of small nations and of
nationalities which lacked the union and the force to make good
their claim to determine their own allegiances and their own forms
of political life.'[14] (Once again, it is not clear why small nations
should be allowed to determine their 'forms of political life' but
Germany should not. It is already possible to discern here the
fatal tendency to treat Germany differently, to deny it both autonomy and equality.)

On 8 January 1918 Wilson had invited Germany 'to accept a
place of equality among the peoples of the world . . . instead of a
place of mastery,' and he had ended his speech by vindicating the
right of all peoples and nationalities 'to live on equal terms of
liberty and safety with one another, whether they be strong or
weak.'[15] The problem was that the peace conference itself treated
the defeated actors as unequal, on the grounds that their lost war
had been a crime and that they therefore did not deserve better.

Wilson was so fond of the notion of equality that, in his fervour,
he did not hesitate to undermine, indeed reject, the great-power
concept. He declared that a general peace 'cannot be pieced together out of individual understandings between powerful states.
All the parties to this war must join in the settlement of every
issue anywhere involved in it'.[16]

Finally, as befitted the spokesman of 'the revolution', Wilson
endowed the notion of progress with a legitimizing quality. He
referred to 'the new world in which we now live'[17] or 'the altered
world in which we now find ourselves',[18] and he opposed it to the
old world tormented by 'the great game, now forever discredited,
of the balance of power'.[19] Wilson described the governments of
the central powers as 'clothed with the strange trappings and

---

[13] Ibid. 434.   [14] Ibid. 438.   [15] Ibid. 435.
[16] Ibid. 437 (11 Feb. 1918).   [17] Ibid. 435 (8 Jan. 1918).
[18] Ibid. 438 (11 Feb. 1918).   [19] Ibid. 439 (11 Feb. 1918).

primitive authority of an age that is altogether alien and hostile to our own.'[20] The German chancellor found himself rebuked by Wilson for allegedly advocating, in his reply to the speech of 8 January, the ways of the past: 'The method [he] proposes is the method of the Congress of Vienna. We cannot and will not return to that ... Is it possible that Count von Hertling ... is in fact living in his thought in a world dead and gone?'[21]

On 4 July 1918 Wilson spoke of the 'deadly grapple' between past and present that the war represented,[22] and on 27 September he even pronounced it to be a 'peoples' war'.[23] 'The counsels of plain men', he declared, 'have become on all hands more simple and straightforward and more unified than the counsels of sophisticated men of affairs, who still retain the impression that they are playing a game of power and playing for high stakes ... Statesmen must follow the clarified common thought or be broken.'[24]

Some months later, on 25 January 1919, Wilson told the second plenary meeting of the peace conference that 'we are not representatives of governments, but representatives of peoples.' He admonished his fellow delegates that

select classes of mankind are no longer the governors of mankind. The fortunes of mankind are now in the hands of the plain peoples of the whole world. Satisfy them, and you have justified their confidence not only, but established peace. Fail to satisfy them, and no arrangement that you can make would either set up or steady the peace of the world.[25]

This speech was endorsed emphatically by the three speakers that followed: David Lloyd George for Britain, Vittorio Emmanuele Orlando for Italy, and Léon Bourgeois for France.[26] But was a 'steady' peace at all compatible with this revolutionary idiom? Could a settlement based on such an idiom be permanent? Wilson was aware that making progress a consensus notion meant that the settlement would have to be revised continually. This was one of the tasks that he assigned to his proposed League of Nations. The peace conference, he told the second plenary session, had to deal with many complicated questions

which, perhaps, cannot be successfully worked out to an ultimate issue by the decisions we shall arrive at here. ... It is, therefore, necessary that

[20] Ibid. 444 (4 July 1918).   [21] Ibid. 437 (11 Feb. 1918).
[22] Ibid. 444.   [23] Ibid. 445.   [24] Ibid. 447 f.
[25] USA, State Department (1942–7: iii. 178, 180).   [26] Ibid. 181 ff.

we should set up some machinery by which the work of this conference should be rendered complete. . . . Settlements may be temporary, but the actions of the nations in the interests of peace and justice must be permanent. We can set up permanent processes.[27]

Application of all these various ideas, Wilson thought, would render possible the transformation of the international system into a veritable society, something that he did not think it had been before. The importance that he attached to the notion of community is reflected in the recurrent description of the ends of the adherents of the old system as 'selfish', whereas the new system and its processes were to be 'unselfish'. 'What we demand in this war', Wilson declared on 8 January 1918,

is nothing peculiar to ourselves [the United States]. It is that the world be made fit and safe to live in, and particularly that it be made safe for every peace-loving nation which, like our own, wishes to live its own free life, determine its own institutions, [!] be assured of justice and fair dealing by the other peoples of the world, as against force and selfish aggression.[28]

A world so constituted would at last be characterized by the 'reign of law' (another key concept for Wilson). Wilson pictured this new society of states as based on the same principles as a democratic domestic society: the third of his *Four Ends* of 4 July 1918 was 'the consent of all nations to be governed in their conduct towards each other by the same principles of honour and of respect for the common law of civilized society that govern the individual citizens of all modern states'. In summing up his speech, Wilson declared that '[t]hese great objects can be put into a single sentence. What we seek is the reign of law, based upon the consent of the governed and sustained by the organized opinion of mankind.'[29]

Wilson spoke of consent, not of consensus. Both his treatment of the German question and his ideas on collective security show that he was confident that consent could be enforced. In fact, this was perhaps the key to all the problems that the conference both encountered and generated. Wilson's ideas were those of an influential school of thought that, from about the turn of the century onwards, had gained increasing popularity in Britain and the United States and which later came to be labelled the 'idealist' school of international relations theory. In line with this 'idealist' thinking,

---

[27] Ibid. 178.   [28] Temperley (1920–4: i. 433).   [29] Ibid. 444.

Wilson believed that the international system could be pacified by introducing into it the peacekeeping mechanisms of domestic society, such as the settlement of conflicts by means of juridic procedures. In this way, the problems of the international sphere would quite literally be 'domesticated'. (One of the major tenets of the 'idealist' school was that war was the result of a lack of other means of resolving conflicts.)[30]

But it is extremely difficult, if not impossible, to enforce the 'reign of law', or, in more general terms, a code of behaviour, if there is no pre-existing consensus that commits the actors to that code of behaviour. This consensus needs to be shared and recognized even by actors that may be tempted to contravene the code of behaviour (or that are thought by others to be doing so). The peace conference did not reflect on this fact. On the contrary, it made matters worse by indulging the notion that the 'reign of law' would be promoted by the punishment of contravening actors (as opposed to their simple defeat—a crucial distinction). In reality, any attempt to inflict punishment on a potentially powerful international actor could only be counterproductive. It could only create resentment, and lead to the rejection of the code of behaviour by that actor. In other words, what punishment promoted was really the destruction of the consensus without which no code of behaviour can function.

While an international actor with little power could be held in check, however much it was antagonized, this was difficult in the case of a large actor like Germany. Attempts to control such an actor could never be more than a short- or medium-term expedient, and one, moreover, that was likely to create even more antagonism. As has often been remarked, the peace conference, in its treatment of Germany, failed to follow Machiavelli's advice that a powerful enemy ought to be either reconciled or destroyed.

2.2. Lloyd George

David Lloyd George, the British prime minister, produced fewer and less resounding utterances on the peace to be concluded than Wilson. But his main contribution, the address to the British trade unions of 5 January 1918, in which he justified the war effort and explained the allied war aims, shows the similarity of his published

[30] See Bull (1972: 30 ff.), Fox (1968: esp. 2 ff.).

views to Wilson's—the more conclusively because his speech pre-dates those of the US president. Like Wilson, Lloyd George talked at some length about the 'general principle of national self-determination'.[31] He insisted that 'government with the consent of the governed must be the basis of any territorial settlement in this war.'[32] Fortunately for propaganda purposes, Czarist Russia's membership of the entente had lapsed in 1917—this enabled Lloyd George to stress that '[t]he democracy of this country means to stand to the last by the democracies of France and Italy and all our other allies.'[33] But he also stressed that Britain had not entered the war 'merely to alter or destroy the imperial constitution of Germany, much as we consider that military autocratic constitution a dangerous anachronism in the twentieth century.' He said that if the constitution were modified, this would 'make it much easier for us to conclude a broad democratic peace with her [Germany]. But, after all, that is a question for the German people to decide.'[34]

Lloyd George agreed with Wilson on the necessity of 'complete restoration . . . of the independence of Belgium', and called for reparations. He said that 'this great breach of the public law of Europe must be repudiated . . . Reparation means recognition. Unless international right is recognized by insistence on payment for injury done in defiance of its canons it can never be a reality.'[35] This shows that Lloyd George, too, made the option of punishment a precondition of 'international right', oblivious to the intrinsic difficulties that this faces in international society.

He, too, stressed the 'equality of right among nations, small as well as great,' and he declared this to be 'one of the fundamental issues this country and her allies are fighting to establish in this war.'[36]

Like Wilson, Lloyd George thought that '[t]he days of the Treaty of Vienna are long past,'[37] that the peace would only be provisional ('whatever settlement is made will be suitable only to the circumstances under which it is made, and, as those circumstances change, changes in the settlement will be called for'[38]), and that some form of international organization was desirable 'as an alternative to war' and in order to bring international society under the

---

[31] Text in Lloyd George (1936: v. 2515 ff., here at 2524).   [32] Ibid. 2520.
[33] Ibid. 2522.   [34] Ibid. 2517 f.   [35] Ibid. 2520.
[36] Ibid. 2519.   [37] Ibid. 2520.   [38] Ibid. 2526.

rule of law. 'After all war is a relic of barbarism, and, just as law has succeeded violence as a means of settling disputes between individuals, so we believe that it is destined ultimately to take the place of war in the settlement of controversies between nations.'[39]

2.3. Clemenceau

Permeated with fervent patriotism and hatred of Germany, the wartime speeches of the French prime minister Georges Clemenceau contain hardly any references to international problems.[40] On 5 November 1918, a week before the armistice, Clemenceau delivered a speech in the French Chamber of Deputies in which he described the war as 'this great humanitarian crusade'.[41] He defined the aim of the French war effort as 'a peace of justice and of right *with the necessary guarantees*'. (My emphasis.) In practice, this meant that his paramount concern was to preserve the wartime coalition even after the peace, in an attempt to protect France against renewed German invasion. Here again, the French national interest had priority over all other considerations. In a ringing appeal for national unity, Clemenceau went so far as to declare that

it is necessary to be French [i.e. a French patriot rather than a 'humanitarian', by which Clemenceau meant an adherent of the new thinking as propounded by Wilson], because France represents that conception of idealism, of humanity which has prevailed in the world, and because one cannot serve humanity at the expense of France.[42]

The French political system (like the Italian one) was hampered by great instability, caused by the fragmentation of the political forces in parliament. The position of the government was therefore permanently precarious. In order to stay in power as prime minister, Clemenceau appealed to heated national feeling as a factor of unity. This, of course, was not conducive to international consensus, and neither was Clemenceau's almost desperate desire to keep the wartime alliance in being, peace or no peace. This desire stemmed from Clemenceau's realization of France's relative weakness *vis-à-vis* Germany, and his belief that international politics was nothing but a barbarous struggle for power. For

---

[39] Ibid.   [40] Clemenceau (1968).
[41] Clemenceau (1938: 7).   [42] Ibid. 6.

Clemenceau, power alone could bring security, and France on its own was not powerful enough. As he was to find, however, the failure of the conference to establish a system-wide consensus, which created doubt as to whether the peace was legitimate, and dissension on what to do with it, had the better even of what France managed to salvage of the alliance.

On 29 December 1918 Clemenceau expounded his thinking in another debate of the French Chamber of Deputies.[43] Clemenceau's remarks on this occasion (which he improvised—the text was not prepared in advance) aroused the anger of President Wilson. They were interpreted as an attempt to vindicate the ways of the past. 'There was an old system', Clemenceau said,

> that seems to be condemned today and to which I am not afraid of saying that I am still to some extent faithful at the present time: countries [and not the international community, as under collective security] organized their defence. That's very prosaic. They endeavoured to have good frontiers; they were armed. It was a terrible burden for the whole population . . . I was saying that there was this old method of solid and well-defended frontiers, armaments, and what was called the balance of power . . . Today, this system seems to be condemned by some very high authorities. I would like to point out, however, that if the balance that has spontaneously come into being during the war had existed before, if, for example, England, America, France, and Italy had reached an agreement to say that whoever attacked one of them was attacking everybody, the war would not have taken place. . . . So there was this system of alliances which I'm not giving up, I tell you that in all frankness, and my guiding thought in going to the conference . . . is that nothing must happen which, in the post-war period, could separate the four powers that were united in the war . . . For this entente I will make every sacrifice.[44]

Clemenceau's point is unconvincing. In fact, there *was* material equilibrium in the European system in 1914 (or, at least, a less imperfect equilibrium than ever before)—which is why the war between the two blocs lasted so long and remained undecided until the United States tipped the balance. But this equilibrium did not prevent the war from breaking out. By referring to the balance of power, Clemenceau was presumably trying to muster some remnants of allegiance to the old consensus notion of that name, but what he really meant was that a *superior* coalition had

[43] Clemenceau (1938). Compare Jordan (1943: 37).
[44] Clemenceau (1938: 19–21).

to be kept in being *permanently* to hold Germany in check. This was not a conception of the balance of power that would have been recognized at Utrecht or Vienna.

It is not surprising that Wilson and his followers were piqued by this statement, the more so because Clemenceau went on to declare that his earlier meeting with Wilson had been marked by diverging views ('I would be lying if I pretended that I agreed immediately with him on all points'[45]). Yet Clemenceau was careful not to reject Wilsonism. 'You want to introduce a new spirit in international relations,' he declared during the same debate. 'So do I [*j'en suis*].'[46] He explained that

I accept for my part all additions of supplementary guarantees with which we will be provided. I go even further. If it is established that these supplementary guarantees are such that we can make sacrifices of military preparedness, I will, as far as I am concerned, make them with pleasure, because I am not keen to impose unnecessary burdens on my country. Only I would ask you to think well. . . . The truth is that, from the most remote ages onward, the peoples have perpetually assailed one another for the satisfaction of their appetites and their egotistical interests. I have not made this history, and neither have you. It is [*Elle est*].[47]

By supplementary guarantees, Clemenceau meant the collective security mechanisms that the proposed League of Nations was to administer. He was saying that he was not opposed to the League, but that he did not trust it as an effective way of guaranteeing the settlement, and that he therefore wanted to keep the wartime alliance anyway.

This attitude was curiously self-defeating, but then so was the concept of collective security itself—the concept under which any aggression by an international actor would be dealt with by a concerted effort of the international community as a whole, permanently organized for that purpose. The mechanisms of collective security could not work unless a great deal of consensus existed in the system. But this consensus was not present, nor did the conference make the situation any better. On the other hand, in a system in which there is sufficient consensus among the actors to make collective security work, such a scheme may be useful, but it is also less necessary. If the consensus is strong enough, any violation will mobilize the actors to defend the notions covered by

[45] Ibid. 29.   [46] Ibid. 32.   [47] Ibid. 23.

this consensus, whether or not there are institutionalized mechanisms for this purpose.

Like Wilson, Clemenceau hoped for a new and better age in international politics, but, unlike Wilson, he did not think that it could be brought about soon. 'Gone are the Talleyrands, the Metternichs, of yesterday, shadows of the days for ever past! Now let the door open to the messengers of the new era.' Thus Clemenceau was to exclaim (with some irony) in his unfinished memoirs *Grandeur and Misery of Victory*.[48] The messengers: but not the era itself.

For the Paris peacemakers, an international set-up supported by a system-wide consensus was something quite divorced, for the time being, from attainable historical reality. This attitude was one of the main causes of the failure of the 1919 settlement. For Wilson, as we have seen, international society meant the 'reign of law' and had yet to be brought about. His principles, Wilson felt, should be applied because they were just, not because there was a consensus on their acceptability that meant that applying them would reduce the potential for serious international conflict. For Wilson, dealing with the problem of international conflict was the task of collective security. In the Wilsonian view, then, principles were not safeguards of stability in the sense that they were vehicles of consensus: instead, the triumph of principles was the end, while stability, if necessary to be brought about through coercion, was a means to that end. Neither Clemenceau nor Wilson understood that, in order to be successful, the peace conference could not simply be a prelude. It would either show international consensus to exist already, or create it, or fail. A consensus not registered then and there was unlikely to develop subsequently.

Clemenceau was not, after all, a conservative reactionary but one of the great exponents of the (moderately left-wing) French *Parti radical*.[49] A speech that he delivered in the French Senate on 25 September 1919, after the Versailles treaty had been signed, is marked by his familiar, mordant 'realism', but also by a revolutionary idiom—somewhat half-hearted but clearly echoing Wilson's. Quoting the chairman of the Senate committee on the peace ('Vous croyez avoir fait la guerre, vous n'avez pas fait la guerre, vous

⁴⁸ Clemenceau (1930*b*: 138).   ⁴⁹ See McCallum (1944: 93).

avez fait la révolution'),[50] Clemenceau exclaimed, 'Yes, this is the beginning[!] of a revolution,' called it 'a revolution of liberty', and referred to 'our liberating action'.[51] But the keyword of the speech is 'solidarity':

This war and this peace are a war and a peace of human solidarity such as had never yet been seen in the world. . . . Today, at this decisive hour, I would like to make plain to you my idea, for I have only one in all this: to show you how [in the Versailles treaty] we have made apparent [*dégagé*] the idea of solidarity, what strength we have given it, what result we expect for it from the application of the treaty.[52]

[If] we want to make a peace of solidarity, if we have fought, despite all difficulties, a war of solidarity, . . . then we must understand what this means. It means that it is not overnight, as if by decree from above, that we will establish solidarity in the world. . . . Time is needed in order for phrases [*verbalisme*], very easily accepted by noble minds [another reference to the adherents of the 'idealist' school and of Wilsonism], to be translated into acts. One of the merits of the treaty is to allow these acts to develop in proportion as the feeling of solidarity will develop among the allies as well as among other nations.[53]

Not that Clemenceau's speech itself, rhetorically effective but obscure in meaning, was free from *verbalisme*. Solidarity, in the sense in which the word is used here by Clemenceau, does seem to presuppose some sort of international society, even though the emphasis is on the necessity for this society to develop rather than on its existing already. Furthermore, the distinction, even after the signature of the Versailles peace, between 'allies' and 'other nations' reflects an attitude typical of the 'idealist' school of international relations: the belief that international society would be created among the more advanced or 'civilized' countries, while others might join if and when their state of development or civilization warranted it. In practice, in 1919 this meant that the League of Nations was, for the time being, to be confined to the victors and the neutral powers, while the defeated actors, not unlike convicted criminals, were only to regain their rights of 'citizenship' after a period of 'probation', so to speak. Finally, the fact that change and progress, not immutability, are identified here as a hallmark of the new order is also characteristic of Wilsonism.

[50] Clemenceau (1938: 167).   [51] Ibid. 169.
[52] Ibid. 172 f.   [53] Ibid. 202.

When on 11 October 1919 the French Senate debated the ratification of the Versailles treaty, Clemenceau declared with remarkable candour that he had discovered at the conference 'parts [*des parties*] of humanity which had eluded me, because I had never been involved in such international conferences and in discussions of this kind.'[54] The following passage from the same speech also shows Clemenceau seeking to keep abreast of the new age:

this quest for idealism, this great urge to escape from this awful material world exposed to extravagant appetites in peacetime and murderous follies in wartime, this idealism born from the war has produced a result which it will be quite difficult to ignore. A time has come when the idealism of the sociologists [the representatives of the 'idealist' school of international relations], who make such noble efforts to keep the world at peace, has found itself face to face with the necessities. The time has come for partitions to be made around the conference table, with the need to safeguard material interests, which, if they are not decisive in speeches, are too often decisive in the world of facts. Idealism and interest have never got on very well with each other, and it has always been the case, as it is at the present time, that always [*sic*] idealism has had to complain of the predominance of interests.[55]

Clemenceau's memoirs, too, are tinged with the progressivist bias characteristic of the period. In the memoirs, Clemenceau speaks disparagingly of the peace treaties of Münster and Osnabrück and of Vienna, and stresses the novelty of the Versailles peace. According to him, this novelty of the Versailles treaty consisted in its being based on right.[56] Once again, this really meant Wilsonism: 'We were left, as our supreme conquest, the right of nations to govern themselves, which is the basis of all civilization.'[57]

Clemenceau's increasing appreciation of 'idealism' also influenced his conception of the balance of power, as the following passage from the memoirs shows:

To sum up, peace is a disposition of forces, supposed to be in lasting equilibrium, in which the moral force of organized justice is surrounded by strategical precautions against all possible disturbances. It [This] is the history of all nations and of all times. Thenceforth right appears

---

[54] Ibid. 244 f.   [55] Ibid. 242.
[56] See e.g. Clemenceau (1930*b*: 149 f., 189, 242).   [57] Ibid. 178.

as an organization of historical forces calling from time to time for reinforcement.[58]

Once again this is rather obscure (and neither, apart from the incorrect 'It is' for 'C'est', is the translator at fault).[59] Nevertheless, the passage indicates an awareness that, somehow, 'moral force' and 'right' did enter into the notion of equilibrium and therefore, by extension, were ingredients of international stability. At the same time the passage is quite in keeping with the Wilsonian view of principles as things that were to be *fought for*, rather than capable of being harnessed to *prevent* conflicts.

It is clear that, in his views on international politics, Clemenceau was really a little confused. At the conference, he devoted himself to a single-minded pursuit of what he perceived to be the national advantage of France. He never realized that, in doing so, he promoted a kind of international system in which any unilateral advantage gained was unlikely to be real and permanent.

2.4. Italy

Italy had originally been allied with the central powers, but when the war broke out it first declared its neutrality and then eventually entered the fray on the side of the entente. It was induced to do so by the 1915 Treaty of London, under which the entente (Britain, France, and Russia) promised Italy substantial territorial gains in the Adriatic and elsewhere in return for its support.

In June 1916 Vittorio Emmanuele Orlando became prime minister of Italy, a post which he held for exactly three years. He fell from power on 19 June 1919, ten days before the signature of the Versailles treaty, and was replaced by Francesco Nitti. Originally Orlando, too, was a believer in the balance of power. In a speech at Palermo on 24 November 1915, couched in a somewhat cryptic but unmistakably conservative idiom, he said:

In the last forty years there had come into being in Europe a regulatory system of peaceful cohabitation between the nations, by means of an equilibrium of forces, capable of determining that reciprocal limit which is the essential prerequisite of every right, domestic or international. This equilibrium had all the more happily ensured the peace, and guaranteed to every people a harmonious sphere of development, because in individual

---

[58] Ibid. 190.   [59] See the original edn., Clemenceau (1930a: 169).

instances the aspirations and needs of the various allied powers [*sic*] could not always, or could not completely, coincide . . . By participating in this system of European equilibrium, Italy promoted its essentially peaceful interests, while at the same time serving a great ideal of civilization: it was actively contributing towards a corresponding [*sic*] conception of the law [*il diritto*] and of the social intercourse of the peoples and asserted its dignity and its status as a great power.[60]

Once it became apparent that both victory and the peace settlement depended on the United States, Orlando's idiom changed drastically. Looking back in 1944, he could write that the nature of the war, which in its initial stages 'could be considered to be of the classical type that aimed at the passage of certain territories from one state to another', was transformed by the intervention of the United States, 'which by itself, and by itself alone, gave to the war a new aspect and introduced spiritual motives [*motivi ideali*] into it.'[61]

Orlando thenceforth devoted his oratorical skills to proving his fidelity to the new creed. In a speech before the Italian Chamber of Deputies on 3 October 1918, he declared that

Only he who closes his eyes and refuses to see can disregard all the spiritual values [*valori ideali*] that have come to exercise an ever-increasing influence on this war, merging all the initial national aspirations, which yet have natural and legitimate motives, into a great collective aspiration; an aspiration which intends to establish the international of the peoples and to create new and powerful guarantees [a reference to collective security] against every form of injustice and arrogance among the nations [*fra le genti*], as set forth by the words of Wilson with all the power and faith of a new gospel [*sic*].[62]

In another major speech, delivered in the Chamber of Deputies on 20 November 1918, Orlando contended that, if material force alone had decided the outcome of the war, the central powers would have won it.[63] Orlando took the opportunity to thank Italy's allies for assisting it in the struggle. When he mentioned the United States, the chamber celebrated President Wilson with one of its (admittedly not infrequent) standing ovations, the spirit of which is captured in the minutes of the session, with their untranslatably effusive superlatives ('Vivissimi generali prolungatissimi applausi

---

[60] Orlando (1923: 28 f.).   [61] Orlando (1946: 45).
[62] Orlando (1923: 259).   [63] Ibid. 276 f.

—Ministri e deputati sorgono in piedi al grido ripetuto di: Viva Wilson!'[64]). For the time being, Wilsonism could count on a groundswell of public approval.[65]

'Everywhere,' Orlando continued his speech of 20 November,

> there triumphs the principle of nationality, which was the purest manifestation of the democratic spirit and found an apostle in one of the glories of Italian democracy, in Giuseppe Mazzini (*Applausi vivissimi—Grida di Viva Mazzini!*). And to the transformation of states corresponds the transformation of governments. The end of the war finds some of the military autocracies no longer alive . . . I have already had the opportunity to say in this chamber that this war was at the same time the greatest political and social revolution (*Vivissimi applausi*) that history records, greater even than the French Revolution.[66]

It is interesting to note here that, despite the evident echoes of Wilson's speeches, Orlando points out facts rather than asserts principles.

A 'new international law, nay, a real international law' was to be instituted, and Orlando did not hesitate to quote the Vulgate to the effect that all things would flow effortlessly from the quest for 'justice' ('quaerite iustitiam, et omnia vobis data erunt'). The Italian people, Orlando claimed, had no imperialistic ambitions at all—none, that is, once their 'legitimate aspirations' had been satisfied.[67]

That proved to be the crux of the matter. Already in his address to a 'Congress of Subject Nationalities' held in Rome in April 1918, Orlando had both assured the delegates of Italy's solidarity *and* reiterated that Italy's 'essential objective in this war' was to have 'defendable frontiers'.[68] It soon became apparent that these frontiers were not defined so as to coincide with the ethnic divides. Later, on 27 November 1918, Orlando denied being embarrassed when he was asked in the Chamber of Deputies in what spirit he was going to the peace conference. 'I believe', he declared, 'that one ought to go to that congress in an Italian spirit [*con animo d'Italiano*]'.[69]

---

[64] Ibid. 282.

[65] See the memorandum of the US ambassador in Rome of 12 Nov. 1918, with enclosures; USA, State Department (1942–7: i. 416 ff.).

[66] Orlando (1923: 283).   [67] Ibid. 288.

[68] Ibid. 174 f. (11 Apr. 1918, but Orlando was quoting his speech before the Italian Senate of 7 Mar.).   [69] Ibid. 305.

The main source of embarrassment was the Treaty of London, the importance of which Orlando sought to minimize in his speech. Signed in April 1915, the treaty was intended to be kept secret, but the Bolshevists discovered it in the drawers of the Czarist administration and publicized it as evidence of the capitalist greed that, in their view, was responsible for the war. Among the territories promised to Italy under the treaty, the town of Fiume in Dalmatia, with its Italian-speaking population, was not included.[70] In his speech, Orlando cited this as proof that Italy was *not* imperialist. In the event, the heightened prominence of the ethnicity criterion simply led the Italian delegation at the peace conference to demand both the territories promised under the treaty *and* Fiume.

For the time being, Orlando declared that Italy acknowledged the need for compromise (here, the minutes indicate cries of 'Bravo!' as well as 'Commenti', or mutterings). Orlando proceeded to confess that the problems of the settlement were so immense as to leave him 'perplexed [*perplesso*]'.[71]

In the Italian Senate on 15 December 1918, Orlando reiterated his loyalty to the Wilsonian principles, but his tone had, by then, become quite different from what it had been only a few weeks earlier:

To these principles it is our intention to be faithful; but to what extent indeed I cannot here foresee or predict. This is not, this must in no way be regarded as, a reservation . . . Rather, we affirm that these principles, for which we have professed, and still profess, the deepest respect, must inevitably, when it comes to applying them in practice, be adapted and made compatible with certain necessities, with certain complex requirements of real life, which neither can nor should be suppressed.[72]

There followed an appeal to the Italian people finally to think of themselves in terms of being a great power (which in itself was perfectly un-Wilsonian). Such a great power should not be tyrannized by some single problem, even if that problem was of great emotional importance. The Italian people should not forget that 'at this moment humanity as a whole is renewing itself and that there are not only economic and territorial questions . . . , but equally the whole ethical and political order of the world' for Italy

---

[70] Text of the treaty in Temperley (1920–4: v. 384 ff.).
[71] Orlando (1923: 307 ff.).   [72] Ibid. 322 f.

to interest itself in.[73] The problem alluded to was that of the Italian claims in the Adriatic and to the South Tyrol, and it is clear that Orlando was fighting a rearguard action in an attempt to salvage what he could of his Wilsonian professions of faith. He did this, not so much perhaps because he felt so deeply committed to Wilsonism, but because he anticipated the difficulties that the clash between the new principles and the demands of Italian popular opinion would cause him.

In the end, the need to preserve his authority at home proved stronger than his deference to the Wilsonian consensus agenda. Matters came to a head on 27 December 1918, when Leonida Bissolati resigned from Orlando's cabinet. Bissolati, a convinced follower both of Mazzini, the nineteenth-century philosopher of nationalism, and of Wilson, was the main exponent of the so-called *rinunciarii* or 'renouncers'—those who opposed the annexation by Italy of non-Italian-speaking territories. In the cabinet, Bissolati had increasingly been at loggerheads with the foreign minister Sidney Sonnino.

Sonnino did not share Orlando's sudden enthusiasm for Wilsonism. He remained a firm, if cautious, advocate of the balance of power, and of Italy's individual national interests. Sonnino's line carried the day against Bissolati and became decisive in forming Italy's attitude at the peace conference.[74]

Sonnino's conception of foreign politics was original in its very eclecticism. It combined frequent and emphatic invocation of progressive-sounding notions—progress, democracy, equality, independence, self-determination, and so forth—with continued and candid adherence to the nineteenth-century idea of a concert of great powers charged with supervising the international system. Sonnino's paramount goal was to secure Italy's status as a member of this club. But he was careful not to antagonize anyone. Unlike Clemenceau or Orlando, he never suggested that 'idealism' and power politics might not be easy to reconcile. In his utterances as foreign minister, both approaches were given equal prominence, and masterfully referred to alternatively as the situation required.

For example, in a remarkable speech delivered in the Italian Chamber of Deputies on 20 June 1917, Sonnino refuted the call which, following the February Revolution in Russia, emanated

---

[73] Ibid. 330 f.　　[74] See Albrecht-Carrié (1966: 70 ff.).

from Petrograd, for a peace without annexations or reparations. Sonnino's point was that a simple return to the *status quo ante bellum* would not permit the instauration of the new order in world politics advocated by President Wilson in his famous 'Peace Without Victory' speech of 22 January 1917. In fact, Wilson's speech called for a cessation of hostilities (the United States had not entered the war at this stage). But Sonnino contrived to adduce Wilson's speech in support of his appeal for continuation of the war effort.[75]

Sonnino declared among other things that 'practical questions can only be solved by practical means'.[76] He elaborated on the complexity of the issues with which the peacemakers would have to deal. Moral concerns, however, were not therefore to be abandoned.

Far from us be any thought, not only of oppression and subjection, but even of humiliation of any race, of any state, near or far, great or small; rather, we are looking forward to cooperating in the establishment of that equilibrium of forces which is the precondition and the guarantee of mutual respect and reciprocal concessions, essential elements of freedom and justice in the social life both of individuals and of peoples. Our aims, I repeat, are aims of liberation and of security ...[77]

In his speech, Sonnino invoked Mazzini: the idea that a unified Italy, from the fullness of its 'moral and material resources',[78] would make an important contribution to European civilization as a whole was borrowed from the nineteenth-century philosopher, as was a certain visionary rhetoric, brilliant and persuasive as well as conveniently vague. But, in the same breath as Mazzini, Sonnino also invoked Garibaldi, the pragmatist and man of action, bent in single-minded devotion on serving Italy before all else. In a speech before the Chamber of Deputies on 25 October 1917, Sonnino affirmed that 'we all want peace, and a peace which is not just a truce.... But there are some essential points on which it is not given to us to compromise,' namely the recovery of the Italian territories still under foreign rule and the securing of defendable frontiers as a safeguard for genuine independence.[79]

In the same speech, Sonnino pointed out that the peace terms should contain in themselves the guarantee of their permanence.

---

[75] Sonnino (1925: 564 ff.). [76] Ibid. 567.
[77] Ibid. 568. [78] Ibid. 567. [79] Ibid. 577.

Like Clemenceau, Sonnino felt that Wilson's proposed League of Nations would be a supplementary rather than a sufficient asset when it came to defending the settlement against future disturbances. But he adopted a sympathetic view of the League, and, rather than stressing military factors, he insisted that the durability of the settlement would depend on its conformity 'with the general precepts of justice, of freedom, and of respect for human dignity.'

The ambiguity of Sonnino's approach did not go unnoticed, and it came under increasing attack. But he was undeterred. 'Our demands on Austria-Hungary', he told the Chamber of Deputies on 23 February 1918, 'correspond to the double concept of ethnicity and of legitimate security by land and sea.'[80] And he reiterated that

We do not pursue imperialistic aims; we want that, given the possibility of the aggrandizement of others as a result of the war, the balance of power be maintained, because an Italy diminished in its position as a Mediterranean power would be heading towards inevitable political decline in the concert of powers . . .[81]

Sonnino went on to state that an equilibrium of forces was needed to support the League of Nations. But his attachment to the concept of balance of power was probably also related to a fear that sacrificing this concept would make the great-power concept redundant as well, thereby depriving Italy of that recognition of greatness which it had been the aim of the Risorgimento to restore to it. After all, throughout the nineteenth century maintaining the balance of power had been the task of the great-power club.

All this was problematic precisely because Sonnino drew on principles so heavily and indiscriminately. Nationalism and cosmopolitanism, 'idealism' and *realpolitik*, such were the ingredients of his own syncretistic code of values. It was useful in speeches, but less so in bargaining. When, at the conference, the need for concrete decisions finally made equivocation impossible, even Sonnino could no longer have his cake and eat it. His delegation was bound to appear unfaithful either to its aims, or to the Wilsonian consensus agenda, or both. In the process, it lost its credibility as well as, to some extent, its bearings. Nitti, Orlando's successor as Italian prime

[80] Ibid. 586.   [81] Ibid. 587.

minister, could write in 1921 that '[a]t the conference Italy had no directing policy. . . . There was no affirmation of principles at all . . . . Italy received least consideration in the peace treaties among all the conquering countries. It was practically put on one side.'[82]

2.5. Germany

Like Italy, Germany was quick to adapt to Wilsonism. The necessity of espousing the Wilsonian 'gospel', both internationally and domestically, was pleaded for example by Prince Max von Baden— who, on becoming German chancellor, had asked the US president for peace (5 October 1918). In a speech before the Reichstag on 22 October, he said:

We have undertaken to be guided no longer by what we ourselves happen to think fit, but by what as the result of frank conference with our enemies is recognized to be just. . . . For the march of justice cannot be stayed at our frontiers, though we should never voluntarily open them to mere force; the principles which we have recognized as binding upon us, raise problems within [Germany] too. . . . The kernel of Wilson's programme is the League of Nations, and its realization depends on a national self-conquest on the part of every single nation. The realization of a just community of nations demands the abandonment of some part of that unlimited independence which up to now was the mark of sovereignty— by us and by others. The spirit in which we accept this necessary development will be decisive for our whole future. If in our inmost hearts we maintain the principle of national selfishness, which till a short while ago was the dominating force in the life of the peoples, then, gentlemen, we cannot look forward to any recovery or revival. . . . But if we have once realized that the meaning of this fearful war is above all the triumph of the idea of justice, and if we pledge ourselves to this idea not reluctantly, not with any inner reservations, but of our own entire free will, we shall find in it a medicine for the wounds of the present and a task for the forces of the future.[83]

This was followed by a call for domestic democratization ('Our aim is the political coming of age of the German people'[84]).

Like Orlando, Prince Max was convinced that Germany had been defeated not so much by force of arms as by its neglect of principles, which in the prince's opinion it should and could have

---

[82] Nitti (1922: 75 ff.).   [83] Baden (1928: ii. 172 ff., here at 173–4).
[84] Ibid. 178.

put forward to justify its actions in the war.[85] In the hour of defeat, it seemed wise to neglect principles no longer and to adopt the Wilsonian creed—because it was triumphant, but also because it was hoped that the 'justice' propagated by President Wilson would protect Germany from the vindictiveness of his European allies.

This was the line advocated by the German foreign office. In a memorandum of 24 November 1918, the head of the group charged with the preparation of the peace negotiations, Bernstorff, wrote:

Because the outcome of the war has been settled by the United States, its position and in particular that of President Wilson has become decisive for the future. The whole world will become economically and financially dependent on the United States. That is why we turned to President Wilson when we were obliged to end the war. That is also why, at the peace negotiations, we will have to seek the political support of the United States and carry out the subsequent reconstruction of Germany with its help. This necessary decision is made easier for us by the fact that Mr Wilson is the only statesman among the leaders of our enemies who has put forward a sincerely pacifist programme and is resolved to carry it out. All the others are open or disguised imperialists. Germany can only recover from the deep scars that this war has inflicted if, for the foreseeable future, it adopts an eminently pacifist policy. It is therefore obvious that we must eagerly endorse and, as much as possible, outdo all Mr Wilson's wishes concerning the League of Nations, disarmament, court of arbitration, freedom of the seas, etc. Only in this way can we hope to hold in check the imperialism of our other adversaries and to compensate in some degree for Germany's present weakness.[86]

This was the familiar strategy of the weak of using the consensus agenda for leverage against their opponents. Foreign Minister Brockdorff-Rantzau, who headed the German delegation at Paris, was prepared to make the Wilsonian idiom fully his own. On receiving the draft terms of peace (and without knowing as yet what that document contained), he said on 7 May 1919:

On this basis [namely the principles put forward by the US president and agreed upon as a *pactum de contrahendo*] you will find us prepared to examine the peace preliminaries which you lay before us, with the fixed purpose of sharing with you the common task of rebuilding that which has been destroyed, of righting the wrongs that have been done, first and foremost the wrong done to Belgium, and of pointing mankind to new

---

[85] Ibid. i. 206 ff.
[86] Germany, Federal Republic of, Foreign Office (1982: 55).

goals of political and social progress. . . . Gentlemen, the lofty conception that the most terrible calamity in the history of the world should bring about the greatest advance in human progress has been formulated and will be realized. If the goal is to be attained, if the slain in this war are not to have died in vain, then the portals of the League of Nations must be thrown open to all peoples of good will.[87]

This plea, that Germany should be admitted to the League, the German delegation repeated on numerous occasions over the following weeks, in an attempt to prevent Germany from being ostracized by international society. Brockdorff-Rantzau realized that, if this happened, the international consensus agenda, and as a result international society itself, would lose its meaning, a development that would lead to a return to war as the only effective arbiter in international politics.

In order to avoid this, Germany, just like the victors, was willing to subscribe to the new principles, but at the same time the victors had to admit it to the society that these principles served. Brockdorff-Rantzau ended his speech on a note of warning:

The German nation is earnestly prepared to accommodate itself to its hard lot, provided the foundations agreed upon for the peace remain unshaken. A peace which cannot be defended in the name of justice [in practice, the Wilsonian consensus agenda] before the whole world would continually call forth fresh resistance. No one could sign it with a clear conscience, for it would be impossible of fulfilment. No one could undertake the guarantee of fulfilment which its signature would imply.[88]

2.6. Russia

This section will be brief. It is intended only as a reminder that Bolshevist Russia had no voice in the making of the settlement. Whether it could have played any constructive role at the conference is doubtful, given both its ideological hostility to capitalism and the domestic weakness of the new regime, engaged in civil war with its opponents. But it should be emphasized that no attempt was made to integrate Russia into the new international system. On the contrary, not only did the allies hope for the overthrow of the Bolshevists, but they even gave (ineffective) military support to the counter-revolutionaries. This attitude obviously did

---

[87] USA, State Department (1942–7, iii. 418 f.).   [88] Ibid. 420.

not make relations with Russia any easier when the Bolshevists eventually prevailed.

Germany was called to the conference to be asked to atone for the war in the shape of huge reparation payments, cessions of territory, and the like; at the same time, it was told that, nevertheless, it would still remain an international pariah for an unspecified period. Russia, on the other hand, was not even so much as spoken to.

There seems to have been insufficient awareness at the conference of what this implied. Germany and Russia were still potentially powerful despite their current weakness. Europe would have been more stable if only one of them had been antagonized, with the other being part of a broad consensus that the settlement ought to be upheld. But with both being antagonized, and put in a position where to them the new international system was an inhospitable, not to say downright hostile, environment, there was little chance of stability.

3. THE CONFERENCE AT WORK

No sooner had the conference convened than it began to be apparent that in many ways the Wilsonian programme was impractical. Disillusionment and constant violation of the Wilsonian agenda led to the failure to provide a basis for stability even by those Wilsonian concepts that were workable and applied.

3.1. Organization of the Conference[89]

The full conference, with seventy plenipotentiaries representing thirty-two countries and more than 1000 delegates in total, was an unwieldy body. Twenty-two delegations came from outside Europe. Besides the United States and Japan, there were the five British dominions (Australia, Canada, India, New Zealand, and South Africa) three more Asian countries (China, the Hejaz (now Saudi-Arabia)), and Siam (now Thailand), eleven countries from Latin America, and one (Liberia) from Africa. Apart from Britain, France, and Italy, Europe was represented by Belgium, Czechoslovakia, Greece, Poland, Portugal, Rumania, and Serbia (officially

---

[89] On this subject, see esp. Temperley (1920–4: i. 236 ff.), and Marston (1944).

'The Kingdom of the Serbs, Croats, and Slovenes', renamed 'Yugoslavia' in 1929).

It was obvious that, whatever Wilson had said on the democratic equality of nations, actors like Siam or Liberia could not usefully take part in the conference on the same footing as, for example, the United States. While the full conference consisted of plenipotentiaries from all the participating states, a weighted vote was introduced by allotting different numbers of plenipotentiaries to different states. Britain, France, Italy, Japan, and the United States each had five; Belgium, Brazil, and Serbia three; twelve more countries were allotted two; and the remaining twelve one. Even this arrangement, however, was not considered by the major actors to be conducive to satisfactory results.

They found it necessary to reserve all decision-making to themselves. This was exactly what had happened at Vienna, and, egalitarian aspirations notwithstanding, made it necessary to reintroduce the great-power concept. The term itself, too evocative of the old order, was not used. Instead, the 'Rules of the Conference', published as an annex to the minutes of the opening session,[90] distinguish between, on the one hand, the 'belligerent powers with general interests' (Britain, France, Italy, Japan, and the United States), and, on the other, the 'belligerent powers with special interests', which included most of the other participants.[91]

In practice, the full conference held only eight meetings, and, despite much grumbling, it had to be content to endorse the decisions made by the major actors. Given the expectations that had been raised earlier, this appeared as a betrayal. If the great-power concept was restored in a thin disguise, the corresponding consensus principle was not. The major actors at Paris were different from the great powers of the Vienna congress. The fact that they were in command did not necessarily mean that they acted as guardians of the system. Clemenceau and Orlando in particular had other worries, as (outside Europe) did Japan. Moreover, the great-power principle could not work anyway as long as actors that qualified for great-power status were not admitted to the concert of powers, and, indeed, were actively antagonized.

[90] Text in USA, State Department (1942–7: iii. 172 ff.).
[91] The document also refers to four 'powers having broken off diplomatic relations with the enemy powers', and to unnamed 'neutral powers' and 'states in process of formation'.

The major actors first constituted themselves as a body called the Council of Ten. In this body, each was represented by two delegates, who were the head of government and the foreign minister (except in the case of Japan, which did not not send its prime minister but another senior official). In an attempt to speed up the work of the conference, the Council of Ten was superseded in March 1919 by the Council of Four, which comprised only Wilson, Lloyd George, Clemenceau, and Orlando. The foreign ministers (including the Japanese) were grouped in a Council of Five, which played only a secondary role. It is apparent from the minutes of the Council of Four that most of the debate took place between Wilson, Lloyd George, and Clemenceau, with Orlando assuming a rather lesser part.[92] When, because of his dispute with Wilson over Fiume, Orlando left the conference in protest (from 23 April to 5 May), the deliberations were not much affected. The peacemaking was essentially in the hands of Wilson, Lloyd George, and Clemenceau.

The draft treaty of peace with Germany was communicated to the sixth plenary session of the conference on 6 May 1919, only one day before it was due to be presented to the German delegation. The conference had little choice but to approve the draft without being able to propose amendments. This high-handed treatment of the smaller actors caused much resentment.

One important question had not been solved when the conference convened, and it was continually put off during the following months. What role were the defeated actors to play in the negotiations?

Originally, the general assumption seems to have been that Germany would take part in the conference as a matter of course. Plans prepared in November 1918 both by the French foreign ministry and Wilson's aide Colonel House allotted seats in the conference to the representatives of the defeated actors.[93] These representatives were not invited, however, because no decision was ever taken on whether the assembly that gathered in Paris in January 1919 was to draw up a preliminary peace, or a final one.

---

[92] For these minutes, see USA, State Department (1942–7: vol. v) (notes taken by the Council's secretary, Maurice Hankey), and Mantoux (1964) (notes taken by the interpreter, Paul Mantoux).

[93] Nicolson (1934: 97). The French proposals in USA, State Department (1942–7: i. 344 ff.).

The armistice concluded with Germany in November 1918 could not be regarded as a preliminary peace, because it was purely military in character. There was, of course, the agreement, reached between the United States and Germany and acknowledged by the allies, that the peace would be based on Wilson's principles as expressed in his speeches. These speeches, however, as we have seen, lacked precision and could usefully have been made more specific before engaging in the main negotiations.[94]

As it was, none of the delegates knew whether the text on which they were working was to be definitive or whether it was to serve as a basis for negotiations with the defeated actors. If the latter was the case, then the draft treaties had to be severe enough to allow for major concessions once the defeated actors were brought in. Wilson was undecided as late as March as to this. In the end, no oral discussions with the 'enemy' delegates were allowed to take place. The reason appears to have been that the draft Treaty of Versailles was so controversial even among the victors themselves. It was feared that the wartime coalition would fall apart if any real discussion with 'enemy' delegates were allowed. The German delegates, practically kept in quarantine and prevented from all physical contact with other delegations, had to make all observations in writing.[95]

Once the precedent had been set, there was no alternative to treating the other 'enemy' delegations in the same way.

3.2. Decisions are Made

The proceedings of the conference were characterized by lack of coordination between its various organs. The committees set up to deal with the various issues did their best in some cases to make one another's recommendations unworkable. In the case of the German treaty, for instance, the Reparations Section sought to extract the very sums from Germany that the Economic Section

---

[94] In his speech quoted earlier, on receipt of what the victors called the 'draft treaty', the German foreign minister, Brockdorff-Rantzau, himself referred to that document as the 'peace preliminaries', implying that he expected further negotiations to precede the drawing up of the final treaty. Official US documents in USA, State Department (1942–7) refer to the conference prior to the presentation of the draft treaty with Germany as 'conference' and thereafter as 'congress', also implying that the 'conference' was originally meant only as a preparatory stage.
[95] On these points, see Hankey (1963: 29, 159), Lansing (1921: 183 ff.), Marston (1944: ch. 11), Nicolson (1934: 95 ff.), Temperley (1920–4: i. 248, 270 f.).

sought to make it impossible for Germany to pay.[96] Overspecial-
ization of the committees allowed the small states, concerned much
more with their own interests than with those of the international
system as a whole, to exert a disproportionate cumulative influence
on the details of the settlement, at the expense of the defeated
actors.[97]

The Council of Four had neither the time nor the technical competence to review and correct all the recommendations that were
passed on to it by the committees. The detailed, but one-sided,
knowledge of the experts tended to supersede the judgement of
the politicians, and consensus notions had a correspondingly smaller
chance of asserting themselves.

But even the Council of Four, in fact, devoted most of its time
to discussing the minutiae of the settlement, and little time to
the principles on which that settlement was to be based, or to the
manner in which they were to be applied. One occasion when
principles were discussed at some length was the meeting of 27
March 1919, and it showed how divisive the issue was.[98] Characteristically, Orlando seems not to have spoken during the entire
meeting, while Clemenceau and Wilson were at loggerheads and
Lloyd George tried to mediate between them. Lloyd George,
at the beginning of the meeting, referred to his Fontainebleau
memorandum of 25 March. The basic idea developed in that
document was that if the victors exploited Germany's current
weakness too much, Germany would sooner or later hit back;
moreover, such treatment was likely to drive it into the arms of
the Bolshevists.[99] At the meeting, Lloyd George also cited the
precedent of Castlereagh and Wellington vetoing the dismemberment of France in 1815. Wilson endorsed this position:

I trust that, in principle, you [Clemenceau] are agreed with Mr. Lloyd
George as to the moderation which must be shown toward Germany. We
do not want to destroy Germany and we could not do so: our greatest
mistake would be to furnish her with powerful reasons for seeking revenge
at some future time. Excessive demands would be sure to sow the seeds
of war. . . . We must not give our enemies even an impression of injustice.

Clemenceau replied that '[m]y principles are the same as
yours; I am considering only their application.' The difficulty, for

[96] Nicolson (1934: 112).   [97] Ibid. 117.   [98] Mantoux (1964: 24 ff.).
[99] Text of the memorandum in Lloyd George (1938: i. 404 ff.).

Clemenceau, was that 'what we regard as just here in this room will not necessarily be accepted as such by the Germans.' And again: 'Their idea of justice, I assure you, is not ours.'

According to Clemenceau, principles therefore had to be upheld by force:

The Germans, a servile people, must have force to sustain an argument. Shortly before he died Napoleon said: 'Nothing permanent is founded on force.' I am not so sure . . . What is true, is that force cannot establish anything substantial unless it is in the service of justice. Every effort must be made to be just toward the Germans; but when it comes to persuading them that we are just toward them, that is another matter. We can, I believe, save the world for a long time to come from German aggression; but the German spirit is not going to change so fast.

The following day, the discussion was about the French claim to the Saar, the legitimacy of which Wilson denied on the grounds that it was incompatible with self-determination.[100] But Clemenceau insisted that

It is a mistake to believe that the world is governed by abstract principles. These are accepted by some parties, rejected by others . . . You wish to do justice to the Germans. Do not believe that they will ever forgive us; they will only seek the chance for revenge . . .

He exhorted Wilson to take into account human feeling rather than only principles. Wilson replied:

I agree with you that feeling is the most powerful force in all this world . . . . Everywhere in the world there is today a passion for justice. . . . This enthusiastic aspiration for just solutions will change into cynical skepticism if the impression is created that we are false to our own rules of justice.

This was correct as well as prophetical. It did not, however, go to the heart of the matter, or refute the point made by Clemenceau that the settlement would inevitably be unacceptable to the Germans. As has been pointed out, even for Wilson principles deserved support exclusively in their capacity as moral imperatives—and not because they provided international society with some means of coordination and cohesion, with common points of reference indispensable to its stability. Lloyd George, as the Fontainebleau memorandum shows, perceived somewhat more clearly that a

---

[100] Mantoux (1964: 41 ff.).

settlement not based on consensus would lack stability. But he was no more capable than Wilson and Clemenceau of the detached, calculating 'cynicism' of a Talleyrand, a Metternich, or, for that matter, a Castlereagh. Like Wilson, therefore, Lloyd George was prepared to admit that, because principles and politics belonged to different and, unfortunately, still antagonistic realms, clashes between them had sometimes to be resolved at the expense of the principles. None of the three grasped that principles might be a more reliable safeguard for order than force. They did, dimly, recognize the dangers of violating the Wilsonian consensus agenda, and yet failed to see that, properly applied, the consensus agenda could make a contribution to peace in its own right.

If the Germans had taken part in the deliberations, it would have been apparent that they endorsed the code and that it was Clemenceau, not they, whose conception of 'justice' differed from the Wilsonian principles. As it happened, the contention that they would never accept these principles was not contradicted until after the treaty had been drawn up, by which time it could no longer be modified substantially.

This does not mean, of course, that the Wilsonian agenda failed to affect the decisions reached. Where Wilson and Lloyd George defended their principles staunchly enough, they were able to prevail over Clemenceau—who had, after all, declared that he would make 'every sacrifice' to remain allied to them.[101] If the supreme strategic necessity, which was to preserve the unity of the victors, implied submission to principles, then lesser strategic desiderata had to be sacrificed. As a result, the Saar was not incorporated into France.

Yet the outcome of the Saar debate was not a successful application of Wilsonism. It was an awkward compromise which may serve as a typical example of the shortcomings of the settlement. Clemenceau succeeded in achieving the separation of the Saar from Germany under a League of Nations mandate—in effect, the Saar was treated much like the German colonies, which were also placed under League mandates and, in practice, attached to the victors' colonial empires. A plebiscite was to be held only after fifteen years, despite the fact that the 650,000 or so inhabitants were all ethnically German and had no obvious desire to be

---

[101] Above, sect. 2.3.

separated from the rest of Germany (there were strikes and in-surgence against the French military administration that ruled the Saar until it was handed over to the League in 1920). In 1922 a local parliament was set up, but it was not given any legislative powers—these remained exclusively with the League administration. In the economic sphere, the treaty transferred the important coal-mines into French ownership as another form of reparations, which, in practice, made at least the subsoil French; and, despite the League mandate, the French government incorporated the Saar into its own customs zone. There were attempts to promote French in the schools, and even to induce the Holy See to remove the Saar from German ecclesiastical jurisdiction and attach it to the French diocese of Metz instead—because the bishops of Trier and Speyer, under whose jurisdiction this Catholic area fell, actively encouraged manifestations of German nationalism on the part of the clergy.

In short, the treaty did not make the Saar French because it was ethnically German, but detached it from Germany as if by right of conquest. It forbade the inhabitants to register their opinion in this matter for fifteen years, during which time the French govern-ment was given the opportunity to interfere. The inhabitants were denied democratic participation in their own government, on the grounds (in effect) that Germany deserved punishment for having been insufficiently democratic before 1918. Ironically, this happened at precisely the same time that the rest of Germany adopted a fully democratic constitution. The whole arrangement was obviously at odds with the recognized official basis of the settlement, Wilson's 1918 speeches. For example, it is unlikely that this is what Wilson meant when he said on 11 February 1918 'that peoples and prov-inces are not to be bartered about from sovereignty to sovereignty as if they were mere chattels and pawns in a game, even the great game, now forever discredited, of the balance of power' (this was the second of the *Four Principles*).[102]

When the plebiscite was held in 1935, hopes that the Saar would opt for France were dashed. The event was easily and massively exploited for National Socialist propaganda purposes, with a 90 per cent vote in favour of Germany despite acute misgivings among the political forces in the Saar about the nature of Hitler's regime.

[102] Temperley (1920–4: i. 439).

The treatment of the Saar is characteristic of the 1919 settlement in that too often the official adoption of the Wilsonian agenda
failed to prevent allied vindictiveness or greed. The assumption
that politics and principles belonged, as yet, to different spheres
favoured the neglect of principles as soon as the negotiations began
in earnest.

Wilson himself anticipated on the decision-making of the conference when, on a visit to Italy in early January 1919, before the
conference had convened, he approved Italy's claim to the strategic Brenner frontier. The most indulgent explanation for this is
that Wilson was simply unaware of the demographic details, which
meant that an extension of the Italian border to the Brenner would
bring a substantial German-speaking population (in the South
Tyrol) under Italian rule.[103] This was obviously incompatible with
the ninth of the *Fourteen Points* of 8 January 1918: 'A readjust-
ment of the frontiers of Italy should be effected along clearly
recognizable lines of nationality.'[104] In other words, Wilson had
committed a serious blunder, which undermined his credibility
even before the conference had opened; and it was not the last.
In a blunder on a larger scale, he (and Lloyd George) connived
at Austria being forbidden from reuniting with Germany, against
Austria's express wishes, in deference to French security interests.
This was perhaps the most flagrant violation, in the name of political expediency, of the principle of self-determination.[105]

Already in the eleventh of his *Fourteen Points*, in a departure
from his usual anti-historical stance, Wilson had suggested that
the settlement of the Balkan question should be in accordance
with 'historically established lines of allegiance and nationality'.[106]
This notion of historicity as a legitimizing factor (a throwback, in
effect, to the Peace of Westphalia, as this concept had played no
role at either Utrecht or Vienna) was in conflict with the principle
of national self-determination. To allow historical considerations
to influence the settlement could only result in more confusion,
and a further widening of the credibility gap besetting the final
settlement.

Czechoslovakia was allowed to retain the 'historic' frontiers of
the Kingdom of Bohemia, and the three million German-speakers

---

[103] Nicolson (1934: 169 ff.).   [104] Temperley (1920–4: i. 434).
[105] See ibid. iv. 391 f.   [106] Ibid. i. 434; above, sect. 2.1.

within these frontiers were not asked their opinion. Defeated Hungary, on the other hand, had to cede two-thirds of its 'historic' territory, complete with some three million Magyars, because the lands in question were inhabited predominantly by non-Magyars. Clinging to the notion of historicity, Hungary explicitly recognized as 'just' that, for historical reasons, the German population in Bohemia should belong to Czechoslovakia, and then used this precedent to protest against the cessions imposed on itself. At the same time, Austria, indignant at the preferential treatment accorded to Czechoslovakia, nevertheless held it to be 'just' that it should receive German-speaking West Hungary.[107]

In reply to the protest by Hungary, the victors wrote that '[e]ven a thousand-year-old state is not built for permanence [*n'est pas fondé à subsister*] when its history is that of a long oppression by a minority avaricious for rule of the races enclosed within its frontiers,' and that '[h]istoric right does not avail against the will of peoples;' in answer to the Hungarian request for plebiscites, the will of the peoples concerned was declared to be self-evident.[108] This might be recognized as an application, if not of the principle of national self-determination in the strict sense, then at least of the ethnicity criterion (a tolerable substitute). But the treatment of Hungary was marred by the punitive streak that did so much to undermine the work of the conference. There was also a strong impression of double-dealing: Hungary was to be dismembered because of its past domination of other ethnic groups, but Prague was, from then on, to rule, not only over the German-speakers in Bohemia, but also over the Slovaks and Ruthenes (as well as a good many Magyars), who did not live in historic Bohemia at all.

In order to create a Hungary that was reasonably homogeneous in ethnic terms, the borders drawn at Paris could perhaps have been a little more generous, but not substantially different. The problem was that the new states, in particular Poland and Czechoslovakia, seemed to conform to exactly the same pattern as the much-condemned old Austria-Hungary—the domination of ethnic minorities by a numerically stronger group. Moreover, it was hard to avoid the impression that there was a hidden strategic rationale for this difference of treatment. Germany and Austria were shorn of the Sudetenland, Alsace-Lorraine, and other territories, and

---

[107] Ibid. iv. 439 ff., esp. 442.   [108] 6 May 1920; quoted ibid. 422.

the two countries were barred from reunification. Hungary was diminished by the transfer of as much of its lands and as many of its inhabitants to other actors as was at all compatible with the criterion of ethnicity. It was obvious that this treatment would not do much to reconcile these countries to the settlement. But Clemenceau was not alone in thinking that they would never recognize the settlement as just whatever the terms, and that it was better therefore to make them as small and weak as possible. Czechoslovakia and Poland, on the other hand, would remain the natural enemies of the defeated actors at whose expense they had been aggrandized, and hence the natural allies of France. This hidden rationale was damaging to the cause of international consensus because it served the exclusive interests of individual actors, in particular France, and not the interests of the system as such.

There is a widespread impression that the unsatisfactory nature of the settlement in central and east Europe was due to a destabilizing effect inherent in the concept of national self-determination as such.[109] But the instability of the settlement had perhaps more to do with the inconsistency with which the principle was applied.[110] The settlement was unsatisfactory not because it was based on the principle of national self-determination, but because it was only partly based on the principle, and because the departures from the principle seemed to be dictated simply by the desire to punish the defeated actors (and, in the process, take advantage of them). The peace treaties were not in keeping with the new Wilsonian consensus agenda.

There would certainly have been problems in any case: ethnic groups were often entangled, and perfect solutions based on the separation of ethnic groups were therefore impossible. But acceptable solutions, perhaps, were not. They would have required that whatever compromises were reached were mutually agreed and supported by consensus. Imposing awkward compromises by means of a dictated peace was certain to create strong mutual antagonism, and hence instability.

As the work of the conference progressed, violations of the consensus agenda accumulated, resulting in widespread and increasing

[109] For the view that self-determination is inherently destabilizing, see e.g. Kedourie (1984).   [110] See Cobban (1969: 57 ff.).

disquiet that things were going wrong. Wilson eventually decided to adopt a particularly intransigent stance *vis-à-vis* the very government that he had previously indulged in his much-remarked mistake over the Brenner frontier. He fiercely opposed Italy's designs in northern Yugoslavia, as if to make up for his earlier consent to Italy's acquisition of the South Tyrol.

The problem was the Treaty of London, mentioned earlier, which had prompted Italy to enter the war on the side of the entente. Britain and France still held themselves to be pledged by their signature, even though the provisions of the treaty, with its references to the balance of power and the need for territorial compensations to preserve it, were quite out of tune with the new consensus agenda as propounded by Wilson. The British and French prime ministers took the view that if Italy insisted on receiving the territories promised to it in the treaty they could not refuse. On 10 February 1920 the president addressed to them a sharply worded memorandum.

It is a time to speak with the utmost frankness. The Adriatic issue as it now presents itself raises the fundamental question as to whether the American government can on any terms cooperate with its European associates in the great work of maintaining the peace of the world by removing the primary causes of war. This government does not doubt its ability to reach amicable understandings with the Associated Governments as to what constitutes equity and justice in international dealings; for difference of opinion as to the best methods of applying just principles have never obscured the vital fact that in the main [the?] several governments have entertained the same fundamental conception of what these principles are. But if substantial agreement to principle . . . is not to determine international issues; if the country possessing the most endurance in pressing its demands [Italy] rather than the country armed with a just cause [Yugoslavia] is to gain the support of the powers; if forcible seizure of coveted areas [an allusion to d'Annunzio's occupation of Fiume in September 1919] is to be permitted and condoned . . . ; if, in a word, the old order of things which brought so many evils on the world is still to prevail, then the time is not yet come when this government can enter a concert of powers, the very existence of which must depend upon a new spirit and a new order.[111]

It is hard to avoid an impression of hypocrisy (heartfelt as it may have been) in reading this. Lloyd George and Millerand (who

---

[111] Temperley (1920–4: v. 422).

had replaced Clemenceau in January) replied that the settlement should no more ignore valid treaties than national aspirations. They pointed out that 'the war began in order to enforce upon Germany respect for the solemn treaty she had made nearly eighty years before in regard to the neutrality of Belgium.'[112]

In fact, from a legal point of view, treaties were traditionally held to be valid *rebus sic stantibus*, which meant that an unforeseen change of circumstances might justify their abrogation. Moreover, such abrogation was required anyway under article 20 of the League Covenant (see below). But, more than a year into the conference, declaring the Treaty of London invalid may have seemed inadvisable.

The British and French prime ministers presumably felt that disowning the Treaty of London at this stage would jeopardize the settlement still further, rather than strengthen it as Wilson seems to have hoped. The new consensus agenda was being applied so arbitrarily and haphazardly that, for the time being, it was clearly not acting as a stabilizing factor. This made it seem unwise to antagonize yet another major actor and to risk pushing it into the ranks of the 'revisionist' powers—those European actors, that is, who were dissatisfied with the settlement.

However, this is precisely what happened anyway. Despite being on the winning side in the war, Italy ended up as a dissatisfied power with a grudge against the settlement. Not only did the peacemakers recreate the pre-1914 division of the European states system into two antagonistic blocs, they even swelled the ranks of the 'revisionist' powers by adding one of the victors to them.

3.3. The Treaties

The chief result of the conference was the five treaties of peace: that of Versailles with Germany (signed on 28 June 1919), that of Saint-Germain with Austria (10 September 1919), that of Neuilly with Bulgaria (27 November 1919), that of the Trianon with Hungary (4 June 1920), and that of Sèvres with Turkey (10 August 1920). The original intention seems to have been to include all five agreements into a single document, following the example of the Congress of Vienna. But in March 1919 it was decided to give priority to the settlement with Germany.[113] The Treaty of Versailles

---

[112] 17 Feb. 1920, ibid. 427.   [113] Ibid. vi. 541; i. 261 f.

was the most important of the five, and the others, described by Lloyd George as 'ancillary treaties',[114] were modelled on it to a greater or lesser extent.

All five treaties were dictated, not negotiated. In every instance, the delegations of the defeated powers were only allowed to present observations in writing. This led to some minor adjustments, but not to any substantial modifications.[115] Foreshadowing the division of Europe into 'revisionist' and 'status quo' powers, each agreement was concluded between two parties only. For example, the Treaty of Versailles was concluded between the 'Allied and Associated Powers' (subdivided into the five 'Principal Allied and Associated Powers' and twenty-two others) on the one hand and Germany on the other.[116]

All five treaties incorporated the Covenant of the League of Nations. The League was to be the embodiment of the comity of nations, but membership was subject to some conditions. Article 1 of the Covenant stated that

Any fully self-governing state, dominion or colony ... may become a member of the League if its admission is agreed to by two-thirds of the Assembly, provided that it shall give effective guarantees of its sincere intention to observe its international obligations, and shall accept such regulations as may be prescribed by the League in regard to its military, naval and air forces and armaments.

Articles 2 to 4 established the democratic structure of the League, which flowed from the equality principle. All member states were to have one vote in the League's Assembly. At the same time, however, the five major victorious powers were given a privileged position, in that they had a permanent seat in the League Council. Article 5 safeguarded the member states' autonomy by laying down that, in general, decisions could only be taken unanimously. The autonomy principle was also served by article 10. It laid the foundation for the mechanisms of collective security, by providing that 'the members of the League undertake to respect and preserve

---

[114] Lloyd George (1938: i. 17).

[115] For these adjustments, see Temperley (1920–4). A convenient summary of the adjustments made to the Treaty of Versailles is found in Finch (1919: 552 f.).

[116] The term 'Associated Powers' was used because for reasons of domestic politics Wilson did not want to describe his cooperation with European powers as an outright 'alliance'.

as against external aggression the territorial integrity and existing political independence of all members of the League.'

International society as represented by the League was to be characterized by what Wilson called the 'reign of law'. Therefore, article 12 stipulated that member states should submit their disputes to arbitration or to enquiry by the Council, and that they could resort to war only if this procedure failed. Article 14 provided for the setting up of the Permanent Court of International Justice. This was an attempt to go beyond the traditional methods of conciliation, mediation, and arbitration for the peaceful settlement of disputes between states, and to introduce, on the international level, judicial procedures directly inspired by municipal law.

Article 19 expressed the idea that the international order established in the aftermath of the war was not to be immutable, but that it should be subject to continual revision: 'The Assembly may from time to time advise the reconsideration by members of the League of treaties which have become inapplicable and the consideration of international conditions whose continuance might endanger the peace of the world.'

In the same vein, article 20 sought to prevent the new international society from relapsing into the ways of the past: 'The members of the League severally agree that this Covenant is accepted as abrogating all obligations or understandings *inter se* which are inconsistent with the terms thereof, and solemnly undertake that they will not hereafter enter into any engagements inconsistent with the terms thereof.'

What the drafters of this article had in mind were the secret alliances of the nineteenth century, but also those concluded during the war, such as the Treaty of London. Thenceforth, such pacts would also be incompatible with article 18 of the Covenant, which (in accordance with the first of the *Fourteen Points*) provided for the publication of all international treaties.

Interestingly, and in contrast with the 1945 United Nations Charter, article 1 of the League Covenant made provision for states wishing to leave the organization. Article 16 threatened with expulsion any member that did not fulfil its obligations. These arrangements illustrate the perceived dichotomy, typical of the 'idealist' school of international relations, between 'civilized' international society on the one hand and a sphere of renegades or outcasts beyond the pale on the other.

The defeated actors were unwilling to accept the opprobrium attached to non-membership, and they made every effort to be admitted immediately to the League. As this request was refused by the victors, the inclusion of the Covenant in the treaties could only appear to the defeated powers as adding insult to injury. (The inclusion is explained by the fact that Wilson agreed to deviations from his principles on the understanding that the other victors supported the League, the establishment of which Wilson felt to be the most important among his intended contributions to world peace. Wilson feared that, if the conclusion of the Covenant was separated from the conclusion of the peace treaties and left till a later date, it would come to nothing. At the same time, he hoped that the League would provide the means for future modification of the settlement.)

The victors reserved membership of the League to themselves and to the neutral actors, while their erstwhile adversaries were put on probation. For the smaller among them, this period was not of long duration: Bulgaria was admitted as early as December 1919 (at a time when it had not even ratified the Treaty of Neuilly), and Austria followed in December 1920. Hungary, however, had to wait until 1922, and Germany did not become a member until 1926. As a result of these delays, the League came to be seen by many, not as a symbol of international society, but as a new repressive 'Holy Alliance' (see quotations further on), a covert way for the victors to remain united against their former foes even in peacetime. The discredit which attached itself to the League in this way obviously did not help the cause of the principles on which the League was based, and added to the instability of the post-war international system.

3.4. The German Reaction

Soon after receiving the draft Treaty of Versailles on 7 May 1919, the German delegation began bombarding the allies with notes of protest. These complaints took a definitive form in the voluminous *Observations of the German Delegation on the Conditions of Peace*.[117] Drawn up in Berlin on 27 May, this text reached the Council of Four two days later. It illustrates the determination with which the German leadership invoked both the Wilsonian

---

[117] USA, State Department (1942–7: vi. 795 ff.).

consensus agenda and the *need* for consensus if the international system was to be stabilized. Of course, the German reasoning was self-serving, and the tone of the complaints was shrill. This does not deprive the German arguments of their objective validity, and, given the treatment meted out to Germany at the conference, the confrontational language, full of alarm and indignation, is understandable. But, obviously, it did not make consensus any easier to attain in practice.

True to the spirit of the age, the *Observations* read in many places like a revolutionary manifesto (indeed, its left-wing rhetoric, which went beyond the more revolutionary utterances even of Wilson, must have put off the allied statesmen, who were not particularly inclined towards socialism). The document proclaimed that '[t]here are natural rights of nations, as there are natural rights of man,' and drew on all the consensus principles of the Wilsonian agenda. Special emphasis was, of course, placed on national self-determination. 'The inalienable basic right of all states', the *Observations* declared, 'is the right to self-maintenance and self-determination.'[118]

But the proposed treaty disregarded the principle of national self-determination, or the related ethnicity criterion, in many instances where its application would have been to the apparent advantage of Germany, most flagrantly with regard to Austria. The *Observations* insisted that 'the right of self-determination of nations must not be a principle which is applied solely to the prejudice of Germany, it must rather hold good in all states alike and especially be also applied where populations of German race wish to be united to the German Empire.' (Somewhat misleadingly, this official translation uses the word 'empire', with its monarchical and imperialist connotations, for 'Reich'. The German term is more neutral, and the Weimar Republic therefore still called itself 'Deutsches Reich'.)[119]

The failure to implement the principle of national self-determination in a consistent way was also a violation of the equality principle. The *Observations*, in protesting against Germany's exclusion from the League of Nations, reminded the victors that '[l]asting peace in the world can only be attained through a League of Nations which guarantees the possession of equal rights to great

[118] Ibid. 810.   [119] Ibid. 823.

and small powers.'[120] The proposed League Covenant was attacked because of its reactionary (that is, un-Wilsonian) nature. For example, the fact was criticized that it gave a privileged position to the big powers, which had permanent seats in the League Council.

That which the treaty of peace aims at creating is rather a continuation of the coalition of [Germany's] enemies which does not deserve the name of a 'League of Nations'. . . . Instead of the long-dreamt-of holy alliance of the peoples it returns to the fatal conception of a Holy Alliance of 1815 . . . One misses the provision of technical bodies and impartial courts existing side by side with the Council which is controlled by the great powers, which can keep the whole civilized world subject to it at the cost of the independence and legal equality of the smaller states. Thus the way is left open for a continuation of the old political system based on force, with all its resentments and rivalries![121]

Democratic renewal and emancipation from an evil past were keynotes of the *Observations* as much as of Wilson's speeches.

The German government are in agreement with the governments of the Allied and Associated Powers in considering that the ghastly devastations which this war has entailed demand the establishment of a new order in the world . . . The restoration and reconstruction of the international order of the world can only be secured if the existing authorities succeed in realizing in a new spirit the great idea of democracy; if, as President Wilson expressed it on the 4th August [in fact, July] 1918, there is 'settlement of all questions . . . on the basis of free acceptance of such settlement on the part of the people thereby affected.' Only those peoples which live free and responsible to themselves in accordance with justice can give each other guarantees for just and honourable relations. But these qualities of justice and honour also require that the peoples should mutually guarantee to each other freedom and life as the most sacred and inalienable of all fundamental laws. No recognition of these principles can be traced in the peace document laid before us; a moribund conception of the world, imperialistic and capitalistic in tendency, celebrates in that document its last dreadful triumph.[122]

The *Observations* expressed bitterness about the fact that Germany's democratic revolution had had no mitigating effect on the peace terms. The document insisted that Germany's new

---

[120] Ibid. 818 f.   [121] Ibid. 812.

[122] Ibid. 818. The quotation from Wilson's speech is retranslated from the German. In the original it read 'settlement of every question . . . upon the basis of the free acceptance of that settlement by the peoples immediately concerned'.

constitutional arrangements were based on 'the strictest principles of democracy', and complained that it was 'impossible to imagine what more stringent conditions could have been imposed on an imperialist government.'[123] In another passage, a 'return to constitutional circumstances in which the will of the German people might be disregarded' was ruled out, and a link was established between domestic affairs and international society.

In view of the inter-connexion which exists today between conditions throughout the world no people can, however, stand alone in its development, but each one, if it is to be an efficient and trustworthy member of the family of nations, needs the support of its neighbours given in full confidence. The new Germany is convinced of her ability to earn that confidence and is therefore entitled to ask for admission to the League of Nations.[124]

Every ingredient of Wilsonism was endorsed and applied in the *Observations*. Self-determination, equality, and democracy were all invoked to suggest a radical break with the past. In summing up, the *Observations* concluded:

The working people of Germany has always wished and still wishes for peace and justice. In this respect Germany feels herself to be at one with all mankind. The noblest spirits everywhere are yearning for the peace of right after the terrible war; if this hope is disappointed, then the idea of right is destroyed for generations to come, and a world order based on morality, impossible. A durable peace cannot be founded on the oppression and enslavement of a great nation. Only a return to the immutable principles of morality and culture and especially to loyalty towards treaties concluded and obligations assumed, can render continued existence possible for mankind. The new peace must be a peace of right and therefore one of free consent. It must therefore in the first place rest on the agreement solemnly entered into by both sides, which was laid down in the notes exchanged [between the US and German governments] between October 3rd and November 5th, 1918.

Justice and the free consent of all parties to the treaty will furnish the strongest—nay, in the course of time the only—guarantees of the treaty that is to be concluded. With the object of founding a new common life based on liberty and labour, the German people turn to those hitherto their adversaries; they demand in the interest of all nations and men a peace to which they can give their consent in accordance with the intimate convictions of their conscience.[125]

[123] Ibid. 805.   [124] Ibid. 882.   [125] Ibid. 883.

3.5. Allied Defence and Persistence

The victors reacted to the German *Observations* on 16 June 1919, with a document entitled *Reply of the Allied and Associated Powers*.[126] This text was even more confrontational, both in its language and in its contents, than the *Observations*. It stated that '[t]he Allied and Associated Powers are in complete accord with the German delegation in their insistence that the basis for the negotiation of the treaty of peace is to be found in the correspondence which immediately preceded the signing of the armistice on November 11, 1918,' that is, the famous exchange of notes between Washington and Berlin.

But the German allegations that the treaty was not in keeping with this agreement were denied energetically.

The Allied and Associated Powers believe that they will be false to those who have given their all to save the freedom of the world if they consent to treat this war on any other basis than as a crime against humanity and right. . . . Justice, therefore, is the only possible basis for the settlement of the accounts of this terrible war. Justice is what the German delegation asks for and says that Germany had been promised. Justice is what Germany shall have. But it must be justice for all. There must be justice for the dead and wounded, and for those who have been orphaned and bereaved that Europe might be freed from Prussian despotism. There must be justice for the peoples who now stagger under war debts which exceed £30,000,000,000 that liberty might be saved. There must be justice for those millions whose homes and land, ships and property German savagery has spoliated and destroyed. That is why the Allied and Associated Powers have insisted as a cardinal feature of the treaty that Germany must undertake to make reparation to the very uttermost of her power; for reparation for wrongs inflicted is of the essence of justice. . . . Somebody must suffer for the consequences of the war. Is it to be Germany, or only the peoples she has wronged? . . . The Allied and Associated Powers therefore believe that the peace they have proposed is fundamentally a peace of justice. They are no less certain that it is a peace of right fulfilling the terms agreed upon at the time of the armistice. . . . [The draft treaty] is frankly not based upon a general condonation of the events of 1914–1918. It would not be a peace of justice if it were.[127]

The *Reply* treated Germany much like a defendant under municipal law. Germany, however, pleaded not guilty, and was

---

[126] USA, State Department (1942–7: vi. 926 ff.).   [127] Ibid. 928 ff., 935.

particularly outraged by article 231 of the treaty—the notorious 'war-guilt clause', by which Germany was made to acknowledge its responsibility for the war. (Similar clauses were later included in article 177 of the treaty with Austria and article 161 of the treaty with Hungary.[128] The inclusion of 'war-guilt clauses' in the Paris settlement marks another break with the past. The other peace treaties considered in this book all contain amnesty clauses, which provided that any injustices committed by any party in the course of the war were to be forgotten from the moment of signature. The wording of such amnesty clauses deliberately omitted to make a distinction between victors and vanquished. They seem to have been a standard feature of European peacemaking.)

A special German memorandum contested the thesis that responsibility for the outbreak of the war lay with Germany alone, and asked that the matter be investigated by an 'impartial commission of enquiry'.[129] The *Reply* in turn undertook to refute the memorandum. Its main argument was that '[t]he whole history of Prussia has been one of domination, aggression and war,' and that '[a]utocratic Germany, under the inspiration of her rulers, was bent on domination.' To demonstrate this, the *Reply* continued, there was no need to have recourse to diplomatic history, since a proof already existed: 'The truth of the charges thus brought against them the German people have admitted by their own revolution.'[130]

This is sophistry. Even as a debate on moral issues the whole exchange was of a poor standard. But the real problem was that such a debate should not have taken place as part of the peace-making process at all, since it was not of a consensus-building nature. If, by the Versailles treaty, Germany indeed obtained 'justice', it was justice reduced to a right of punishment. For all its declared Wilsonian progressivism, to a large extent the settlement was rather more concerned with punishing past wrongdoings than with building a better future. We have already discussed the danger of such an approach to the problem of international stability.

On the whole, the Council of Four was unmoved by the German objections. Although Wilson was the chief promoter of the

---

[128] See Marks (1976: 13).

[129] 27 May 1919; USA, State Department (1942–7: vi. 781 ff.). The memorandum was signed by Hans Delbrück, Albrecht Mendelssohn-Bartholdy, Max von Montgelas, and Max Weber. [130] Ibid. 959 ff.

new principles, he lacked the impartiality in applying them that was the prerequisite for their being a factor of stability. This aspect of his personality was captured by Lloyd George when he wrote of Wilson that '[h]is radiant charitableness towards mankind turned to flame when it came into contact with heretics.'[131] As for Clemenceau and Orlando, they felt that too much of their respective national interests had been sacrificed to abstract principles already, and that further concessions were out of the question. Italy, it is true, was affected less by the Versailles treaty than France. But it could hardly support a rigorous application of principles with regard to Germany when it intended to disregard them itself over Yugoslavia and the South Tyrol. Neither of the two prime ministers realized that what was needed was not a compromise between principles and national interests, but a compromise between national interests compatible with the prevailing consensus principles.

Among the Four, Lloyd George was the only one to express misgivings about the treaty.[132] He proposed modifications which his colleagues (especially Clemenceau) were unwilling to accept. Indeed, given the inconsistency of Lloyd George's suggestions, it is difficult to see how they could have been accepted without calling the whole settlement in question. If the 'injustice' of the treaty was admitted on one point, how could it be defended on others? If Germany was granted membership of the League, how could the victors still insist on the payment of enormous reparations or on the particularly humiliating demand for the extradition and trial by the victors of the deposed emperor? For these were items which even Lloyd George did not intend to sacrifice. Far from legitimizing the treaty, piecemeal concessions would only have exacerbated the struggle for revision. Short of drafting a new treaty, there was no choice but to push ahead with the existing one.

If the Germans withheld their 'free consent', there were means to compel them—the blockade of the sea ports (which was starving a population that was also being decimated by epidemics), the large numbers of prisoners of war whose repatriation could be delayed, or the threat of further occupation of German territory from the existing bridgeheads. In Berlin, faced with the allied ultimatum, the government fell. The new government that took its

---

[131] Lloyd George (1938: i. 231).
[132] On the attitude of Lloyd George, see Gilbert (1966: ch. 5).

place submitted to the inevitable. The German note of acceptance was sent on 23 June 1919:

Yielding to overwhelming force, but without on that account abandoning its view in regard to the unheard-of injustice of the conditions of peace, the government of the German Republic therefore declares that it is ready to accept and sign the conditions of peace imposed by the Allied and Associated Powers.[133]

4. NEGATIVE CONSENSUS OR THE PEACE THAT FAILED

As early as 1919 there was a widespread feeling that things were going seriously wrong. The peace terms were nowhere greeted with enthusiasm. Their authors were placed on the defensive not only by the Germans, but even by their own compatriots. Virtually everybody who was at all interested in politics (and in the wake of the war there were few who were not) either considered the settlement to be too harsh or too lenient. Over the years, the view prevailed that the terms were too harsh, an indication that the new consensus agenda, which they infringed, was indeed supported widely. But by that time it was too late. Mistakes had been made that could no longer be rectified. Any attempt to do so—the policy of appeasement in particular—tended to make matters worse. If the contemporary utterances on the settlement have a common denominator, it is the feeling that history had got out of hand and that catastrophe lay in wait.

Following the divulgation of the draft treaty of Versailles, disillusionment prevailed in both the British and the US delegations. As early as 8 May 1919 the US secretary of state, Lansing, summed up his impression as follows:

The terms of peace were yesterday delivered to the German plenipotentiaries, and for the first time in these days of feverish rush of preparation there is time to consider the treaty as a complete document.

The impression made by it is one of disappointment, of regret, and of depression. The terms of peace appear immeasurably harsh and humiliating, while many of them seem to me impossible of performance.

[133] Quoted Hankey (1963: 181).

The League of Nations created by the treaty is relied upon to preserve the artificial structure which has been erected by compromise of the conflicting interests of the great powers and to prevent the germination of the seeds of war which are sown in so many articles and which under normal conditions would soon bear fruit. The League might as well attempt to prevent the growth of plant life in a tropical jungle. Wars will come sooner or later.

It must be admitted in honesty that the League is an instrument of the mighty to check the normal growth of national power and national aspirations among those who have been rendered impotent by defeat. . . .

This war was fought by the United States to destroy forever the conditions which produced it. These conditions have not been destroyed. They have been supplanted by other conditions equally productive of hatred, jealousy, and suspicion. In place of the Triple Alliance and the Entente has arisen the Quintuple Alliance [the five permanent members of the League Council—Britain, France, Italy, Japan, and the United States] which is to rule the world. The victors in this war intend to impose their combined will upon the vanquished and to subordinate all interests to their own. . . .

It is useless to close our eyes to the fact that the power to compel obedience by the exercise of the united strength of 'The Five' is the fundamental principle of the League. Justice is secondary. Might is primary. . . .

We have a treaty of peace, but it will not bring permanent peace because it is founded on the shifting sands of self-interest.[134]

In his book on the peace conference, Lansing goes on to state that in May 1919 there was a consensus among leading British statesmen, as well as in the British delegation, that the treaty was a bad one. Evidence for this is furnished by Harold Nicolson, a member of the British delegation. 'The more I read [the draft treaty with Germany],' Nicolson wrote on 28 May, 'the sicker it makes me . . . If I were the Germans I shouldn't sign for a moment.'[135] And on 8 June: 'There is not a single person among the younger people here who is not unhappy and disappointed at the terms. The only people who approve are the old fire-eaters.'[136]

Discontent was not only expressed in private. Members of the US delegation protested and one of them, William C. Bullitt, resigned on 17 May.[137] In the British delegation, a similar step was

---

[134] Lansing (1921: 244 f.).   [135] To Vita Sackville-West, Nicolson (1934: 350).
[136] To his father, ibid. 359.
[137] Lansing (1921: 242, 246). Lansing had to deal with manifestations of protest, oral or in writing, from several other members of the US delegation. Bullitt's letter of resignation to Wilson of 17 May 1919 is in Bullitt and Freud (1967: 234 f.).

in preparation. On 26 May John Maynard Keynes, main representative in Paris of the British Treasury, addressed a letter to his chief, Austen Chamberlain. Keynes made no bones about his opinion of the treaty:

> We have presented a draft treaty to the Germans which contains in it much that is unjust and much more that is inexpedient. . . . It is now right and necessary to discuss it with the Germans and to be ready to make substantial concessions. If this policy is not pursued, the consequences will be disastrous in the extreme. . . . The prime minister is leading us all into a morass of destruction. . . . How can you expect me to assist at this tragic farce any longer, seeking to lay the foundation, as a Frenchman puts it, 'd'une guerre juste et durable'.[138]

On 28 May, after a lunch with Keynes, Nicolson noted in his diary that Keynes was 'very pessimistic about the German treaty', and that he considered it 'not only immoral but incompetent'.[139] Keynes resigned on 7 June, and spent the following months writing a book on the settlement. Entitled *The Economic Consequences of the Peace*, the book appeared in December 1919. It blamed the victors for being bad economists.

On the German side, Foreign Minister Brockdorff-Rantzau, faithful to his warning of 7 May, refused to put his signature to the treaty and stepped down on 22 June. Other high-level politicians contemplated doing so, too. 'Dine with [Jan Christiaan] Smuts,' Nicolson recorded on 24 June. 'He has at last consented to sign the treaty, but under protest and against his conscience.'[140]

With Louis Botha, Smuts represented South Africa at the conference. One of the most prominent supporters of the new consensus agenda, he issued a statement explaining his position on 29 June.[141] He reiterated his reservations in his farewell message on leaving England of 17 July.[142] There, he stated that '[t]he protest which I issued on signing the peace treaty has called forth a vast correspondence, which shows a widespread agreement with the views I hold on that document'. But he urged that '[i]n spite of the apparent failure of the peace conference to bring about the real and lasting appeasement of the nations to which we had been looking forward, our faith in our great ideals should be kept untarnished.'

---

[138] Quoted Gilbert (1966: 50).   [139] Nicolson (1934: 350).
[140] Ibid. 364.   [141] Temperley (1920–4: iii. 74 ff.).   [142] Ibid. 77 ff.

James Headlam-Morley, a member of the British delegation, described the signing of the Versailles treaty on 28 June:

There was very little ceremony or dignity. The plenipotentiaries all walked in casually with the crowd. . . . When they were all seated, the German delegates were brought in; they passed close to me; they looked like prisoners being brought in for sentence . . . The Germans signed first and then all the other delegates. . . . When the signing was finished, the session was closed, and the Germans were escorted out again like prisoners who had received their sentence. Nobody got up or took any notice of them, and there was no suggestion that, the peace having been signed, any change of attitude was to be begun. Looking back, the whole impression seems to me, from a political point of view, to be disastrous. . . . As a matter of fact, what was really being done was not merely to make peace with Germany, but to sign the Covenant of the League of Nations, but of this no one seemed to think. . . . Just the necessary note of reconciliation, of hope, of a change of view, was entirely wanting.[143]

Harold Nicolson, on the same 28 June, closed his diary of the conference with the words 'To bed, sick of life.'[144] This option, however, was not available to everyone. While Orlando had fallen from power on 19 June, Wilson, Clemenceau, and Lloyd George still had to defend the treaty before their respective parliaments and electorates. This proved no easy task, since there was a general impression that the settlement had settled nothing.[145] Parodying what had been the victors' declared objective, Colonel Josiah Wedgwood (like Keynes) described the treaty as 'a just and durable war' in the House of Commons.[146] Even Lloyd George himself, not long after leaving office in 1922, openly asked 'Is It Peace?' This was the title under which in 1923 he published a collection of commentaries on the current international situation. He heaped blame on the French for their chauvinism, and identified disrespect for the principle of self-determination as a major

[143] Headlam-Morley (1972: 178 f.).   [144] Nicolson (1934: 371).
[145] Wilson's speech on presenting the treaty to the Senate is in Senate Document No. 50, 66th Congress First Session; quoted Finch (1919: 554 ff.). For Clemenceau's and Lloyd George's speeches, see Temperley (1920–4: iii. 80 ff. and 83 ff.). Clemenceau (on 30 June 1919) avoided referring to the international implications of the treaty. He combined vindictive, exultant nationalism with an urgent appeal for domestic unity. Lloyd George (on 3 July) made a more reasoned, and much longer, attempt to allay the misgivings of both 'doves' and 'falcons'. He described the treaty as a peace not of vengeance, but of discouragement, based on the necessity not to let the German 'crime' go unpunished.
[146] Quoted McCallum (1944: 51 f.). Wedgwood spoke on 6 June 1919.

flaw of the settlement. Lloyd George was also unhappy about the League:

Undoubtedly the great weakness of the League comes from the fact that it only represents one half the great powers of the world. Until the others join you might as well call the Holy Alliance a League of Nations. . . . The League to be a reality must represent the whole civilized world. . . . That was the original conception.[147]

Lloyd George was unsure whether the treaty should be upheld or not. Resorting to another frequently used comparison, he pointed out that '[w]hen you have walked some distance into a quicksand, and are sinking deeper and deeper with every step you take, it is always difficult to decide whether you are more likely to reach firm ground by pressing forward or by going backward.'[148]

The quicksand metaphor (also used by Lansing in his condemnation of the draft treaty quoted earlier) was originally popularized by Wilson, in his famous 'Peace Without Victory' speech—made on 22 January 1917, when the United States had not yet entered the war. In this speech, another manifestation of his gift of prophecy, the president had warned that

Victory would mean peace forced upon the loser, a victor's terms imposed upon the vanquished. It would be accepted in humiliation, under duress, at an intolerable sacrifice, and would leave a sting, a resentment, a bitter memory upon which terms of peace would rest, not permanently, but only as upon a quicksand.[149]

Among the most prolific critics of the settlement was Francesco Nitti, who followed Orlando as Italian prime minister and held that office until June 1920. He subsequently published a whole series of works on the settlement, producing torrents of worried reflection. His two main books, immediately translated into German, French, and English, are L'Europa senza pace ('Peaceless Europe', 1922) and La decadenza dell'Europa ('The Decadence of Europe', 1923).

---

[147] Lloyd George (1923: 200). There was clearly some confusion among the 1919 peacemakers about the nature of the Holy Alliance. In fact, it was open for every single European sovereign to sign; moreover, all did (in the case of the British prince regent, informally by means of a written declaration of support). Only the Pope refused.
[148] Ibid. 79.   [149] Wilson (1924: i. 352).

Nitti blamed the victors for not having honoured their commitment to the Wilsonian agenda. He deplored that self-determination was denied to Germans and Magyars, condemned the violation of German sovereignty and equality especially by the dictatorial powers vested in the Reparations Commission, and repeatedly declared the entente or the League to be a 'new Holy Alliance'. He was in agreement with Keynes and with Colonel Wedgwood that the settlement provided for 'a state of permanent war', and warned that Europe was on the eve of further violent conflicts 'unless some means be found to replace the present treaties, which are based on the principle that it is necessary to continue the war, by a system of friendly agreements whereby winners and losers are placed on a footing of liberty and equality'.[150]

Nitti noted that the settlement had disunited Europe. (It is significant that the word 'Europe' appears constantly in his books, whereas it had been practically absent from the negotiations.) 'Europe', Nitti declared, 'will be able to make up for her losses in lives and wealth. . . . But one thing she has lost which, if she does not succeed in recovering it, must necessarily lead to her decline and fall: the spirit of solidarity.'[151]

Deploring that '[c]ontinental Europe is now a reproduction of the Balkan peninsula on a large scale,'[152] and that 'every part of Europe is in a state of flux,'[153] Nitti found the only stable pattern to be the division of the continent into two camps—winners and losers. In short, he diagnosed the fragmentation and breakdown of the international society of Europe and the continued prevalence of various brands of us-and-them thinking over any sense of community.

Nitti reminded his readers that '[t]here are no peoples always victorious,'[154] and that a settlement that left strong antagonism and resentment was doubly dangerous: 'For as everyone who takes vengeance does so in a degree greater than the damage suffered, if one supposes for a moment that the conquered of to-day may be the conquerors of to-morrow, to what lengths of violence, degradation and barbarism may not Europe be dragged?'[155]

Nitti was worried that Germany and Russia, excluded from the concert of Europe, would not remain for ever in their current

---

[150] Nitti (1922: 23).   [151] Ibid. 17.   [152] Nitti (1923: 26).
[153] Nitti (1922: 129).   [154] Ibid. 239.   [155] Ibid. 67.

state of weakness: 'What will then happen to a Poland which pretends to divide two peoples who represent numerically and will represent in other fields also the greatest forces of continental Europe to-morrow?'[156]

Nitti thought that 'when war is over nothing should be put into a peace treaty except such things as will lead to a lasting peace, or the most lasting peace compatible with our degree of civilization.'[157] Unfortunately, however, and despite the prevailing disdain for the 'immoral' statecraft of the past, the peace of 1919–20 was retrograde when compared to that of 1814–15. This is what Nitti had in mind when he chose the title *The Decadence of Europe*.

In comparing the treaties of 1814–15 with those of 1919–20 . . . one is overcome with sadness. The men whom we have been accustomed to regard as the mouthpieces of the past, the sovereigns by divine right, the ministers of absolutism, the diplomatists of the old school and the old spirit, such as Metternich, reveal themselves to us as men encircled with moral nobility and political grandeur, compared with those who, a century later, declared, in the name of the entente, that they represented democracy and civilization. What a difference there was in their sentiments! There was then no hatred towards the vanquished, from whom all the acts of violence and injustice had come; no unbridled greed, but a firm desire to restore peace with justice, an almost anxious solicitude to avoid fresh wars and fresh failures. Thus, a century later, Europe appears not only morally debased, but so far removed from the Europe of that time, so far inferior, that one cannot conceive how so great a decadence has been possible. . . . Europe has taken a big step backward in the path of civilization . . . the new treaties have . . . severed the bonds which centuries of common effort had forged.[158]

The opening chapter of *The Decadence of Europe* is devoted to a detailed comparison of the two settlements. For Nitti, the Treaty of Versailles revealed its absurdity in punishing Germany for contemplating the 'crime' of hegemony, while at Vienna, France was reintegrated into the European system as if Napoleon had never happened.

To Germany, vanquished in 1918, nothing more was credited than *intentions* of empire and expansion—intentions, which, moreover, were and are common to not a few of the victors. . . . She did not dominate any European nation, she had annexed no territory, she had forced no German

[156] Ibid. 144.   [157] Ibid. 91.   [158] Nitti (1923: 23 f.).

prince on to any throne. Still less had she invaded other countries, or compelled the armies of free peoples to struggle and to fight for the glory of Germany. No comparison is therefore possible with the Napoleonic domination, which did not exist merely in intention, but in fact.[159]

Abandoning the 'idealist' school's preoccupation with 'justice', Nitti went so far as to write:

No right-thinking person has nowadays [1921] any doubt as to the profound injustice of the Treaty of Versailles and of all the treaties which derive from it. But this fact is of small importance, inasmuch as it is not justice or injustice which regulates the relations between nations, but their interests and sentiments.[160]

The antithesis between 'justice' on the one hand and sentiments on the other is clearly somewhat inaccurate, since it was precisely the debate on the 'justice' of the treaties that aroused such passionate sentiments among the nations concerned.

Excessive preoccupation with 'justice' obviously encourages a self-righteous blindness to what virtue, and therefore ground for consensus, there may reside with the opponent. This is clearly not conducive to the successful resolution of conflicts. Nitti devoted considerable effort to dispelling the idea 'that there exist in Europe two groups of nations, one which stands for violence and barbarism—the Germans, the Magyars and the Bulgarians— while the other group of Anglo-Saxons and Latins represents civilization'.[161]

He pointed out that during the three centuries preceding the world war Germany had been involved in fewer military conflicts than Britain and France, and he refused to believe in an innate German preference for dictatorial regimes:

Not only am I of the opinion that Germany is a land suited for democratic institutions, but I believe that after the fall of the empire [i.e. the monarchy] democratic principles have a wider prevalence there than in any other country of Europe. . . . the democratic parties . . . , if they are loyally assisted by the states of the entente [but why should there still have been an entente!], can not only develop themselves but establish a great and noble democracy.[162]

[159] Ibid. 35 f. Emphasis in original.   [160] Nitti (1922: 253).
[161] Ibid. 256 f.   [162] Ibid. 257.

5. THE GERMAN PROBLEM EXACERBATED

Unfortunately, the victors of 1918 did nothing (to put it mildly) to help the cause of democracy in Germany, which suffered fatal damage from being associated with the settlement. In these circumstances, the widespread suspicion among the victors that the democratization of Germany was somehow not 'real' became a self-fulfilling prophecy.

No doubt this suspicion was in itself dictated, to some extent, by the desire to punish. But it was also nourished by Germany's behaviour before and during the war, which gave rise to the impression that Germany was a peculiarly ruthless and aggressive international actor that could never be trusted. The idea was, and is, widely shared that German aggressiveness was the result of a society supposedly organized along reactionary and authoritarian lines. (I say 'supposedly' because it seems to me that the extent to which this was the case, and the extent to which Germany differed in this respect from other west European countries, is often exaggerated.) Had there been more effective democratic control of German politics, this theory runs, Germany would have acted less aggressively in the international arena. But did not a functioning democracy require a certain amount of democratic tradition, and was this not conspicuously absent in Germany's case? Nor could it be created overnight: hence, the new German republic had to be distrusted.

Whatever its merits, this approach overlooks the constraints placed on Germany by its awkward position in the international system—as an international actor recently risen to a position of potentially hegemonial strength, and therefore regarded by its neighbours with suspicion. This created a situation (strongly reminiscent of France's in the seventeenth century) of rivalry and mutual suspicion that was very difficult to overcome. *Both* sides felt under threat—but Germany felt that it had more to fear because it was not yet fully accepted in its new position, and because of the danger of the other actors combining against it. Once again, in this instance, aggressive behaviour was not at all the result of self-assurance, but of deep-seated insecurity. Regardless of what other factors may have been at work, this one certainly exerted a powerful influence on Germany's behaviour. But it was not identified or understood, let alone addressed. On the contrary, the settlement worsened the situation considerably in this respect.

As we have seen, people like Prince Max von Baden or Prime Minister Orlando thought that Germany had lost the war on the propaganda front. In fact, it is not at all clear what a German propaganda campaign might have looked like. The entente could advance democratic notions for its propaganda discourse (albeit only belatedly—after Russia had dropped out and the United States had stepped in)—notions that had a universal rather than narrowly national appeal. No such notions were available to Germany.

Germany was hampered by insecurity about its international standing and was inclined to overcompensate with fiery rhetoric and sabre-rattling. A further impediment was an awareness of the outdated nature of Germany's constitutional arrangements, that peculiar alliance between parliamentarism and old-style monarchism contrived by Bismarck. (Awareness did not necessarily mean conscious avowal—although Max von Baden, in his Reichstag speech quoted earlier, explicitly referred to democratization as the 'political coming of age of the German people'.) For this reason as much as from geopolitical considerations, the pre-1914 Reich had felt on the defensive *vis-à-vis* Britain and France (as developed and successful as Germany, but with more modern political institutions). Germany had not, at that stage, felt fundamentally different from the western powers. Once the war had begun, however, the break with the western powers greatly increased the tendency to concentrate on what, supposedly, set Germany apart. Much emphasis was placed, for example, on the alleged dichotomy between virtuous German 'culture' and decadent western 'civilization', between cosy patriarchal *gemeinschaft* (community) and plutocratic western *gesellschaft* (society), etc.[163]

It is significant that, when the war broke out, no one in Germany seems to have felt much need for ideological defence against Russia—a country far more autocratic than Germany. The fact that the effort at ideological self-justification was directed mainly against the western democracies is a clear indication that these were secretly or subconsciously seen as role models, however vehemently this was denied.

As a result, German political discourse during the war was firmly locked into a chauvinist vein. Unlike the entente after 1917,

---

[163] For a review of manifestations of this line of thinking, see Krockow (1990: esp. 100 ff.).

Germany could not transcend this chauvinism in its rhetoric. In order to retain its self-esteem and identity in the face of the threat posed to it by the allies, it had to persuade itself that its less-than-fully-democratic set-up was part of what made it different in a positive sense, in other words superior. Needless to say, this relentless assertion of German superiority in the name of notions held to be peculiarly German, rather than commonly shared by people anywhere, was counterproductive abroad.

This helps to explain why the German war plans relied on overcoming resistance by purely military, if need be brutal, means regardless of the propaganda cost—as illustrated by the notorious decision to unleash unrestricted submarine warfare. (Considerations of this kind did not necessarily motivate the responsible decision-makers on a conscious, articulate level—even a purely intuitive awareness of the logic of the situation would have engendered the attitude in question.) The same logic found expression in the fact that the September 1914 German war aims relied for the creation of a stable post-war order on German military domination of the continent, rather than on mutually accepted principles.[164]

Among the most serious shortcomings of the 1919 settlement was that it exacerbated the feeling that Germany was different, set apart from mainstream 'western' civilization. In Germany, the settlement nurtured resentment against the political culture of the victors much as the war itself had done. The victors were seen, not only to have threatened and defeated the old monarchical order, but also to have humiliated the new republic deeply. This perpetuated and strengthened the notion that there was no common ground between Germany and 'western' civilization, and helped to pave the way for a political movement (National Socialism) that would promise revolutionary modernization all round while also presenting itself as a potent counter-charm to hostile 'western' democratism.

Would a different treatment of Germany in 1919 have consolidated the Weimar democracy? There is good reason to answer this question in the affirmative. The post-1870 order in Germany did not rest on the most solid of foundations. On the contrary, it

---

[164] Compare Fritz Fischer's views on the subject and the debate these views caused. Fischer (1967; 1975).

was particularly vulnerable to loss of prestige. There was no constitutional principle, no universally accepted abstract concept of domestic legitimacy to back it up. In many ways, it was an archaism with a democratic façade. What legitimacy it possessed stemmed originally from the military triumph of 1870 and the subsequent German 'unification' (a somewhat dubious term for a process that also involved the military expulsion of Austria from Germany). Bismarck presented this to German opinion as the fulfilment of long-held aspirations—aspirations that originally had a strongly democratic aspect, and of which he was wary in the extreme. Subsequently, the new Reich was able to pride itself on its economic and scientific achievements. In countless exalted speeches, the emperor William II industriously celebrated this progress. He did not forget to highlight his own role in promoting it, insubstantial as it may have been in practice—his famous assertion, 'herrlichen Zeiten führe ich euch noch entgegen' ('they are marvellous times towards which I will yet lead you') springs to mind.[165] The naïvety of the rhetoric can leave little doubt that he felt what he said.

But, at the same time, this was a logical stance for him to take; the order which he represented, and to which he owed his position and power, depended for survival on keeping the people impressed with the prestige that it generated. A similar rationale of buying the people off (so to speak) underlay the model social-welfare legislation initiated by Bismarck, in the hope that it would take the wind out of the sails of the opposition Social Democratic Party. The SPD vigorously contested the established social and political order—and in 1914 it was the strongest party in the Reichstag. In sum, post-1870 Germany functioned by virtue of a sort of ersatz legitimacy, which substituted nationalism and prestige for constitutional principle.

This did not make Germany unique. Nationalism and the generating of prestige—military, economic, or scientific—were exploited everywhere to strengthen the existing order, undermined by what Marxist theory terms the 'class struggle'. In France and Britain, too, the existing order, with its class system, was 'undemocratic', in the sense of non-egalitarian, and contested by the left.

---

[165] Speech before the Brandenburg regional parliament (Provinziallandtag), 24 Feb. 1892, quoted Krockow (1990: 17 f.).

But the German government was still less democratic, still less egalitarian, and, therefore, even more vulnerable to being deprived of prestige—and it went on to lose the war. It is striking that in November 1918, quite literally from one day to the next and without any struggle, not only the emperor, but his twenty-one fellow German princes disappeared into political oblivion as if through a trapdoor. This illustrates the extent to which the old order had already outlived itself. Anything which, in this situation, could be presented as a winning political recipe had a solid chance of success.

History provides much evidence that the best opportunity for political change is when a regime has just suffered a major military defeat. One striking example, involving international actors already considered in this book, is the constitutional development of Sweden and France in the eighteenth century. When in 1715 Louis XIV died peacefully in his palace of Versailles, his great aim of aggrandizing France and firmly establishing it as the foremost European power had been accomplished. The recent Utrecht peace had brought the international community's definitive acceptance of his achievement. By the same token, the absolutist nature of the French monarchy was established equally firmly for the next two or three generations—until the 1789 revolution brought it down. In Sweden, Charles XII also concentrated all power in his own hands. But in 1718 he was killed by a bullet under the walls of the Norwegian fortress that he was besieging, in a (quite literally) last-ditch effort to salvage what was left of Swedish imperial grandeur. Thereupon, the pendulum in Sweden swung away from absolutism to the other end of the constitutional scale, removing all power from the monarchy. In this instance, too, the effect lasted for the next two or three generations (until Gustaf III's 1772 coup restored royal rule).

It has already been made clear that the notion that international actors can be 'punished' for what they do is dangerous. Stability is promoted, not through penalties, but through conciliation (which is not the same as appeasement). By appearing to punish the new democratic Germany for the alleged moral turpitude of the old order, the victors helped to resuscitate the glowing embers of anti-democratism. As a result, the settlement left the Weimar Republic smouldering; ten years later the world economic crisis had little difficulty in bringing it down and making way for a new revolutionary ideology, National Socialism. This new ideology was rabidly opposed to the 'western' thinking of which Versailles had come to be seen as the despicable symbol. It was helped by widespread acceptance of the 'stab-in-the-back' legend, according to which it was not the old order that had brought disaster on Germany, but the democratic revolutionaries, the 'November criminals', as they came to be branded by the nationalist right. In this way, the German defeat of 1918 did not benefit the new order that was established as a result, but, instead, benefited its opponents, whose numbers were swelled by resentment of the settlement.

Only a peace between equals can last. Only a peace the very principle of which is equality and a common participation in a common benefit. The right state of mind, the right feeling between nations, is as necessary for a lasting peace as is the just settlement of vexed questions of territory or of racial and national allegiance.

What would such a peace, advocated by Wilson on 22 January 1917, before he was himself drawn into the turmoil, have looked like?[166]

There is no denying that a consensual peace with Germany, based on strict application of the Wilsonian agenda, would have appeared not only not to punish, but, indeed, to reward Germany for the war—a circumstance that made such a peace even less of a realistic possibility than it would have been otherwise. If national self-determination had been implemented fully, the unity of most German-speakers, including those in the former Habsburg lands, would have superseded the Bismarckian unification. In 1870 this Greater Germany was politically unattainable, because it was incompatible with the continued existence of the Habsburg Empire. But, after the disintegration of that empire as a result of the war, historical logic made the Greater Germany an almost inescapable political imperative—something that it was dangerous to disregard. It is clear that, by handling the issue in the way that they did, the peacemakers greatly increased the German threat that they were trying to control. Suppose that a democratic Greater Germany had come into being as a result of the conference. It is inconceivable that the cession of non-German-speaking territories would then have had the humiliating impact that it did. Nor would the enemies of the new democratic order have been able to strengthen

---

[166] Wilson (1924: i. 352).

their position by invoking injured national pride. Moreover, if Prussia, with its alleged militarism, was held to be responsible for what had happened, then it would have made sense to dilute it as much as possible in an enlarged Germany, which it could not control to the same extent. A stable, democratic, self-respecting Germany (as stable as the 'class struggle', exacerbated by the war in all parts of Europe, permitted) would have been a useful asset for maintaining a reasonably stable Europe.

This is, of course, the very distribution of territories brought about (without war) within twenty years of Versailles anyway. But, as it was, this happened in circumstances that made a debased, vindictive Germany a tremendous threat to Europe. It took another, even more terrible, war to swing the pendulum the other way and to bring about the other extreme: the Germany of the post-Second World War era, reduced territorially much further than it had been in 1919 and broken up into less than fully sovereign successor states—what Clemenceau would have liked to see in 1919.

6

Summary and Update

The 'classical' European states system, at whose evolution since the mid-seventeenth century we have looked in this book, was not created in one piece. Originally, as we have seen, its structure was to a considerable extent outside the scope of abstract, programmatic principles. Such principles evolved only slowly and fitfully, gradually including more and more aspects of the system in their purview. Sanctioned by custom, structural features that the European system had already possessed in medieval times were eroded only slowly. Indeed, this process of erosion has not been completed even today. In many cases, traditional features of the system have been relegitimized successively by different consensus principles. This is very noticeable, for example, when we look at the identity of the international actors. In many cases, there is a certain continuity here in spite of changing structural principles—even though, in every case, the nature of the actors, as determined by their domestic set-up, has changed drastically over the centuries.

In this final chapter, I propose to review briefly the three fundamental aspects of the structure of the international system—the identity of the actors, their relative status *vis-à-vis* one another, and the distribution of territories and populations between them. We will look at the way in which the consensus principles affecting these aspects of structure have evolved in the period covered by this book. In particular, we will look at international developments since the 1919 Paris Peace Conference in the light of our findings so far.

1. IDENTITY OF THE INTERNATIONAL ACTORS

There was no abstract criterion for membership of the international system of Europe before the early nineteenth century. Both at Münster and Osnabrück and at Utrecht, membership of the system was on a *de facto* basis. Adherence to some type of Christianity was, indeed, a necessary prerequisite for membership, but it could not determine the identity of the actors. There were no consensus notions on which potential international actors wishing to assert themselves could have relied to boost their cause. New actors could come into being only by means of determined military insurrection. It did not even matter whether actors were trying to establish themselves for the first time, or whether they had already enjoyed autonomous status in the past. The Swiss and the Dutch, who had not been independent before, had to engage in fierce and protracted struggles (in the late Middle Ages and in the sixteenth and seventeenth centuries respectively) in order to shake off Habsburg rule and assert themselves as international actors in their own right. (They did this despite the fact that, in both cases, it had not even been the original intention.) But even Sweden in the sixteenth century and Portugal in the seventeenth century only regained their independence (from Denmark and from Spain respectively) through purely military means. All four bids for membership in the international system were unassisted by any consensus notions operating at system level.

Contrary to what is often assumed, dynastic legitimacy (the idea that, on the whole, only actors ruled by members of certain ancient leading families could claim rightful membership of the international system) played little or no role in international relations before the French Revolution. This was so regardless of the domestic importance that dynastic legitimacy might have in the case of individual actors.

Dynastic legitimacy did furnish the first abstract criterion for membership of the system, but this was not until the early nineteenth century. By that time, the major republican actors in the system had disappeared with the exception only of Switzerland. Talleyrand, at the Congress of Vienna, advanced dynastic legitimacy as a means of restoring stability to the European system after the upheavals triggered by the French Revolution. But, as we have seen in Chapter 4, the idea that dynasticism was both the hallmark of the pre-revolutionary order and the secret of its stability was a fallacy based on wishful thinking. Moreover, the abstract, programmatic rationale that Talleyrand employed to promote the concept of dynastic legitimacy was in itself characteristic of the new era, of the systematic political thinking that had also produced the French

Revolution. The 'spontaneous pattern of obligation' (Kissinger 1957) on which the pre-revolutionary order had largely rested could not be restored.

By the end of the First World War, dynamic, populist political thinking had spread so widely that national self-determination became the accepted criterion for membership of the system. Since then, international actors have been considered rightful members of the international system only if they could also be considered as enjoying the acceptance of the populations living within their boundaries, or at least of the major part of these populations (minority dissent may affect the legitimacy of boundaries, but will not normally affect the legitimacy of the actors as such).

At the end of the First World War, the structure of the international system was, as yet, quite incompatible with this new Concept. During the seventy years that separate the Paris Peace Conference from the time of writing, it has often looked as if the concept of national self-determination could be violated with impunity for the sake of power-political considerations. If we look at this stretch of time as a whole, however, we realize that every apparent defeat of the principle has so far only been temporary. In the long run, the principle has invariably prevailed. The history of the transformation of the international system, both in Europe and globally, since the end of the First World War is perhaps the most powerful testimony to the impact that consensus notions can have on the structure of the international system.

New actors established themselves in Europe after the First World War, in the name of national self-determination. The collapse of Czarist Russia led to Finland, Estonia, Latvia, Lithuania, the Ukraine, Georgia, Armenia, and Poland declaring their independence. Poland was also helped by the defeat of Germany and Austria-Hungary, and the disintegration of the Habsburg Empire also resulted in the creation of Czechoslovakia.

The Ukraine, Georgia, and Armenia were quickly brought back under Russian rule, the three Baltic states were repossessed by Moscow in 1940, and Poland came under Russian domination again after the Second World War (along with Czechoslovakia and other east European actors). Of all the international actors that had broken away from Russian rule, only Finland was able to retain its independence. But what looked like a major defeat for national self-determination was only a temporary set-back. Indeed, lip-service was always paid to the principle, and exerted a degree of influence on the restructuring of Europe even when the principle was violated at the same time. Unlike Czarist Russia, the Soviet Union was a federation which gave nominal autonomy to its constituent republics. Significantly, too, Stalin and his successors refrained from incorporating Poland, Czechoslovakia, Hungary, Rumania, and Bulgaria into the Soviet Union.

This tribute to the principle of national self-determination, however nominal, facilitated relations with non-Communist international actors. Even though the political structure that the Soviet government gave to its empire conformed to the principle only nominally, it still provided a fair amount of protection from criticism—for it meant that Moscow could only be criticized for its behaviour, and not for maintaining a political structure that was at odds with a very prominent principle of the international consensus agenda. Hostile interpretations of Soviet behaviour could always be rejected, and political acts denied. Something as fundamental as political structure could not be disguised as easily. It was therefore preferable to bring it into line with the consensus agenda, and to use its semiotically powerful paraphernalia—for example, flags, borders marked on maps, or eye-catching procedures such as the protocol surrounding state visits—in support of the fiction that Russia's behaviour was in line with that agenda, too.

In the end, however, this nominal structure created for propaganda purposes facilitated the collapse of the Soviet Empire. When the pressure for reform, created largely by a disastrous economic situation, became overwhelming in the late 1980s, the nominal structure was easily turned into an actual one. All the non-Russian republics have now seceded and become international actors in their own right. At the time of writing, then, all the power-political vicissitudes that beset potential actors trying, in the name of national self-determination, to escape from Russian overlordship have been undone.

At the Paris Peace Conference, self-determination was largely denied to German-speaking populations. As a result, an international actor came into being that did not want to be one at first —Austria, which would have merged with Germany if it had been at liberty to do so. Hitler 'remedied' this oddity, as well as uniting other German-speaking territories to Germany. Despite concern caused by his style and methods, he did not encounter determined opposition—because, by and large, his behaviour was in line with the consensus agenda, which recognized claims based on the principle of national self-determination (or, at any rate, on the ethnicity criterion). Significantly, it was only when Hitler's attack on Poland revealed his adherence to that principle to have been merely a façade for arbitrary expansionism (the old enemy of international stability) that war was declared on him by other major actors that were attached to the status quo.

Hitler's defeat brought about the domination of the European system by the two great powers of the Cold War era, the United States and the Soviet Union. To some extent, this meant a reversion to a formula first adopted by the Congress of Vienna, which had made the policing of the system by recognized great powers the mainstay of international stability (we will return to this point). It also meant that, for the next four-and-a-half decades, this great-power principle entered into competition with the principle of national self-determination and prevented it from operating fully. This is another reason why the Soviet Union got away with maintaining its empire for so long.

In the years after 1945 Germany was denied self-determination once more. But the diminution and division of Germany was this time in application of the great-power principle and accepted for the sake of international stability—until the end of the Cold War. As I will explain in more detail further on, this turning-point led to the disintegration of one great power (the Soviet Union), deprived the other (the United States) of its own great-power status as a result, and, in this way, made the great-power principle inoperative again. The inevitable comeback of national self-determination that has resulted has led to the reunification of Germany in 1990. (Austria after 1945 was happy to remain separate, because at that time it found it inopportune to be associated with the disgraced Germany. Unlike the situation after the First World War, its status as an international actor after 1945 has been in line with its own wishes.)

Further west in Europe, other international actors were affected equally deeply by secessionist movements invoking the principle of national self-determination. In west Europe itself, only three new international actors have come into being in this century— Norway in 1905, Iceland in 1918, and Ireland in 1922 (though one might take the view that Ireland and Iceland only became fully independent when they shook off their ties with, respectively, the British and Danish crowns and declared themselves republics—Iceland in 1944 and Ireland in 1949). But after 1945 the colonial empires of Britain, France, the Netherlands, and Portugal all disintegrated under the impact of the principle, causing a dramatic increase of the number of international actors at the global level.

The reason why the West European colonial powers were unable to retain their empires for as long as the Soviet Union did was because none of them were great powers any more. They were not essential to international stability. Therefore, none of them could rely on the support of those powers that were (the United States and the Soviet Union) to protect them from demands to implement national self-determination. The Soviet Union only protected itself in this way, while doing its utmost to disguise the fact that it was really a colonial power, too. (Semiotically, this was facilitated by the fact that, unusually, its own colonial dominions were contiguous with the metropolis, not located overseas as was the case with the other empires.)

Neither did the United States wish to be seen to support the cause of colonialism. As we saw when we looked at the Congress of Vienna, a great power characteristically perceives itself to be accountable to the international community; if it did not, this would jeopardize its status. Only on one occasion did the United States allow itself to be drawn into a colonial conflict in support of the metropolis—when France managed to present its own struggle against Vietnamese nationalism as a fight against Communism and Soviet hegemony, justifying US intervention. The result was a total disaster that did considerable damage to the United States' standing in the world (both in terms of prestige and economically).

2. RELATIVE STATUS OF THE INTERNATIONAL ACTORS *VIS-À-VIS* ONE ANOTHER

The consensus agenda may also furnish criteria governing the relative status of the international actors *vis-à-vis* one another. At the time of the Peace of Westphalia, the twin principles of autonomy and of equality of the actors gained much ground. Autonomy meant independence from any hierarchic superior, such as, in the Middle Ages, the Emperor or the Pope. At Münster and

Osnabrück, certain remnants of the old hierarchic set-up remained, such as the diplomatic precedence of the Emperor's representatives over those of other actors. The French crown contested this symbolical privilege, not because it favoured the equality principle but because it coveted the Emperor's position for itself. By the time of the Peace of Utrecht, by and large such pretensions were shelved, and the idea tended to prevail that all actors in the system, regardless of their size and history, had equal rights and were entirely self-determined.

Utrecht may have marked the high point of this trend towards total autonomy of the actors and towards total notional equality between them. This made functional sense because the power of states in early eighteenth-century Europe was determined not so much by their population or size but by their economic muscle. Under the social set-up then prevailing in Europe, armies were made up of mercenaries, who were both expensive and bothersome to recruit and keep together. This meant that even territorially small actors, like the Dutch or Venice, could play a major role in international politics—because their wealth enabled them to pay for sizeable armies.

This became impossible after the French Revolution. Changes in the social order of Europe resulted in a different kind of warfare, which in turn caused modifications of the structure of the international system. Revolutionary France, predicated on the notion that the masses should participate in the political process, was able to introduce universal conscription. This provided it with huge armies that were relatively easy to finance and to replenish. France's adversaries had to match these huge armies. As a result, the gap between the power of the more populous states and that of the less populous ones widened. A handful of big states suddenly found themselves vastly more powerful than they had been before, and it was clear that this new-found power could have disastrous consequences for international stability if it were not checked somehow or even harnessed to protect the stability of the system.

The Congress of Vienna saw the introduction of a two-tier set-up into the international system. The five biggest actors in the system formed a kind of managing committee and invested themselves with the responsibility for maintaining international stability. This was the beginning of the great-power concept, referred to throughout the nineteenth century as the 'concert of Europe'.

It should be stressed that this was very much a new phenom-enon. Frequently, the expression 'great power' is used regardless of the period being dealt with, but this leads to nineteenth-century assumptions about what a great power is and does being read into historical processes in which such assumptions were not present. A misleading interpretive overlay is the result. (This is only one example of a typical shortcoming of historical or political analysis, which consists in uncritically using assumptions for analysis that in reality did not affect, or, at least, did not affect decisively, the phenomena under consideration.)

There have always been big powers, of course. But both at Münster and Osnabrück and at Utrecht, the big powers had little sense of special rights and responsibilities. Traditionally, efforts to define the concept of great power have drawn on power-political categories. However, in the classical European system, a great power was not just any big power, but a power recognized as having special status.

What sets a great power apart is really the shared assumptions in the system concerning that power's status. How essential such assumptions are can be shown by comparing the Congress of Vienna to the Paris Peace Conference a century later. At Vienna, the special status of the great powers was acknowledged by all actors, albeit perhaps reluctantly. There was no choice, for two reasons: first, because all those actors qualified for great-power status recognized one another as possessing that status, without even excluding defeated France, and secondly, because combined they were so vastly superior to all other actors. Because they were big and united (at least when it came to presenting a common front to the smaller actors), the smaller actors had no choice but to acquiesce in great power leadership. And because the great powers, keenly aware of the necessity of 'moderation', used their privileged position prudently, they succeeded in persuading the smaller actors that this new set-up was beneficial for all, or at least not detrimental to the smaller actors.

At Paris, the situation was different. Wilson had made himself the spokesman of a campaign against the old consensus agenda, including the balance-of-power and the great-power principles. But, at the conference, the equality of all states propagated by Wilson turned out to be as much of a functional impossibility as it had been at Vienna. In the end, the peace was dictated, not by the great powers, but—a crucial distinction—by some of the big powers with an insufficient mandate to do this.

The big powers were unable to justify their special status convincingly. The great-power principle had never been equipped with much of an explicit theoretical foundation even in its heyday. At the Congress of Vienna, the great powers had achieved tacit acceptance of the principle on purely pragmatic grounds and by treating the smaller actors with remarkable solicitude; indeed, they made sure that almost all the smaller actors benefited materially from the leadership of the great powers through being awarded additional territory. Thereafter, there was enough goodwill between the great powers and the smaller actors to allow the privileged position of the great powers to continue unchallenged.

But when after 1918 progressivist, populist political thinking finally gained the upper hand over the conservatism that had prevailed since the Congress of Vienna, a new consensus agenda was needed. This new consensus agenda had to be abstract and programmatic rather than being based on pragmatism. The great-power concept, never endorsed in any very programmatic way, was actively discredited in the run-up to the Paris conference. At the conference itself, the big powers were far from united. Those among them that had been defeated—Germany and Russia—did not even participate. France and Italy pursued private goals at the conference, with reckless disregard for international consensus. The 1919 peacemakers lacked the (albeit rather intuitive) understanding of the great-power principle that the Vienna peacemakers had possessed. This contributed to the disastrous failure of the 1919 settlement. Three potential great powers (Germany, Italy, and Russia) out of six (if the United States is included) were uncommitted to the maintenance of the settlement, or even actively seeking its undoing.

For the great-power concept to work in practice, it is essential, first, that all actors qualified for great-power status are also recognized as possessing that status; secondly, that, between them, these actors are in control of the entire system, in the sense that they are able to alter its structure substantially should they wish to do so; thirdly, that the potential threat that they pose both to the system and to one another is such that they are thereby induced to cooperate; and fourthly, that there is consensus in the system that the great powers behave acceptably.

These conditions were not fulfilled in the European system of the 1920s and 1930s. The great-power concept was also inoperative at world level, because at that time only one actor, the United States, was in a position of strength such as to be capable of policing the system. British and French strength was, in comparison, more apparent than real. But the United States could not control the entire system by itself. This would have amounted to a very burdensome hegemony, doomed to failure by creating potent resentment. Even if US strength had been harnessed to the collective security mechanisms of the League of Nations, as originally planned before the United States withdrew once more into isolationism, this would not have worked either, because the high degree of system-wide consensus that the League would have required in order to succeed was not present.

Consequently, quite apart from the penchant for isolationism that had been inherent in US domestic political culture from its inception, the United States could not have played a great-power role even if it had wanted to. Since there was little consensus in the system, a single actor could never have dealt with all the problems arising from that. And if consensus had existed in sufficient measure to make the task less onerous, then no such actor would have been required. For functional reasons, therefore, the United States' failure in the 1920s and 1930s to play a great power role was really inevitable.

But by 1945, as a result of the Second World War, the Soviet Union had risen to a position where it was a serious threat both to the United States and to the international system as a whole. The great-power concept could come back into operation. Because of the earlier de-legitimization of the term 'great power', a new one was coined—'superpower'. (That a 'superpower' is not necessarily an actor of overwhelming absolute strength is apparent from the increasing usage in recent years of the rather odd expression 'regional superpower'. This shows that what is meant is really very much akin to the old term 'great power'.)

It was the danger of a potential clash between the United States and the Soviet Union that led Washington and Moscow to co-operate, at least to the extent that they avoided open war between them. Despite their confrontational rhetoric, they never challenged the post-1945 structure of the international system in any fundamental way. In a system with several great powers, the twin phenomena of great power rivalry, even hostility, on the one hand, and the need for great power cooperation on the other, are rendered less immediately obvious by the complexity of the mutual relations between several actors. In the post-1945 bipolar system, where great-power relations existed only between two actors, the functional link between great power competition and great-power cooperation was evident in the very visible alternation of periods of heightened tension with that peculiar product of the Cold War era, *détente*.

While the Cold War lasted, the smaller actors by and large accepted the tutelage of the great powers (and the ones that did not were not in a position to threaten the overall stability of the international system). Those actors that belonged to the Soviet camp did not have much choice—the autonomy that they were allowed to retain did not extend that far. Those actors that belonged to the western camp were afraid of the Soviet Union, and therefore accepted voluntarily the tutelage of the United States. The great powers themselves were happy to be afraid of each other, because only the mutual threat that they posed to each other and to each other's client actors justified their hegemonial status as protectors of their own client actors. If that mutual threat were taken away, they would cease to be great powers, because, unlike the great powers in the nineteenth-century European system, their demographic weight and their other resources were not so great, in relation to the other actors, as to give them unquestioned preponderance in the international system in any case.

As a result, the United States leadership found itself somewhat inconvenienced by the collapse of the Soviet threat. Its attachment to the bipolarity of the Cold War system is shown by the reluctance (one is tempted to say: the regret) with which the Reagan administration eventually conceded that Gorbachev's offer to end the Cold War was genuine, and the rather neurotic manner in which the Bush administration, faced with the rapid disintegration of the Soviet Union, later insisted that the United States had become 'the only superpower'. The United States is, indeed, the strongest single power in the present international system. But no international actor can be a great power (or a 'superpower') all by itself. The United States has not yet understood the difference between being a great power and merely being an unusually big one.

The gradual triumph, after the Peace of Westphalia, of autonomy and equality also led to the evolution of that best-known consensus principle of the classical European system, the balance-of-power principle. It stands to reason that balance-of-power politics are more difficult if there is a hierarchy of actors. Inequalities of ranking between actors will encourage the lower-ranking actors to become the automatic clients of the foremost ones, which is an impediment to a balance-of-power system of the eighteenth-century type (based on flexible alliances). It is not surprising, therefore, that in the half-century after the Peace of Westphalia, at a time, that is, when the French crown at least still strove for pre-eminence over the other actors, the balance-of-power concept gained prominence only slowly. The concept only triumphed at the Congress of Utrecht, which saw both the Bourbon dynasty and the Habsburg dynasty abandon their hegemonial pretensions. It was at this juncture that the balance-of-power concept became universally accepted as a structural principle of the European system and as the preferred safeguard for ensuring the overall stability of that system. At the Congress of Vienna, too, the balance-of-power principle was extremely prominent in the peacemakers' utterances.

As a structural principle, the balance of power meant two things. In one sense, far from being concerned with the exact distribution of forces, it was a No to hegemony. In this respect, it was really an elaboration of the principles of autonomy and equality. By the Peace of Utrecht, the idea that there was no place in the system for hegemonial ambitions on the part of any actors was formally accepted even by all the major actors. At Vienna, this idea was modified to allow a limited, joint hegemony to be exercised by the biggest actors in the name of the great power principle.

So, to the extent to which the balance of power principle was concerned with the status of the international actors, in the eighteenth century it simply proscribed hegemony. In the nineteenth century it was modified, by the great-power principle, to admit only a certain form of hegemony. But in the latter part of the nineteenth century the balance-of-power principle went into decline, along with the great-power principle itself.

As the nineteenth century wore on, nationalism began to spread even to the ruling élites, including those of the great powers; indeed, it became one of the mainstays of their domestic legitimacy. As a result, the great-power principle was more and more undermined. The aggressive nationalism that permeated the international climate tilted the balance between great-power competition and great-power cooperation increasingly in favour of competition, making cooperation more arduous. Around the turn of the twentieth century domestic opinion in all the great powers had become so inflamed with nationalism that governments could no longer afford to be seen to be on too good terms with one another. In the eyes of nationalist domestic opinion, too much international cooperation by the governments would have appeared as a betrayal.

Not surprisingly, the pressure on the governments of the great powers to be confrontational in their dealings with at least some of the governments of the other great powers created a constant expectation of some major conflict. Apprehension about this looming conflict led to intense scrutiny of the resources at the disposal of the various great powers, and of the manner in which these resources were likely to develop in the future.

It was precisely this fixation with the distribution of forces that spelled the end of the balance-of-power principle as a vehicle of international consensus. In the eighteenth and nineteenth centuries, as we have seen, the balance-of-power concept operated as a consensus principle because concern about the actual distribution of forces was never taken very far. The balance-of-power principle coexisted with great inequalities in the distribution of forces even between the major actors. Paradoxically, around the turn of the twentieth century, this distribution was probably more even than it had been at any point in the past. Yet this did not help the cause of international consensus, quite simply because governments could not afford international consensus.

In order to be prepared for the major conflict that most people felt to be inevitable, the great powers obviously could not afford to be on bad terms with all their fellow great powers at once. Quite inevitably, the prevailing climate of confrontation led to a pronounced tendency to think in terms of friends and foes. Nationalist opinion was content as long as there were some foes. With beautiful logic, the six great powers (Austria-Hungary, Britain, France, Germany, Italy, and Russia) eventually found the constellation that combined the option of maximum confrontation with maximum mutual support. They divided themselves neatly into two camps of three. (It is true that Italy remained in a somewhat ambiguous position—it was allied to the central powers, but also cultivated some links with the entente. But it was the least important among the six, which meant that its eventual switching of sides in the war made relatively little practical difference.) Having found this constellation, the great powers locked into it until the conflict actually broke out. The two camps were matched remarkably evenly, as the conflict itself proved. Equilibrism triumphed. But as a consensus principle, as a factor of stability, the balance of power was dead.

President Wilson, the most important among the 1919 peacemakers, and his adherents denigrated the balance-of-power concept, holding it responsible for the 1914 war. But many people, foremost among whom was Clemenceau, the French prime minister, remained convinced equilibrists, and they had some success in bringing equilibrist thinking to bear on the settlement. Unfortunately, equilibrism is incompatible with the concept of national self-determination, and while self-determination had become the new master principle of the international consensus agenda, the balance-of-power concept did not figure on that agenda any more. This inevitably meant that, to the extent to which the balance-of-power concept was applied by the peacemakers, the settlement remained unsupported by a system-wide consensus.

It is sometimes asserted that the 1919 settlement was unsatisfactory because it failed to restore a European balance of power. Indeed, the settlement left even the diminished Germany, barred from uniting with Austria, in a stronger position in relation to its neighbours than it had had in 1914. Then, Germany's eastern neighbours had been the Russian and the Austro-Hungarian Empires. In 1920 these had given way to a number of weak successor states. However, it should have become clear by now that the instability of the settlement did not result from this uneven distribution of forces, but from the continuing lack of consensus among the international actors. This left the door wide open for the next general war.

The balance-of-power principle was not brought back even after the Second World War, despite the fact that the great-power principle was restored for the duration of the Cold War. It may be that the concept of MAD or mutual assured destruction, which meant that each of the two post-1945 great powers had the means to annihilate the other with a nuclear strike even if it was the one that was attacked first, contributed to the stability of the international system. But it is doubtful whether the 'equilibrium of terror' can be interpreted as an application of the balance-of-power concept. It may have acted as a vehicle of consensus in that it was a strong reminder for both sides of the undesirability of an all-out clash between the great powers. But consensus on this point existed independently of MAD. This is shown by the fact that MAD was not achieved until the 1960s—not, that is, until the worst crises in East–West relations were over.

The 'overgrown military establishments in time of peace' (to use Wellington's expression) that were maintained by the two great powers and their satellites after the Second World War have probably never done more than waste their time and everybody's money. Their clienteles—and many others, too—were convinced of the need for each side at least to match the military potential of the other. But what really preserved international stability was the consensus among the key international players (especially the two great powers, of course) that the structure of the international system was acceptable. Both great powers derived immense benefits from the bipolar set-up of the international system; neither welcomed the gradual erosion of this bipolarity. The stability of the Cold War system was due in large part to the successful operation of the great power principle, complete with great power tension. Stability was also contributed to by the operation of the principle of national self-determination, where this was compatible with the great-power principle (national self-determination giving way to great-power cooperation where there was a conflict between the two, as the history of Germany after 1945 shows particularly clearly). This no longer left any room for the balance-of-power principle.

3. DISTRIBUTION OF TERRITORIES AND POPULATIONS

There is another sense in which the balance-of-power principle was structural. The international actors also resorted to it to work out a mutually acceptable distribution of territories and populations. In this respect, however, the principle was of limited usefulness. Saying that no one should get too much gives no very precise indication of quite what anyone should get where. In order to answer that question, it was necessary to supplement the balance-of-power principle.

At Utrecht, the peacemakers could fall back on custom (much of the existing structure of the system surviving the war) and on what we have called the security principle, under which redistribution of territories was acceptable to the extent to which it increased the security of individual actors from attack. At Vienna, the balance-of-power principle *qua* criterion for the redistribution of territories was supplemented by the great-power principle. Under this principle, the smaller powers accepted the decision of the great powers. The great powers among themselves might have diverging views on how to redraw boundaries in line with equilibrist thinking, but they *had* to agree among themselves, no matter how difficult and tense the process, because they were the great powers. Their joint hegemony imposed on them an obligation to reach agreement between them, if they were to maintain their privileged position.

At Paris, finally, the principle of national self-determination also took over from the balance of power as the universally acknowledged criterion for determining boundaries.

We have already traced the fortunes of this principle in the twentieth century, since it is not only capable of determining boundaries but of who the boundaries should be between—capable of determining the identity of the international actors, in other words. It is a very powerful principle, which has led to a dramatic transformation of the international system, in Europe and even more so outside Europe, in a fairly short space of time. It embodied what the Vienna peacemakers called 'the revolution', harnessing as it does the dynamic forces of populism (in the shape of nationalism). It is not surprising, then, that it has brought revolutionary change to the world. But is it also capable of bringing lasting stability?

Intrinsically, it is probably no more and no less capable of doing so than any of the other major consensus principles that we have identified in this book. None of these principles has ever been called upon to maintain international stability on its own. Stability has always relied on the operation of two or more principles, which may modify one another in their practical effects. With regard to national self-determination, it is clear, in particular, that where claims to self-determination conflict with one another, some other concept will be needed to achieve consensus.

We have already seen how in this century national self-determination coexisted with the great-power principle during the

Cold War. Moreover, the need for some concept to regulate national self-determination has led to the evolution of a new consensus principle, a principle that is of great importance in the present-day international consensus agenda.

This is the principle of the inviolability of borders, under which borders cannot legitimately be changed unilaterally or by military means. This principle figures, for example, in the 1975 Final Act of the Conference on Security and Cooperation in Europe, in the treaties concluded between West Germany and various east European states in the context of West Germany's *Ostpolitik*, and, outside Europe, in the celebrated 1964 declaration of the Organization of African Unity validating the existing borders between its member states.

The evolution of this new principle was made possible by the formal proscription of aggressive warfare between states (warfare not undertaken in self-defence) that has become more and more accepted in the twentieth century and which is enshrined, for example, in the Charter of the United Nations. Under this principle, borders can only be changed by mutual agreement, and any actor seeking to *impose* a change of borders unilaterally can be quite sure of strong international criticism. This is one reason why Saddam Hussein's recent outright annexation of Kuwait produced such a strong reaction by the international community, while the more discreet appropriation of Lebanon by Syria has not aroused the international community at all. Israel, too, is unlikely to achieve a tranquil existence while it insists on determining its borders unilaterally. Within the European system, Serbia has been branded as an aggressor by the international community for not accepting the borders that it inherited from the former Yugoslavia. When the Soviet Union disintegrated, Russia at one point announced claims on Ukrainian territory, only to retreat, for the time being at any rate, in the face of strong criticism.

As far as the European system is concerned, the prospects for international stability are probably better, at the time of writing, than they have been at any previous stage in its history, including even the nineteenth century. There is enough consensus in what is now a subsystem of the larger world-wide system to make it unlikely that, in the foreseeable future, Europe should again be subjected to armed international conflict on a major scale.

Except in the former Yugoslavia, and in localized (so far) areas of the former Soviet Union, the discrepancy between ethnic claims and the actual international structure of Europe is probably too small to contain the potential for open warfare. Moreover, what the Vienna peacemakers called 'the revolution' seems to be largely over domestically. Nationalism may have come back to haunt us with ugly manifestations of its strength, but, unlike the nineteenth century and the first few decades of the twentieth, at the present time it is not instrumentalized to prop up a distribution of political power in the domestic sphere that otherwise would lack popular acceptance. This is what made nationalism so extremely dangerous to international stability before by obstructing international cooperation.

The strong basic consensus on which the present set-up of the European system rests helps the process of European integration. This process may eventually extend to the entire continent an international structure—the European Community—that is similar, in many respects, to the German subsystem of the seventeenth and eighteenth centuries. Already, the European Community has, in fact, more or less achieved that 'reign of law' that was at least partly realized in the Holy Roman Empire, and dreamt of at Paris. It is only now, on the basis of a solid international consensus, that this 'reign of law' has become possible in Europe as a whole.

APPENDIX

Kissinger on the Polish–Saxon Question

In his work on the Vienna congress, Kissinger seems a little confused in his treatment of Metternich's two communications of 22 October 1814, addressed respectively to Hardenberg and to Castlereagh, and in which the Austrian minister reluctantly offered to be complaisant over Saxony if Prussia helped to check Russia.

In analysing the note to Castlereagh, Kissinger writes that the British minister in his eagerness to secure Metternich's support 'ignored an enigmatic reservation: that Prussia's annexation of Saxony should not lead to a "disproportionate aggrandizement", a condition clearly impossible of fulfilment if Prussia first regained her Polish provinces.'[1] In fact, the expression 'disproportionate aggrandizement', which looks like a quote, is Kissinger's own—it is not found in Metternich's text. In that document, the passage that Kissinger clearly has in mind—the only possible one—stipulates, as a condition for Austria's consent to the annexation of Saxony,

que ce sacrifice serve à la reconstruction de la Prusse et à la consolidation de sa force, mais qu'il ne soit pas une compensation pour son acquiescement à des vues d'aggrandissement, à des opérations politiques aussi dangereuses pour les deux états que contraires à la lettre des traités.

[that this sacrifice contribute to the reconstruction of Prussia and to the consolidation of its strength, but that it must not serve as a reward for its [Prussia's!] acquiescence in designs of aggrandizement, to political operations which are as dangerous for the two states [Prussia and Austria!] as they are contrary to the letter of the treaties.][2]

In other words, Metternich is actually referring here to the necessity to prevent the disproportionate aggrandizement of *Russia*. This is just a restating of the basic message of the whole note—that Prussia should only obtain Saxony if it put up opposition to the expansionist designs of Russia. The reference to 'dangerous political operations' is an allusion to Russia's exploitation of Polish nationalism. Read correctly, then, this is not a reservation at all, let alone enigmatic—it is Kissinger who overlooked something here, not Castlereagh.

Kissinger then goes on to analyse the note to Hardenberg, claiming

---

[1] Kissinger (1957: 158).   [2] Chodźko (1864: iv. 1940).

that 'his eagerness to obtain Saxony blinded Hardenberg and caused him to overlook still another subtle reservation, that Metternich's offer was conditional not on the *fact* of resistance in Poland but on its *success*.'[3] This is unfair on Hardenberg. He could not overlook what Metternich, in his note, does not say. In fact, the note to Hardenberg says very little on Poland and Russia, while holding forth at length on the unfavourable and unsettling impression that the absorption by Prussia of the whole of Saxony would make on the other German powers. Metternich exhorts Prussia urgently to be content with just some Saxon territory. Failing this, Austria's acquiescence in the annexation is explicitly made dependent on the acceptance by Prussia of Austria's strategic desiderata *in Germany*, in particular the non-acquisition by Prussia of the fortress of Mainz. This is indeed declared a *sine qua non*, but not the *success* of the stance to be taken against Russia.[4]

Kissinger appears to have mixed up the two notes. It is the final paragraph of the one addressed to Castlereagh, and that alone, that may, if one so chooses, be construed as Metternich making his offer dependent on the actual thwarting of Russia's Polish designs:

Je suis chargé . . . de vous inviter, Mylord, à vous joindre à moi et à faire usage de toute votre influence pour engager les cours de Russie et de Prusse à consentir à des arrangements aussi équitables que nécessaires pour le repos de l'Europe, et que l'empereur [d'Autriche] regarde comme conditions expresses de son consentement, sans lesquelles il ne peut se croire aucunement lié.

[I have orders . . . to invite you, My Lord, to join me in using all your influence to induce the Russian and Prussian courts to consent to arrangements which are as equitable as they are necessary for the repose of Europe. The emperor [of Austria] regards them as explicit conditions for his consent, and without them he cannot consider himself bound in any way.][5]

The 'arrangements' to which the text alludes are not, in fact, specified in the note to a degree that would have made it possible to say with any certitude whether or not they had been implemented successfully. All that the note really says, in very general language, is that, in deciding the Polish–Saxon issue, the balance of power should be preserved both in Germany and in Europe, and that Saxony should be sacrificed only as a last resort. Besides, too much should not be read into this in any case. The whole scheme was Castlereagh's idea, and Metternich was making a point of supporting it only reluctantly. It is natural, therefore, that he should have insisted, *with Castlereagh*, that the scheme had better work, too. If Metternich had seriously intended to make this a *sine qua non* in a quasi-legal sense, he should have put this condition, preferably in a

[3] Kissinger (1957: 158). Emphasis in original.
[4] Chodźko (1864: i. 316 ff.).   [5] Ibid. iv. 1940.

much more precise formulation, *to Hardenberg* (which is perhaps why Kissinger—wrongly—remembered him as having done so).

Kissinger may have drawn on Webster, who also speaks of Metternich's 'grudging assent on the Saxon point, on the explicit [*sic*] understanding that Poland was saved and Mainz was kept out of Prussian influence.'[6] The footnote to this refers to Metternich's note to Hardenberg—wrongly, since, as we have seen, that note does not contain the 'explicit' understanding that Webster claims. An understanding concerning Poland is only adumbrated in this note. It only says that the Emperor of Austria 'counts on [*compte sur*]' Prussian 'support [*appui*]', as well as 'absolute conformity of the line taken by the two courts on the Polish issue'. That is all.[7] Moreover, Webster's formulation 'that Poland was saved' seems rather ill-chosen, given that it was the *partition* of Poland that was to be saved.

[6] Webster (1950: 347).   [7] Chodźko (1864: i. 317, 319).

REFERENCES

CHAPTER 1: GENERAL REMARKS

BLANNING, T. C. W. (1986), *The Origins of the French Revolutionary Wars* (London).

BRIDGE, F. R., and BULLEN, R. (1980), *The Great Powers and the European States System* (London).

BULL, H. (1977), *The Anarchical Society: A Study of Order in World Politics* (Basingstoke).

COHEN, R. (1981), *International Politics: The Rules of the Game* (London).

HOLSTI, K. J. (1991), *Peace and War: Armed Conflicts and International Order 1648–1989* (Cambridge).

KENNEDY, P. (1989), *The Rise and Fall of the Great Powers: Economic Change and Military Conflict from 1500 to 2000* (London). (References in this book are to the Fontana paperback edn.)

KISSINGER, H. A. (1957), *A World Restored: Metternich, Castlereagh and the Problems of Peace 1812–1822* (Boston, Mass.).

McKAY, D., and SCOTT, H. M. (1983), *The Rise of the Great Powers 1648–1815* (London).

CHAPTER 2: THE PEACE OF WESTPHALIA

APW, see Braubach and Repgen.

Baltische Studien (1832–) (Herausgegeben von der Gesellschaft für Pommersche Geschichte und Altertumskunde, Stettin).

BAYLE, P. (1683), *Pensées diverses ... à l'occasion de la comète qui parut au mois de décembre 1680* (Rotterdam).

BECKER, W. (1973), *Der Kurfürstenrat: Grundzüge seiner Entwicklung in der Reichsverfassung und seine Stellung auf dem Westfälischen Friedenskongreß* (Münster).

BRAUBACH, M., and REPGEN, K. (eds.) (1962–), *Acta Pacis Westphalicae* (*c.*60 vols. planned) (Münster).

BREUCKER, G. (1879), *Die Abtretung Vorpommerns an Schweden und die Entschädigung Kurbrandenburgs: Ein Beitrag zur Geschichte des Westfälischen Friedens* (Halle).

LE CLERC, J.(?) (ed.) (1725–6), *Négociations secrètes touchant la paix de Munster et d'Osnabrug ... [1642–1648]*, 4 vols. (The Hague).

DICKMANN, F. (1985), *Der Westfälische Frieden*, 5th edn. (Münster).

FEINE, H. E. (1932), 'Zur Verfassungsentwicklung des Heil. Römischen Reiches seit dem Westfälischen Frieden', *Zeitschrift der Savigny-Stiftung für Rechtsgeschichte, Germanistische Abteilung*, 52: 65–133.

FIEDLER, J. (ed.) (1866), *Die Relationen der Botschafter Venedigs über Deutschland und Österreich im siebzehnten Jahrhundert*, i (Vienna).

KRAUS, A. (1984), *Die Acta Pacis Westphalicae: Rang und geisteswissenschaftliche Bedeutung eines Editionsunternehmens unserer Zeit, untersucht an Hand der Elsaß-Frage (1640–1646)* (Opladen).

LORENZ, G. (1969), *Das Erzstift Bremen und der Administrator Friedrich während des Westfälischen Friedenskongresses: Ein Beitrag zur Geschichte des schwedisch-dänischen Machtkampfes im 17. Jahrhundert* (Münster).

LUNDGREN, S. (1945), *Johan Adler Salvius: Problem kring freden, krigsekonomien och maktkampen* (Lund).

MCKA., D., and SCOTT, H. M. (1983), *The Rise of the Great Powers 1648–1815* (London).

MEIERN, J. G. VON (ed.) (1734–6), *Acta Pacis Westphalicae Publica: Oder Westphälische Friedens-Handlungen und Geschichte*, 6 vols. (Hanover).

DU MONT, J. (ed.) (1728), *Corps universel diplomatique du droit des gens*, v and vi (Amsterdam).

MOSER, J. J. (1767), *Von der Garantie des Westphälischen Friedens; nach dem Buchstaben und Sinn desselbigen* (Stuttgart).

ODHNER, C. T. (1877), *Die Politik Schwedens im Westphälischen Friedenscongress und die Gründung der schwedischen Herrschaft in Deutschland* (Gotha).

PETRI, F., SCHÖFFER, I., and WOLTJER, J. J. (1991), *Geschichte der Niederlande* (Munich).

POELHEKKE, J. J. (1948), *De vrede van Munster* (s'-Gravenhage).

REPGEN, K. (1956), 'Der Päpstliche Protest gegen den Westfälischen Frieden und die Friedenspolitik Urbans VIII.', *Historisches Jahrbuch der Görres-Gesellschaft*, 75: 94–122.

RUPPERT, K. (1979), *Die kaiserliche Politik auf dem Westfälischen Friedenskongreß (1643–1648)* (Münster).

STOLPE, S. (1982), *Drottning Kristina* (Stockholm).

SYMCOX, G. (ed.) (1973), *War, Diplomacy, and Imperialism, 1618–1763* (New York).

WIGHT, M. (1977), *Systems of States*, ed. H. Bull (Leicester).

ZEUMER, K. (ed.) (1904), *Quellensammlung zur Geschichte der deutschen Reichsverfassung in Mittelalter und Neuzeit* (Leipzig).

CHAPTER 3: THE PEACE OF UTRECHT

BAUDRILLART, A. (1890), *Philippe V et la Cour de France*, i (Paris).

BLACK, J. (ed.) (1987), *The Origins of War in Early Modern Europe* (Edinburgh).

BOLINGBROKE, see ST JOHN.

COBBETT, W. (ed.) (1810), *Parliamentary History of England. From the Norman Conquest... to the Year 1803*, vi (London).

COLBERT, J.-B. [Marquis de Torcy] (1756), *Mémoires de M. de *** pour servir à l'histoire des négociations depuis le Traité de Riswick jusqu'à la Paix d'Utrecht*, 3 vols. (The Hague).

—— (1757), *Memoirs of the Marquis of Torcy, Secretary of State to Lewis XIV: Containing The History of the Negotiations from the Treaty of Ryswic to the Peace of Utrecht*, 2 vols. (London).

—— (1884), *Journal inédit de Jean-Baptiste Colbert, Marquis de Torcy, Ministre et Secrétaire d'Etat des Affaires Etrangères, pendant les années 1709, 1710 et 1711*, ed. F. Masson (Paris).

DICKINSON, H. T. (1970), *Bolingbroke* (London).

FRESCHOT, C. (ed.) (1714–15), *Actes, mémoires, et autres pièces authentiques concernant la Paix d'Utrecht: Seconde édition augmentée et corrigée*, 6 vols. (Utrecht).

GAEDEKE, A. (1877), *Die Politik Österreichs in der Spanischen Erbfolgefrage*, 2 vols. (Leipzig).

HILL, B. W. (1988), *Robert Harley: Speaker, Secretary of State and Premier Minister* (New Haven, Conn.).

LAMBERTY, G. DE (ed.) (1728–30), *Mémoires pour servir à l'histoire du XVIII siècle*, vi–viii (The Hague).

LEGRELLE, A. (1888–92), *La Diplomatie française et la succession d'Espagne*, 4 vols. (Paris).

LÜNIG, J. C. (ed.) (1713), *Das Teutsche Reichs-Archiv: Zweite Fortsetzung der Continuation des Partis Generalis* (Leipzig).

McINNES, A. (1970), *Robert Harley: Puritan Politician* (London).

ROUSSEL DE COURCY, M.-R. (1889), *Renonciation des Bourbons d'Espagne au trône de France* (Paris).

ST JOHN, H. [Viscount Bolingbroke] (1798), *Letters and Correspondence ... of The Right Honourable Henry St John, Lord Viscount Bolingbroke, during the time he was Secretary of State to Queen Anne*, ed. G. Parke, 2 vols. (London).

—— (1844) *Works*, 4 vols. (London).

STURGILL, C. (1987), 'From Utrecht to the Little War with Spain: Peace at Almost Any Price Had to Be the Case', in Black (1987), 176–84.

TORCY, see COLBERT.

WEBER, O. (1891), *Der Friede von Utrecht: Verhandlungen zwischen England, Frankreich, dem Kaiser und den Generalstaaten 1710–1713* (Gotha).

CHAPTER 4: THE CONGRESS OF VIENNA
APPENDIX

CASTLEREAGH, see STEWART.

CHODŹKO, J. L. (published under the pseudonym 'Comte d'Angeberg') (ed.) (1864), *Le Congrès de Vienne et les Traités de 1815*, 4 vols. with continuous pagination (Paris).

D'ANGEBERG, see CHODŹKO.

GENTZ, F. VON (1873), *Tagebücher*, i (Leipzig).

—— (1876), *Dépêches inédites du Chevalier de Gentz aux Hospodars de Valachie pour servir à l'histoire de la politique européenne (1813 à 1828)*, i, pub. by the Comte Prokesch-Osten Fils (Paris).

—— (1913), *Briefe von und an Friedrich von Gentz*, iii(1), ed. F. C. Wittichen and E. Salzer (Munich).

GRIEWANK, K. (1954), *Der Wiener Kongreß und die europäische Restauration 1814/15* (Leipzig).

GULICK, E. V. (1982), *Europe's Classical Balance of Power* (Westport, Conn.).

HUBER, E. R. (ed.) (1961), *Dokumente zur deutschen Verfassungsgeschichte*, i (Stuttgart).

HUMBOLDT, W. VON (1903), *Gesammelte Schriften*, xi (Berlin) (repr. 1968).

JAUCOURT, A.-F. DE (1905), *Correspondance du Comte de Jaucourt . . . avec le Prince de Talleyrand pendant le Congrès de Vienne*, pub. by his grandson (Paris).

KISSINGER, H. A. (1957), *A World Restored: Metternich, Castlereagh and the Problems of Peace 1812–1822* (Boston, Mass.).

KLÜBER, J. L. (ed.) (1815–18), *Acten des Wiener Congresses in den Jahren 1814 und 1815*, 8 vols. (Erlangen).

—— (1835), *Acten der Wiener Congresses in den Jahren 1814 und 1815*, ix (suppl. vol.) (Erlangen).

METTERNICH, C. W. N. L. VON (1880–4), *Nachgelassene Papiere*, ed. R. von Metternich and A. von Klinkowström, 8 vols. (Vienna).

—— (1880–2), *Memoirs of Prince Metternich*, ed. R. von Metternich and A. von Klinkowström, 5 vols. (London). (This is a partial trans. of the preceding work.)

MÜNSTER, G. H. VON (1868), *Political Sketches of the State of Europe from 1814–1867* (Edinburgh).

STEWART, R. [Viscount Castlereagh] (1853), *Correspondence, Despatches, and other Papers, of Viscount Castlereagh . . .*, ed. C. W. Vane, 3rd Series. *Military and Diplomatic*, 4 vols. (London).

TALLEYRAND, C.-M. DE (1881*a*), *Correspondance inédite du Prince de Talleyrand et du Roi Louis XVIII pendant le Congrès de Vienne*, ed. M. G. Pallain (Paris).

—— (1881*b*), *The Correspondence of Prince Talleyrand and King Louis XVIII: During the Congress of Vienna*, ed. M. G. Pallain, 2 vols. (London).

—— (1891–2), *Memoirs*, ed. de Broglie, 5 vols. (London).

TREITSCHKE, H. VON (1875), 'Preußen auf dem Wiener Congresse', *Preußische Jahrbücher*, 36: 655–714.

—— (1879), *Deutsche Geschichte im Neunzehnten Jahrhundert*, i (Leipzig).

—— (1882), *Deutsche Geschichte im Neunzehnten Jahrhundert*, ii (Leipzig).

WEBSTER, C. K. (ed.) (1921), *British Diplomacy 1813–1815: Select Documents dealing with the Reconstruction of Europe* (London).

—— (1934), *The Congress of Vienna 1814–1815* (London).

—— (1950), *The Foreign Policy of Castlereagh 1812–1815* (London).

WELLESLEY, A. [Duke of Wellington] (1861–5), *Supplementary Despatches, Correspondence, and Memoranda of Arthur Duke of Wellington*, viii–xii, ed. by his son (London).

—— (1838), *The Dispatches of Field Marshal the Duke of Wellington . . .* , ed. Gurwood, vol. xii (London).

WELLINGTON, see WELLESLEY.

CHAPTER 5: THE PEACE CONFERENCE OF PARIS

ALBRECHT-CARRIÉ, R. (1966), *Italy at the Paris Peace Conference* (Hamden, Conn.).

BADEN, MAX VON (1928), *Memoirs*, 2 vols. (London).

BAILEY, T. A. (1963), *Woodrow Wilson and the Lost Peace* (Chicago).

BULL, H. (1972), 'The Theory of International Politics 1919–1969', in Porter (1972), 30–55.

—— and WATSON, A. (1984) (eds.), *The Expansion of International Society* (Oxford).

BULLITT, W. C., and FREUD, S. (1967), *Thomas Woodrow Wilson . . . A Psychological Study* (London).

CLEMENCEAU, G. (1930a), *Grandeurs et misères d'une victoire* (Paris).

—— (1930b), *Grandeur and Misery of Victory* (London).

—— (1938), *Discours de paix* (Paris).

—— (1968), *Discours de guerre* (Paris).

COBBAN, A. (1969), *The Nation State and National Self-Determination* (London).

CROCE, B., ORLANDO, V. E., and SFORZA, C. (1946), *Per la pace d'Italia e d'Europa* (Rome).

Federal Republic of Germany, see Germany, Federal Republic of.

FINCH, G. A. (1919), 'The Peace Negotiations with Germany', *American Journal of International Law*, 13: 536–57.

FISCHER, F. (1967), *Germany's War Aims in the First World War* (London).

—— (1975), *World Power or Decline: The Controversy over 'Germany's Aims in the First World War'* (London).

FOX, W. T. R. (1968), *The American Study of International Relations* (Columbia, SC).

GERMANY, FEDERAL REPUBLIC OF, FOREIGN OFFICE (1982), *Akten zur Deutschen Auswärtigen Politik 1918–1945*, Serie A. *1918–1925*, i (Göttingen).

GILBERT, M. (1966), *The Roots of Appeasement* (London).

HANKEY, M. (1963), *The Supreme Control at the Paris Peace Conference 1919: A Commentary* (London).

HEADLAM-MORLEY, J. (1972), *A Memoir of the Paris Peace Conference 1919*, ed. R. Bryant, A. Cienciala, and A. Headlam-Morley (London).

JORDAN, W. M. (1943), *Great Britain, France, and the German Problem 1918–1939: A Study of Anglo-French Relations in the Making and Maintenance of the Versailles Settlement* (London) (new impression 1971).

KEDOURIE, E. (1984), 'A New International Disorder', in Bull and Watson (1984), 347–55.

KEYNES, J. M. (1920), *The Economic Consequences of the Peace* (London).

KROCKOW, C. VON (1990), *Die Deutschen in ihrem Jahrhundert 1890–1990* (Reinbek bei Hamburg).

LANSING, R. (1921), *The Peace Negotiations: A Personal Narrative* (London).

LLOYD GEORGE, D. (1923), *Is It Peace?* (London).

—— (1936), *War Memoirs*, 5 vols. (London).

—— (1938), *The Truth about the Peace Treaties*, 2 vols. (London).

MCCALLUM, R. B. (1944), *Public Opinion and the Last Peace* (London).

MANTOUX, P. (1964), *Paris Peace Conference 1919. Proceedings of the Council of Four (March 24–April 18)* (Geneva).

MARKS, S. (1976), *The Illusion of Peace: International Relations in Europe 1918–1933* (London).

MARSTON, F. S. (1944), *The Peace Conference of 1919: Organization and Procedure* (London).

METTERNICH, C. W. N. L. VON (1880–4), *Nachgelassene Papiere*, ed. R. von Metternich and A. von Klinkowström, 8 vols. (Vienna).

—— (1880–2), *Memoirs of Prince Metternich*, ed. R. von Metternich and A. von Klinkowström, 5 vols. (London). (This is a partial trans. of the preceding work.)

NICOLSON, H. (1934), *Peacemaking 1919* (London).

NITTI, F. S. (1922), *Peaceless Europe* (London).

—— (1923), *The Decadence of Europe: The Paths of Reconstruction* (London).

ORLANDO, V. E. (1923), *Discorsi per la guerra e per la pace*, ed. A. Giannini (Foligno).

—— (1946), 'La leggenda della vittoria mutilata', *Corriere di Roma*, 19 Nov. 1944, in Croce et al. (1946), 43–9.

PORTER, B. (1972) (ed.), *The Aberystwyth Papers: International Politics 1919–1969* (London).

SONNINO, S. (1925), *Discorsi parlamentari*, iii (Rome).

SRBIK, H. VON (1925), *Metternich: Der Staatsmann und der Mensch*, 2 vols. (Munich).

TEMPERLEY, H. W. V. (ed.) (1920–4), *A History of the Peace Conference of Paris*, 6 vols. (London).

USA, STATE DEPARTMENT (1942–7), *Papers Relating to the Foreign Relations of the United States: 1919. The Paris Peace Conference*, 13 vols. (Washington DC).

WILSON, W. (1924), *The Messages and Papers of Woodrow Wilson*, ed. A. Shaw, 2 vols. (New York).

INDEX

Aachen (congress) 123, 171, 213, 221, 239, 248
actors, *see* international actors
absolutism 192, 219–20
Adler Salvius, *see* Salvius
Aire 143
Aix-la-Chapelle, *see* Aachen
Alexander I (Czar of Russia) 168, 171, 227
  and the balance of power 225, 229
  attacked by Castlereagh 176–7, 178
  and dynastic legitimacy 191, 214
  and the great-power-concept 239–40
  ideological orientation 181, 188–9, 192–3, 220, 221–2
  and the Polish-Saxon issue 169, 180–1, 187, 195, 196, 206, 231, 238, 242–4
  and public opinion 191, 192–3
  wishes to improve Russia's standing in Europe 178–9, 180–1, 244
Alsace:
  and the Peace of Westphalia 21, 50, 67, 68–71, 76
  and the Peace of Utrecht 142
  and the Vienna congress 201, 203
  and the Paris peace conference 288
Althusius, Johannes 36
amnesty clauses 299
Anjou, Duke of, *see* Philip V
Anne (Queen of Britain) 154, 162 n.
  as addressee of official communications 139, 149
  proposed as arbiter 119
  and the balance of power 124–5
  and the Elector of Hanover 122
  and the London Preliminaries 98
  and Louis XIV 108, 117
  survival essential for peace settlement 155, 156
Anne of Austria (Queen of France) 29, 75, 76
Annunzio, Gabriele d' 290
Anstett, Johann Protasius von 180

Anton Ulrich (Duke of Braunschweig-Wolfenbüttel) 136
appeasement 301
Aragón 103
Armenia 318
Assoziation der Vorderen Reichskreise 141 n.
Auersperg, Leopold Graf von 148
Ausgleich (Austria-Hungary) 252
Australia 279
Austrasia (kingdom) 66, 69
Austria:
  and the Peace of Westphalia 39, 75
  and the War of the Spanish Succession 94, 138
  and the Paris peace conference 287, 288, 291, 294, 295, 299, 319
  as an international actor in the 19th and 20th century 231, 249, 312, 320, 329
  nature of the Austrian monarchy 104, 184–5, 223, 252
  see also Austria–Hungary
Austria, House of, *see* Habsburg
Austria–Hungary 252, 275, 288, 329
Austro-Italian War (1859) 241
Austro-Prussian War (1866) 241
autonomy 321–2, 326–7
  at Münster and Osnabrück 77–82, 85, 87
  at Utrecht 120–1, 140, 232
  at Vienna 184, 234
  at Paris 257, 258, 292
  and national self-determination 255
Autun 166
Avaux, Claude de Mesmes, Comte d' 20, 86
  author of circular to the estates 44 n., 79
  on the delegates of the estates 48
  encounter with Mecklenburg envoy 37
  intervention in negotiations over Pomerania 63
  religious zeal 29
Avignon 203

Baden (grand-duchy) 213
Baden (Peace of) 99, 161
Baden, Prince Max von, *see* Max von Baden
balance-of-power concept 10, 43, 327–31
  at Münster and Osnabrück 80–2
  at Utrecht 102, 115, 123–39, 228, 232
  at Vienna 175–7, 194, 195–6, 223–33, 237, 245
  at Paris 258, 264–5, 268–70, 273, 274, 275, 290, 323
  compared to great-power principle 234
  compared to principle of national self-determination 255
Baltic States 249
Bar (duchy) 92
Barcelonnette 147
Barraux, *see* Fort Barraux
barrier concept 140–7, 150, 174, 228
Bavaria (electorate, later kingdom) 31, 38, 75
  delegation at Münster 69, 74
  and the War of the Spanish Succession 91, 119, 138
  at the Vienna congress 168, 218, 238
  see also Maximilian; Max Emanuel
Bayle, Pierre 71–2
Belgium:
  and the War of the Spanish Succession 90, 95, 96, 103, 109, 118–19, 133, 138, 140, 141–2, 143, 228
  and the Vienna congress 169, 170, 174, 204, 227, 246
  and the Paris peace conference 257–8, 262, 277. 279, 280, 283, 291
Bentham, Jeremy 2
Bergeyck, Jean de Brouchoven, Comte de 164–5
Bernstorff, Johann Heinrich Graf von 277
Berry, Charles, Duke of 93, 127, 132, 156, 159, 162 n.
Besnardière, *see* La Besnardière
Béthune 143
bipolarity 326, 330
Bismarck, Otto Fürst von 231, 250, 252, 310, 312

Bissolati, Leonida 273
Blenheim (Battle of) 96
Bohemia 18, 104, 109, 207, 287–8
Bolingbroke, Henry St John, Viscount 97, 119, 142, 199, 228, 243
  and the British kingdoms 104
  and the Dutch 144
  judgment of French policies 156–7, 158–9
  desires moderate peace 152–3, 155
  and the notion of a European system 110
  impeached 156
  and the notion of 'interest' 100, 101, 111, 114–18
  and the Italian situation 137
  gives order to Ormonde to quit war 98
  and popular opinion 104–5
  and the renunciation issue 125–30
  and the issue of the Savoy barrier 144–6
  and Spain 163, 164
  and Torcy 99
  views on Utrecht peace 153–5, 160
  and the Wittelsbach issue 118
Bolshevism 249, 254, 272, 278–9, 283
Bonaparte, *see* Napoleon
Bonn 218
Bonnac, Jean-Louis d'Usson, Marquis de 131
Botha, Louis 303
Bothmer, Johann Caspar Freiherr von 149, 150, 158
Bouchain 143
Bourbon (dynasty):
  and the War of the Spanish Succession 89, 90, 93, 94, 95, 96, 104, 117, 121, 124, 127, 130, 131, 134, 156, 161, 232, 327
  and the Vienna congress 168, 173, 192, 214, 217, 220
Bourgeois, Léon 259
Brandenburg (electorate) 39, 45 n., 51, 56, 60, 61, 62, 107
  delegation at Osnabrück 56, 61, 62, 63, 65 n., 75
  see also Prussia
Bratislava 245
Brazil 280
Breisach 66, 68, 142
Bremen 51, 52–6, 65, 212
Brenner question 287, 290

Briançon 145
Bridge, F. R. 12
Brienne, Henri-Auguste de Loménie,
    Comte de 28, 41, 67, 69, 76, 83
Bristol, The Bishop of, see Robinson,
    John
Brittany, Louis, Duke of 126
Brockdorff-Rantzau, Ulrich Graf von
    277–8, 282 n., 303
Brun, Antoine 35, 87 n.
Bulgaria 291, 294, 308, 319
Bull, Hedley 11
Bullen, Roger 12
Bullitt, William C. 302
Burgsdorff, Conrad Alexander
    Magnus von 32, 33
Burgundian Circle 12, 33–5
Burgundy 34, 35
Bush, George 326
Buys, Willem 152

Cammin (bishopric) 65
Canada 98, 279
Cardinal-Infante, The 13
Castelldosrius, Manuel Sentmanat y
    Lanuza, Marqués de 103–4
Castlereagh, Robert Stewart, Viscount
    172, 173, 182, 185, 186, 187, 231,
    283, 285, 334–5
    and the balance of power 175–6,
    226–7, 228
    circular note on Poland 179–80
    and the Czar 176–7, 193
    and dynastic legitimacy 214–19
    and the great-power concept 234–5,
    238
    and the Holy Alliance 188
    and the Ottoman Empire 188
    and the Polish-Saxon issue 169,
    181, 193, 195–8, 205–6, 230–1,
    242–4, 334–5
    and public opinion 193–4, 197–9,
    205
    and the right of conquest 197, 204,
    205–7
    and the Second Peace of Paris
    198–9, 201–3
    stubbornness 177–8
    and Talleyrand 175, 238
Catalonia 17, 77, 105, 109
central powers 252, 258–9, 269, 270
Chamberlain, Austen 303
Chambon, Joseph 166–7

Charles II (King of Spain) 90, 92,
    113–14, 116, 148
    death 93
    first will in favour of Bavaria 91
    second will in favour of Bourbon
    dynasty 92–3, 94, 100, 104, 124,
    133, 161
    German influence at court 148
Charles IV (Duke of Lorraine) 68
Charles V (Emperor) 14, 66, 94, 135,
    136–7
Charles VI (Archduke of Austria,
    then Emperor) 151, 155, 161, 165
    and the Catalans 109
    criticized by France 117
    not mentioned in Hague alliance
    96
    compared to his father Leopold 134
    and the second partition treaty 92
    advocates severe peace 147–9, 158
    implications of succession to
    Imperial throne 97, 126
    and the Utrecht negotiations 98, 99,
    122, 134–5
    and the will of Charles II 93, 94
    and the Wittelsbach issue 118–20,
    138
Charles X (King of France) 210, 216
Charles X (King of Sweden) 88
Charles XII (King of Sweden) 90,
    124, 165, 313
Charte 220
Châtillon (peace talks) 176
Chaumont (Treaty of) 168 n., 224,
    239, 246 n.
Chigi, Fabio (Papal envoy at
    Münster) 18, 80, 85
China 249, 279
Christendom, Christian
    Commonwealth of Europe,
    Christianity:
    and the Peace of Westphalia 22, 26,
    27–30, 42–3, 47, 53, 63, 66, 74, 80,
    83, 84, 85, 88
    and the Peace of Utrecht 103,
    110–11, 112, 113, 114, 135, 151,
    158
    and the Vienna congress 181,
    188–9, 191, 193, 223, 236
    as a criterion for membership of
    the international system 88, 223,
    317
    see also religion

Clancarty, Richard Le Poer Trench, Earl of 175, 215
class struggle 312, 315
Clemenceau, Georges 273, 275, 280, 281, 289, 304, 315, 329
  general views on First World War and peace settlement 263–9, 283–5, 300
  replaced by Millerand 291
Cohen, Raymond 11
Cold War 320, 326, 330, 332
Colbert, see Torcy
collective security:
  at Münster and Osnabrück 27, 40–2, 47, 233, 239
  at Utrecht 151–2, 233, 239
  at Paris 260, 264, 265–6, 270, 292, 325
Cologne (electorate) 96, 117, 119, 218
Commonwealth, see English Commonwealth
Communist Manifesto 251
Conference on Security and Cooperation in Europe 332
Congress of Subject Nationalities (1918) 271
conquest, see right of conquest
conscription 236, 322
Contarini, Alvise 18, 82–3
Cooke, Edward 193
Cornejo, Feliz 162
Council of Five (1919) 281
Council of Four (1919) 281, 283, 294, 299
Council of Ten (1919) 281
Cracow 212
Crimean War 241
Croatia 104
Cromwell, Oliver 77
cuius regio eius religio (doctrine of) 12, 40
custom as a source of consensus 43–5, 47, 72–3, 78, 100, 102–3, 190, 232–3, 316, 331
Czartoryski, Adam Jerzy, Prince 169, 180
Czechoslovakia 249, 279, 287–9, 318, 319

Daily Courant 150
Dalmatia 169, 272
Dartmouth, William Legge, Earl of 97 n., 145, 146

Dauphin:
  (Louis, Dauphin de France [the 'Grand Dauphin']) 91–2, 93
  (Louis, the future Louis XV) 126, 130, 159, 160 n.
Dauphiny 145
Decapolis 71 n.
Delbrück, Hans 299 n.
Denain 99
Denmark 52, 53, 54, 56, 61, 88, 109, 168, 170, 207, 317, 321
  intervention in Thirty Years War 16, 18
  proposed as mediator at Osnabrück 18
depersonalization 251
Descartes, René 24
détente 326
dictatorship:
  contrasted with kingship 207, 209–10, 219
Directoire 167
Dithmarschen 208
Doge 209
Douai 143
Dutch Republic, see Netherlands
dynastic legitimacy 175, 191, 207–23, 233, 317–18
  not applicable to Poland 194
dynastic solidarity (absence of in 17th century) 74–7
dynasticism 76, 211, 219, 317

Edict of Restitution 16
elective monarchies 45, 109, 207–8, 209
Electors, see Holy Roman Empire
Emperor, see Charles VI; Ferdinand II; Ferdinand III; Leopold I; Holy Roman Empire
English Commonwealth (1649–60) 77, 209
Enlightenment 250
entente (1907–20) 252, 262, 269, 302, 306, 310
equality 321–2, 326–7
  at Münster and Osnabrück 82–9
  at Utrecht 120–3
  at Vienna 234
  at Paris 258, 262, 292, 295–6, 297
  and national self-determination 255
equilibrium, equilibrism, see balance of power

equilibrium of terror 329–30
Erfurt 230
Estonia 318
ethnicity criterion 272, 275, 288, 289, 295, 320
Europe (concept) 110–11, 172, 182–3, 306
European Community 9, 333
Exilles 145, 146

Fascism 251
February Revolution (Russia) 252–3, 273
female suffrage 249
Fenestrelle 145, 146
Ferdinand II (Emperor) 16, 17, 37, 52
Ferdinand III (Emperor) 17, 20, 44, 62, 85
    and the armistice question 21
    protests peaceful intentions 25–6
    seeks rapprochement with Saxony 33
    and the issue of Bremen-Verden 53–4, 55
    and the issue of Alsace 68
    and the Catholic radicals 53
    and the alliance with Spain 74, 75
    conciliatory attitude towards the estates 80
    and questions of rank 82
Ferdinand IV (King of Naples and Sicily) 170, 217, 218
Ferdinand Joseph (Prince of Bavaria) 91–2
Feuillade, see La Feuillade
Final Act of Vienna 170, 213, 227, 239, 246
Finland 170, 180, 249, 318
First Peace of Paris, see Paris
First World War 249, 250, 251, 318
    compared to Thirty Years War 252
    as a revolution 249–50, 266–7, 271
Five Particulars, The 255
Fiume 272, 281, 290
Florence 84
Fontainebleau memorandum 283, 284
Fort Barraux 145
Four Ends, The 255, 260
Four Principles, The 255, 286
Fourteen Points, The 254, 255, 256, 257, 287, 293

France:
    compared to Germany 88, 147, 309
    intervention in negotiations over Pomerania 62–3
    as a monarchy 209, 210
    role in Thirty Years War 17, 26–7, 35–6, 58
    position and policies after Thirty Years War 88–9
Franche-Comté (Freigrafschaft Burgund) 35
Francis I (Emperor of Austria) 171, 184, 185
    and the Holy Alliance 188
    and the Saxon issue 197
    adopts new title 213
    hosts Vienna congress 168
Franco-Prussian War (1870) 241
Frankfurt (free city) 212
Frankfurt, Declaration of 224
Frederick (Prince of Denmark) 52–3, 54–5, 65
Frederick Augustus (King of Saxony) 169, 205, 213, 217–18, 245–6
Frederick William (Elector of Brandenburg) 33, 56, 58, 76
    and the Pomeranian issue 51, 56, 59, 61–2, 64–5
    seeks to revive the Protestant 'Union' 32
Frederick William I (King of Prussia) 106–7
Frederick William III (King of Prussia) 188, 195–6, 230–1, 244, 245
Freiburg-im-Breisgau 142
French Revolution 166–7, 194, 201, 203, 209, 216, 271, 317–18, 322
    effect on French strength according to Wellington 202
    creates new intellectual climate 228
    populism its essential feature 250–1
    a struggle between principles 173
    and representative democracy 210
    undermines custom as a source of consensus 232–3
    and the nature of warfare according to Liverpool 243
frihetstid 209

Garibaldi, Giuseppe 274
Gaultier, François 145

Geertruidenberg (peace talks) 96, 97, 114–15, 143, 147, 152, 158
Geneva 246
Genoa 84, 209, 212
and the Vienna congress 223, 246–7
Gentz, Friedrich von:
on Austrian policy 224
translates documents for Castlereagh 177
view of Castlereagh 176, 178
view of the Czar 192
author of draft declaration (Feb. 1815) 186, 235
on the situation of Europe (1818) 248–9
view of French role at Vienna congress 174
and public opinion 191
criticizes Prussian policy 183
view of the Saxon issue 205
Georg Ludwig (Elector of Hanover) 122, 149, 155
Georgia 318
Germany:
aims in First World War 257, 311
attitude preceding Paris peace conference 276–8
compared to France 88, 147, 309
constitutional question (1918) 256–7, 258, 262, 296–7
national feeling at time of Peace of Westphalia 30–1, 32, 33–5, 36–7, 38, 39, 40, 42, 52–3, 73–4, 75
national feeling at time of Vienna congress 198
national feeling and the First World War 310–11
position in European system and effect of Versailles treaty 309–15
reaction to draft Treaty of Versailles 294–7, 298–9, 300–1
since 1945 315, 320, 332
German Confederation 170, 196–7, 220, 229
German Liberty 46, 78–9, 120
Gibraltar 98, 161
Golden Bull 45 n.
Gorbachev, Mikhail 326
Great Northern War 90
great-power concept 88, 321, 324, 327–8
absent before the 19th century 323

at Vienna 168, 226, 229, 232–47, 322–4, 331
at Paris 252, 258, 272, 273, 275, 280, 292, 323–4
and the Cold War 320, 330
compared to balance-of-power principle 234
and national self-determination 255, 320, 330, 331
Greece 279
Gregorian calendar 15
Guipúzcoa 92
Gulick, E. V. 195–6, 226
Gustaf Adolf (King of Sweden) 16, 19, 24, 57, 58
Gustaf III (King of Sweden) 313

Habsburg (dynasty) 49, 213, 222, 317
and the Thirty Years War 16–17, 19, 27, 28, 36, 37, 41, 44, 66, 67, 79
role at Münster and Osnabrück 19–20, 75
and the War of the Spanish Succession 90, 91, 94, 96, 104, 106, 119, 123, 135, 136, 138, 147–8, 228, 327
and the Vienna congress 169–70, 201, 223, 231
before the First World War 249, 252, 314
and Alsace 21, 62, 68–71, 76, 201
and Burgundy 35
origins of 13
Hague Alliance 95–6, 97, 114, 115, 117, 121, 126, 140
Hague, The (peace talks) 96, 97
Halberstadt (bishopric) 65
Hamburg 25, 212
Hankey, Maurice 281 n.
Hanover (electorate, later kingdom) 39, 56
and the Vienna congress 213, 214, 218, 231, 238
Hanover (dynasty) 155
see also Georg Ludwig
Harcourt, Henri de Lorraine, Marquis d' 113
Hardenberg, Carl August Fürst von 183, 193, 205–6, 224–5, 245
replies to Castlereagh's note on Poland 182
demands punishment of France 200

Hardenberg (*cont.*)
  and the German Act of
    Confederation 220
  and the Polish-Saxon issue 195–6,
    197, 334–5
Harley, Robert, *see* Oxford, Earl of
Hauterive, Alexandre-Maurice Blanc
  de Lanautte, Comte d' 203
Headlam-Morley, James 304
Heidelberg 154
Heinsius, Anthonie 111, 125, 141, 145,
  148, 151
Hejaz 279
Hertling, Georg Friedrich Graf von
  259
Hesse 231
Hesse-Darmstadt (grand-duchy) 213
Hesse-Kassel (landgraviate, later
  electorate) 108, 213
Hitler, Adolf 10, 250, 286, 319–20
Höchstädt (Battle of) 96
Hoffmann, Johann Philipp 109 n.
Holsatia 54
Holstein-Oldenburg 213
Holsti, Kalevi R. 12
Holy Alliance 188–9, 222, 294, 296,
  305, 306
Holy Roman Empire 9, 27, 71, 184,
  213
  and the War of the Spanish
    Succession 96, 99, 101 n., 136
  and the Utrecht peace 99, 118, 122,
    142, 143–4, 161
  division into 'circles' 12–13, 33, 65
  constitutional arrangements 16, 31,
    32, 36, 38, 39, 40, 42, 44, 45,
    46–7, 48–9, 53, 65, 82, 133
  Council of Cities 18
  Council of Electors 18, 31, 45, 47,
    48, 50, 74, 82, 85, 147 n.
  Council of Princes 18
  ranking of the Emperor 82, 83, 120,
    121, 321–2
  title of the Emperor 14–15, 82, 104,
    121
  compared to European Community
    333
  general policy of the estates at
    Münster and Osnabrück 31–2, 36,
    38, 46, 78, 80
  legalism of the estates 48
  religious arrangements 12, 16, 40,
    44

containing republican forms of
    government 208, 209
  right of alliance of the estates 46–7
  see also Reichstag
Holy See 203, 213, 286
House, Edward M. 281
Humboldt, Wilhelm Freiherr von
  182–3, 220
Hungary 104, 109, 136, 207, 249, 252,
  319
  and the Paris peace conference
    288–9, 291, 294, 299
  see also Austria–Hungary
Hussein, Saddam 332

Iceland 249, 320–1
'idealist' school of international
  relations 260–1, 267, 268, 293,
  308
India 279
industrial revolution 251
international actors:
  definition 1–2
  relative insulation 7
international law 48
international legitimacy 50
international organizations 3
  as international actors 2
international society, definition of 10
inviolability of borders 332
Ireland 104, 249, 320–1
  compared to Poland 180
Israel 332
Italy 328–9
  and the War of the Spanish
    Succession 136–8, 142, 228
  and the Vienna congress 169–70,
    181, 246–7
  and the Paris peace conference
    269–76, 279, 280, 287, 290, 300,
    324
  see also Genoa; Naples; Sardinia;
    Sardinia-Piedmont; Sicily; Venice

James II (king of Britain) 95
James (III) Stuart 95, 108
Japan 279, 280, 281
Jaucourt, Arnail-François, Comte de
  191, 217
Johann Kasimir (Duke of Pfalz-
  Zweibrücken) 25 n.
John George (Elector of Saxony)
  32–3

John William (Palatine Elector)
Joseph I (Emperor) 97, 126
Julian calendar 15

Kamień Pomorski (Cammin)
 (bishopric) 65
Kapodistrias, Ioannes Antonios,
 Count 180, 201
Kayser, Abraham 37–8, 51 n.
Kehl 142
Kennedy, Paul 12, 13
Keynes, John Maynard 303, 304, 306
kingship 45, 207–10, 213, 219–20, 221,
 249
 see also republicanism
Kinsky, Franz Ulrich Graf von 159 n.
Kirchner, Michael Achaz von 119
Kissinger, Henry A. 10, 185, 199, 223
 view of the Polish-Saxon issue 196,
 243–4, 334–6
Kristina (Queen of Sweden):
 and the administrator Frederick
 54
 and the Brandenburg elector 58,
 64, 76
 and the Oxenstiernas 19–20, 23–4
 desire for peace 22–4
 views on religion 30
 and Salvius 19–20, 25, 30, 60, 81
Kuwait 332

La Besnardière, Jean-Baptiste de
 Gouey, Comte de 171 n.
La Feuillade, Louis d'Aubusson,
 Duc de 155
Laharpe, Frédéric César 180
Landau 203
Lansing, Robert 301, 305
Latin America 279
Latvia 318
Lawless, Patricio 117 n.
League of Nations 151, 265, 275, 304,
 325
 and the abrogation of treaties 291
 provisions of Covenant 292–4
 German critique of Covenant
 295–6
 German eagerness to adhere 276,
 277, 278, 295, 297
 likened to Holy Alliance 296, 305,
 306
 initially confined to victors and
 neutrals 267, 294, 300

intended for continual revision of
 peace settlement 259
 criticized by Lansing 302
 criticized by Lloyd George 305
 administers Saar territory 285–6
Lebanon 332
Legrelle, Arsène 103
Leipzig 230–1
Leninism 251
Leopold I (Emperor) 100, 123–4, 135,
 148, 159 n.
 consolidates his position in the
 Empire 123, 136
 and the Hague Alliance 95–6
 occupies Milan 95
 rejects partition schemes 92
 succeeded by Joseph I 97
 writes to Palatine elector 133–4
 instruction for Wratislaw 134
Lessing, Gotthold Ephraim 13
levée en masse 236
Liberia 279, 280
Lille 143
Lithuania 318
Liverpool, Robert Banks Jenkinson,
 Earl of 193
 and dynastic legitimacy 219
 and public opinion 194
 urges moderate stance towards
 Russia 242–3
 wishes to preserve Saxony 193–4
 and the Second Peace of Paris
 199–200
Lloyd George, David 259, 281, 304
 and the Adriatic issue 290–1
 and the issue of Austria 287
 critique of settlement 305
 as an advocate of moderation 283,
 284–5
 address to trade unions 254, 261–3
 on Versailles treaty 292
 on Wilson 300
Lodi (Peace of) 82
Lombardy 91, 169
London Preliminaries 98, 125, 143,
 147–8, 150, 152–3, 154
London (Treaty of) 269, 272, 290–1,
 293
Longueville, Henri II d'Orléans,
 Duke of 20, 29, 45, 75
Lorraine 50, 67–8, 92, 142, 288
Louis XIII (King of France) 42,
 86 n.

Louis XIV (King of France) 97, 100, 130, 232, 313
  and Queen Anne 108, 117
  and the balance of power 123–4, 125
  and the barrier concept 141, 142, 143
  envisages Belgian republic 109
  faced with Charles II's will 93–5, 103–4
  expansionism of 77, 88, 139, 147, 148, 149–50
  and the Geertruidenberg peace talks 157–8
  seeks influence in Germany 136
  accused of wishing to subjugate Germany 105–6
  attitude towards legal questions 162–3
  role in negotiations at Münster 85–6
  on Oxford University 163
  willingness for peace 96, 159–60
  and Philip V 98, 131, 161–4
  provocative policies after acceptance of Spanish succession 95–6
  policy of 'reunion' 71
  number of troops fielded 58 n.
  does not seek universal dominion 108
  seeks to avoid war over Spanish succession 90–3, 113–14, 116
  and the Wittelsbach issue 117–20
Louis XVIII (King of France) 172, 191, 198, 202, 206, 210, 222–3, 227, 239, 246 n.
  recalled by Talleyrand (1814) 167, 213–14
  forced by Talleyrand to grant constitution 220
  second restoration (1815) 170, 200, 215–19
  to be protected by allied occupation troops 221
Louis-Philippe (King of France) 210
  see also Orléans
Lübeck 54, 212

Machiavelli, Niccolò 261
McKay, Derek 12
Magdeburg (archbishopric) 65
Magyars 252, 288, 306, 308

Mainz (electorate) 53, 75
Mainz (fortress) 335, 336
Mantoux, Paul 281 n.
Maria Anna of Austria (Queen of Spain) 148
Maria Anna von Pfalz-Neuburg (Queen of Spain) 94, 148
Max von Baden, Prince 276–7, 310
Max Emanuel (Elector of Bavaria) 91–2, 96, 117–120, 136, 138, 141 n.
Maximilian (Elector of Bavaria) 54
Mazarin, Jules:
  and the balance of power 80
  and Catalonia 77, 109
  views on the English and republicanism 77
  and the policies of the German princes 36, 38
  religion versus raison d'état 28–9
  exhorted by Salvius to intensify war effort 21
Mazzini, Giuseppe 271, 273, 274
Mecklenburg 37–8, 51–2, 213
membership of the international system 76–7, 88, 102, 223, 233, 316–17, 318
Mendelssohn-Bartholdy, Albrecht 299 n.
Menorca 98
Metternich, Clemens Fürst von 172, 174, 205, 206, 242, 266, 285, 307
  favours a Bourbon restoration 214
  author of the Declaration of Frankfurt 224
  and the question of French territorial cessions 200–1
  and the German Act of Confederation 220
  and the issue of Hesse-Kassel 213
  and the Holy Alliance 188
  and the Ottoman Empire 188
  and the Polish-Saxon issue 169, 181, 184–5, 193, 195–7, 218, 229–31, 245–6, 334–6
  avoids commitment to principles 185–6, 204, 222–3
  and public opinion 190–1
Metz (bishopric) 67–8, 142, 286
Milan 91, 92, 95, 96, 133, 140
Millerand, Alexandre 290–1
Minden (bishopric) 51
Modena 169
monarchical principle 221–2

Moniteur universel 172, 187, 191
Montgelas, Max Graf von 299 n.
Münster, Ernst Graf von 214, 215, 238
Murat, Joachim 170, 216–17
Murcia 103
mutual assured destruction 329

Naples 96, 140–1, 222
  and the Vienna congress 170,
    216–17, 218
Napoleon 171, 174, 176, 179, 190, 191,
    194, 201, 221, 224, 229, 236, 307
  quoted by Clemenceau 284
  changes international system 232
  and Murat 170
  and Prussia 182
  returns from Elba 167, 170, 192,
    206, 215, 217, 239, 246 n.
  his rule a populist dictatorship 219,
    250
  and Talleyrand 167, 213
  adopts imperial title 212–13
Napoleon III 219
national feeling:
  in early 18th-century Europe
    104–6, 121
  in the 19th and 20th centuries 251,
    255
  and the Paris peace conference 263
  see also Germany
national self-determination:
  and the balance of power 329
  in the view of Clemenceau 268
  demanded by German delegation at
    Paris 295, 297
  as a way of dealing with the
    German question 314
  and the great-power principle 255,
    320, 330, 331–2
  advocated by Lloyd George 262,
    304
  unevenly applied by Paris peace
    conference 287, 288, 289, 304
  since the Paris peace conference
    318–20, 331–2
  in Wilson's speeches 255–7
  not a consensus notion at time of
    Vienna congress 198
National Socialism 251, 286, 311, 313
nationalism:
  after the end of the Cold War 333
  older than the French Revolution
    184

  in 17th- and 18th-century Germany
    9, 30, 39, 74
  and national self-determination 331
  and National Socialism / Fascism
    251
  populist nationalism and the decline
    of mercenary armies 236
  and socialism 251
  in Sonnino's speeches 275
  causes international tension in the
    19th century 250, 251–2, 312,
    327–8
Nesselrode, Carl-Robert Graf von
    180, 187, 242
Netherlands, The 33, 56, 61, 77, 88,
    111 n., 209, 236, 317, 321, 322
  in Thirty Years War 17
  at Münster and Osnabrück 57, 64,
    74, 78, 84–7
  and the War of the Spanish
    Succession 91–2, 94–9, 100, 109,
    115, 116, 124, 126, 130, 138,
    139–40, 141–2, 143–4, 147,
    149–50, 151–2
  and the Vienna congress 169, 204,
    213, 218, 227, 231, 246
Netherlands, Spanish, *see* Belgium
Neuilly (Treaty of) 291, 294
New Style 15
New Zealand 279
Nice 146
Nicolson, Harold 302, 303, 304
Nieuwpoort 95
Nitti, Francesco 269, 275–6, 305–8
Nördlingen (Battle of) 16, 19, 58
Northern War (Great) *see* Great
    Northern War
Norway 170, 180, 249, 320

Old Style 15
orbis christianus, see Christendom
Organization of African Unity 332
Orlando, Vittorio Emmanuele 259,
    275, 276, 280, 300, 305, 310
  role in Council of Four 281, 283
  general views on First World War
    and peace settlement 269–73
  falls from power 304
Orléans, Philippe II, Duke of (regent
    of France) 127, 156, 161, 162 n.
Orléans, Louis Philippe, Duke of
    215–16
  see also Louis Philippe

Ormonde, James Butler, Duke of 154
Ostend 95
Ostpolitik 332
Osuna, Francisco Maria de Paula
  Téllez-Girón y Benavides, Duke
  of 165
Ottoman Empire 28, 29
  and the Vienna congress 188–9
  see also Turkey
Oxenstierna, Axel, Count 23, 24, 25,
  60
  role in Thirty Years War 17, 19,
  58–9
  views on Westphalian peace
  settlement 19–20, 22, 57, 59
Oxenstierna, Johan, Count 19, 23,
  29–30, 56, 57, 58
  role in negotiations over Pomerania
  60–1
Oxford, Robert Harley, Earl of 199
  competes with Bolingbroke 155
  and the Dutch barrier 144
  correspondence with Heinsius 111,
  125, 151
  impeached 156
  seeks to remove Philip V from
  Spain 129–30
  share in Utrecht settlement 99 n.
Oxford University 156, 163

pacta sunt servanda (doctrine of) 101
Palatinate 203
Palatine elector, *see* John William
Papal envoy at Münster, *see* Chigi,
  Fabio
Papal States 170
Paris (First Peace of) 200, 229, 235
  balance-of-power rhetoric 224
  and the great-power concept 236–7
  general summary 167–8
  in Talleyrand's view 174–5, 198
  in Wellington's view 202
Paris (Second Peace of) 167, 188, 206,
  230, 239
  debate over terms 170, 198–203
  general summary 170
Paris peace conference:
  organization 279–82
Parlement de Paris 162
Parma (principality) 169
Parti radical 266
peaceful settlement of disputes 41–2,
  47–8, 151, 261, 263, 293

'Peace Without Victory', *see* Wilson
Peñaranda, Gaspar de Braccamonte y
  Guzman, Conde de 86
Permanent Court of International
  Justice 293
Perpignan 66
Persia 181
Pfalz-Neuburg, *see* Maria Anna
Pfalz-Zweibrücken, *see* Johann
  Kasimir
Philip V (King of Spain) 97, 104–5,
  119, 148, 156–7, 158
  named as heir by Charles II of
  Spain 93
  cedes Belgium to the Elector of
  Bavaria 118
  condition of his recognition as king
  96
  likely to inherit French crown 106,
  126
  proclaimed King of Spain 95
  Spanish patriotism of 105
  emphatic invocations of the 'public
  good' 112–13
  and the renunciation issue 127–32
  represented at Utrecht by Louis
  XIV 98
  resists Utrecht settlement 160–5
Poland 61, 107, 207
  a quasi-republic 209
  and the Vienna congress 169, 176,
  179–80, 181, 182, 184, 185, 187,
  191, 194, 195–6, 198, 205–6, 212,
  223, 229, 241, 242–5, 334–6
  and the Paris peace conference 249,
  279, 288–9, 307
  in the 20th century 318, 319, 320
Pomerania 51, 56–65, 76, 79
Pope 53, 208, 305 n.
  role at Münster and Osnabrück 18,
  39
  and the Holy Alliance 189
  see also Chigi, Fabio; Holy See
popular opinion 104–5, 273
populism:
  and conservatism 233, 324
  and the causes of the First World
  War 250–2
  and kingship 210, 219
  and military organization 236
  and national self-determination 255,
  256, 318
  and nationalism 184–5, 251–2, 331

and the Paris peace conference 253
a threat felt by the Vienna
  peacemakers 185, 190
Portugal 90, 168, 237, 249, 279, 317,
  321
  in the Thirty Years War 17
  and the War of the Spanish
    Succession 96
  at Utrecht 99, 101 n., 117, 127
Pozzo di Borgo, Charles André,
  Comte de 180
Pragelas (Pragelato) 145
Prague (Peace of) 47 n.
Prior, Matthew 155, 156
procedural rules, definition of 5
Prussia 315
  and the Holy Roman Empire 49
  and the Utrecht Peace 99, 101 n.,
    106-7, 108
  explanation of behaviour at Vienna
    182-3
  position after the Vienna congress
    231
public opinion:
  at the Vienna congress 189-201,
    204-5, 206
  see also popular opinion
punishment in international relations
  10-11, 154, 158, 199, 261, 262,
  299, 313

Quadruple/Quintuple Alliance 222,
  238

Rastatt (Peace of) 99
Ratzeburg (bishopric) 52
Razumovsky, Andrey Kyrillovich,
  Count 180, 242
Reagan, Ronald 326
Regent, The (of France) (Philippe II,
  Duke of Orléans) 161
Reichsexekution 48-9
Reichshofrat 49
Reichskammergericht 49
Reichstag:
  (pre-1806) 16, 18, 35, 65, 69-70
  (post-1871) 256, 312
reparations:
  imposed on France (1815) 203
  at Paris (1919-20) 262, 282-3, 286,
    298, 300
Reparations Commission 306

religion:
  and the Peace of Westphalia 12, 16,
    17, 18, 27-30, 40, 41, 44, 48, 51,
    61, 62, 66, 70, 75, 76, 83
  and the Vienna congress 187-9,
    191, 246
  invoked in peace treaties, see
    Trinity
  see also Christendom
representative democracy 210
republicanism 77, 210, 220
republics:
  in the ancien régime 74, 77, 109,
    208-9
  in 19th-century Europe 212, 213
respublica christiana, see Christendom
Rhineland 169, 180, 200, 217-18, 227
Richelieu, Armand-Jean du Plessis,
  Duc de 27, 36, 40-1
Richelieu, Louis François Armand de
  Vignerot du Plessis, Duc de 203
right of conquest 286
  at Münster and Osnabrück 49-51,
    53, 65, 68
  at Vienna 182, 197, 204-7
Rijswijk (Peace of) 94, 95, 113
Riksråd (Swedish Council of State)
  19, 20, 22, 23, 59, 60 n., 80 n.
Riksdag (Sweden) 209
rinunciarii 273
Risorgimento 275
Robinson, John (Bishop of Bristol)
  118
Roman Republic 209
Rorté, Claude de Salles, Baron de 84
Rosenhane, Schering 19, 29, 56, 57
Rumania 279, 319
Russia 332
  and the Great Northern War 89, 90
  and the great-power principle at
    Vienna 239-45
  inferiority complex at Vienna
    congress 180-1
  and the Paris peace conference
    278-9
  see also Soviet Union
Ruthenes 288

Saar question 284-7
Saavedra Fajardo, Diego 50
Saint-Germain (Treaty of) 291
St John, Henry, see Bolingbroke
Saint-Venant 143

Salvius, Johan Adler 19–20, 23, 44 n.,
    51, 54, 56, 76, 88, 110
  and the autonomy of the German
    estates 78–9
  and the balance of power 81–2
  on French policy 84
  role in negotiations over Pomerania
    59–60, 61, 62, 63, 64
  views on religion 30
  social background 25
  views on Westphalian peace
    settlement 19, 20, 24–5, 57–8,
    59
San Marino 213
Sardinia 118–19, 142, 161
Sardinia-Piedmont (kingdom) 222,
    246–7
Saudi-Arabia 279
Savoy:
  at Münster 84, 85, 86
  and the War of the Spanish
    Succession 96, 99, 103, 106, 108,
    112, 118, 127, 130–1, 137, 138,
    141, 142, 144–7, 162 n., 163–4
  and the Vienna congress 246
Saxe-Coburg, Ernst, Duke of 187,
    214
Saxony (electorate, later kingdom) 31,
    33
  and the Vienna congress 169, 172,
    180, 184, 187, 191, 192, 193, 194,
    195–8, 204–7, 214, 217–18, 223,
    229–31, 245–6, 334–6
Saxe-Weimar (grand-duchy) 213
Sayn-Wittgenstein, Johannes VIII,
    Graf von 56, 65
Schwerin (bishopric) 52
Scotland 104
Scott, H. M. 12
Second Socialist International 252
Second World War 325, 329, 330
security:
  at Münster and Osnabrück 78, 81,
    89
  at Utrecht 102, 139–47, 232, 331
  at Vienna 200
  at Paris 264, 274, 275
  see also collective security
self-determination, see national self-
    determination
Serbia 279, 280, 332
Servien, Abel, Marquis de Sablé et de
    Boisdauphin 20, 28, 67, 76, 86–7

Sèvres (Treaty of) 291
Shrewsbury, Charles Talbot, Duke of
    119, 156–7, 158–9
Siam 279
Sicily:
  and the War of the Spanish
    Succession 96, 103, 106, 112, 118,
    138, 140–1, 142, 145, 161, 162,
    163
  and the Congress of Vienna 170,
    217, 222
Silesia 49
Sinzendorf, Philipp Ludwig Wenzel
    Graf von 122, 135–6, 150
slave trade 98
Slovaks 288
Smuts, Jan Christiaan 303
Social Democratic Party (Germany)
    312
socialism 251, 295
Socialist International, see Second
    Socialist International
Sonnino, Sidney Barone 273–5
South Africa 279
South Tyrol 273, 287, 290, 300
sovereignty 78, 257–8, 276
Soviet Union 319, 320, 321, 325–6,
    332–3
Spain 222, 317
  role in Thirty Years War 16–17, 27,
    35, 62, 77
  role at Münster and Osnabrück 19,
    34, 35, 50–1, 74–5, 83, 86–7
  role at Vienna 168, 170, 237, 238,
    246
  division into several kingdoms
    103
  recognizes English parliament 76
Spanish Netherlands, see Belgium
Spanish Succession, War of the
    (history) 90–9
Speyer 154, 286
'stab-in-the-back' legend 314
Stackelberg, Gustav Ernst Graf von
    180
Stadhouders 91, 209
Stadion, Johann Philipp Graf von
    190–1
Stalin, Joseph 319
Stalinism 251
Stanhope, Alexander 94
States-General of the United
    Provinces, see Netherlands

Stein, Heinrich Friedrich Carl Freiherr vom 180
Stewart, Charles 176
Stolpe, Sven 30
Strafford, Thomas Wentworth, Earl of 122 n., 126, 129, 150, 153
Strasbourg 70–1
strategic boundaries 202, 228
structure of the international system, definition of 3
structural principles, definition of 5–6
Stuart (dynasty) 95, 155
Sudetenland 288
Sultan 28, 123
superpower concept 325, 326
supranational organizations 3
supranational cooperation, examples of 9
Sweden 249, 317
  role in Thirty Years War 16–17, 21, 58 n.
  position and policies after Thirty Years War 88–9
  and the Vienna congress 168, 170, 180, 237, 246
  and the Baltic 16, 57, 59, 67
  constitutional arrangements 207, 209
  Council of State, see Riksråd
  recognizes English parliament 76
  compared to France 209, 313
  thinness of power base 25, 31, 58–9, 67
Switzerland 78, 207–8, 213, 317
  and the Vienna congress 170, 245, 246
Syria 332
Szczecin 64

Tallard, Camille d'Hostun de la Baume, Duc de 113–14, 123
Talleyrand, Charles-Maurice de, Prince 181, 187, 197, 245–6, 266, 285
  and the balance of power 225–9
  early career 166–7
  and Castlereagh 175, 178
  and the Czar 191, 192, 214, 240
  and dynastic legitimacy 207, 211–23, 233, 317
  view of First Peace of Paris 198
  general views on peace settlement 171–5

achieves full great-power status for France at Vienna 169, 237–8, 239
  and the Ottoman Empire 188
  and public opinion 191–2
  in line with public opinion over Saxony 195
  and the Second Peace of Paris 170
Tarnopol 229
Thailand, see Siam
Thirty Years War (history) 16–17
Tiberius 45
Torgau 230
Torcy, Jean-Baptiste Colbert, Marquis de 91, 99, 228
  and the barrier concept 141–7
  and the will of Charles II 93–4
  seeks peace based on consensus 152–3
  on peace concluded under duress 157–8
  and the Italian situation 136–7
  and popular opinion 104, 106
  'public-good' rhetoric 111–12, 114–19
  and the renunciation issue 125–31, 156–7
  discussions with Sinzendorf 135–6
Toruń 231
Tory Party 97, 124, 130, 132, 143, 144, 150–6
Toul (bishopric) 67–8, 142
Tournai 143
Trauttmansdorff, Maximilian Graf von 20, 21, 75
  and the issue of Alsace 70
  and the issue of Bremen-Verden 53, 54
  and the Pomeranian issue 56–7, 60, 62, 64, 65
  and the Peace of Prague 47 n.
Treitschke, Heinrich von 183
Trevelyan, George Macaulay 100 n.
Trianon (Treaty of the) 291
Trier 218, 286
Trinity (invoked in peace treaties) 27–8, 29, 110, 187
Triple Alliance 252, 302
Triple Entente, see entente
Trotsky, Leon 254
Turkey 181, 249, 291
Tuscany 141, 169
Tyrol 141
  see also South Tyrol

Ukraine 318, 332
United Kingdom (creation of) 104,
    180
United Nations 9, 293, 332
United Provinces, *see* Netherlands
United States:
    and the Paris peace conference 253,
        264, 270, 277, 279, 280, 282, 302,
        310
    since 1920: 320, 321, 325–6
Ursins, Marie-Anne de la Trémoille-
    Noirmoutier, Princesse des 130 n.,
    131 n.

Valencia 103
Venaissin 203
Venice 209, 236, 322
    and the Peace of Westphalia 18,
        82–3, 84
    and the Vienna congress 169, 212,
        223
Verden 51, 52–4, 65
Verdun (bishopric) 67–8, 142
Versailles (Treaty of) 151, 291–2, 314,
    315
    interpreted by Clemenceau 266–7,
        268
    controversy over 299–305, 307, 308
Victor Amadeus II (Duke of Savoy),
    see Savoy (and the War of the
    Spanish Succession)
Vietnam 321
Volmar, Isaac, Freiherr von Rieden
    20, 45, 70, 75, 84

War of the Spanish Succession
    (history) 90–9
war-guilt clauses 299
Wartenberg, Franz Wilhelm Graf von
    30, 53
Waterloo (Battle of) 170, 245
Weber, Max 299 n.
Webster, Charles K. 194–5, 198, 336
Wedgewood, Josiah 304, 306
Weimar Republic 295, 311, 313
Wellington, Arthur Wellesley, Duke
    of 175, 188, 245–6, 283, 330
    urges moderation towards France
        201–2

and the second restoration of Louis
    XVIII 215
and the question of Murat 217
commands allied occupation troops
    in France 221
Wessenberg, Johann Philipp Freiherr
    von 184 n.
Whig Party 97, 130, 147, 150, 152,
    155, 156
Wight, Martin 49
William I (Elector of Hesse) 213
William II (German Emperor) 300,
    312, 313
William III (King of Britain) 91,
    94–5, 124
Wilson, Woodrow 106, 253, 263, 275,
    280, 281, 282, 286, 293, 295, 296,
    304, 323, 329
    and the Adriatic issue 290–1
    and the issue of Austria 287
    and the Brenner question 287
    and Clemenceau 264, 265, 266,
        283–5
    as perceived in Germany 276, 277
    lack of impartiality 299–300
    popularity in Italy 270–1, 273
    and the League Covenant 294
    concordance of views with Lloyd
        George's 261–2
    and the role of principles 266,
        283–5
    'Peace Without Victory' speech
        274, 305, 314
    programmatic speeches 254–61
Wiser, Franz Melchior Freiherr von
    159 n.
Wismar 51
Wittelsbach (dynasty) 91–2, 96,
    117–20
Wittgenstein, *see* Sayn-Wittgenstein
World War I, *see* First World War
World War II, *see* Second World War
Wratislaw, Johann Wenzel Graf von
    134
Württemberg (kingdom) 16, 213

Yugoslavia 249, 279–80, 290, 300,
    332
    see also Serbia